D1215164

This work addresses the challenge of contemporary materialism for thinking about God. The book examines
contemporary theories of consciousness and defends a
nonmaterialist theory of persons, subjectivity and God. A
version of dualism is articulated that seeks to avoid the
fragmented outlook of most dualist theories. Dualism is
often considered to be inadequate both philosophically
and ethically, and is seen as a chief cause of denigrating the
body and of promoting individualism and skepticism.
Charles Taliaferro defends a holist understanding of the
person–body relationship in which the two are distinguishable yet integrally related. This integrated dualism is
spelled out in a way that avoids the ethical and philosophical problems associated with other dualistic accounts,
especially in their Platonic and Cartesian forms. A defense
is then made of the intelligibility of thinking about God as
nonphysical, yet integrally present to creation.

CONSCIOUSNESS AND
THE MIND OF GOD

CONSCIOUSNESS AND THE MIND OF GOD

CHARLES TALIAFERRO

Associate Professor of Philosophy,
St. Olaf College, Northfield, Minnesota

CAMBRIDGE
UNIVERSITY PRESS

Published by the Press Syndicate of the University of Cambridge
The Pitt Building, Trumpington Street, Cambridge, CB2 1RP
40 West 20th Street, New York, NY 10011-4211, USA
10 Stamford Road, Oakleigh, Melbourne 3166, Australia

First published 1994

Printed in Great Britain at the University Press, Cambridge

A catalogue record for this book is available from the British Library

Library of Congress cataloguing in publication data

Taliaferro, Charles.
Consciousness and the mind of God / Charles Taliaferro.
p.   cm.
Includes index.
ISBN 0 521 46173 1 hardback
1. God – Proof.   2. Dualism.   3. Materialism.   4. Consciousness.
1. Title.
BL182.T351994
212′.1 – dc20   93-42897   CIP

ISBN 0 521 46173 1 hardback

Contents

Acknowledgments

I gratefully acknowledge all who have commented on earlier versions of this book, including Thomas Chance, Richard Creel, Jil Evans, Steve Evans, Rick Fairbanks, Kay Hong, Pauline Marsh, Patrick Richmond, Jonathan G. Rinehart, Daniel N. Robinson, David Vessey, Andy Ward, and Linda Zagzebski, with special thanks for encouragement and support from Tom Morris, Roger Trigg, and Richard Swinburne. I am grateful to the National Endowment for the Humanities for supporting a year's research and the Pew Foundation for a semester's release from teaching to work on the project. I am indebted to Dee Bolton at St. Olaf College and to Grazyna Cooper and the crew at the Oxford University Computer Centre for their assistance in preparing the typescript. I thank the fellows of Oriel College for their hospitality for eighteen months of research and writing. The book is dedicated to the SSJE (the Cowleys), of whom I am an associate, and to Ann, Danial, Jared, Jessica, and William. Most important, this book is dedicated to Jil with love.

Introduction

How we think about ourselves can determine how we think about God, and how we think about God can affect our self-understanding. Virtually all the major world religions insist upon the cardinal importance for all of us to know ourselves. Ernst Cassirer went so far as to characterize the duty to "know thyself" in Judaism, Buddhism, Confucianism, and Christianity as a categorical or absolute imperative.[1] The vital importance of knowing oneself is an especially central theme in Christian spiritual texts, poetry, theology, and philosophy. Christian mystics, such as Meister Eckhart, have held that self-knowledge is crucial to spiritual development; it is in some sense prior to knowledge of God. Well before him, Augustine interwove self-exploration and strenuous philosophical reflection on the mind of God in the *Confessions*. For Augustine, the pursuit of self-knowledge and the knowledge of God occur together naturally and virtually simultaneously. In his classic work *On the Trinity*, Augustine even proposed that our internal, mental life of memory, intellect, and will could be recognized as a mirror, vestige or distant reflection of the inner, three-part life of God. Our interior life is an echo of God's.

Today many philosophers would endorse something like Augustine's and Eckhart's insistence upon the link between our view of God and our view of the self, but conclude that deep philosophical reflection on what it is to be a person, to act intentionally and to have conscious experience, undermines any

---

[1] Ernst Cassirer, *An Essay on Man* (New Haven: Yale University Press, 1944), chapter I.

I

substantive view of God and, indeed, of religion as a whole. A wide range of these philosophers have argued for a radically materialist notion of persons, one which tends to throw our everyday notion of lived experience overboard or at least to inch it toward the railing. In western tradition God is typically conceived of as an immaterial, spiritual being. God is a nonphysical, powerful, intentional agent present throughout the cosmos without being identical with it or with some material object in it. God is not, in Ernst Haeckel's colorful phrase, "a gaseous vertebrate."[2] As a spiritual reality God does not have mass, weight, volume, electrical charge, atomic number, and so on. God is no mere assemblage of physical parts, or some kind of formal, abstract set with all and only material members, but the creative power responsible for the cosmos' origin and continued existence. If a materialist view of the cosmos, according to which *all* of reality is fundamentally physical, is correct, then the traditional understanding of God is incorrect. Even those materialist philosophers who have not dismissed the mental (and who are criticized by more radical partisans as timid or pre-scientific) have placed the traditional under-standing of the self and God in jeopardy, because of their exclusively physical conception of reality. As far as *traditional* Christianity is concerned, it appears that T. L. S. Sprigge is right: while it "is not true that to be an atheist is to be a materialist ... in effect to be a materialist is to be an atheist."[3] The same is true for traditional forms of Islam and Judaism.

   Just as the scientific community has dispensed with demonic activity or supramechanical vitalistic forces called entelechies in their theories about the cosmos, some philosophers and natural scientists now wish to dispense with the mental world of intentions, motives, and awareness (a world that is often referred to as "folk psychology") in their explanatory theories of human

---

[2] Haeckel cited by Emil Brunner in *Christianity and Civilization* (London: Nisbet, 1948), p. 15.
[3] T. L. S. Sprigge, *Theories of Existence* (Harmondsworth, Middlesex: Penguin, 1985), p. 35. Sprigge is referring here to a comprehensive materialism, according to which all of reality is material. We shall see later that some theists are materialist in their view of humans and other animals, but immaterialists in their view of God.

behavior. They seek either to identify the mental with the physical or to eliminate the mental altogether. Paul Churchland lays out the implication of his eliminative materialism with marked clarity:

> Our common-sense psychological framework is a false and radically misleading conception of the causes of human behavior and the nature of cognitive activity ... Folk psychology is not just an incomplete representation of our inner natures; it is an outright misrepresentation of our internal states and activities.[4]

In place of our ordinary, "folk" understanding of ourselves as centers of consciousness and agency, philosophers like Churchland want to substitute a more scientifically refined picture. Richard Rorty gives a specific example of this desired physicalist substitution, wherein talk of pain, for example, is supplanted by talk of nerve fibers.

> The absurdity of saying "Nobody has ever felt a pain" is no greater than that of saying "Nobody has ever seen a demon," if we have a suitable answer to the question "What *was* I reporting when I said I felt a pain?" To this question, the science of the future may reply "You were reporting the occurrence of a certain brain process, and it would make life simpler for us if you would, in the future, say 'My C-fibres are firing,' instead of saying 'I'm in pain.'"[5]

Rorty believes that the case for such a substitution will unfold with the same force as displayed in a scientific treatment of demons. The scientist answers the witch doctor's question "What was I reporting when I reported a demon?" by saying "You were reporting the content of your hallucination, and it would make life simpler if, in the future, you would describe your experiences in those terms."[6] Paul and Patricia Churchland, Willard Quine, Stephen Stich, and others have endorsed related proposals calling into question the propriety of appealing to beliefs, desires, and sensations as mental states in the explanation of events.

[4] Paul Churchland, *Matter and Consciousness* (Cambridge, Mass.: MIT Press, 1984), p. 43.
[5] Richard Rorty, "Mind–Body Identity, Privacy, and Categories," *Review of Metaphysics* 19:1 (1965), 30.   [6] *Ibid.*, 31, 32.

Many objections to recognizing some immaterial feature of ourselves apply with equal force to recognizing some immaterial aspect of the cosmos or, as it were, behind the cosmos conserving it in existence. Philosophers have objected to an incorporeal concept of God on grounds such as: intentional agency is not truly explanatory of events; if there were a nonphysical agent it would be too dissimilar from physical things for there to be any causal relation between them; the very idea of a nonphysical thing is conceptually absurd. These are some of the many objections philosophers have wielded against classical theism, the same objections which are wielded with as great a force against the belief that we ourselves either are nonphysical, spiritual beings or contain a nonphysical part called a soul. John Macquarrie underscores the theological importance of our philosophy of human nature. "If we have abandoned dualism when we are thinking of finite beings, does it make sense to retain it on the cosmic level in thinking of God and the world? It has no more plausibility there."[7]

Richard Rorty explicitly links together his judgment about God and persons or minds. According to Rorty, both "God" and "mind" must go from any clear-headed theory of the cosmos. He writes that the immaterial, classical understanding of God is faulty principally because it is an extension of a faulty understanding of ourselves. To view ourselves as in some measure nonphysical is to uphold a "blurry," ill-formed self-image.[8] And in a similar fashion, Kai Nielsen, Adel Daher, Antony Flew, Paul Edwards, and others to be discussed below (despite their intramural differences) criticize classical theistic notions of God because the foundational ideas of self and mind which inform the classical model, are no longer viable.[9] Classical

---

[7] John Macquarrie, Foreword to *God's World, God's Body* by Grace Jantzen (Philadelphia: Westminster Press, 1984), pp. ix, x.
[8] Rorty, "Mind as Ineffable," in *Mind in Nature*, Nobel Conference XVII, ed. by Richard Q. Elvee (San Francisco: Harper & Row, 1981), pp. 85, 87.
[9] Kai Nielsen, *Scepticism* (London: Macmillan, 1973), as well as his more recent "God, Disembodied Existence and Incoherence," *Sophia* 26:3 (October 1987) and *An Introduction to the Philosophy of Religion* (New York: St. Martin's Press, 1982), especially pp. 36–37; Adel Daher, "Does Religion Have its Own Logic?," *International Logic Review* 12:1–2 (December 1981); Paul Edwards, "Some Notes on Anthropomorphic

theism was based upon a useful, but false self-understanding. Get rid of blurry, folk psychology, so they argue, and we will soon be rid of blurry, folk religion.

In the great monotheistic religious traditions, God is not, of course, depicted with precisely the same attributes as created persons; God is not a super *homo sapiens*. And at important junctures in the development of these religions, theists have gone to great lengths to insist that God differs from us in that God is eternal, while we are temporal; God is not made up of parts, we are; God has no sense organs, we do; God creates galaxies from nothing, we only shape things that already exist; God is without origin and incorruptible, we are neither. In the central conviction that God exists necessarily, while we exist contingently it might appear that the God of classical theism resembles abstract propositions like "$7 + 5 = 12$" which are necessarily true far more than God resembles us. But God is also believed to know about the world, to be an all-good agent, to reshape things which already exist, to love the cosmos. Theists will diverge on how to understand these features as ascribed to God, but it is evident that these ascriptions make up central items in the folk-psychology framework that is under attack in much contemporary philosophy. Theists refine terms like "intelligence," "agency," and "emotions" as applied to God, but surely the theistic enterprise requires that we have some conceptual handle on our own intelligence, agency, and emotions before religious refining can take place. And if the

---

Theology," in *Religion, Experience and Truth*, ed. Sidney Hook (New York: New York University Press, 1961) and "Difficulties in the Idea of God," in *The Idea of God*, ed. E. Madden *et al.* (Springfield, Ill.: C. C. Thomas, 1968), p. 48. See also Anthony Flew's contribution to *Does God Exist?* by Flew and T. Miethe (San Francisco: HarperCollins, 1991), and J. C. A. Gaskin's *The Quest for Eternity* (Harmondsworth, Middlesex: Penguin, 1984). Paul Churchland entitles one reason for accepting dualism "the argument from religion" (*Matter and Consciousness*, p. 13), an argument he hastily dismisses (pp. 14, 15). The crucial role of the philosophy of mind for the philosophy of God has been widely noted historically. See, for example, Thomas Reid, *Lectures on Natural Theology*, ed. by E. H. Duncan (Washington, D.C.: University Press of America, 1981), p. 2. Descartes endorsed a similar view. See *Descartes: Philosophical Letters*, trans. A. Kenny (Oxford: Clarendon Press, 1970), p. 252. Worries about the intelligibility of conceiving God as nonphysical have a long history. Witness Sextus Empiricus' discussion of the topic in *Against the Physicists* (third century AD) and, still earlier, Cicero's *The Nature of the Gods* (first century BC).

eliminative materialism of the Churchlands, Rorty, and Stich holds sway, it is difficult to see how such theistic refining can even get started.

Philosophers in the Christian tradition earlier in the twentieth century appreciatively grasped the link between the concept of God and persons. William Temple, A. E. Taylor, and F. R. Tennant would not have been surprised that the materialist turn in our understanding of persons would lead to a turning away from classical theism. The goal of balancing theories of persons and God is not ignored by some contemporary philosophical theists. Thus, Alvin Plantinga, Richard Swinburne, and Keith Ward (among others) have each drawn upon philosophically developed theories of persons in spelling out and defending theism. Each has sought to articulate and defend a conception of persons in sharp contrast to materialistic reductionism.

But because of widespread philosophical dissatisfaction with any type of dualistic treatment of persons, not all Christian theologians have embraced a distinction between persons (mind or soul) and material bodies, God and the world. The intellectual temperament toward dualism is negative indeed, and captured in Daniel Dennett's comment that "dualism is not a serious view to contend with, but rather a cliff over which to push one's opponents."[10] As a result, some Christian theologians articulate postdualist notions of the person and the God–world relation. While theistic philosophers like Peter Van Inwagen, Bruce Reichenbach, and (at one time) Stephen T. Davis have defended materialist notions of human persons alongside a traditional immaterialist picture of God, this combination is far from the consensus position. The attempt to localize and contain materialism has not commanded the field. Grace Jantzen rejects both the dualist distinction between the mind and body and the classical distinction between the cosmos and an incorporeal God. Instead, she proposes that we conceive of God and creation along material lines, affirming the single reality of God

---

[10] Daniel Dennett, "Current Issues in the Philosophy of Mind," in *Recent Work in Philosophy*, ed. Kenneth Lucey and T. R. Machan (Totowa: Rowen and Allenheld, 1983), p. 157.

and the world. Adrian Thatcher applauds nondualist trends in anthropology and theology: "The blurring of the distinction between spirit and matter also blurs the distinction between God and the world and ... theology is better for it."[11] He holds that a nondualist view of persons is actually better placed to articulate central Christian notions of creation, incarnation, and resurrection. Patrick Sherry and Nicholas Lash both see the rejection of dualism as a prerequisite to developing an adequate understanding of God. Lash comments that "For the consistent dualist, God is either an idea or a ghost," and Sherry castigates dualist-motivated theology for its imagining God to be "more like a Super-Frankenstein than the God of Abraham, Isaac and Jacob."[12] The theologian Fergus Kerr is equally hostile to dualism. In *Theology After Wittgenstein* he campaigns for a thorough abandonment of traditional dualism, a theory he thinks has had a nearly catastrophic effect on religious belief. "In all traditions, Christian theologians are to be found who work with a concept of the self that needs to go to the cleaners ... Therapy is required to free us from the inclination to compare ourselves, unfavorably of course, with bodiless beings, whether angels or machines."[13]

The disenchantment with dualism has contributed to a revival of the Aristotelian understanding of the person. This anthropology, especially as refined in the thirteenth century by Thomas Aquinas, has historically often appeared as an attractive alternative to outright mind–body dualism. The demise of dualism at the hands of current philosophical critics is heralded by some theologians as a vindication of Aquinas' saner Aristotelianism, which sees the soul as the form of the body, over against Augustine's more radical dualism in which the soul has

[11] Adrian Thatcher, "Christian Theism and the Concept of a Person," in *Persons and Personality*, ed. A. Peacocke and G. Gillett (Oxford: Basil Blackwell, 1987), pp. 183, 184. See also Jantzen, *God's World, God's Body*. Work by Jantzen, David Paulsen, and Ishtiyaque Haji which attempts to retain theism while rejecting an incorporealist idea of God recalls the radical theism of Thomas Hobbes (seventeenth century).

[12] Lash, "Materialism," *A New Dictionary of Christian Theology*, ed. A. Richardson and J. Bowden (London: SCM, 1983), p. 353; Sherry, *Spirit, Saints and Immortality* (London: Macmillan, 1984), p. 13. Sherry seems to be using "Frankenstein" as the name of the monster rather than its creator (a very common confusion).

[13] Fergus Kerr, *Theology after Wittgenstein* (Oxford: Basil Blackwell, 1988), p. 187.

a body as its container. Far more extreme theologically is the move by Gary Legenhausen, who uses the case against dualism to argue that God is best thought of in altogether impersonal terms. "Persons persuaded by the arguments of the physicalists that mind is dependent upon body might be tempted by atheism. Such persons might reason that since mind is dependent on body, God, who is mind without a body, cannot exist. But given the impersonalist view of God, it is possible to draw a different conclusion, namely that God exists but does not have a mind."[14]

Rejection of theism as an outworn world view resting upon a mistaken view of persons has also marked a more skeptical theological movement. Perhaps the most radical departure from classical theism in recent years is undertaken by theologians who seek to preserve religious language and some practices (religious ethics, prayerful meditation, liturgy) while either bracketing or rejecting outright the notion that God exists. Thus, D. Z. Phillips and others construe Christian beliefs as expressing a form of life which may be embraced without believing that God exists. Gordon Kaufman has also developed a conception of religious imagination and ethics that is cut off from the claim that there is a God.[15] In some respects this revisionist stand resembles one branch of materialism which insists upon the practical indispensability of conceiving human behavior in terms of beliefs and desires, even though beliefs and desires are not recognized by them as actually existing states.[16] Some theological revisionists treat the physicalist movement as no more dangerous to religious life than the Copernican revolution or Darwinism. When Copernicus displaced the view that the earth is the center of the cosmos and Darwin advanced his evolutionary theory, many thought Christian belief was doomed. If Christian belief can incorporate a Copernican view

---

[14] Gary Legenhausen, "Is God a Person?," *Religious Studies* 22 (1986), 322.
[15] At times, Kaufman's view of God seems close to Dennett's view of beliefs.
[16] Wilfrid Sellars' paper "Philosophy and the Scientific Image of Man" is among the most important in twentieth-century Anglo-American philosophy to press for a distinction between the practical and theoretical which allows for such a demarcation, *Science, Perception and Reality* (London: Routledge & Kegan Paul, 1963).

of the cosmos and the theory of evolution in biology, then why, it is argued, can't it incorporate a physicalist view of the person and the rest of reality?

So, in the wake of current attempts to reform our understanding of intelligence and agency, philosophers and theologians have tended either to revitalize and defend the classical theistic model or reject it outright or subject it to radical reinterpretation. Before I outline the place of this book in the ensuing debate, consider further two central areas of contemporary work in the philosophy of religion that bring to the fore the critical need for taking theories of the person seriously. The first involves the treatment of arguments for God's existence and the second involves the revival of Anselmian philosophical theology.

All the classical arguments employed to justify belief in God have been systematically attacked on the grounds that the concept of a nonphysical personal God is incoherent. Jonathan Barnes' principal objection to the ontological argument is that it is "becoming increasingly clear that persons are essentially corporeal."[17] For similar reasons Thomas McPherson rejects the argument from design – an argument that the purposive character of the world is evidence of a purposive Creator. "The Argument from Design stands or falls by the analogy between human purposing agents ... and a presumed divine purposing agent ... The Argument from Design, as an argument by analogy, cannot even get off the ground unless it is possible to give sense to the notion of a human purposing mind."[18] McPherson deems that the problems afflicting our belief in human purposiveness challenge belief in Divine purposiveness. Anthony Kenny's analysis of the design argument exhibits with great clarity the interwoven character of theism and the philosophy of mind. He concedes that *if* the notion of an incorporeal purposive agent is intelligible, the argument from design is successful in providing some evidence for God's existence. But as Kenny thinks it is far from clear that such

[17] Jonathan Barnes, *The Ontological Argument* (London: Macmillan, 1972), pp. 84, 85.
[18] Thomas McPherson, *The Argument from Design* (New York: St. Martin's Press, 1972).

incorporeal life is intelligible, he concludes that the argument
has little force.[19] T. R. Miles rejects arguments in support of
theism based upon religious experience largely because he finds
the notion of a nonmaterial causal agent conceptually unacceptable.[20]

The most recent development in philosophical theology may
be termed the Anselmian Revival, after St. Anselm of the
twelfth century. Modern-day Anselmians take as their principal
concern the philosophical defense of God as supremely excellent.
God is said to be unsurpassably great, maximally perfect, or, in
Anselm's language, a being greater than which cannot be
conceived. As this is played out in the work of many Christian
philosophers, we begin to see in the literature an increasingly
clear, carefully articulated conception of God and perfection.

I am convinced that this is a fruitful, important move in
philosophical theology, and it will be taken seriously in this
book. But it needs to be appreciated that this revival rests upon
assumptions about persons, minds, and matter, foundational
assumptions that are under vigorous attack. We may discover a
formal analysis of perfect or maximal knowledge, and perhaps,
as I argue in Chapter 5, we may formulate a consistent
Anselmian conception of God as possessing supreme cognitive
excellence. But suppose that some contemporary physicalists
are correct that knowledge is identifiable with certain neural,
brain states such that for a subject to know anything she or he
must have a certain neurophysiological structure. What, then,
becomes of the supposition that there is an all-knowing, perfect
Creator? Are we to imagine that a perfect, all-knowing God
must have some massive, perfect material brain? Doubts about
the conceivability of nonphysical states and activities feed
doubts about the classical notion of God and erode the work of
Anselmians.

Clearly, then, the debate over the philosophical case for
theism must include or rely upon an investigation into our
conceptions of ourselves, consciousness, possible forms of personal life, agency, purpose, value, and the material world.

---

[19] Anthony Kenny, *Religion and Reason* (Oxford: Basil Blackwell, 1987), p. 84.
[20] T. R. Miles, *Religious Experience* (London: Macmillan, 1972).

These notions are central to a theistic understanding of the cosmos, for, as Keith Ward aptly summarized the theistic world-view, "To believe in God is to believe that at the heart of all reality, of this very reality in which we exist, is spirit, consciousness, value, reason and purpose."[21]

In *Consciousness and the Mind of God* I seek to develop a coherent, reasoned understanding of ourselves as psycho-physical creatures. My project is to focus and defend what Rorty dismisses as the blurry folk notion of ourselves and to assess critically what Thatcher sees as the desirable blurring of the spirit–matter distinction. I endeavor to bring the results of such work on the character of consciousness and agency to bear upon developing and elucidating a classical theistic under-standing of God and the cosmos. My goal is to advance an alternative to the materialist naturalism now in vogue. Along the way I consider the merits of different forms of materialist and nonmaterialist accounts of God and created persons. We are not limited intellectually to a choice between either embracing theism on the one hand or, on the other, endorsing an extreme eliminative materialism – the theory endorsed by Stich, Churchland, *et al.* that eliminates or denies outright the existence of such mental states as beliefs, hopes, and fears. There is a dizzying array of other alternatives. I focus on what I believe to be the more promising, widely held theories, but I make no pretense to examine exhaustively all the religiously relevant views of consciousness, persons, and the material world. The tasks taken up in this book range from critically analyzing contemporary theories of matter to speculative theorizing about a conceivable afterlife. Can any form of classical Christianity survive if we view all persons as thoroughly material beings? Is it philosophically and scientifically defen-sible to view persons as nonphysical? What could be meant by the claim that there is a personal God present everywhere? How can an incorporeal God be close to anything?

The book concentrates upon foundational issues concerning the metaphysical status of human persons and God, but I also

---

[21] Keith Ward, *Holding Fast to God* (London: SPCK, 1982), p. 5.

address the ethical implications of some theories of mind and go on in Chapter 6 to suggest ways in which classical theism extends our treatment of ethics and personal identity. The thesis that there is a God has profound repercussions. If theism is recognized to be true, God's existence is not easily isolated from our other beliefs about the cosmos. To borrow a distinction of Ernst Cassirer's, theistic convictions involve maximal beliefs as opposed to minimal beliefs; maximal beliefs being those that have a larger impact on our other convictions.

Up to this point, I have stressed the importance of the philosophy of mind for the philosophy of God, emphasizing the threat one poses for the other. I think there is no doubt about this threat, or any doubt that the radically materialist conception of reality threatens more than theistic religious beliefs; it also threatens ethics and our very self-image. I also wish to voice a more positive motive for this book. I see the book as more than part of a defensive strategy. Rather, I believe constructive gains can be made for a theistic world-view by taking the philosophy of mind seriously.

Like all such projects, this one has limitations, some obvious. I do not explicitly assess great nontheistic concepts of God as found in Hindu tradition, for example, though much of what follows has implications for a Hindu concept of self. A study of consciousness that contrasts eastern and western religious thought in explicit terms will have to take shape in another project.[22]

Because much of this project and the questions raised about the nature of ourselves and God are foundational and, I think, philosophically prior to articulating the customary arguments for God's existence, there is a heavy emphasis on establishing the coherence and clarity of certain key tenets in a theistic vision of the cosmos. Without the coherence of these notions in place, we are handicapped in debating the ontological argument with Barnes, the design argument with McPherson and Kenny, and the argument from religious experience with Miles. More is

---

[22] I address some of the issues at stake in *Contemporary Philosophy of Religion* (Oxford: Basil Blackwell, forthcoming).

done in this book on the philosophy of mind and related areas to establish the coherence of belief in God and to draw out some of its implications in the theory of values, thus setting the stage for further work.[23]

I have written the book with the nonexpert in mind. Some exposure to philosophy and theology is important, but I explain technical terms and most historical references as they are introduced to enable upper-level undergraduates and interested nonacademics to enter the debate. My hope is that this book will be of use to those who have specialized in one, but not all the disciplines covered, enabling a theologian to gain background in the philosophy of mind or assisting someone in the philosophy of mind to consider the theological bearing of her or his work.

I employ the term "classical theism" to indicate the general position I embrace, a view I later specify as integrative theism. By classical theism I mean the view that there is an omniscient (all-knowing), omnipotent (all-powerful), good, purposive being who has created and conserves this cosmos. According to classical theism, the created world is contingent, whereas the Creator necessarily exists; God does not exist by virtue of the causal power of any other being. God is not a corporeal, material being, though for reasons to be discussed later, this is not incompatible with the Christian affirmation that God became incarnate as a human being with a material body.

---

[23] Once theism is granted initial intelligibility, other areas of theological inquiry may be explored that it is not possible to treat here, such as critically assessing process theology. My conviction that God suffers and is subject to passion places me in alliance with many process theologians, though I do not subscribe to Whiteheadian notions about God's polar nature and several other key points. All things considered, I think contemporary physicalism represents the most serious threat to classical (and process) theistic conceptions of God and persons. Note Raymond Tallis' remark about Derrida: "If, as many modern thinkers seem to believe, mental contents such as qualia can be defined in terms of, and their essence reduced to, their causal relations to inputs mediated by sensory endings and to behavioral outputs, then consciousness is utterly emptied. Next to such interpretations of the mind, even Freudian, Durkheimian, Derridian and Helmholtzian marginalizations of consciousness seem positively humanistic," "A Critique of Neuromythology," in *The Pursuit of Mind*, ed. Tallis and H. Robinson (Manchester: Carcanet, 1991), p. 108. For a challenging critical review of deconstruction philosophy, see John Ellis' *Against Deconstruction* (Princeton: Princeton University Press, 1989) and Raymond Tallis' caustic but challenging *Not Saussure: A Critique of Post-Saussurean Literary Theory* (London: Macmillan, 1988).

Although much of what follows would be acceptable to theists in
Islamic and Jewish tradition, sections of Chapters 4 and 6
address issues of special concern for Christian theism.

I employ the term "classical" to distinguish the view
defended here from recent theologies which may be aptly called
Neotheist, such as Grace Jantzen's theory that God and the
world are a single reality, a view I consider in Chapter 4. I
identify as classically theistic only some of the Divine attributes
traditional theists recognize. Other attributes, such as Divine
simplicity (the Divine nature does not involve distinct attributes; there are no real distinctions between attributes within
God, though there may be in our thinking about God),
immutability (God is not subject to change), and eternity (God
is not in time) are not included so as to emphasize those
attributes which I think are especially relevant to the present
project. I believe God to be in time and subject to change; I
shall not argue over such matters in the text, however, and will
indicate when appropriate if my arguments depend critically on
any such assumptions. Those who believe God to be simple,
immutable, and eternal need not find themselves at cross
purposes with the case I advance for a less ambitious theism.
Advocates of this form of theism still have a stake in answering
the charge that it is incoherent to believe God is both
nonphysical and yet omnipotent, omniscient, good, active in
the world, and omnipresent. The text includes some treatment
of the notion that God has passions, a notion which has not
always been well received in traditional Christianity. As I
believe God does have passions, the use of the term "mind" in
the title of this book should not be read as signaling any
endorsement of an overly intellectual conception of God. The
position I finally adopt is essentially classical theism plus the
affirmation that God is integrally present in the world as a
passionate, affective agent, a view I shall call integrative theism.

I employ nongender-specific terms whenever possible. The
terms "physical," "material," and "corporeal" are used
interchangeably, as are "physicalist" and "materialist." There
is no nuanced distinction of meaning intended here, though I
note for the record that some writers have delimited the physical

(which covers matter and energy) from the material (matter alone). Using the terms in that way, one can say that the physical forces acting on matter are immaterial. For present purposes, however, I will follow a common practice of making the term "material" stand as generically as "physical," so if there were a universe of pure energy with no matter in it we could still describe this alternatively as a physical or material universe.

The view of the person–body relationship I defend is dualistic, and may even be called Cartesian dualism, though I am anxious to distance the view I embrace from what is often associated with these terms. I wish to distinguish my view from Descartes's insofar as he exaggerated the independence of mind from body. He thought certain forms of our intellectual reflection, which occur regularly, are not causally dependent on the brain. Moreover, Descartes adopted a mechanistic view of the body and denied that nonhuman animals have conscious experiences. Neither stance seems compelling to me; I am convinced there are good reasons to attribute conscious experience to at least some nonhuman animals. I also disclaim a view critics associate with Cartesianism – that persons are naturally immortal and therefore survive the destruction of their bodies in virtue of their own innate power. As it happens, Descartes did not hold this view, though he did believe that, by the grace of God, human persons do not pass out of existence with the destruction and death of the body. I follow the historical Descartes here, but not the immortalism associated with Cartesianism. We *can* be destroyed by biological death, but are not so destroyed because God preserves us, notwithstanding the organic dissolution of our bodies. The term "dualism" alone is also fraught with other associations I repudiate. It is often linked with a world-denying, body hatred and castigated as a paradigm case of patriarchal hierarchicalism. Dualism is also commonly thought of as chaining us to an intolerably isolated, atomistic view of individuals, a world of private minds capable of only the most tenuous, doubt-ridden relationships. The theory of person and body defended in *Consciousness and the Mind of God* has none of these repercussions.

In an effort to distinguish the view I defend from this array of associations, I employ the term "integrative dualism" to describe my stance. Initially I aim to articulate and defend dualism without noting the "integrative" rider, but as I refine what I take to be the most plausible reading of the person–body relationship, "integrative dualism" will be the preferred term. The term is awkward, but I think it is no worse than many alternatives like neodualism, progressive, nonmonarchical dualism, or a dualism which is either modest, moderate, soft, holist, thin, weak or post-Cartesian. Moreover the term "integrative dualism" highlights my concern to offset the perennial charge that a dualist view of persons must leave us with a fragmented view of the world. I defend the compatibility of dualism with treating the person and body as a single unit in ethical, social, political, and aesthetic contexts, as well as most scientific ones. Integrative dualism is in accord with theological accounts that insist upon the interwoven nature of the mental and physical, God and the world. Such an integrated viewpoint is in keeping with many of the Church's early theologians, of whom Aelred Squire says "Theirs is neither a holy naturalism, nor an empty headed supernaturalism."[24] Following them, I want to acknowledge the interrelated but distinct realities of both the material and the immaterial. The overriding aim of this book may be summed up as a defense of the view that persons are not identical with their bodies and God is not identical with the cosmos, and yet persons and bodies, God and the cosmos, exist in a profoundly integral union. Integrative dualism and integrative theism will themselves be articulated as closely related.

A brief note about ultimates: no philosopher can do without assuming something, some principle, state or relationship, as basic or primitive in his or her work. At least at the outset of any philosophical inquiry we must provisionally assume that some notions or ideas are intelligible. There is nothing unphilosophical about this. Not all terms can be explained in an illuminating fashion by appeal to other terms. Earlier I referred

---

[24] Aelred Squire, *Asking the Fathers* (New York: Paulist Press, 1973), p. 128.

to Rorty and others who discard "God" along with "mind." The tendency to dismiss these notions is often due to critics adopting at the outset different assumptions about what is ultimate or basic in the cosmos, or what can be a proper starting point to begin reasoning about ourselves, the cosmos, and God. The early chapters of this book offer reasons for considering the existence of consciousness, the world of lived experience, as a viable, robust place for us to begin our philosophical reflection, reflection which (unless I am terribly mistaken) does not lead us to dismiss this world of consciousness as an illusion or a chimera with no place in a sober, hard-nosed view of the world. D. M. Armstrong concludes "it is the scientific vision of man, and not the philosophical or religious or artistic or moral vision of man, that is the best clue we have to the nature of man."[25] In effect, I argue that what Armstrong characterizes as the scientific vision is not supreme, but must take its place alongside philosophical, religious, artistic and moral visions. I believe that a more comprehensive vision will prove to be our best clue, not just to our own nature, but to the nature and mind of God.

Finally, a broadly based form of realism is assumed in what follows. That is, I assume that it is philosophically legitimate to argue about the truth and falsehood of different theories about God and ourselves. Much of the materialist challenge to classical theism presupposes a realist outlook – the truth of materialism entails the falsehood of theism. I believe that a realist, objective understanding of truth and falsehood is eminently defensible, though to review here all the *pro/contra* considerations involved would make this project too unwieldy.[26] If such a realist

---

[25] D. M. Armstrong, "The Nature of Mind," reprinted in *Readings in Philosophy of Psychology*, vol. I, ed. Ned Block (Cambridge, Mass.: Harvard University Press, 1980), p. 193. Armstrong's work is addressed later, but I note here the peculiar nature of his claim about science. It seems to me there is nothing in science *qua* science that does or can vindicate a claim like Armstrong's. Rather, his is a philosophical claim. Accepting the scientific account must itself be finally a philosophical decision, and this undermines the assertion that the ultimate grounds for choosing are scientific.

[26] See, for example, Roger Trigg's *Reality at Risk*, 2nd edition (London: Harvester Wheatsheaf, 1989), and *Understanding Social Science* (Oxford: Basil Blackwell, 1991). Some of those who oppose a realist view of truth do not have an impoverished notion of the mental, but a very rich, protean one. They may place, in Trigg's phrase,

treatment of truth is discredited, does the project of *Consciousness and the Mind of God* lose all value? I do not think so. If you believe that instead of truth and falsity, we may legitimately refer only to the relative justification of beliefs or to the propriety of beliefs within the confines of historically delineated traditions, the arguments of this book still have currency within those parameters. The reasons I advance for the truth of integrative dualism and the intelligibility of integrative theism may be employed, with some alterations, to argue for the justification of such beliefs or their defensibility within the context of certain traditions of inquiry.

The order of topics and the conclusions argued for are as follows:

Chapter 1: "Consciousness." Basic philosophies of the physical and mental are outlined and defined. I introduce some of the principal reasons why materialism is such an impressive theory and has achieved the hegemony it has in the current intellectual climate. Specifically I focus on the scientific grounds for materialism and its unified character. It is the unified nature of materialism that creates such a formidable challenge to a dualist philosophy that leaves the mental and physical in mysterious bifurcation. A materialist strategy of reduction is examined and an argument is laid out, the aim of which is to dislodge an ostensibly commonsense conviction that the mental and physical are irreducibly distinct. Important, additional reasons in favor of materialism are explored in succeeding chapters, as the aim of Chapter 1 is to launch the central philosophies at hand, to identify what I take to be some of the more central reasons in favor of materialism, and to initiate a dualist rejoinder. Reasons for and against materialism will eventually take the shape of a cumulative argument on either side. Our choice between comprehensive world-views rarely amounts to our assessment of a single argument, but appears to involve an array of considerations that are interrelated and variegated.

reality at risk, but I believe that some of their work places a radically materialist world-view at greater risk than world-views that recognize consciousness.

In proposing a dualist rejoinder in Chapter 1, I advance a criterion that differentiates mental and physical properties, and defend the legitimacy of appealing to subjective experience in replying to the arguments for materialism. I conclude with suggesting a way in which theism can provide a unified philosophical framework within which to understand the interwoven character of physical and mental life. Of course, to some critics, this will seem hopelessly quixotic, supporting the obscure with the even more obscure. The plausibility of materialism leads many people to regard theism as implausible, and one does not improve the credentials of one suspect witness by having his or her testimony corroborated by an equally suspect witness. However, I set out here the bare outline of what is developed in various stages throughout the book, as dualism and theism are articulated in related, integral terms. A dualist theory of the person in partnership with theism can, I believe, provide a substantially unified world-view to offset materialist complaints about the notoriously disjointed character of dualism. My view of theism and dualism is akin to what one patriot said about his companions during the American Revolution: they should hang together, for otherwise they will hang alone.

Chapter 2: "The Material World." Materialist arguments are canvassed that dualism rests upon an untenable theory of meaning and reference, that it invites an intolerable skepticism, and that its picture of the human person is intellectually opaque. The latter complaint arises from the charge that dualism rests upon a peculiarly empty notion of the mental; dualists tell us what the mental is not (it is nonphysical), without telling us what the mental is. A materialist version of functionalism is considered as a powerful alternative to dualism. In reply, I distinguish integrative dualism from other forms of dualism, and argue for its tenability over and against the above objections. Materialist versions of functionalism are criticized on the ground that they are unable to do justice to our subjective, conscious experience. Attention is given to how our concepts of the mental and physical, person, body, and human being may be refined. Theism is again brought to bear in an effort to develop a dualist response to materialist arguments, this time in response to the claim that dualism violates what may be called the public character of the mental.

Chapter 3: "Persons and Bodies." Reasons are advanced for viewing human persons as nonphysical, yet materially embodied in an integrative union. I reply to objections that dualism faces intractable problems in accounting for mental–physical causal interaction and for the individuation of persons. I consider and reject the proposal made by some materialists that human persons are physical, but could become nonphysical.

Chapter 4: "God and the World." The chapter begins with an overview of some of the historically important Christian conceptions of the person, including dualist as well as materialist. I then argue that important religious objections to dualism and the classical God–world distinction are not binding. This chapter is especially concerned with distancing integrative dualism from competing forms of dualism associated with Descartes and Plato. The work of earlier chapters is brought to bear to defend the coherence of believing that God is nonphysical and to resist theological materialism.

Chapter 5: "The Omnipresence of God." As the early chapters argue for an integrated dualism, I go on to develop a form of integrated theism. The key notions of Divine agency and knowledge are analyzed in articulating the theistic conviction that God is everywhere present throughout the cosmos. The relationship between the arguments for theism and dualism are clarified.

Chapter 6: "Integrative Theism." The concepts of psychological nearness and detachment are explored. Dualists are sometimes accused of promoting an excessively detached, disengaged notion of the self. I seek to identify different respects in which a kind of psychological detachment can be a virtue, essential to the development of personal life, and also to identify ways in which detachment can cripple and destroy. Balance is needed, and I examine what this amounts to in a psychospiritual sense within the framework of integrative dualism. I aim at overturning the charge that the idea of God as an incorporeal being cannot do justice to the religious experience of God's intimate presence. I defend the view that God has sorrow and pleasure in the world, and use this to expand the theistic understanding of God's ubiquity and the proximate, interior presence of God.

Conclusion: Summary of integrative dualism and theism and final remarks.

The early chapters, then, contain the main analysis and reply to materialism and the articulation of integrative dualism. Once a version of dualism is developed that avoids the atomism, body denigration, and hyper-privacy associated with Cartesianism, the path is all the clearer to explore a related integrative theistic philosophy which avoids the atomism, cosmic denigration, and isolationism often associated with traditional theism.

CHAPTER I

Consciousness

The starting point of philosophical theology is man himself, the common humanity that is known to each of us men existing in the world. The analysis of our own existence will draw attention especially to those structures and experiences which lie at the root of religion and of the life of faith.

John Macquarrie[1]

BETWEEN EXTREMES

Philosophers have not always regarded consciousness with suspicion. Some have treated consciousness itself and the inner world believed to be revealed to conscious attention – a world of desires, purposes, sensations, emotions, and judgments – as basic, evident realities. According to these philosophers, consciousness is not some motley illusion with no reality behind it. On the contrary, the world of conscious experience is the least peculiar, least precarious realm to investigate. The world of matter has seemed more of a riddle to unravel than the realm of mind. For it appears, or at least it has appeared to many philosophers in the past, that the mental world of conscious, subjective experience is immediately present or given. We do not have to engage in a weighty inferential process to determine, say, whether we are in gripping pain. Introspection (which literally means looking into or looking within) discloses our feelings and emotions with a unique surety; the etymology of

---

[1] John Macquarrie, *Principles of Christian Theology* (New York: Scribner, 1966), p. 51.

22

the word "consciousness" hints at the certainty available in conscious life, being derived from the Latin term, *conscientia*, for knowledge (knowing something with others). We may well know about the material world, but this has seemed to require comparatively greater work, having to be gained through conjecture and experiment, than knowledge of our own mental states.

Confident recognition of consciousness has marked many philosophical theories, but it was especially the hallmark of much idealist philosophy which flourished in the late nineteenth and early twentieth centuries. According to a prominent, representative version of idealism, all ostensibly material objects are actually units of conscious experience, the manifestation of one or many minds.[2] An idealist may employ this theory to analyze claims about material objects such as the assertion that there is a book in front of you as a claim about a wide range of experiences that you and others are having or would have, including the sensory awareness of black and white shapes, tactile sensations like the sensed resistance to pressure, maybe even the smell of paper. Some idealists dismissed as a hopeless confusion the notion of a material object that is independent of or separable from an experiencing subject. Idealists have coped in different ways with the (apparently) evident fact that objects like trees and galaxies can exist apart from particular experiencing subjects like you and me. At this juncture, some idealists have claimed that there is an overriding conscious mind, God or the Absolute, in which the sense experiences unfold that constitute trees, oceans, and the entirety of material reality.

To those schooled in some forms of philosophical Hinduism or of Buddhism, whether formally or through growing up in a culture in which either religion flourishes, idealism will not seem as odd as it does to the average "modern" westerner. To many,

---

[2] A. C. Ewing's *Idealism: A Critical Survey* is still a superb introduction to idealism (London: Methuen, 1933). Versions of idealism differ widely in their analysis of the self, consciousness, sensations, beliefs, desires and so on, as witnessed by comparing Bradley and Berkeley. The form of idealism I allude to in this and later chapters is closer to Berkeley's.

it appears that idealism is thoroughly refuted by the success of the natural sciences. On this front, it is worth noting that idealists themselves have insisted that the success of science is not at all an embarrassment. The early twentieth-century logician-philosopher Charles Peirce thought of the natural sciences as taking place within an altogether mental world. "The one intelligible theory of the universe is that of objective idealism, that matter is effete mind, inveterate habits becoming physical laws."[3] In the hands of some idealists, the sciences are seen as principally ordering and regimenting past and present sense experiences. Laws of nature turn out to cover recurring patterns of experience. Idealism is not without champions today, T. L. S. Sprigge and John Foster among them. One of my own teachers, Peter Bertocci, was a vigorous defender of idealism; he contended that "the qualitative structure of all being is psychic or mental as well as goal-directed."[4]

According to many idealists, the commonsense, ordinary notion of a material object is a theoretical construction of our own. We become accustomed to thinking of material objects existing independently of experience. This informal assumption becomes such an habitual, humdrum affair that it appears natural, almost instinctive, to believe that we live among experience-independent entities. We lose track of the fact that the belief in such material objects is a convenient hypothesis. Today, precisely the opposite move has been introduced by some philosophers. They argue that the realm of consciousness, our sensations and beliefs as we ordinarily think of them, is a theoretical construct. Just as idealists held that positing an experience-independent material world is a fiction, some materialist philosophers characterize our ordinary grasp of beliefs, desires, and so on as a well-entrenched yet false ideology.

At the opposite end of the philosophical spectrum from idealism, psychological categories have little prestige. Marvin

[3] C. S. Peirce in *The Collected Papers of Charles Sanders Peirce*, ed. Charles Hartshorne and Paul Weiss (Cambridge, Mass.: Harvard University Press, 1965), vol. I, p. 24.

[4] Peter A. Bertocci, "The Perspective of a Teleological Personalistic Idealist," in *Contemporary American Philosophy*, ed. John E. Smith (London: George Allen & Unwin, 1970), p. 248.

Minsky counsels a cautious, wary approach to the mental world as we ordinarily conceive of it.

Though prescientific idea terms like "believe," "know" and "mean" are useful in daily life, they seem too coarse to support powerful theories; we need to supplant rather than to support and explicate them. Real as "self" or "understand" may seem to us today, they are not (like milk and sugar) objective things our theories must accept and explain; they are only first steps toward better concepts.[5]

Daniel Dennett likewise seeks to dispel confidence in the world of beliefs. Why might we want to talk about beliefs? Not just "because they are there," for it is far from obvious that they are there. Beliefs have a less secure position in a critical scientific ontology than, say, electrons or genes.[6] Steven Stich proposes that our ordinary notion of beliefs and desires, which he calls folk psychology, has no place in a serious account of human life. Introducing his radical book *From Folk Psychology to Cognitive Science* Stich writes: "My focus will be on the folk psychological concept of belief, and my central thesis will be that this concept ought not to play any significant role in a science aimed at explaining human cognition and behavior."[7] A similar claim may be found in work by Willard Quine, Paul Churchland, and Patricia Churchland.[8] These philosophers adopt a stance opposite idealists who would return the compliment by charging that the materialist understanding of objects – whether of electrons and genes or milk and sugar – is too coarse to support powerful theories of reality. The materialist's idea of a physical object is not as clear and well grounded as sensory experience

[5] Marvin Minsky, "Decentralized Mind," *Behavioral and Brain Sciences* 3 (1980), 439.
[6] Daniel Dennett, *Brainstorms* (Cambridge, Mass.: MIT Press, 1978), p. xx.
[7] Stephen Stich, *From Folk Psychology to Cognitive Science: The Case Against Belief* (Cambridge, Mass.: MIT Press, 1983), p. 5.
[8] Quine's position in *Word and Object* (Cambridge, Mass.: MIT Press, 1960) is representative: "If we are limning the true and ultimate structure of reality the canonical scheme for us is the austere scheme that knows... no propositional attitudes but only the physical constitution and behavior of organisms," p. 221. At a later point, in *Quiddities: An Intermittently Philosophical Dictionary*, Quine seems less dismissive (Cambridge, Mass.: Harvard University Press, 1987), pp. 132–133, but this hardly seems like a retraction of his earlier views. Note p. 133 especially: "Whatever it precisely may be, consciousness is a state of the body, a state of nerves." Cf. Paul Feyerabend, "Mental Events and the Brain," *Journal of Philosophy* 60 (1963).

and, thus, not a notion that ought to be used in accounting for human cognition and behavior. To put it crudely, idealists supplant matter with mind, whereas materialists like Stich supplant mind with matter. Many idealists would not hesitate to reverse Churchland's claim: "There is no doubt at all that physical matter exists, while spiritual matter remains a tenuous hypothesis."[9]

Midway between the extremes of radical idealism and the austere materialism just documented lies dualism. The dualist joins the idealist in recognizing a realm of conscious awareness, a realm which is not itself physical, and joins the materialist in recognizing a distinct realm of objects which are not the contents of consciousness. As such, dualism seems to represent a marriage between partners who are forever in tension. A dualist resists the allure of either account alone, each of which purports to provide a more unified picture of reality.

Dualism is frequently characterized by its friends and foes alike as common sense, the philosophy of the "person on the street." Michael Levin, a materialist, puts the point baldly: "Mankind's official view of itself is dualistic."[10] After all, *contra* idealism, it appears – at least at first – that the radically

---

[9] Churchland, *Matter and Consciousness*, p. 18.

[10] Levin, *Metaphysics and the Mind–Body Problem* (Oxford: Clarendon Press, 1979), p. 64. Many opponents of dualism admit that it is the commonsense or at least commonly held theory of the person in the West, the metaphysics of the ordinary person on the street. See Thomas Hobbes, *The English Works of Thomas Hobbes of Malmesbury* (London: John Bohn, 1839), vol. IV, p. 62; Daniel Dennett, *Content and Consciousness* (London: Routledge & Kegan Paul, 1969), pp. 3–5 and *Consciousness Explained* (London: Allen Lane, 1991); David Lewis, "An Argument for the Identity Theory," *Journal of Philosophy* 63 (1966), 25; Thomas Nagel, "Physicalism," *Philosophical Review* 74 (1965), 340; Brian O'Shaughnessy, *The Will*, 2 vols. (Cambridge: Cambridge University Press, 1980), vol. I, p. 29; Richard Rorty, *Philosophy and the Mirror of Nature* (Princeton: Princeton University Press), p. 17; J. J. C. Smart, "Materialism," *Journal of Philosophy* 60 (1963), 661; and Derek Parfit, *Reasons and Persons* (Oxford: Oxford University Press, 1984), pp. ix-x, 219. Donald Davidson, Wilfred Sellars, and William Lycan insist that we must explain why it seems that the mental is distinct from the physical, why people are tempted to embrace Cartesian dualism. See Davidson's "Mental Events," in *Experience and Theory*, ed. Lawerence Foster and J. W. Swanson (Amherst: University of Massachussetts Press, 1970) and William Lycan's *Consciousness* (Cambridge, Mass.: MIT Press, 1987), p. 42. As noted in Chapters 3 and 4, dualism, or beliefs that entail dualism, are also widely spread in eastern cultures and among indigenous peoples, for example Native Americans.

materialist view is too extreme: sensations, emotions, and beliefs seem to exist and appear to be distinct from, though closely related to, physical bodies and material processes. Feeling pain and believing $2 + 2 = 4$ seem distinct from neural and other bodily processes, and dualist philosophers typically appeal to such apparent disparity in an effort to establish some presumption in favor of their views.

Of course our initial, pre-philosophical picture of ourselves may be an enormous mistake, however firmly installed as a commonplace assumption. Moreover, the pre-philosophical view of the mental and the physical is not well defined and precise. At first, a formal, radically dualist stance (you are not your body, but an embodied, nonphysical mind) may seem as odd as a radically materialist one (beliefs and desires do not exist). So, let us initially characterize dualism very broadly, subject to later refinement, without making any reference to souls or immaterial minds. Dualism is the view that the mental is distinct from the physical. Thus far, there is nothing about dualism to suggest anything specifically religious, and accepting dualism would not be incompatible with thinking of ourselves as biological animals. As for the latter, the dualist will hold that being a warm-blooded animal like a *homo sapiens* involves physical *and* mental life.

At the start, we can characterize the physical in terms of the natural sciences. An object, property, or process is physical if it is posited and described by sciences such as physics, chemistry, and biology. Galaxies, atoms, subatomic particles, DNA, enzymes, neurons, and so on, are all physical. The mental may be demarcated by offering examples. Believing, doubting, hoping, desiring, feeling, sensing, and the like are all mental activities and states. If, in addition to believing, doubting, hoping, desiring, feeling, and sensing, there are beliefs, doubts, hopes, desires, and sensations, then these are also examples of the mental. The prospects of a more rigorous depiction of the mental and physical will be explored in the next chapter. At the outset, then, dualism may be thought of as the thesis that the mental, as we have delineated it, is distinct from the physical; it is neither identical with, nor constituted by, that which is posited and described by the natural sciences. The intuitive appeal or commonsensical character of dualism emerges if you imagine a neurologist scanning your brain and claiming to have discovered that your beliefs about Winston Churchill are not just causally related to, but are the very same thing as, brain states, properties, and connections. If you think there are beliefs, and if you think that it would be odd to discover them in the physical realm like this, you have at least some quasi-dualist sympathies. Similarly, if you think that your feelings of, say, anxiety or exhilaration involve something more than specific brain states and various bodily relations and processes, you may be disposed to dualism. Insofar as dualism is part of common sense, I think it should be added that common sense is not just dualistic in orientation, but tied to what philosophers technically refer to as interactionist as opposed to epiphenomenalist and occasionalist versions of dualism. Dualistic interactionism is the view that the mental and physical causally affect one another. Epiphenomenalism is the thesis that the causal relation is only one way: the physical affects the mental but not *vice versa*. According to occasionalism, there is no direct causal relation between the mental and physical at all, but both are harmonized and coordinated by God.[11] Occasionalism has had few adherents, because of its extravagant conception of causation and magisterial supertheism, while epiphenomenalism seems to be at complete odds with everyday convictions about our bringing about material changes in the world, thus leaving interactionism as the most commonly adhered to form of dualism. From a pre-philosophical point of view it would be odd to think that no changes in the material world depend on people's thoughts, feelings, and desires. I consider shortly whether dualist interactionism does indeed possess any initial intuitive support from "common sense" and, if so, whether this is philosophically important.

There are roughly two versions of materialism that are in wide currency today, each of which poses a challenge to dualism. The first form of materialism is the radically elimi-

---

[11] The best-known defender of occasionalism was Nicolas Malebranche (1638–1715).

native sort already sketched, as propounded in different ways by Stich, the Churchlands, Rorty, Quine, and others. These materialists charge that the mental realm as we ordinarily conceive of it does not exist and should be eliminated outright from serious theorizing about reality. Folk psychology may be practical, serving many purposes, but it is not genuinely explanatory or descriptive of what exists. I shall refer to this account as eliminative materialism. The second theory is best termed identity materialism because it acknowledges the reality of the mental but insists the mental can be reduced to, or somehow identified with, the physical. This second school of materialism has yielded different accounts of how the mental is construed. One version of the identity strategy is to liken the relation between the mental and physical to the relation between clouds and water vapor. Clouds are made up of water vapor as mental states like feeling pain are made up of various physiological events, different nerve patterns for example. Accordingly, this strategy permits its followers to affirm the existence of clouds and pains while at the same time insisting that these are not something other than water vapor and neurological matter respectively. In recognizing the mental, identity materialists hope to avoid being dismissed because of what Donald Davidson calls the "nothing-but reflex," for example How can you possibly claim that loving another person is *nothing but* brain and other bodily processes?[12] Although identity materialists assert that a person should be seen in exclusively physical terms, they hope to avoid the knee-jerk criticism that their account treats the mental as a theoretical delinquent. Loving and other mental activities exist, and yet they turn out to be thoroughly material processes. Some philosophers adopt what I am referring to as the identity theory, but call their theory nonreductive or compositional materialism.

Special notice needs to be taken here of a theory that is sometimes labeled materialist, though it is far more commonly

---

[12] Donald Davidson, *Actions and Events* (Oxford: Clarendon Press, 1980), p. 214. But compare B. F. Skinner on love in *Recent Issues in the Analysis of Behavior* (Columbus: Merrill, 1989), pp. 5–7.

considered a form of dualism. According to this theory there are only physical objects, yet some of these objects, preeminently human persons, have mental properties that are not physical. The theory is materialistic insofar as it denies the existence of any nonphysical individual things, and, because of this, it is occasionally called supervenient materialism. Even so, its more common designation is dualist as it challenges both identity and eliminative materialism on the grounds that beliefs and sensory states are not identical with, nor do they constitute, anything physical. The theory satisfies the characterization of dualism I have suggested we begin with, and is often referred to in the literature as the dual-aspect theory, property dualism, and feature dualism. When it is important to delineate the theory from more developed forms of dualism (those that accept nonphysical individuals, minds, souls, selves, or persons) I shall call it the dual-aspect theory.

These three camps, eliminative materialism, identity materialism and the dual-aspect theory, mirror three forms of idealism. An eliminative idealist holds that there are no material objects whatever. These eliminativists argue that the very concept of a material object should be jettisoned as incoherent or, if admitted as coherent, rejected as having no application in the real world. An idealist identity theorist accommodates reference to material objects but claims that ostensible material objects are actually the contents of consciousness. Although difficult to classify, the great eighteenth-century British idealist George Berkeley may have adhered to this last position. He countenanced talk of physical objects, so long as we understand the very essence of such objects to involve their being perceived.[13] It is difficult to locate idealists who adhere to their own

---

[13] Berkeley certainly countenanced reference to mountains, rivers, houses, and such, allowing the philosophically naive to call these material objects. His concern was that when we do philosophy we realize "What are the aforementioned objects [mountains, *et al.*] but the things we perceive by sense, and what do we perceive besides our own ideas or sensations; and is it not plainly repugnant that any one of these or any combination of them should exist unperceived?" (*Principles of Human Knowledge* 1.4). Berkeley's considered philosophical outlook was uncompromisingly idealist, however. "Nothing properly but persons, i.e. conscious things, do exist; all other things are not so much existence as manners of the existence of persons" (*The*

version of the dual-aspect theory, believing that there are physical properties and only nonphysical objects, though perhaps the seventeenth-century Dutch philosopher Baruch Spinoza came close to doing so.[14]

In this book I use the term "dual-aspect theory" only to refer to the nonidealist version of the theory, though I make one exception by noting the contrary version in the following list of views discussed so far.

MENTAL		MENTAL-PHYSICAL		PHYSICAL
Eliminative idealism	Dual-aspect theory	Dualist interactionism	Dual-aspect theory	Eliminative materialism
Identity idealism		Dualist epiphenomenalism		Identity materialism (also called nonreductive and compositional materialism)
		Dualist occasionalism		

I do not want to give the impression that this schema of classification and the terms adopted are the only ones feasible. What I have called eliminative materialism is sometimes called mental nihilism or the disappearance theory. It is worth noting

Philosophical Commentaries 24; 1, p. 10). Because of Berkeley's theistic version of idealism, in which material objects turn out to exist independently of our own perceptions though not God's, I am inclined to regard him as more of an identity theorist, preserving a large segment of our common assumptions about the objects around us. Nontheistic phenomenalists in the idealist camp seem to me more like eliminativists insofar as they do not allow for this degree of perceiver-independence.

[14] Spinoza held that the ultimate reality which he called God or nature has matter as one of its many attributes; God or nature is not material in and of itself. As an aside note, if Spinoza's metaphysics is coherent, then Fred Feldman seems to be mistaken in his analysis of physical properties. Feldman holds that "F is a physical property = df. Necessarily, if something X, has F at some time, t, then X is a physical object at t," *A Cartesian Introduction to Philosophy* (New York: McGraw-Hill, 1986), p. 166. Spinoza believed that God or nature has physical (material) attributes (properties) and yet is not itself a physical object. There may be some dispute about whether Spinoza should be considered an idealist, and not a neutral monist. Neutral monism is discussed in Chapter 6. For an idealist reading of Spinoza, see T. L. S. Sprigge's "Spinoza: His Identity Theory," in *Philosophy Through its Past*, ed. Ted Honderich (Harmondsworth, Middlesex: Penguin, 1984).

that whether the dual-aspect theory is labeled in textbooks a brand of materialism or a brand of dualism often seems to reflect the vantage point of the one doing the classification. From the perspective of an eliminative materialist, the view I am calling the dual-aspect theory may appear to be lavishly dualist, while an ardent Cartesian dualist might regard the theory as so timid and bland that it is best considered to be merely garden-variety or soft materialism. I have depicted the dual-aspect theory as dualist, but it should be borne in mind that it does not wander as far from the materialist stronghold as more developed forms of dualism. It is also worth underscoring at the beginning that it is not always easy to identify who in the history of philosophy held which theory. There are notorious difficulties with respect to Aristotle's writings, for example, and determining whether Aristotle should be considered a dual-aspect theorist, a more substantive dualist ("a card carrying dualist," in Daniel Robinson's phrase), or an identity materialist. Bernard Williams describes Aristotelianism as "a polite form of materialism," but one can build a case for describing Aristotle as a begrudging, uneasy dualist.[15] Such problems in locating different philosophers will beset virtually every classification schema.

Because the current philosophical climate is principally materialist rather than idealist in character, the major preoccupation in these opening chapters will be with the case for and against materialism. I also focus on materialism because, in light of the considerations on display in the Introduction, I believe it represents the most serious challenge to classical theism. A survey of reasons why many embrace materialism will serve as an accurate representation of reasons why some philosophers think of dualism as extinct, omitted from the customary taxonomy of live, intelligent options. I begin by

---

[15] Bernard Williams, "Hylomorphism," *Oxford Studies in Ancient Philosophy* 4 (1986), 195. It is clear that Aristotle is no Cartesian dualist, but some worry whether he isn't too close to Descartes's camp for comfort. For a brilliant introduction to Aristotle's work, see Dan Robinson's *Aristotle's Psychology* (New York: Columbia University Press, 1989). Also see Robert Heinamen's discussion of whether Aristotle is best viewed as a dualist in "Aristotle and the Mind–Body Problem," *Phronesis* 35:1 (1990).

outlining an important materialist strategy for reducing the mental to the physical, and then examine a series of pro-materialist arguments that are largely inspired by the promise of modern science.

A MATERIALIST STRATEGY; REDUCTION
FROM TOP TO BOTTOM

Daniel Dennett is one of the more prominent, current anti-dualists, so it is fitting to begin with an overview of his work and the behaviorist background to his and many other forms of materialism. Dennett concedes that at the outset it seems that beliefs and desires exist, that they account for our purposive activity, and that all this provides *some* grounds for dualism. He grants that describing ourselves in terms of beliefs and desires is practical and perhaps even indispensable for a range of activities in ordinary life, but he goes on to insist that there are different levels of explanation and that belief–desire explanations are only viable at what he depicts as "the top level." At the top we can account for things in terms of sophisticated intentions, what Dennett calls intentional system characterizations, but these explanations can then be explained in terms of deeper and deeper accounts in which intentions play less and less of a role. Ultimately intentional explanations give way to nonintentional, purely physicalist accounts of human and other forms of conscious, sentient life. Explanations are nonintentional if they make no reference to any intentional attitudes or activities like believing, desiring, hoping, fearing, and so on.

Though not itself a form of behaviorism, Dennett's work may be seen as an off-shoot from early versions of behaviorism, the view that mental states and activities refer to material behavior. Perhaps the most popularly acclaimed behaviorist since the 1950s has been B. F. Skinner, who propounded an uncompromising version of materialism, and it will be useful to sketch briefly Skinner's stance, from which Dennett takes his cue.

Skinner thought psychological, internal feelings, attitudes, and sensory awareness have no important role to play in the

determination of human behavior.[16] He had several complaints
against mentalist notions of consciousness and reasons why they
were not scientifically "well behaved." Principally, he advanced two complaints against folk psychology. The first was
that folk psychology is vacuous. In the final analysis, explanations in folk psychology proceed by the equivalent of positing
an invisible internal agent – an homunculus or little man – to
account for the behavior of the bigger, better visible agent
before us. Consider, for example, Sigmund Freud's explanation
of human behavior in terms of id, ego, and super-ego. In
Freudian theory these three entities were imagined to function
as though they were separate agent-like selves or little people
struggling for supremacy, making war and peace, within the
greater self. Skinner deemed this positing as easy as it was
unhelpful. "The fictional nature of this form of inner cause is
shown by the ease with which the mental process is discovered
to have just the properties needed to account for behavior."[17] I
do X because I have certain matching desires and beliefs and a
will to do X. This account seemed to Skinner to be no more
illuminating than the standard sample of pseudo-explanations
whereby the sleep-making effects of opium are explained on the
grounds that opium has sleep-making power. Skinner's second
complaint is that folk psychology leaves psychology itself
unaccounted for. According to Skinner, a folk-psychological
account of intelligent activity brings curiosity to an end, for the
whole point of scientific inquiry is to explain intelligence. The
positing of homunculi-like entities does more to enshrine
intelligence than explain it. Skinner held that even if the
explanations of folk psychology are not vacuous, they still lead
us nowhere. Imagine that a Freudian account of someone's
behavior is accepted, according to which the ego was impaired
by the id's drives. Now, we have the task of explaining, in turn,
why the ego and the id behave the way they do. Folk psychology

[16] Despite his marginalizing of mental states here, Skinner was not an eliminativist. See
Richard Creel's very fine paper, "Radical Epiphenomenalism: B. F. Skinner's
Account of Private Events", *Behaviorism* 8:1 (1980), 31–53. It is fitting to begin with
a discussion of behaviorism, as many materialist schemas are advanced as making
improvements on it.
[17] B. F. Skinner, *Science and Human Behavior* (New York: Macmillan, 1983).

thereby seems saddled either with initiating an endless regress of explanations in terms of sub-egos and sub-ids or with just leaving unexplained some brute mental reality. Insofar as accounts of the psychological remain in the domain of the psychological, we have yet to get to the philosophical and scientific bottom of things.

Dennett judged this dismissal of the mental to be problematic, but not because our conscious experience of acting in the world or possessing beliefs and desires constitute some distinct, full-bodied citizenship in a sober account of what exists. Thus, Dennett's critical departure from Skinner is quite different from that of others, who insist that behaviorists overlook the evident feel or subjective character of mental life. Rather, Dennett contends we should permit mini-agent or homunculi talk such as Freud's; there is no reason for the materialist to dispense with all talk of agency. "Psychology without homunculi is impossible," Dennett writes.[18] To think of persons as intentional systems is fitting and not altogether vacuous. However, Dennett's aim is to employ talk of homunculi only with an important proviso. We explain the behavior of homunculi in terms of smaller homunculi, homunculi who are less intelligent, less bright. Progress is made if we can account for things of high intelligence in terms of "a team or committee of relatively ignorant, narrow-minded, blind homunculi."[19] The final pay-off is to get to levels of homunculi so low that they can be replaced by the purely physical, the mechanical. Thus, Dennett shares with Skinner the view that a science of human nature will not be successful until intentional system characterizations give way to exclusively physical, nonintentional accounts. Ultimately we must get rid of the homunculi, for while we cannot do psychology without them, "psychology with homunculi is doomed to circularity or infinite regress."[20]

An analogy may be useful. Consider a corporation such as IBM. Why did IBM introduce the computer XY? Little is gained in the way of an answer if we reply that IBM believed

[18] Dennett, "Artificial Intelligence as Philosophy and as Psychology," in *Brainstorms*, p. 123.   [19] *Ibid.*, p. 122.   [20] *Ibid.*, p. 122.

that the XY was profitable and acted on that belief, though this provides an informative description as a decent starting point. We do a little better when we explain the action of IBM in terms of what various departments of the corporation research, the history of the Board of Directors, and the like. These items (departments and boards) can also be broken down into smaller units. Why did Ms. Stewart vote to market the computer? Dennett's strategy is somewhat analogous. He countenances talk of intentionally undertaking projects on the grounds of certain beliefs and desires as a preliminary description of what occurs so long as he can then look for a more fine-grained, deeper analysis of what occurs.

Eventually this nesting of boxes within boxes lands you with homunculi so stupid (all they have to do is remember when to say yes or no when asked) that they can be, as one says, "replaced by a machine." One discharges fancy homunculi from one's scheme by organizing armies of such idiots to do the work.[21]

Our account of IBM's behavior in terms of other committees may always leave us with some level of intentionality, whereas Dennett wants ultimately to dispel reference to intentional agency in his final account of human behavior.

This is called a "top-down" strategy. We begin with a level of sophistication and intellection which appears to be radically different from physical events. We start at the top with commonsense talk of intentionally doing things, entertaining beliefs, and the like.[22] Still, this talk is tentative. It need not be uncritically included in our final theory as to what really exists. Dennett's concern to save the mental only temporarily is summed up in his book *Brainstorms*.

We can, then, "agree" with Skinner when we read him between the lines to be asserting that no satisfactory, psychological theory can rest on any use of intentional idioms, for their use presupposes rationality, which is the very thing psychology is supposed to explain. So if there is progress in psychology, *it will inevitably be, as Skinner suggests, in the direction of eliminating ultimate appeals to beliefs, desires, and other intentional*

---

[21] *Ibid.*, p. 124. See also pp. 80, 81, and chapter 1 of *Consciousness Explained*.
[22] Dennett, *Brainstorms*, p. xx.

items from our explanations ... But ... there is no reason why intentional terms cannot be used provisionally in the effort to map out
functions of the behaviour control system of men and animals, just so
long as a way is found eventually to "cash them out" by designing a
mechanism to function as specified.[23] (My italics)

Like a factory that becomes so automated that the human
workers are ultimately replaced by machines, the scientific
analysis of human behavior proceeds to develop greater and
greater power, until ultimately one's settled nonpsychological
account of why people act the way they do is able to replace our
appeal to beliefs and desires. When we employ intentional
idioms to "explain" events, we are said to be taking out a
theoretical loan. We are leaning on terms which themselves need
to be accounted for, and Dennett thinks the only way for our
explanations to get out of the red and into the black is to reach
explanations which are freed from appeal to our felt desires and
beliefs.

Intentionality abstracts from the inessential details of the various
forms intelligence-loans can take (e.g. signal-readings, volition emit-
ters, librarians in the corridors of memory, egos and superegos) and
serves as a reliable means of detecting exactly where a theory is *in the
red* relative to the task of explaining intelligence; wherever a theory
relies on a formulation bearing the logical marks of intentionality,
there a little man is concealed.[24]

Bedrock, *bona fide* explanations of events must be of a physical
sort that makes no use of mentalist talk of intentions, desires,
and so on. Employing Dennett's scheme of cashing out top-level
intentional descriptions in terms of increasingly simpler ones,
we come ever closer to realizing purely physical explanations.
Person-level, psychological characterizations are ultimately to
be seen as decomposed into sub-personal, nonpsychological
characterizations. As Paul Ziff reports: "The current mental-
istic schema is gradually giving up the ghost. Our intellectual
concepts, thinking, planning, experimenting, all are tottering;

[23] Dennett, "Skinner Skinned," *Ibid.*, pp. 61, 62.
[24] Dennett, *Brainstorms*, p. 12. See also his "Three Kinds of Intentional Psychology" in
Reduction, Time and Reality, ed. R. A. Healey (Cambridge: Cambridge University
Press, 1981). Dennett's comments on intentionality are not always clearly consistent.

intelligence looks to be not importantly different from a trait of mechanical morons with lightning-like access to prodigious memories, computers."[25] In *Consciousness Explained* Dennett articulates his own project in explicit, simple terms. "Only a theory that explained conscious events in terms of unconscious events could explain consciousness at all."[26]

Dennett's strategy illustrates a way in which philosophers can recognize the mental at one level, and yet reduce it to the physical without remainder by taking incremental explanatory steps, without adopting Skinner's more direct route. Having offered this rough depiction of a physicalist stratagem, let us consider several lines of argument prompting us to make the move from what Dennett depicts as top to bottom. After surveying the rationale for materialism, I canvass some of the resources available to the dualist in mounting a rejoinder. The opening salvo of materialist arguments focus on the philosophical significance of scientific investigation, the overall explanatory unity of materialism, and an argument that our folk-psychological understanding of sensations is ripe for theoretical replacement by more respectable physical notions. All three areas are closely related, and constitute a cumulative case for materialism. In Chapter 2 other arguments in favor of materialism are considered that appeal to linguistic meaning, reference, and the theory of knowledge. In various ways these latter arguments build upon the unified character of a materialist philosophy to be examined here.

EMPIRICAL EVIDENCE

Materialists such as Daniel Dennett, Paul Churchland, Richard Rorty, Michael Levin, Sydney Shoemaker, and others have maintained that sufficient empirical data either exist already or will soon to establish that the mental does not constitute a realm distinct from the physical world. The natural sciences, especially neuroscience, have brought to light the enormous role of

---

[25] Paul Ziff, "The Simplicity of Other Minds," *Journal of Philosophy* 62 (1965), 584.
[26] *Consciousness Explained*, p. 454.

material forces in shaping our development. Churchland assesses the bearing of these findings on our theory of human nature:

> If there really is a distinct entity in which reasoning, emotion, and consciousness take place, and if that entity is dependent on the brain for nothing more than sensory experience as input and volitional executions as output, then one would expect reason, emotion, and consciousness to be relatively invulnerable to direct control or pathology by manipulation or damage to the brain.[27]

We have detected very little, if any, psychological invulnerability to physical forces, and the more vulnerable we discover ourselves to be (it is argued), the more evidence we have of our being thoroughly material. Churchland likens a materialist account of the mental to what he takes to be analogous scientific advances.

> The red surface of an apple does not *look* like a matrix of molecules reflecting photons at certain critical wave-lengths, but that is what it is. The sound of a flute does not *sound* like a sinusoidal compression wave train in the atmosphere, but that is what it is. The warmth of the summer air does not *feel* like the mean kinetic energy of millions of tiny molecules, but that is what it is. If one's pains and hopes and beliefs do not introspectively seem like electrochemical states in a neural network, that may be only because our faculty of introspection, like our other senses, is not sufficiently penetrating to reveal such hidden details.[28]

As I observed earlier, dualists have been wont to appeal to our subjective experience as part of their case against materialism. Don't we know that having certain experiences differs radically from the physiological states identified by materialists? Churchland and others construe this dualist posture as a stubborn resistance to scientific advance.

While materialists of virtually every stripe agree that the sciences threaten a nonphysical account of human nature, they disagree at points about the precise form of materialism which emerges as best supported. Identity materialists stress the discovery of close correlations between the mental and physical,

[27] Paul Churchland, *Matter and Consciousness* (Cambridge, Mass.: MIT Press, 1984), p. 20.   [28] *Ibid.*, p. 15.

using this correlation to establish the identity of the two. If what we take to be two items are invariably conjoined, "they" display the same effects, and "they" are brought about by the same causes, why persist in positing two items, rather than simply one? Sydney Shoemaker advances a criterion of identity that would enable us to treat evidence of correlation as evidence of identity. He argues that mental and physical events are identical if they have the same causes and the same effects. "Properties are identical, whether in the same possible world or in different ones, just in case their co-instantiation with the same properties gives rise to the same causal powers."[29] This criterion seems to be at work in a systematic, fertile way in the sciences. It would be agonizingly anti-scientific to refuse to acknowledge that water is H_2O if one had reason to believe that each behaves exactly the same in causal contexts (water boils at 100 degrees Celsius, so does H_2O, and so on). With a causation-based criterion of identity in place, some materialists claim that the sciences have virtually established the truth of materialism. After all, it is widely agreed that the sciences have demonstrated the close causal tie between the mental and physical. Few dualists would deny that neurological processes affect feelings, emotions, and thoughts. If neurology can establish that so-called mental properties and their matching physical properties are brought about by the same causes and give rise to the same effects, then it is reasonable to conclude that mental properties are actually physical. Shoemaker and many other identity theorists do not take the extra step, however, of concluding that there are no such things as mental properties. As an identity materialist, Shoemaker is convinced, for example, that these folk items do exist.

As identity-materialist philosophers look to correlations between the mental and physical to establish the identity of the former with the latter, eliminativists like Stich place a great deal

---

[29] Sydney Shoemaker, "Causality and Properties," in *Time and Cause*, ed. Peter Van Inwagen (Dordrecht: Reidel, 1980), p. 122. Shoemaker's concern is with properties; Donald Davidson endorses a similar causal account of individuation when it comes to events. See his paper "The Individuation of Events," in *Essays in Honor of Carl G. Hempel*, ed. N. Rescher (Dordrecht: Reidel, 1969). The criticism that is later raised against Shoemaker applies against Davidson.

of weight on cases in which there fails to be any systematic correlation. Many, though not all, identity theorists want to achieve a scientific analysis of mental life, identifying laws linking what we call beliefs and desires with their underlying physical constituents.[30] Eliminative materialists, on the other hand, try to show how the whole framework of beliefs and desires is inadequate, or at least unnecessary, both in describing and explaining human behavior. Stich highlights case studies by social psychologists in which it appears that the ordinary conception of ourselves as agents provides an inadequate explanatory framework. There are cases in which a person's reported beliefs, motives, and desires are implausible candidates for explaining behavior, and Stich suggests that such failures of folk psychology should lead us to question whether any beliefs, desires, and so on exist at all. I consider some of Stich's cases later. Stich agrees with Churchland that folk psychology is very much like what we now recognize to be false theorizing about the world in other areas.

Folk astronomy was false astronomy and not just in detail. The general conception of the cosmos embedded in the folk wisdom of the West was utterly and thoroughly mistaken. Much the same could be said for folk biology, folk chemistry, and folk physics. However wonderful and imaginative folk theorising and speculation has been, it has turned out to be screamingly false in every domain where we now have a reasonably sophisticated science. Nor is there any reason to think that ancient camel drivers would have greater insight or better luck when the subject at hand was the structure of their own minds rather than the structure of matter or of the cosmos.[31]

Identity theorists give the camel drivers slightly more credit but neither they nor eliminativists allow them enough credibility to be of service to dualism.

The materialist program, and the difference between eliminative and identity materialism, can be seen in relation to Ockham's razor, named after the fourteenth century philosophical theologian William of Ockham. According to the

[30] Donald Davidson is an example of an identity theorist who wants to resist positing psychophysical laws. See "Mental Events."
[31] Stich, *From Folk Psychology*, pp. 229, 230.

principle of Ockham's razor, one should omit from one's theoretical explanations any items that are not necessary to explain the relevant data. Both eliminative and identity theorists agree that it is not necessary to posit a nonphysical mind and nonphysical psychological properties to explain human behavior. But while identity theorists insist that we should not omit psychological phenomena (when appropriately identified as physical realities) from our view of human life, eliminativists think Ockham's razor can be used to shave off even this last vestige of our folk world. Eliminativists wield Ockham's razor with greater vigor than do identity theorists.

THE MENTAL IS JUST A THEORY ARGUMENT

As Dennett seeks to displace our pre-philosophical, common-sense understanding of intentionality to make room for ultimately nonintentional, physical processes, Paul Churchland endeavors to displace our ordinary conception of sensory experience. As with many other materialists, his central, initial task is to discount the idea that our experience constitutes a realm distinct from the world of material objects and events. Churchland introduces a thought experiment designed to show that when dualists seek to vindicate their stance by appealing to sense experience, this is not a case of appealing to pre-theoretical evidence. If it were, then the evident subjective character of sense experience would constitute a stubborn obstacle to the project of eliminativism. Against this, Churchland contends that our ordinary understanding of sensations is itself theory-laden. Churchland's strategy can be formulated succinctly: If sensory states are nontheoretical, then there cannot be creatures who have what Churchland calls transposed modalities. There can be such creatures. Hence it is false to think of sensory terms as nontheoretical.

Churchland's thought experiment of transposed modalities is as follows. Imagine that there are creatures we may call infrared cousins who are similar to us in every respect except that they have no tactile sensations. Instead, they have extraordinary visual capacities enabling them to perceive the middle-range temperatures of ordinary objects. They assent to the following list of temperature beliefs.

a. Fires are hot.
b. A warm thing will warm up a cooler thing, but never the reverse.
c. If a body is warmer than a second body, and that second body is warmer than a third body, then the first body is warmer than the third body.
d. Food keeps better in a cold place.
e. Hot things cause painful burns.
f. Rubbing things makes them warmer.[32]

To increase the plausibility of his thought experiment Churchland describes their large eyeballs, refracted lenses, and sensitivity to some wave lengths of electromagnetic radiation.

Since the vigor with which any body radiates in the far infrared is a more or less straightforward function of its temperature, and since images of these bodies will be formed on the retinas of the kind of eyes described, their possessors will be quite prepared, physiologically, to perceive visually the temperatures of common bodies, since the "brightness" of the corresponding image will be a function thereof.[33]

The creatures' language is indistinguishable from ours except that our temperature vocabulary of "cold," "hot," "warmer than," and so on is used in visual observations. They do not possess any color words, including "black," "gray," and "white." Churchland describes their visual field in some detail, comparing it with our sensory experience.

To make matters interesting, let us suppose finally that, so far as the intrinsic nature of their visual sensations is concerned, the world "looks" to them much as it looks to us in black-and-white prints of pictures taken with infrared-sensitive film ... That is to say, on viewing a very hot object they have what we would describe as a sensation of an incandescent white object, and on viewing a very cold object they have what we would describe as a sensation of a black object, and so on. They, of course, describe these sensations quite differently – as sensations of heat, of coldness, and so on.[34]

[32] Paul Churchland, *Scientific Realism and the Plasticity of the Mental* (Cambridge: Cambridge University Press, 1979), pp. 8–9.   [33] *Ibid.*, p. 8.
[34] *Ibid.*, p. 9.

Churchland argues that if the meaning of simple observation terms such as being "warm" and so on is given or fixed by sense experience, then the creatures' subscription to the above list of temperature beliefs is mistaken. According to his character-ization of the commonsense view, "we must insist that their terms cold, warm, and hot really mean black, gray, and white respectively rather than cold, warm, and hot."[35] But if we substitute color predicates for temperature predicates in the creatures' language we derive a large body of false statements, for example Snow is black, fires are white. "To insist on this sensation-guided translation is, I suggest, to make a joke of a perfectly respectable and very powerful sensory modality."[36] Truth is preserved in translation only in certain accidental cases, for example when a black object happens to be cold. He contends that it is more reasonable to believe these creatures see temperatures, and therefore that the meanings of temperature-observation terms are not fixed by sensations. If they were fixed by sensations, then either our temperature beliefs or the creatures' beliefs (or both) are false. Since observation terms are not fixed by immediate experience, they are theoretical in character and are fixed instead by clusters of theoretical assumptions, however inchoate and unexamined.

Churchland's argument taken alone does not, of course, establish that sensations do not exist. After all, one may well believe that our folk psychology is a theory, but a correct theory for all that. But if successful, Churchland has given the dualist pause, as he has set the stage for a materialist, theoretical account of our sensory, mental life. Moreover, this thought experiment can give pause to identity materialists as well who share with dualists the conviction that sensations and beliefs do exist. As an eliminativist, Churchland wants to prepare us for finally rejecting the whole folk theory.

---

[35] *Ibid.*, p. 10.   [36] *Ibid.*, p. 10.

THE APPEAL TO UNITY

Churchland's thought experiment may seem even more odd
than Dennett's, but the function of both and the appeal to the
success of science is to pave the way for a unified theory of what
exists. In the eyes of its critics, dualism produces a bifurcated,
cloven picture of nature with no clear way to theoretically
corral the mental and physical, whereas a materialism like
Churchland's gives us a way of by-passing altogether the
problem of how the mental interacts with the physical. One
reason for adopting some form of materialism, then, is that the
most likely alternative, dualism, is worse. It not only posits a
reality not needed to account for human behavior, but is unable
to account satisfactorily for the relation between the nonphysical and physical realms. Gilbert Ryle articulated the
problem for dualists some years ago in his important book *The
Concept of Mind*:

There was from the beginning felt to be a major theoretical difficulty
in explaining how minds can influence and be influenced by bodies.
How can a mental process, such as willing, cause spatial movements
like movements of the tongue? How can a physical change in the optic
nerve have among its effects a mind's perception of a flash of light?[37]

Jerry Fodor provides a sober depiction of the dualist's predicament: "If you think, as Descartes did, that minds are
immaterial substances, you ought to be worried (as Descartes
was) about how there can be mental causes of behavioral
effects."[38] Daniel Dennett thinks the problem here is so grave
that the avoidance of dualism constitutes for him something like
a dogmatic requirement. "This fundamentally anti-scientific
stance of dualism is, to my mind, its most disqualifying feature
and is the reason why ... I adopt the apparently dogmatic rule
that dualism is to be avoided *at all costs* ... If dualism is the best
we can do, then we don't understand human consciousness."[39]

Some identity materialists admit there are serious difficulties
with empirically demonstrating that the mental is identical with

[37] Gilbert Ryle, *The Concept of Mind* (London: Hutchinson, 1949), p. 19.
[38] Jerry Fodor, *Representations* (Cambridge, Mass.: MIT Press, 1981), p. 2.
[39] *Consciousness Explained*, pp. 37, 39.

the physical in general and, more specifically, with providing sufficient reason for how it comes to be that particular mental states are identical with particular physical ones. Part of the problem lies in the ostensibly interwoven, holist character of the mental, whereby various aspects of one's mental life are interdefinable. Our mental terms are customarily defined by other mental terms: hope is defined as certain expectations and beliefs, love as a blend of belief, desire, and pleasure, and so on. As Davidson, himself an identity theorist, characterizes it, mental states like beliefs and intentions have "no echo in physical theory."[40] It is therefore difficult for identity theorists to envisage discretely formulated psychophysical laws. How are we to carve up the appropriate bits of our mental life and match these with the appropriate material process? Eliminativists take this as their clue to wield Ockham's razor, cutting off what is not imbedded in well-defined physical theory, whereas identity theorists counsel moderation. But both agree that dualism is in immensely greater trouble, for materialists only presume that there is one general class of entities, whereas dualists posit two and leave it an utter mystery how they are interrelated. It is partly because of the more streamlined, unified character of materialism that all the dualist construals of mental–physical interaction are so confidently overturned and absorbed, whether or not the dualists try to exploit the holist character of the mental. As noted earlier, the dualist emphasis on the correlation between the mental and physical is taken by Shoemaker and others as evidence of a materialist identity theory. Dualists who try to block such a move by emphasizing the holist nature of the mental and the consequent anomalous nature of mental–physical interaction play into the hands either of eliminativists who charge that the mental is dispensable or of identity theorists who charge that the identity of the mental and physical is itself anomalous.[41]

[40] Davidson, *Actions and Events*, p. 231.
[41] Such an anomalous position amounts to claiming that each mental event is identical with some physical event, but that while laws of nature may be formulated governing all physical events, there are no laws that connect the mental with the physical. While the anomalous theory need not construe the identity of specific mental and physical events as vague, it may well do so.

At the close of this initial survey of materialist arguments, it is worth noting that materialism is often assumed to be true in a variety of fields outside the philosophy of mind. The adequacy of this assumption is sometimes taken by critics to be yet one more reason for rejecting dualism. As Ockham's razor is never far away, dualism is often faced with the task of showing that it is indispensable, for if we *can* dispense with it, some philosophers argue that simplicity demands we *ought* to jettison it and settle for the greater unity provided by materialism. Consider, for example, the philosophy of language in which it is largely assumed that a satisfactory account of meaning must be materialist, notwithstanding the challenges facing a materialist semantics.[42] Typically, in the study of language we distinguish between semantics and syntax; the former focuses on meaning or content, whereas the latter concerns the formal features of terms or systems of communication. Some materialists allow only for the syntactic character of terms to play a causal role in accounting for human behavior, leaving meaning *qua* meaning and content to one side. The nonsemantic causal relations neatly fit within the broadly uniform physicalist view of nature. It is partly because of this orientation that many materialists look to computational models of human intelligence, for the computer is thought of as primarily a syntactic, not semantic-driven, machine. In this way intentional explanations of language usage give way to nonintentional computational ones. This amounts to a kind of eliminativism insofar as meaning *qua* meaning is concerned. The point to observe here is that any evidence for the adequacy of such a materialist program is often taken to be evidence that dualism is not needed *tout court*. If an acceptable philosophy of language is feasible without dualism, why not carry out an equally unencumbered philosophy of mind? At first glance, language usage represents a serious challenge to materialism – with its entourage of categories that include belief, meaning, and intentionality – and, if materialism can meet the challenge, this would represent further reason for abandoning dualism.

---

[42] This is an assumption running throughout work by Michael Devitt, for example.

To summarize the prevailing attitude of many philosophers, the dualist story of human behavior seems regressive and backward. One recent introduction to the philosophy of mind warns about the danger of "back-sliding" into dualism.[43] As the most radical challenge to dualism comes from eliminativists, it is fitting to end this section by attending to one of their representatives. In the course of articulating the importance of a unified world view, Churchland berates the stagnancy and shallowness of folk psychology in contrast to the powerful unified theory of materialism.

> What we must say is that [folk psychology] suffers explanatory failures on a epic scale, that it has been stagnant for at least twenty-five centuries, and that its categories appear [so far] to be incommensurable with or orthogonal to the categories of the background physical science whose long-term claim to explain human behaviour seems undeniable. Any theory that meets this description must be allowed to be a serious candidate for outright elimination.[44]

Why cling to a dualist theory which seems so retrograde and dissipated in comparison with a unified, scientifically articulate materialism?

DUALIST REJOINDER; MENTAL AND PHYSICAL PROPERTIES

I think it must be granted that materialism has great explanatory power, and that many of the philosophical-scientific points made on its behalf have substantial merit. There is a significant advantage to a unified theory of the cosmos, as opposed to one that posits disparate elements with no clear account of their relationship, and it is clearly important to take scientific advances seriously, as materialists have done. But the reasons for adopting materialism sketched thus far, and others to be considered in the following chapters, fail to convince me. In this and the next chapter my aim is to defend a dualism of mental and physical properties, a stance shared by the dual-

---

[43] *The Philosophy of Mind* by Peter Smith and O. O. Jones (Cambridge: Cambridge University Press, 1986), part III.

[44] Paul Churchland, "Eliminative Materialism and Propositional Attitudes," *Journal of Philosophy* 78 (1981), 1.

aspect theory as well as by more developed versions of dualism. If a dualism of mental and physical properties is indefensible, clearly a more extreme dualism between persons and bodies is in serious trouble.

In launching a response to the case for materialism, more needs to be said about the initial propriety of dualism as a commonsense philosophy or a view with any rudimentary, presumptive plausibility. I mentioned earlier that it at least appears as though we have beliefs and the various items posited by folk psychology and that this is something which most critics, both eliminative and identity materialists, admit. Dennett, for example, allows that it is legitimate to begin with the assumption of a top level of intentionality; the arguments from science and Churchland's thought experiments also presume the ostensible intelligibility of our ordinary, folk world.

I propose that we approach the philosophy of human nature by taking appearances seriously, trusting them until we have reason to distrust them. When we do take appearances seriously, we take up what may variously be described as the first-person or subjective point of view, according to which there is a discernible feel or awareness we have as conscious beings of our own states and activities. We seem to believe certain things, and appear to have a range of sensations, emotions, desires, and so on. Some call the felt awareness of such states as feeling pain or sensing blue *qualia*, from the Latin *qualis*, meaning what kind of. This subjective, descriptive approach to consciousness is championed by some members of the phenomenological movement, especially popular in the first half of this century in Europe and in many parts of North America. The phenomenological movement was and remains diverse but is united by a concern to capture descriptively how things appear to us. My own allegiance within this strand of philosophy is to what is called phenomenological realism.[45] I submit that a phenomenological

---

[45] Phenomenological realists, include Adolf Reinach, Alexander Pfaender, Dietrich von Hildebrand, Fritz Wenish, and Josef Seifert. Phenomenological realism is more in line with Husserl's very early writings and not given over to his later antimetaphysical, Kantian project. A good overview of the field is Herbert Spiegelberg's two-volume work, *The Phenomenological Movement* (The Hague: Martinus Nijhoff, 1960).

approach to human nature supports the view that there are pains, beliefs, desires, and so on, and that they are not identical with any of the physical properties and configurations proposed by materialists. There may well be reasons for dismissing the phenomenological gambit on behalf of dualism, but let us begin by getting clearer about why it might be thought initially that a phenomenological approach to the mental tends to support dualism.

Consider the question of when to recognize a single object or property and when to recognize two or more. Imagine a case in which you are not sure whether you saw the same car or different cars of similar design and color on two occasions. You would be warranted in thinking there were two cars if you were justified in believing that there was something true of the first (such as that it was built out of steel in Japan) that was false of the other (it was built out of wood in Norway). Note that this would not just be warrant that your concept of the first car differs from your concept of the second; it would be evidence of there actually being two cars that you use various concepts to refer to. The beliefs you have that would justify concluding that there were two objects may involve constitutional issues about the objects' intrinsic features or extrinsic, less fundamental ones (the first car is exclusively owned by Miriam, the other by Eric).

Are we justified in believing that there is something true of pains, beliefs, desires, and so on, not true of physical properties and states? It seems to me that the answer is yes. Mental properties like being in pain can be conceived and grasped phenomenologically without conceiving of the physical properties with which they are supposed to be identical, and *vice versa*. There is something true of mental properties and states – they possess an apparent phenomenological character – not true of physical properties. This is not to deny that the relevant physical processes and neural states can be conceived of at the same time. Certainly they can be, but the crucial point is that it appears that in conceiving of the mental we do not thereby conceive of the physical, and in conceiving of the physical one is not conceiving of the mental. To conceive of the mental and the physical simultaneously is not to conceive of just one kind of property. No matter how hard I focus on my believing Mexico to be south of Canada, say, or my sensing pain, I do not thereby observe a section of my cerebrum or central nervous system. The neural wiring and its complex material features are not themselves disclosed to my introspection. Analogously, I can conceive of the relevant complex neurology without thereby conceiving of the mental states with which they are supposedly identical. There is a phenomenological character to the mental that is not evident as one among the many other physical properties of the brain or body as a whole.

The strategy I am proposing here is hardly an entirely innovative one in the debate between materialists and dualists. Materialists of all stripes are familiar with some form of dualist argumentation that appeals to subjective phenomenology, and most materialists acknowledge the *prima facie* difficulty of eliminating the mental or of identifying it with the physical. What I hope to bring to light in what follows is that contemporary materialists do not take this appeal to the subjective character of experience with sufficient seriousness. Some materialists dismiss this appeal with an almost patronizing air, perhaps, in part, because the argument from phenomenology can be developed recklessly and fallaciously. In any case, I contend that the version of the argument which I, along with others, employ has considerable weight and that the objections lodged against it have yet to overturn its formidable plausibility. Let me further defend the method proposed here for demarcating the mental and physical and then address the avalanche of materialist arguments we have canvassed.

The criterion of identification utilized in the argument draws upon what is formally referred to as the *principle of the indiscernibility of identicals* and may be stated rather abstractly as: If X is Y, then whatever is true of X is true of Y. (For technical reasons we need not grapple with until Chapter 3, this principle is distinct from a related principle called *the identity of indiscernibles*.) It is the viability of the principle at hand, the indiscernibility of identicals, that allows us to conclude that if we have reason to believe something is true of X that is not true of Y, then we have reason to believe that X is not Y. In tailoring a criterion of individuation to this specific philosophical investigation, I explicitly note the role of reasons for accepting beliefs. This is because our identifying and distinguishing properties will always be from specific vantage points, relying (ideally) on the best evidence we have available at the time. As my initial concern is with the credentials of a dualism of properties, I shall formulate the criterion with respect to properties rather than concrete individual things. I submit that: For any property X and any property Y, if I have reason to believe that I can conceive of X without conceiving of Y, I have reason to believe that X and Y are not identical.[46] The term "property" is not meant to play a highly technical role: terms like "attribute," "feature," or "aspect" would do as substitutes. The term "property" is not meant to exclude formally what we think of as states and processes; one can construe states and processes as types of properties, for example the property of being in such and such a state or process. While dualism can be advanced using a variety of classifications (we may translate what follows in terms of mental and physical *facts* or *events*), employing the notion of properties is simple, less cumbersome, and a useful starting point.

This criterion leaves open the possibility that one can be mistaken in delimiting properties. On the basis of this principle I may have reason to believe something false, but that is hardly a serious flaw as there are many instances when proper norms of evidence may lead one to embrace false conclusions. (There

---

[46] A further defense of my account of differentiating properties and individuals is given in Chapters 2 and 3. Essentially, my account is in accord with R. M. Chisholm's in *Person and Object* (La Salle: Open Court, 1976) and "Leibniz's Law in Belief Contexts," in *Contributions to Logic and Methodology in Honor of J. M. Bochenski*, ed. A. T. Tymieniecka (Amsterdam: North Holland, 1965), pp. 243–250. See also Richard Swinburne's treatment of properties, especially for his critique of Davidson's criterion of event identity in *The Evolution of the Soul* (Oxford: Clarendon Press, 1986).

Some philosophers distinguish between a host of different ontological categories in which properties, attributes, aspects, relations, processes, states, events, facts, states of affairs, sets, individuals, substances, bare particulars, aggregates, heaps and more are all offered separate treatment. I am concerned, however, not to utilize any more technical categories and arguments than necessary in these early chapters. The reasons I advance for accepting dualism can be reformulated using other categories, though it can also be developed with only the categories of properties, individuals, and states of affairs which may or may not obtain. In my view, these are the most basic ontological categories.

may be good, *bona fide* evidence for me to believe falsely that Jones works for the CIA.) In my view, the greater the reason we have to think we can conceive of X without Y, the greater the reason we have to believe that X and Y are not identical.

In the case of the mental and physical, I believe I can conceive of auditory sound experience (listening to an old Beatles' tune, say) without conceiving of the accompanying sinusoidal compression wave trains, the motion of my eardrum membrane, and so on. The reasons I have for this conviction are reasons for my believing in the distinctness of the auditory experience and the physical processes themselves, and not just reasons for believing that our concept of listening to the Beatles is not identical with our concept of the acoustic spectrum and the rest. Compare the earlier observation about believing that there are two cars present with believing that our *concept* of one car differs from our *concept* of the other. I may rightly wonder whether two cars were at the scene of some crime rather than one, without this amounting to my wondering merely about the concepts I use when referring to the car(s). In both the criminal and philosophical investigation we are interested in more than the relation between concepts. In the automotive case my interest in the relevant concepts is derived from my interest in what we are trying to conceive, and similarly with the mental–physical case. It is crucial to appreciate that the criterion we are applying to the philosophy of the mental and physical is located in terms of our convictions about the world itself and what we believe to be the case. The dualist application of our criterion for property identification is couched, not in terms of our conceiving of abstract *possibilia*, but in terms of what we have reason to believe actually exists.

Accepting the criterion of identification I propose does not commit one to dualism at the outset, and it does not preclude a radical skepticism in the philosophy of mind. Thus, it is possible for one to accept this principle of identification and hold that we lack sufficiently good reason to reach *any* conclusions at all about the relationship between the mental and the physical. I emphasize, too, that if one both accepts the criterion *and* endorses its non-skeptical, dualist applications, one has not thereby established that the mental and physical are causally unrelated, or invulnerable to each other's influence. Most dualists are interactionists and would have no philosophical objections whatever to believing that sinusoidal compression wave trains in certain circumstances lead to auditory experiences.

The criterion of identification advanced here does not have a role that is strictly isolated, only of use in the philosophy of mind. Distinct properties can bear a host of different relations to one another and the criterion of identification has what I believe to be a well earned role to play in our understanding of these relations in the philosophy of knowledge, ethics, aesthetics, mathematics, and other areas. Consider, for example, a mathematical case of distinguishing properties and identifying their relationships. I can conceive of the property of being the successor of 5 without conceiving of being the smallest perfect number (the smallest number equal to the sum of its divisors including one, but not including itself), and yet both are essential properties of the same number: 6. The fact that the property of being 5's successor can be conceived of without conceiving of being the smallest perfect number gives us sufficient grounds for concluding that these are distinct, nonidentical properties. Children probably first grasp that 6 is 5's successor before having an inkling that 6 has an *additional* property: being the smallest perfect number. In the philosophy of knowledge we argue over whether conceiving of the property of being knowledge is to conceive of a complex property: being a justified, true belief. In ethics, there are arguments over whether the property of being good is distinct from the property of being approved of by an ideal observer, with opposing sides claiming that to conceive of the first property is (or is not) to conceive of the latter. Such arguments employ a pattern and strategy similar to those used in arguing whether being in a mental state is the very same thing as being in a physical state.[47]

---

[47] Debates over the identity of properties sometimes take the form of imagining possible states of affairs in which one property is present and the other (ostensibly identical) property absent. This method of proposal and counter-proposal of thought experiments is central to the example and counter-example method of analytical

As the above cases suggest, I am not presuming that "conceiving" in the criterion of identification must be read exclusively as "picturing" or "imagining" in the sense of forming a visual image of some kind. Rather, "conceiving" is to be construed broadly to include thinking, grasping, entertaining, examining, as well as picturing and imagining. All sorts of considerations may come into play to provide evidence that one can conceive of some property without conceiving of another, only some of which might involve the forming of visual images.

In an effort to avoid the notion of conceiving, some may be tempted to opt for linguistic criteria of identification. Consider, for example, the proposal that the mental and physical are not identical if discourse about the mental cannot be translated into discourse about the physical. I have two concerns about such linguistic strategies, with only the second approaching a serious reservation.

First, I worry that a linguistic demarcation of properties does not have the existential import of the conceptual criterion. That is, with the conceptual criterion, we are planted (whether firmly or lightly) on the grounds of what we have reason to believe is the case about sound, music, brain states, and so on. The linguistic criterion seems more open to the charge that it is of little use in drawing substantive conclusions in the philosophy of mind, for even if it is true that physical discourse and mental discourse are not inter-translatable, this is perfectly compatible with the eliminativist thesis that there is no reality that the folk, mental discourse refers to. It is for this reason that some critics maintain that the irreducibility of the mental and physical does not have any implications for believing that there is a difference between actually existing mental and physical phenomena. This reservation about the linguistic criterion is not serious, however, for if one first provides reasons for treating discourse about the mental and physical as truly referring to features of

philosophy. The method helps sharpen our understanding of the identity of different properties and their relationships, for example does the presence of one property explain the presence of another? I address the relevant methodological concerns at stake at various points in the next two chapters.

the world *and* that the discourse about the one is not translatable into discourse about the other, then the linguistic and conceptual criteria appear to be on equal ground.

My second reservation stems from my conviction that the conceptual criterion is the more basic of the two. It is on the basis of our realizing that to conceive of (grasp, think about) one property is not to conceive of another, that we have reason to believe that our discourse referring to the various items at hand is not translatable. The reason we have for believing that colors are not types of virtues and that giraffes are not periods of time or mathematical points rests upon our conceptually grasping the incompatible features of the items involved. The fact that our true, referential sentences about each do not preserve the same meaning when the various terms are utilized as translations (the meaning of our terms "giraffe" and "mathematical point" make it absurd to assert that "a giraffe is a mathematical point") is based on the more basic fact involving our conceptual abilities. In my view, we would not have the linguistic ability to introduce talk of points, giraffes, the mental and physical, without possessing the relevant conceptual powers. Our sentences can only be as well defined as the concepts we use them to express. In the next chapter I address such linguistic considerations in more detail. At this point in our investigation, however, the linguistic criterion need not be ruled out. If you prefer to employ such a criterion, the various arguments that follow *pro* and *contra* materialism may be adjusted along linguistic lines. Reasons offered to the effect that conceiving of the mental does not involve conceiving of the physical (and *vice versa*) may be taken to be reasons for recognizing that discourse about the mental is not translatable into discourse about the physical. Some evidential relations are two-way. As evidence of nontranslatability can be evidence of conceptual differentiation, so evidence for conceptual differentiation can function as evidence for nontranslatability.

To avoid misunderstanding, it is crucial to emphasize that the conceptual criterion advanced here by no means commits us to the absurd conclusion that if we can conceive of the property being the 42nd President and not have any grasp of the property being Al Gore's running mate, then it follows that the 42nd President is not Al Gore's running mate. As noted earlier, my concern at this stage is to distinguish properties, not the bearer of properties. Hence, while the criterion proposed would establish (correctly, I believe) that the properties being the 42nd President and being Al Gore's running mate are not identical, it does not establish that both properties are borne by different individuals. As it happens, a single individual, Bill Clinton, has both properties. It is often because we distinguish non-identical properties that we wrongly assume there to be two bearers of the properties at hand. So, it is because I can distinguish the properties being a Roman orator known by many people as Tully from being someone who denounced Catiline and who is known by many people as Cicero that I am enabled to reach the mistaken view that Tully and Cicero are different people, whereas there is only one person known by virtue of possessing these different properties. To bring us back from these analogies to the philosophy of mind, my concern at this juncture is only to distinguish mental from physical properties, leaving it an open question for now as to whether these distinct properties are had by the same object, perhaps the physical body as a whole, the brain, or some part of it.

Because of the importance of the criterion proposed for responding to the initial barrage of materialist arguments, I defend it further against five objections, some more weighty than others, and then address the arguments from Churchland, Dennett, Shoemaker, *et al.*

(1) Objection: The proposed criterion establishes the existence of infinitely many properties, since there are infinitely many aspects of things we can conceive of independent of others, for example I have the property of being shorter than seven feet, the property of being shorter than eight feet, and so on *ad infinitum*. Surely a more parsimonious criterion for distinguishing properties is in order.

Reply: Why think there are a finite number of properties? It is plausible to suppose there are infinitely many numbers and that numbers are types of properties, e.g. being one, being two, *ad infinitum*. I believe there are indefinitely many properties and see no oddity in recognizing that I have the property of being shorter than seven feet, being shorter than eight feet, and so on.[48] Parsimony is desirable in some contexts, but it should not mandate conflating into one category objects (or properties) that we have reason to believe are distinct. The proposed criterion for differentiating properties does not conflict with the scientific goal of parsimonious explanations. I do not conclude from the fact that I have infinitely many properties that each plays a distinctive causal role in explaining my existence. Scientific explanations focus on only a narrow range of properties. Presumably an explanation of my size will involve various properties concerning genes and environment without needing to include the indefinitely many other properties I possess that are not relevant to the investigation.

(2) Objection: The proposed criterion fails to recognize the important difference between distinguishing properties at an abstract level and distinguishing actual *instances* of properties. That is, it is one thing to establish abstractly that a mental property like being in pain differs from a physical property like being in a neural state, and another to establish that a particular instance of pain is not the very same thing as a neural state. An analogy may prove useful. Presumably, there is some difference between the properties of being a sculpture and being marble. We can conceive of one without the other and, admittedly, the English expressions "marble" and "sculpture" have different meanings or senses. Nonetheless, it could turn out (as it actually has turned out) that a single thing, the *Pietà*, for example, is a marble sculpture. Why rule out the possibility that certain physical properties are mental, notwithstanding the fact that mental and physical properties differ at an abstract level of description? If we allow for this, then the proposed criterion for distinguishing properties in terms of conceivability accomplishes very little. A materialist can allow that mental and physical terms have different meanings or refer to different properties or

---

[48] Michael Loux provides what I think are strong reasons for recognizing numbers and other abstract objects as necessarily existing entities: see his *Substance and Attribute* (Dordrecht: Reidel, 1978). See C. I. Lewis for a defense of the view that objects have infinitely many properties, *C. I. Lewis: Collected Papers* (Stanford: Stanford University Press, 1970), p. 439.

types, and yet hold that the mental terms employed to describe ourselves actually refer to the very same things (instances or tokens) as physical terms, namely neurological states. A difference between concepts or notions does not entail a difference in the object being referred to. Philosophers sometimes refer to properties or kinds as "types" and instances of such properties or kinds as "tokens." Thus philosophers have called the following position the token identity theory: while mental and physical properties differ at an abstract level as types, every token of the mental is physical.

Reply: Does this objection reveal an oversight or problem with the criterion? I do not think so. Apropos of the analogy, I believe that the properties being a sculpture and being marble are distinct and that for any object, the *Pietà*, say, that is at once a sculpture and constituted by marble, it possesses these features as distinct, nonidentical properties. We can use different expressions to pick out the same object, as when I identify the *Pietà* by saying "Look at that sculpture" or "Notice that marble," but it is important to appreciate that if the descriptive expressions employ different properties, then they attribute different properties to the thing being referred to. If properties are distinct at what a critic might call an *abstract* level, then I think we have reason to believe that the *instances* of those properties are also distinct. In the case at hand, in which each property is aptly used distinctly to select the *Pietà*, I would say that the *Pietà* is thereby attributed with having two distinct properties. Not only does the thing we call the *Pietà* have the property of being marble, but it also has the property of being a sculpture. One can conceive of its being a sculpture without conceiving of its being marble, and one can conceive of the object being marble without realizing it has the property of being a statue. Arguably, the object in St. Peter's could retain its property of being marble but cease to possess the property of being a sculpture, should it be severely damaged. Moreover, even if you insist that the thing we call the *Pietà* could not survive its loss of either the properties of being marble or of being a statue, it by no means follows that you must treat the instances of the two properties themselves as identical. Your

stance can instead be represented as insisting that both
(nonidentical) properties are essential properties of the *Pietà*.
While you claim not to be able to conceive of the *Pietà* lacking
either property, it is still the case that you can conceive the one
property which it has essentially, attending to one aspect or
feature of the *Pietà* (its having the property of being a sculpture)
without conceiving of another of its essential properties (its
being marble).

The gist of my reply is to deny that there is a wide gulf
between the abstract and the particular, the uninstantiated and
the instantiated, when it comes to identifying properties. If the
properties being red and being hot may be separately conceived
either in the abstract or in their concrete instantiation, then
they are distinct properties on both the abstract and concrete
plane, even if it happens that the only time an object is red, it is
hot and *vice versa*. Of course we may have good practical
grounds for constructing a single notion to cover the conjoining
of both properties (in which the term "red-hot" stands for the
co-instantiation of being red and being hot), but this would not
somehow make them identical.

While I have been insisting upon a strong criterion of
identification across the abstract and particular, another reply
to the objection is available. For the sake of argument let us
concede that there is a disparity between type and token when
it comes to differentiating properties, and that it is possible for
properties to differ abstractly but not in their token instanti-
ations. The criterion is not thereby shown to be dubious, for it
can be employed in a fashion that is sensitive to the level of
analysis at issue. That is, we can couch the criterion in terms of
the reasons available to believe that the token properties differ
(I have reason to believe token property X differs from token
property Y if I have reason to believe I can conceive of one
without the other), and similarly for the level of types. The
points made earlier about conceiving of the phenomenological
character of the mental sound experience *vis-à-vis* the different
wave trains can easily be construed in such specific terms.[49]

---

[49] For further discussion of the token–token theory see John Foster's *The Immaterial Self*
(London: Routledge, 1991), chapters 4–6.

(3) Objection: As shown above in Churchland's thought experiment, Stich's appeal to empirical data and the like, we simply do not possess a sufficiently clear, firm, phenomenological grasp of mental properties in order to distinguish them from physical properties as you propose. Our notion of the mental is tenuous and untrustworthy both when it comes to thinking of it in the abstract as a type and in more concrete token manifestations. Consider the significant problems your criterion faces when it comes to identifying many scientifically interesting properties. Take, for example, the properties being water and being H_2O. These appear to be distinct, and your criterion would rule them as such, for surely many pre-scientific persons conceive of one property without conceiving of the other. Nonetheless, subsequent scientific study reveals the two properties to be the same.

Reply: The criterion I propose is in a modest form: If I have reason to believe I can conceive of X without conceiving of Y, I have reason to believe X and Y are not identical. Having reason to believe something does not always amount to knowledge, and I grant that persons may have reason to believe there are two properties or things, being water and being H_2O, when there is only one. So, the water case would not show that the proposed criterion is false, nor would it expose the criterion as a flawed characterization of our thinking about the world in scientific and nonscientific contexts. Evidence for the identity of water and H_2O is evidence that to conceive of being water is to conceive of being H_2O. The main thrust of the objection here is an important one, however. If we have reason to believe that our phenomenological grasp of mental states is indeed underdetermined and substantially open-ended, then we have reason to be suspicious of the dualist use of the criterion for property-differentiation. Is my grasping what it is like to hear music sufficiently defined and specific that I can be sure that to conceive of such auditory properties is distinguishable from conceiving of the physico-chemical correlative properties? Part of applying the criterion of property-differentiation to the philosophy of mind involves taking this question seriously, and it will be a main concern in the next two chapters. Accepting the criterion does not by any means make dualism a foregone conclusion.

It is worth noting in conjunction with this reply that the proposed criterion for property-differentiation helps us articulate a related matter. It can help us see that identifying water and H_2O does not entail conflating all the various properties of water *qua* H_2O. If water is H_2O, then whatever property is had by water is had by H_2O, but it does not follow that all the properties had by the single object are really just one property. It is still plausible to see that the property of being colorless is distinct from being flavorless, which is not identical with properties like being a constituent of living bodies, being the main constituent in lakes and oceans, and so on. The criterion for property-differentiation helps us capture the distinctiveness of these properties involved, for each property may be separately conceived. It is partly because such properties are distinct, as are others like being such that it is called "water" in English, that persons are able to know something about water without knowing water is H_2O.[50]

I conclude that the third objection does not show that the criterion for property-differentiation is flawed.

(4) Objection: Assuming your criterion does not differentiate properties that are really identical, it is nonetheless defective because cases arise when your criterion would identify properties that are actually distinct. Imagine a curved, three dimensional material structure that is of uniform thickness, one inch say. Imagine, further, that the curve forms a concave surface on one side and a convex surface on the other. It is reasonable to think the properties being concave and being convex which are instantiated here are different. After all, one can bounce a ball

---

[50] Saul Kripke contends that it is an empirically discoverable necessary truth that water is a compound of hydrogen and oxygen. In light of scientific evidence, no thought experiments in which there seems to be water but without such a constitution carries weight with him. Even so, Kripke does not conflate all the distinct properties of water, and he allows that other compounds might simulate the "characteristic feel, appearance and perhaps taste" of water. The criterion I defend helps articulate the distinctions involved, for example he can conceive of many of the properties we associate with water without conceiving of water. Kripke, *Naming and Necessity* (Cambridge, Mass.: Harvard University Press, 1980), especially p. 128.

against the concave surface without doing so on the convex. But using your criterion it is not clear that there are two properties, for to conceive of one property (being a three-dimensional, concave object of uniform, one-inch thickness) is to conceive of the other (being a three-dimensional, convex object of uniform, one-inch thickness).

Reply: Whatever reason the objector has for thinking there are two properties here may be employed by the proponent of the conceptual criterion with equal success. Insofar as these properties are distinguishable on the basis that something may be done involving one property that does not involve the other, the properties may be distinguished on the basis that one property may be conceived of without conceiving of the other. If I can conceive of bouncing a ball against one side of the object rather than the other, then the conceptual criterion will secure the distinction between the respective property surfaces – the one surface being such that it bulges toward the point where the ball hits it, while the other surface does not have this property.

(5) Objection: Your criterion employs the mental term "conceiving." If eliminative materialism is correct, then our whole way of thinking about the mental world including our conception of conception needs to be revised. The proposed criterion employs the language of folk psychology to defend folk psychology. In a sense, then, it is no surprise your criterion tends to support some form of dualism. For all that, you wind up begging the question against eliminative materialism at the start.

Reply: If talk of conceiving and referring to properties as they appear to us is question begging, then such question begging seems inevitable. How else can one proceed? Stich and other eliminativists are compelled to develop their rejection of folk psychology in the language of folk psychology. For their sake, it is good that talk of belief, conceptions and thoughts are intelligible at least initially. Otherwise we would not be able to understand the arguments they put forward against the existence of beliefs, desires, and so on. So, I do not think there is anything particularly heinous about the proposed criterion in virtue of its appeal to our ability to conceive so long as we are prepared to revise our criterion in the face of compelling objections.[51]

I now review in order the preliminary case for materialism outlined above.

A DUALIST STRATEGY

Consider, then, Dennett's program of reducing the top-level, intentional realm to increasingly simple-minded intentional relations until we get to blind, narrow-minded, relatively ignorant homunculi, finally jettisoning them at the bottom.

One response to Dennett's proposal would be a flat-out denial that it makes any sense. Gilbert Ryle opposes research programs that analyze persons into increasingly sub-personal units like homunculi. Although Ryle was a hostile opponent of dualism, his stance here may be of service to dualists and others who oppose Dennett's form of reduction.

This picture of a man's mind as being somewhat like the War Office, comprising lots of semi-autonomous departments, having sometimes little and sometimes much to do with one another, is pure mythology. It is I who remember or forget, I who calculate and infer, I who smell and hear things, I who invent fairy stories, I who feel pangs of guilt, and so on. It is not mysterious bits of my mind that do these things for me, in the way in which my solicitor or my chimney sweep or my electric oven do things for me.[52]

---

[51] A substantial problem eliminative materialists face is that to communicate and argue for their position, it is necessary for them to use the language of folk psychology. This comes close to providing a self-refutation of their stance. Arthur Danto has questioned the intelligibility of claiming to disbelieve in intentionality in "Science as an Intentional System," *Behavioral and Brain Sciences* 6 (1983), 359–360. Lynne Baker presses this objection against eliminativists in *Saving Belief* (Princeton: Princeton University Press, 1987), as has John Foster in *The Immaterial Self*, p. 19. As for the objection that my use of intentional idioms to distinguish properties begs the question, it is important to appreciate that all philosophical reflection must proceed on the basis of some assumptions. Critics who do not share these may well charge that important questions are begged in that the assumptions are held to be true without argument. In response, I maintain that it is intellectually appropriate to begin philosophizing on the basis of how things appear to be the case, and that *because* it appears that we can conceive of things and hold beliefs there is nothing awry in trusting these until we have positive reason for doing otherwise. At least at the beginning of inquiry, I think Ernest Sosa is quite right that "some questions demand begging," "Serious Philosophy and Freedom of Spirit," *Journal of Philosophy* 84:12 (1987), 714.   [52] Ryle, *On Thinking* (Oxford: Basil Blackwell, 1979), p. 52.

But while I heartily endorse Ryle's stance here, it will not work initially to counter Dennett's top-down reduction.

I think Ryle is quite right that when a person does things like remember, we do not construe this as a claim like "Some part in a hierarchically arranged organization that the person constitutes is doing the remembering *instead* of the person or on the person's behalf." But what Ryle does not speak to is the claim that a person is composed of this material organization such that a person's remembering *amounts to* the hierarchy functioning in the appropriate manner. In remembering things, feeling guilt, inventing fairy stories, and so on, we have good scientific grounds for assuming that many physiological substances, properties, and processes are involved which are, in a sense, functioning in an hierarchical pattern. Dennett clearly wants to draw on the full force of this impressive scientific backing. I believe that Dennett's program of reduction would be quite plausible on one condition, the condition that the phenomenological appraisal of consciousness is altogether discredited. Dennett's strategy works quite well when employed to account for what it means (in some metaphorical sense, anyway) for IBM and War Offices to think, to remember, and feel. This is because there is no phenomenology involved in such cases. IBM *qua* corporation does not have feelings in the sense that you or I do. So, here I want to address a consideration more fundamental than a fully articulated, phenomenological self-awareness. Let us imagine that Ryle's cautionary note may be discounted and that Dennett is correct that a person's *self*-awareness is actually composed of micro-agents, homunculi-like forces of descending intelligence. Does his proposal account for the bare phenomenology of awareness?

I do not think so. Dennett's proposed explanation of a person's psychological life along a gradually diminishing scale does nothing to displace the conviction that at whatever level of consciousness we imagine, if there is a level of consciousness, there is a phenomenologically apparent awareness or subjective experience, however primitive. Even a very modest mental property such as might be possessed by the most obtuse of Dennett's homunculi presents a problem. To establish that this modicum, mental realm is identical with the physical, then – given the criterion for property-identification defended above – we will need reasons to believe that to conceive of the mental is to conceive of the physical here, and the hypothesizing of homunculi gives us no reason to think we can make this leap from mental properties to physical. Why would it be any more plausible to believe that a simple mental state like being in pain is physical than a more complex state like feeling anguish about institutional racism? The way to make the crucial move away from recognizing consciousness as an irreducibly psychological reality is left dangling in Dennett's thought experiment of less and less intelligent homunculi.

That this crucial move is nontrivial has been supported by Raymond Tallis, Colin McGinn, and others who have argued that the presence or absence of consciousness is absolute. "Consciousness is either there or not," Tallis insists. "You can't be a little bit conscious any more than you can be a teeny-weenie bit pregnant."[53] And McGinn writes:

In the case of life there is a gradual transition from the plainly inanimate to the indisputably living; but in the case of consciousness we cannot take such a gradualist view ... The emergence of consciousness must be compared to a sudden switching on of a light ... and we conceive the minds of lowly creatures as consisting in ... a small speck of consciousness quite definitely possessed, not in the partial possession of something admitting of degrees.[54]

A critic might try to lessen the force of the Tallis–McGinn thesis by claiming it involves a merely verbal point. Is there a substantive disagreement between us if I describe stupid homunculi as only possessing consciousness to a meager, limited degree and you describe them as possessing consciousness *tout court* (no degrees) but a consciousness with only meager, limited content? Even if this is written off as a matter of convention, I believe Tallis and McGinn rightly underscore the radical

[53] Raymond Tallis, *The Explicit Animal* (London: Macmillan, 1991), p. 31.
[54] Colin McGinn, *The Character of Mind* (Oxford: Oxford University Press, 1982). Alastair Hannay also stresses the need for physicalists to take seriously the subjective vantage point, whatever its meager appearance. "However theoretically redundant the individual perspective proved to be, however small this baby born out of physicalist wedlock, it would still be incumbent on the physicalist to find it a home in the physicalist universe," *Human Consciousness* (London: Routledge, 1990), p. 9.

difference between possessing consciousness and failing to possess it, a demarcation that Dennett and others do not help us across. To make such a move, we need to consider other materialist arguments which may be brought to bear in surmounting the phenomenological challenge.[55]

EMPIRICAL EVIDENCE REVISITED

What of the accumulation of empirical data and the analogy materialists draw between folk psychology and other folk domains that have been supplanted by the natural sciences? I believe they accomplish far less than Churchland and others expect. Materialists point out how the sciences establish that something like being in pain may *appear* to be different from a brain state, while it is *really* the very same thing. But how are we to assess the project of a total identification of *all* appearances themselves with a physical ground floor where there are no appearances because there is no consciousness? One cannot claim "Appearances only appear to be appearances: there are actually no such things" without being left with appearances of appearances to account for. No matter how many steps back we take of appearances having appearances (like tiny homunculi behind others who are behind others), one does not eliminate this surd of conscious awareness. I shall develop this point briefly with reference to four materialists, Churchland, Lycan, Dennett, and Rorty.

(1) The tenacity of subjectivity comes to light in the passage from Churchland's work, cited above in the section "Empirical Evidence", in which he assimilates the identification of pain and electrochemical states to the identification of red surfaces with wave lengths, sounds with sinusoidal compression wave trains, and so on. Churchland's examples are readily construed

---

[55] Dennett may claim that our intentional states simply lack the kind of phenomenological character I am assuming, and in this and the next chapter I endeavor to draw attention to reasons why we should resist his claim. I believe that the same shortcoming I attribute to Dennett afflicts other forms of homuncular functionalism. See, for example, Jerry Fodor's "The Appeal to Tacit Knowledge in Psychological Explanation," *Journal of Philosophy* 65 (1968), 627–640, and Lycan's "Form, Function, and Feel," *Journal of Philosophy* 78 (1981), 24–50. A theist drawn to a version of the design argument might take heart from Lycan's liberal identification of teleological features.

in a form which counts against his position. If pains *seem* different from neurological states and sounds *seem* different from sinusoidal compression wave trains, there are at least ways in which each *seems* or appears. Whatever else exists, is there not at least an auditory "appearance" or a seeming-to-hear something? These appearances – these looks-like, sounds-like, feels-like – themselves require recognition and explaining. I have no difficulty whatever attending to the music next door. I may be grateful about the sinusoidal compression wave trains which enable me to hear the tune. But what reason is there for us to accept the claim that auditory experience *is* the wave train, or a motion in my brain? Few dualists doubt that our color sensory experiences are brought about (in part) by certain physical processes, and the same is true for Churchland's cases of sound, feeling, pains, hopes, and beliefs. But it is altogether different, and more tenuous, to claim that what sound and so on *are* turns out to be what Churchland identifies.

(2) The difficulty some materialists have with psychological appearances is also evident in William Lycan's treatment of subjective reports. In the following passage, Lycan dismisses reasons to believe there are after-images and sense data. "Sense data" is a technical philosophical term for the objects of sensation, as when one sees a red patch in one's visual field. An after-image is a visual sensation that lingers after the removal of the physical object that stimulated it, for example the after-effects of seeing a flash of light. Typically these are treated as being brought about by a discharge of the receptors of the retina.

A believer in actual sense-data such as green after-images may protest that he can see the after-image he is having, that it is right before his eyes, and that nothing could be more obvious to him than its actual existence. But how might the believer defend this last claim against the competing hypothesis that it merely looks as though there were something green before him when in reality there is not?[56]

[56] Lycan, *Consciousness*, p. 88. J. L. Mackie raises an objection similar to mine in "Mind, Brain, and Causation," in *Midwest Studies in Philosophy*, ed. Peter French *et al.* (Minneapolis: University of Minnesota Press, 1979), pp. 19–29. So does Eddy Zemach in "Churchland, Introspection, and Dualism," in *Philosophia* 20:3 (December 1990), 329, 330.

It may well be that the believer need give no further defense at
all for I can well imagine a "believer" being justified in
responding: "All I can say is that I am seeing a green after-
image. You are not offering a redescription of what I am seeing,
like correcting my judgment that I am seeing an Englishman
whereas you think I am seeing a Frenchman. I am sorry that my
report of seeing this green after-image fails to convince you, but
what more can I say?" But laying aside this response (and
returning to sense data later), note that Lycan still preserves the
notion of "looking as though there is something green." This
further removed stage of looking by no means removes the
phenomenal *qualia* or appearance-quality of experience.
Rather, Lycan seems instead to offer us some reason to
acknowledge the tenacity of phenomenal appearances, even if
these be the appearances of appearances. An analogy may be
useful. Imagine a philosopher who argues that there is no such
thing as change, but only changing appearances. So long as
philosophers admit that appearances change, they acknowledge
that there is change and have yet to eliminate it.

The problem I seek to document here does not rest on
treating appearances as objects or substantial things. Consider
cases where appearances are plausibly considered *ways of being
appeared to*, rather than objects. A book may appear old, for
example, without there being an object called an old appearance. For a person to appear intelligent does not require
that there is an appearance that is itself intelligent. Both cases
involves reference to the way something seems to observers. So
long as one grants that there is an experiential *the way something
appears*, one has granted a foothold for subjectivity and, I
believe, created a problem for materialism.[57]

(3) The recalcitrance of phenomenologically evident subjectivity found in Churchland's and Lycan's work is also in
Dennett's. Dennett comments that "there seems to be phenomenology, but it does not follow from this undeniable, universally

---

[57] This is why, in my view, James Cornman does not advance the cause of materialism
by virtue of his adverbial theory of sensations in *Materialism and Sensations* (New
Haven: Yale University Press, 1971). Interestingly enough, one of the key proponents
of the adverbial theory, Roderick Chisholm, holds that sensory states (ways of being
appearing to) are nonphysical.

attested fact that there really is phenomenology."[58] The admission of apparent phenomenology is dangerously phenomenological, however. As Galen Strawson has observed, "For there to seem to be phenomenology – for it to seem to one that one is feeling velvet, tasting pineapples, burning one's finger, and so on – just is for there to be phenomenology."[59] I think it is because of Dennett's failure to treat adequately the challenge of phenomenology that his attempts at reductive, explanatory schemes in *Consciousness Explained* seem to leave us on either side of the divide, so to speak. That is, we are treated to instances where it appears that the physical controls the mental, or that certain mental processes contribute to other mental processes, or that complex physical processes are accounted for in terms of simpler ones. What we do not have is a plausible instance where phenomenologically apparent mental properties turn out to be the very same thing as physical properties.

(4) I believe Rorty also underestimates the importance of the phenomenological character of the mental. He writes:

> We can say that although in one sense there just are no sensations, in another sense what people called "sensations", viz., neural states, do indeed exist. The distinction of senses is no more sophisticated than when we say that the sky does not exist, but that there is something which people call the sky (the appearance of a blue dome as a result of refracted sunlight) which does exist.[60]

His last example of the blue dome only has intelligibility insofar as one acknowledges the existence of appearances (or ways something appears). Insofar as the two cases are indeed parallel, Rorty seems saddled with there being *a way that neurons seem*, neurons seem or appear to be what people call "sensations".

Consider another analogy and a thought experiment Rorty employs to dispel the appeal of dualism. I believe these wind up leaving the materialist either with greater mysteries than those found in dualism or with analogies that fail to illuminate because they assume the very things Rorty is trying to establish.

---

[58] *Consciousness Explained*, p. 365.
[59] "The Self as Software," *Times Literary Supplement*, August 21, 1992, p. 5. Dennett would presumably protest that all he is committed to is the existence of information here, not subjective *qualia*, but this strikes me as implausible.
[60] *Philosophy and The Mirror of Nature*, pp. 117–118.

He asks: "Why should we be troubled by [the] point that if the brain were blown up to the size of a factory so that we could stroll through it, we should not see thoughts?"[61] He likens the puzzlement we find at not seeing thoughts to a problem of textual interpretation.

To say that we cannot observe intentional properties by looking at the brain is like saying that we cannot see a proposition when we look at a Mayan codex – we simply do not know what to look for, because we do not yet know how to relate what we see to a symbol system. The relation between an inscription – on paper or, given the hypothesized concomitance, in the brain – and what it means is no more mysterious than the relation between a functional state of a person, such as his beauty or his health, and the parts of his body.[62]

Consider the last set of analogies first. How mysterious is the functional relation between the parts of a person's body and their beauty or health? That depends on how you define beauty and health. I suggest that any robust understanding of our health must take into account our psychological life. It would be odd to think of a person as perfectly healthy if he or she were schizophrenic or severely manic-depressive. "Beauty" is also something that may plausibly be construed as involving both the mental and physical. Would a person be thought of as beautiful (without qualification) if his or her mental life were in shambles, locked in a virtual gridlock of vicious, bitter feelings, cruel hate, and so on?[63] Insofar as the notions of beauty and health involve both mental and physical features, one may well conclude that determining the relation between these and a person's physical body is no more mysterious than the general mystery of how the mental and physical are related. *But they are no more mysterious, because they are no less mysterious.*

With respect to Rorty's illustration about the factory, I suggest that we should be worried if our aim is to identify the

---

[61] *Ibid.*, p. 26.   [62] *Ibid.*, pp. 25, 26.

[63] On another front, Rorty's example also appears to invoke the "mystery" of mental–physical relations. Attributing beauty to someone's body (and/or personality) is plausibly interpreted as a claim about how the body (or whatever) either does or should give aesthetic pleasure to one who observes it. I defend an objectivist account of beauty and ugliness in terms of pleasure and displeasure in "The Ideal Aesthetic Observer," *The British Journal of Aesthetics* 30:1 (1990), 1–13.

mental with micro-physical processes. Of course, materialists may identify thoughts, not with micro or macro particular *objects*, or *parts* of the brain, as much as with micro or macro *processes*. The enlarged brain thought experiment still highlights the challenge facing the materialist of accounting for the phenomenologically evident character of thought, accounting for how it is that thinking about factories, say, can be the very same thing as the physiological processes posited in the materialist schema. Eliminativists will, of course, not be troubled by failing to see thoughts, because they do not recognize them (*qua* folk, mental notions) at all, but for the identity theorist and those who take the phenomenology of experience seriously this conclusion will be unacceptable.

As for Rorty's other analogy, a dualist can surely be sympathetic with his point about the Mayan codex in *one* respect. If there is mental–physical interaction, the precise causal relations linking the two are not obvious, and the research goal of dualist neurologists is not unlike trying to decipher a codex, linking the codex with a language already understood. Note, however, that for the dualist neurologist this is not a matter of discovering that the physical is really the mental, analogous to the way one might discover the English translation of the Mayan, or discover that what we thought was Mayan was actually a version of English.[64]

Let us now consider Stich and others on the empirical case for materialism. We have observed that materialists themselves are not in consensus about the import of the relevant empirical data, some concluding that it supports eliminativism while others see gains for the identity theory. In my view, eliminativism is the least supported. Stich's analogy between folk psychology and other folk disciplines seems extraordinarily weak. The advances we make in the sciences themselves, the overturning of astrology, folk biology, *et al.* have all taken place within the broad framework of what Stich means by "folk

---

[64] While Rorty's analogy of the Mayan text may seem congenial to the materialist program, it can be used to underline the serious challenge it faces. On a fairly standard treatment of propositions, according to which propositions are abstract objects, it would be odd indeed if we ever could see them.

psychology. " It is very difficult even to imagine the sciences proceeding, if there are no such things as beliefs and desires (the main denizens of folk psychology). Scientists have worked on gaining clearer and better-grounded beliefs about the natural world. Camel drivers of the ancient world may have had many false beliefs, but it is difficult indeed to imagine that neither they nor any of us have had any beliefs whatever.

The experimental data which Stich thinks unveil deep problems with folk psychology are not, in my view, very compelling. In his book against beliefs, Stich cites two cases in which there is evidence that subjects give false accounts of why they performed an action. In one case, insomniacs are given placebo pills which they are told will have certain effects. When the effects happen as predicted by the social psychologists and the subjects are informed that the pills were in fact placebos, the subjects tend to invent reasons for their behavior which are more respectable than being prey to the social psychologist's manipulation. "The core idea of dissonance research is that if subjects are led to behave in ways they find uncomfortable or unappealing and if they do not have what they take to be an adequate reason for enduring the effects of this behavior, then they will come to view the effects as more attractive."[65] Stich's second case is similar, involving subjects who are administered electrical shocks in the course of learning material. Subjects wind up behaving in ways which they are told later were prompted by causes which they tend to find demeaning. The outcome is that the subjects invent more attractive motivating causes which prompted their behavior. I fail to see the reason for Stich's inference from these types of cases to the conclusion that our whole belief–desire framework is liable for elimination. Surely we do on occasion misdescribe our motives. Why think we always do? As John Foster has observed: "These putative deficiencies in folk psychology do nothing to impugn the reality of the mental realm which it is trying to characterize. To suppose that they do is as crazy as supposing that, by exposing the faults of classical mechanics, modern science has brought us

---

[65] Stich, *From Folk Psychology*, p. 232.

nearer to a nihilist view of the physical world."[66] Note, too, that the results of the experiments Stich cites lend themselves rather easily to explanations within folk psychology. Wasn't the reason why the subjects in both experiments invented more attractive hypotheses for their behavior that they found the alternatives undesirable? The subjects' misdecription of their own beliefs and desires suggests that this was due to still other beliefs and desires about what they found embarrassing and appealing. Cases of self-deception are a commonplace in folk psychology (and rightly so, I shall maintain later).

If the accumulation of empirical data does not support eliminativism, what about the identity theory? The greater threat to dualism seems to me to be posed by those who recognize the mental and physical as nomologically (that is, lawfully) related for, with the help of Shoemaker's criterion of identity, cited earlier, the ordered pairing of mental and physical properties would be evidence of mental–physical identity. If what appear to be two properties have the same causes and effects, there is actually only one property, not two. Would the co-instantiation of physical and mental properties in similar causal contexts give us any reason to identify the two?

I do not think so. Co-instantiation between anything, whether inside of causal contexts or not, is a necessary but not sufficient condition for identity. Many properties are co-instantiated without being identical. Consider the following pairs: being triangular and being trilateral, being a certain shape and being a certain size, being the successor of five and being the smallest perfect number. Shoemaker's criterion seems inadequate for a number of other reasons as well. Most importantly, his criterion seems to be circular. He offers us a way to identify properties by appealing to causal powers. But causal powers are themselves properties. Thus, Shoemaker does not offer us a noncircular, illuminating account of identifying properties. Rather, his criterion presupposes the ability to individuate properties. If one still wishes to adopt Shoemaker's criterion, a dualist can accommodate it so long as a broad

---

[66] *The Immaterial Self*, p. 25. Foster does not exploit these weaknesses in the physical sciences in his defense of idealism.

notion of cause and effect is involved. Thus, a dualist can argue that physical and psychological properties have distinct causal effects in at least the attenuated sense that thinking about psychological properties has different affects on us than does thinking about physical properties. When I think about a psychological property like being in anguish for a year, I am caused to respond differently than when I entertain the correlative physical property like being a central nervous system in certain specific configurations for a year.[67]

The empirical findings of the neurosciences have clearly demonstrated what Churchland has called the vulnerability of consciousness to material processes. This vulnerability is precisely what many dualists expect. Obviously our whole mental life is causally bound up with the well-being of our material constitution. But this does not mean our mental life is itself material, or that our material bodies are not sometimes vulnerable to our mental life, our aims, emotions, sensations and such. Even if the sciences established only one-way causal relations in which the mental is at the beck and call of the physical but not *vice versa* (epiphenomenalism), this would not reduce the mental to the physical. The recognition that there is a mental level of experience in causal relation with the physical would itself imply a kind of dualism, even if this does not amount to interaction. John Searle accurately points out that strict supervenience, according to which the physical always determines the mental, does not vindicate reductionism or physical–mental identity.

From the fact that a property is supervenient on the behavior of lower level elements it simply does not follow that there is nothing there except the behavior of the lower level elements. In the case of, for example, consciousness, we have a supervenient, but nonetheless nonreducible property. That, indeed, is the difference between, for example, heat and consciousness. Consciousness is a separate and nonreducible property.[68]

---

[67] On the causal role of such beliefs see Jung's *Modern Man in Search of a Soul* (London, 1933), pp. 258f. For additional criticism of causal theories like Shoemaker's see *Identity and Essence* by Baruch Brody (Princeton: Princeton University Press, 1980).

[68] *John Searle and his Critics*, ed. E. Lepore and R. Van Gulick (Oxford: Basil Blackwell, 1991), p. 182.

So, one can allow that Quine is correct ("Nothing happens in the world, not the flutter of an eyelid, nor the flicker of a thought, without the redistribution of physical states") and still insist there are thoughts and a phenomenologically evident subjectivity.[69] Searle, an advocate of the kind of phenomenological stance I adopt here, is quite rightly not persuaded by the materialism of Rorty, Armstrong, and Churchland.

Armstrong holds what I take to be the amazing view that our perceptual experiences have no internal phenomenological properties at all. On this account, there is nothing that it feels like to see something, or touch something or taste something. When Armstrong uses the word "consciousness," it seems clear that he does not mean what I mean, nor what I take the rest of us to mean, by consciousness. He is simply talking about a kind of inner registering of our bodily states. Conscious states as such for Armstrong have no internal phenomenological feel, no "what it is like" internal phenomenal properties.[70]

The problem facing identity and eliminative materialism is this stubborn, evident, phenomenological appraisal we have of our own conscious states. Such an appraisal constitutes a serious challenge to assembling a materialist theory based upon empirical data. More will be said on the import of the empirical data in the last section of this chapter.

MENTAL THEORY AND MENTAL DATA

But is all this appeal to the phenomenology of the mental too glib? Has Churchland offered us good reasons why we should treat our subjective appraisal of color sensations as part of a

---

[69] *Theories and Things* (Cambridge, Mass.: Harvard University Press, 1981), p. 98.

[70] *John Searle and his Critics*, p. 184. I am treating Searle as an ally of dualism here, but in the end Searle embraces a broadly based physicalism. He opposes the materialism of Armstrong, Churchland, Dennett, and others, because these theories leave no room for subjective, phenomenological awareness. Searle believes that if we broaden our understanding of what may count as physical, we may see that "conscious states are simply higher level features of the brain," Searle, *The Rediscovery of the Mind* (Cambridge, Mass.: MIT Press, 1992), p. 14. But how high can physical features be before it makes more sense to consider them nonphysical? Chapter 2 takes up the issue of how to define the mental and physical in more exact terms than we are using provisionally in Chapter 1. Thought experiments I introduce in Chapters 2 and 3 count against views like Searle's that identify consciousness with brain properties.

speculative theory, rather than evidence or data that may confirm or disconfirm theories? Churchland's thought experiment raises several issues that we do well to consider. His argument may be especially appealing to theists, for many theists believe God knows about the world in ways very different than we do. Classical theologians like Anselm, Maimonides, and Aquinas held that God knows the world without having any sense organs and without any sense experience, for example. Those of us who believe in the possibility of such high, powerful cognitive ability may be loath indeed to deny the possibility of Churchland's interesting infrared cousins. Churchland could well ask those of us who are theists why we should strain at a gnat, denying transposed modality awareness, while swallowing the camel of Divine cognition.

Recall that Churchland has argued that if the meanings of mental terms are fixed by immediate experience, then terms like "hot" must be grounded in the felt sensation of hotness. If so, then a creature who had no felt sensation of hotness could not grasp the meaning of the term "hot." Because there could be such creatures (infrared cousins), it follows that mental terms are not fixed by immediate experience. Churchland forces us to judge the list of infrared cousin beliefs either false or true; if false, then those adopting the thesis of sensory-immediacy seem peculiarly narrow, excessively conservative; if true, then the thesis of sensory-immediacy seems mistaken and our sensory terms are ripe for the Churchland reduction of them to purely physical states.

I think there is a way to construe the beliefs of infrared cousins as true beliefs without abandoning the thesis of sensory-immediacy. We can both acknowledge the possibility of infra-red cousins and insist that sensory terms are not merely theoretical. Consider a fuller translation than Churchland offers of the infrared cousin's temperature terms in our color vocabulary.

a′ Fires are white.
b′ A gray thing will make something dark brighter, never the reverse.

c′ If a body is brighter than a second body, and the second
    body is brighter than a third body, then the first body is
    brighter than the third body.

d′ Food keeps better in a black place.

e′ White things cause painful burns.

f′ Rubbing things makes them brighter.

According to some extreme, I think implausible, form of what
philosophers call naive realism, either our beliefs about fires and
other items are false or the infrared cousin's beliefs are false or
both. In such a realist schema, the color of an object is perceiver-
independent, so that an object is either red or white irrespective
of any reference to ordinary perceivers. When I see the log as red
I am seeing a feature of the log which is as perceiver-
independent as its particular spatial extension. So, if naive
realism is accepted, we seem caught in the vice of Churchland's
argument. But why accept such extreme realism?

    It is not at all puzzling that some object, a log burning, may
cause me to see it as red whereas it appears to be white to a
creature with refracted lenses and whose retinas consist solely of
rods sensitive to electromagnetic radiation at some wave length
in the far infrared. Ordinary conditions for color perception by
human beings differ from ordinary conditions for color perception by the creatures envisioned by Churchland. According
to a plausible account of color properties, part of what it means
to claim that an object is red is to claim that it will stimulate
certain color sensations under ordinary conditions, causing the
subject to have red sensory experiences. In the lives of
Churchland's creatures, fires *are* white, food *does* keep better in
black places, and so on. The log does appear to be white to them
and red to us. We may understand their ostensible list of
temperature beliefs as color beliefs with a clear conscience;
neither their suitably translated list nor ours turns out to be
false. I conclude that Churchland has not established that our
cousins see temperatures.

    At this point Churchland could take a different approach
and simply insist at the outset that our talk of hot and cold really
only refers to physical magnitudes, a matter of the mean energy

level of molecules, for example. I am certain that if this is all there is to temperature, kelvin cousins (another branch of our epistemic family tree) can be envisioned. Under ordinary conditions I cannot detect visually all the respective 2×10^n molecules and their feverish activity in the drop of coffee sizzling away on the coffee maker. Kelvin cousins can, and, *ex hypothesi*, they thereby take in visually all there is to the hotness of coffee. But there is little in the kelvin cousin thought experiment to convince the ordinary person, let alone even a half-hearted sympathizer with recognizing sensations and consciousness as real and noneliminable, that all there is to thermal experience of heat is feverish molecular activity (however it is to be accounted for in thermodynamics). Obviously hot and cold talk was born long before molecule talk. I believe we came to call objects hot and cold because of our own thermal sensory experience. It at least appears that my stove deserves to be called hot because it brings about in me searing pain when I rest my hand on it. It is this older (and still very much alive) language of sensory states of felt awareness that Churchland *qua* eliminative materialist has targeted.

At least at this stage of our inquiry I have been pleading that we give folk psychology a chance and speak of such things as the temperature of an object in a way that includes a thermosensory character. In Chapter 2 we will consider arguments other than Churchland's that oppose a dualist, phenomenological identification of sensations based upon the theory of language; thus far, my effort is to note the commonsense, initial plausibility of the dualist reply over against Churchland's specific points. Rather than leave the matter here, however, let us go on to consider why we should think that infrared cousins (or anyone, for that matter) cannot see temperature as described. Why believe that certain sensory modes are exclusive and do not admit of Churchland transposing? I have shown that Churchland's thought experiment has not provided solid grounds for construing folk psychology as mere theory, but perhaps folk psychology can be shown to be inadequate for reasons that emerge in the analysis of the issues involved. Its inadequacy may emerge in its inability to answer these questions clearly and in its being replaceable by an alternative, clear, perhaps physicalist, schema.

I believe the answer to the above query may be treated within the context of a dualist, phenomenological account of the mental. The exclusivity of our modes of awareness (why we cannot, strictly speaking, see hotness) stems from the exclusivity or distinctiveness of sensory states themselves. Seeing is visual, tastes involve gustatory sensations, feeling hot and cold involve tactile feelings, and so on. Of course we may use our terms "to see," "to taste," "to feel" in an extended fashion as when we discuss so-and-so's taste in art. But strictly speaking, seeing as a sensory modality must involve visual sensations or undergoings. If the only sensory modality I enjoy is hearing, I will not be a seeing person in the relevant sense. I may still see the point of an argument, but that would not involve visually sighting a conclusion following a host of premises. Visual states or feelings are not auditory states or feelings. To hear the middle C is not to have a blue sensory experience. Likewise, our thermal sensations of hot and cold are distinct from the twists and turns of our visual field. If the only sensory feelings one had were thermal in nature and not visual, then one would not see *qua* enjoying visual points of view. Likewise, if one had no thermal feelings but only visual points of view, then, *ex hypothesi*, one would not have tactile states of hot and cold. One cannot visually see the temperature of objects *qua* their thermosensory properties, because visual states are distinct from tactile states.

It may be objected that the above schema is overly narrow. Is it not the case (and not just some remote science-fiction possibility) that some of us can see that an object is hot without actually undergoing tactile heat sensations? Surely we make such observations as a matter of course, but such observations involve judgments and presuppose underlying assumptions about the systematic, regular correlation between temperature and visual appearance. The temperature is not thereby the same thing as its visual appearance, and the hotness I feel when my hand is on fire is not the same as the red glow I see surrounding my flesh. One "sees" that the log is hot, but one does not see the thermosensory hotness.

The moves I am proposing here and earlier do not require that thermal and color sensations be treated as objects (often called sense data in the literature) as opposed to ways or modes of sensing. A number of philosophers have sought to avoid a sense-data schema, and have instead proposed that sensing involves a kind of adverbial state. Recall the point made above when addressing Lycan's work about appearances and ways of appearing. According to an adverbial theory of sensations, seeing a blue object involves a subject seeing it bluely, not seeing a blue sense datum. For the record, I note that I accept a sense-data view of color sensations, but an adverbial account of tactile feelings. That is, I think hot sensations involve feeling a certain way, but seeing blue objects involves a visual field of sense data. But it will not be crucial here, or elsewhere in the book, to choose between one of these more specific characterizations of sensation. The response to Churchland and the account of modal exclusivity is just as warranted whether we treat thermal and visual sensing in adverbial or substantive terms.

My depiction of modal exclusivity still faces a challenge. Certain properties of objects may be ably displayed to more than one sense modality. Thus, an object's figure, its roundness, may be felt and seen. Why allow some features to be "poly-modal" and not others? Even if we cannot taste colors, how can we rule out there being some additional sensory modality able to encompass the others? Perhaps the folk psychologist seems modal-phobic here. Maybe we can S (S being some sixth or seventh sense) the object's array of properties. Surely (someone like Churchland could argue) this brings to light the plasticity of human psychology, the brittleness of narrow mentalism.

I think we may account for some properties being poly-modal on the grounds that there is no real exclusivity of sensory states in such cases as there is with color, smell, taste, and so on. Take the shape and motion of an object. We may enjoy the sight of round objects moving across our visual field and we may feel round objects moving swiftly by us. Neither the tactile nor the visual has a monopoly on the roundness of an object; the object's figure may be displayed in both theaters, so to speak. This is why both kelvin cousins and I may have access to the temperature *qua* molecules in motion of an object. Problems arise only when one claims to see the thermosensory character of the object without this being a truncated way of expressing the fact that one may judge an object to be hot based upon its visual appearance and one's independent grasp of the correlation between visual appearance and heat.

However, the suggestion that creatures can be envisioned who possess cognitive equipment which vastly outstrips our own is less easy to settle. There is no little speculation in religious literature about God knowing the world's states, its sensible features and all, without having sensory experiences. Does the coherence of Divine cognizers reveal that our sensory talk is replaceable or plastic? Does the coherence of supernatural cognizers provide any reason for thinking our sensory talk is dispensable (in principle) so that even we could replace language of hot and cold sensations with physicalist talk of molecular motion?

The coherence of "Divine cousins" such as that Divinity envisioned by Anselm, Maimonides, Boethius, and Thomas Aquinas would establish that tactile and visual sensory under-goings are not the only (exclusive) ways in which an intelligence may grasp what it is to feel warm and see blue. Anselm, Aquinas, and company claimed that God knows of the world's full character without undergoing sensations. There are no Divine sense data, much less sense organs. Maybe they are correct. Perhaps Divine cousins could lack noses and all other sense organs, and yet still grasp by supernatural means how gaseous effluvia smell to creatures who have noses and olfactory membranes. What follows?

It does not follow that our sensory states of tactile experiential undergoings are illusory or that it is likely such undergoings are entities we posit as hypotheses to account for behavior. It would follow, however, that our sensory experiences are replaceable in a certain respect. Not all forms of intelligence need to rely upon the sensory experience we do in order to grasp what is involved in such experiences for sentient creatures. A God lacking in sensory thermoreceptors could conceivably know what it is like for me to feel hot without God ever feeling hot. But it remains the case that our Divine cousins do not visually see temperatures *qua* the thermosensory searing I undergo while sitting on a hot stove. The Divine cousins have taken an epistemic high road and, I would add, the coherence of our Divine-cousin-talk rests upon the coherence of supposing there could be a distinct, extraordinary means of cognition that does not involve our commonplace sensory modes. With respect to the sensory endurance of heat and seeing color, it is impossible (strictly speaking) to see visually all there is to thermosensory heat and to feel *qua* thermosensory tactile feeling all there is to the visual appearance of blue. Just as presumably even God cannot taste someone's intelligence, God and Divine cousins cannot visually see tastes, taste colors, or feel sounds. Classical Christian theists as well as Islamic and Jewish were careful to stress this point. Maimonides is representative. He spoke of God's access to the world as a kind of perception but he was careful to note that this did not involve visual sensations. "[God] is equally elevated above all the five senses ... By saying God sees, we mean to state that He perceives visible things; 'He hears' is identical with saying 'He perceives audible things'; in the same way we might say, 'He tastes and He touches,' in the sense of 'He perceives objects which man perceives by means of taste and touch.'"[71] Allowing for supreme Divine cognition such as this does not force us to think of sensory terms as theoretical.

If our observation terms are merely theoretical in character, and persons do not have reliable subjective awareness of their sensory states and of the world itself, Churchland's argument from transposed modalities and our speculations about kelvin and Divine cousins have not brought this to light. While our sensory life may not be as cognitively praiseworthy as Divine cognitive life, this should in no way tempt us to be suspicious that our sensory experience is a theoretical construct with only a tenuous claim upon our allegiance.[72]

[71] Moses Maimonides, *The Guide for the Perplexed*, trans. M. Friedlander (New York: Dover, 1956), p. 63. Michael Beaty and I defend the intelligibility of such Divine cognition in "God and Concept Empiricism," *Southwest Philosophy Review* 6:2 (July 1990).

[72] Churchland's argument is philosophically fascinating, but certainly not the first to contend that what we take to be subjectively apparent is a theoretical construct. For

DUALISM AND THEISM

What of the appeal to unity? I believe there is a great advantage to a unified conception of the natural world, and being free from the Herculean task of philosophically and scientifically linking disparate ontological realms. In this chapter I have defended the view that, for better or worse, we have good reason for distinguishing the mental and physical at least at the level of properties, and, if successful, we do face the task of forging an understanding of how the two are interrelated. I do not think materialism and idealism are the obvious beneficiaries of the appeal to unity, however, for there is a way in which a dualism of mental and physical can be construed as part of an overriding theistic view of the cosmos. Dualism may be taken up in a comprehensive, nontheistic naturalism which sees the mental as somehow naturally emergent from the physical, but a theistic outlook will provide a fuller model of explanation in which the natural emergence of the mental from the physical, and indeed the very constitution and powers of the physical world itself, is seen as stemming from a deeper, underlying cause. Let me outline this proposal over against Dennett's strategic thought experiment.

While Dennett sought a top-down reduction of consciousness and intelligence, a theist can advance a contrary move, developing a schema of explanation that draws upon increasingly rich notions of consciousness and intelligence. Recall that Dennett would regard such a direction of explanation as fruitless and empty. "The account of intelligence required of psychology must not of course be question-begging. It must not explain intelligence in terms of intelligence, for instance by assigning responsibility for the existence of intelligence in creatures to the

a good overview of the background of this debate see J. J. Ross' *The Appeal to the Given* (London: George Allen & Unwin, 1970). In my defense of recognizing subjective sensory experience here and elsewhere I am not supposing that our knowledge of these states is always infallible and incorrigible. My goal is nonetheless to defend the *prima facie* evidential credibility of our subjectively apprised sensory experience. I believe it provides an indispensable point of reference for our subsequent theorizing about such subjective states and human nature (for example should the sense data or adverbial *theory* be preferred?).

munificence of an intelligent Creator."[73] But why is this? If the invocation of a Creator was to compete with the scientist, by altogether supplanting scientific analysis, then one can appreciate Dennett's line. But a theistic view of the cosmos need not have such an implication; the munificence of God may be understood as God's creating and sustaining a cosmos of vast, interwoven complexity in which the physical and mental are firmly embedded. God's creating such interrelationships among the mental and physical is what enables the sciences to have the success they have, in terms both of doing science at all and of scientifically understanding the brain's role in our psychophysical life. Are there compelling reasons for accusing those of us who invoke higher orders of intelligence and consciousness in this way of question-begging? Are there decisive reasons for regarding nonintentional explanations as more lucid or perspicuous (more in the black, to talk in Dennett's budgetary fashion) than those which employ intentional factors? I shall adopt an artificial device in suggesting how a theistic construal of the mental and physical might go, by putting the issues in the voice of Dennett's imagined alter-ego. I think Dennett's material invites us to consider what an equally confident, brazen anti-Dennett might say in response. My own sense is that much of what follows is true, though a full vindication of these claims (or Dennett counter-claims, if you like) will require some hedging and further argument.

Alter-ego: "We must come up with some account of nonmental, nonconscious, material events and processes. To explain them in terms of each other is vacuous and brings curiosity to an end. Every time we explain events in a mechanical fashion, I believe our theoretical accounts are in the black. Let us reverse Dennett's top-down strategy. For every simple, ostensibly mechanistic event, let us imagine that there is a blind, relatively ignorant agent effecting the change. Water boils at 100 degrees C at sea level because of some homunculus's constructional, purposive activity. Then let us imagine that whole clusters, teams, or committees of these agents are

[73] *Brainstorms*, p. 83.

orchestrated by the desires and aims of yet more intelligent agents. Imagine these clusters of agents are ordered not as a Chinese box with one homunculus inside another, but as a pyramid where all the lower agents are orchestrated by a supremely intelligent agent, God. We have a noncircular account of nonintentional, mechanistic processes. In fact, the bottom-up strategy can be effected more elegantly than the way we have with a pyramid of agents. There is a short-cut: simply conceive outright of the physical workings of the cosmos as the outcome of the reasoned, purposive agency of a single intelligence, God. We can expect (and at times require) that physics and the other sciences proceed with descriptions of natural phenomena without referring to personal agency, but this by no means saddles us with leaving nonagentive explanations as somehow themselves unexplained. The underlying, cosmic agent should be thought of as powerful enough to account for the complex, uniform character of the world. Surely this is a simple hypothesis with the resources available to account for the merely mechanistic. I need not stop theorizing at the stark, unilluminating position that causal relations cannot involve meaning, content, reference, beliefs and desires. Finally, I can account for dumb merely syntactic relationships by an all-encompassing, supreme intelligence.

Some materialists want to reduce the intentional to subintentional computational relations. I want to head in the other direction and account for the computational in terms of the intentional. To parody a passage from Ziff cited earlier, the current materialistic schema is gradually losing its steely hold. Our conception of wave motion, gravitational fields, and such as forces that lack an underlying intelligent force sustaining them, are tottering; physical laws of nature look to be not importantly different from the expressed will of a powerful, intelligent agent. Why break human intelligence down to neuroanatomy when we can explain neuroanatomy and human intelligence together in terms of a higher, purposive agent?

The bottom-up strategy need not generate idealism, for it can preserve the status of physical objects as not themselves being constituted by consciousness, albeit their very existence and possession of causal powers is accounted for by the underlying power of a conscious being, God. It can also avoid occasionalism, a view briefly alluded to earlier in which God coordinates mental and physical activity to simulate interplay without allowing for direct mental–physical causal interaction. In my schema, God does not act on creation in a piecemeal fashion, moving the mental and physical in utter causal independence, but God has created and now sustains a causally complex, interconnected cosmos. Theism does not so much displace neurophysiology as provide it with an underlying metaphysical account within which to understand both the mental and the physical. Some discount this theistic strategy because they have only the dimmest appreciation for the unsurpassable power and intelligence theists ascribe to God. Witness, for example, Brian O'Shaughnessy's comment:

Well, four centuries of triumphant advance by the rock-bottom physical sciences of physics cannot but leave some mark on philosophy. When you can predict the wave length of a spectrum line to eight decimal places it is rather more difficult to believe that the underlying reality of everything is spiritual, e.g. an immaterial Deity. After all, should a Deity be so fastidious?[74]

What is the root difficulty here? O'Shaughnessy seems to suggest that it would be easier to believe in an immaterial God if the physical cosmos were less precise and predictable, perhaps more of a vague, approximate demarcation of objects as opposed to the universe as we find it. But why enjoin such a limited notion of God? Would theism be a more reasonable world-view if we could only predict wave lengths to three decimal places? Classical theism advances the belief that God is supremely great, omniscient, and omnipotent. When would an omniscient being's knowledge be fastidious, that is, excessively concerned with detail? Supposing there is a Divine reality involves none of the oddity of O'Shaughnessy's limited God, and allows us to account for the physical sciences, wave lengths and all.

Later in this book I will try to bolster this bottom-up strategy,

[74] Brian O'Shaughnessy, *The Will*, vol. I, p. xvii.

developing a theistic understanding of the laws of nature. One feature of the theistic strategy, giving it a slight edge at least as far as clarity goes, is its clear appeal to God as a real being whose activity is purported to be truly explanatory, whereas Dennett's invocation of homunculi is part of an imaginative thought experiment for materialism. He does not think there really are little people (and subpeople) called homunculi who exist in a descending bureaucratic order. The thought experiment is supposed to pave the way for a more straightforward, physicalist account by providing a model for explaining intelligence in terms of descending levels of intelligence. John Searle, among others, has duly questioned the status of these homunculi.

Now what I want to know is, what exactly do these homunculi believe at each and every level? The thesis on its face is fantastic and of course we are not supposed to take it literally. We are not supposed to ask who are these homunculi, how old are they, what are their names, etc. But the bit about progressively more stupid beliefs, though part of the fantasy, is meant literally. Otherwise no explanation has been given. Until these obvious questions are answered we have no idea what the thesis is, but from Armstrong and Dennett we get no answer.[75]

I hope to show later that a theistic account of natural laws and the cosmos, replete with conscious and nonconscious forces, is a viable alternative to the original Dennett strategy and that it is not at all antiscientific. One can ask the kinds of questions Searle does concerning God's intelligence, God's identity, God's relation to time, the names of God in various religions, and so on. But before giving further consideration to the philosophy of theism, more work needs to be done to secure the plausibility of distinguishing the mental and physical. Explaining causal interaction between the mental and physical by appealing to the causal power of God will seem (at this stage anyway) to many critics desperate and unilluminating, compounding rather than dispelling mystery. More needs to be said on behalf of the dualist appeal to the phenomenology of experience, and

---

[75] *John Searle and his Critics*, p. 185. See also Brian Hebblethwaite, *The Ocean of Truth* (Cambridge: Cambridge University Press, 1988), p. 109.

we have yet to develop a dualist reply to the problem of causal interaction.[76]

[76] An earlier version of my assessment of Churchland's work appeared in "The Argument from Transposed Modalities," *Metaphilosophy* 22:1, 2 (1991), 93–100. A version of an argument for theism based upon an appeal to simplicity which I have sketched in the final section of this chapter has been vigorously defended by Richard Swinburne in *The Existence of God* (Oxford: Clarendon Press, 1979), chapters 8 and 9 especially. See also R. M. Adams' "Flavors, Colors and God," in *The Virtue of Faith* (New York: Oxford University Press, 1987). In *Does God Have a Nature?* Alvin Plantinga writes that: "The very causal laws on which we rely in any activity are no more than the record of God's regular, constant and habitual dealings with the stuff of the universe he has created" (Milwaukee: Marquette University Press, 1980), p. 3. For a good overview of theistic treatments of natural laws see Francis Oakley's *Omnipotence, Covenant and Order* (Ithaca: Cornell University Press, 1984), chapter 3. See, too, Del Ratzsch's "Nomo(theo)logical Necessity," *Faith and Philosophy* 4:4 (October 1987), 383–402, and Alfred Freddoso's "The Necessity of Nature," in *Midwest Studies in Philosophy*, ed. Peter French *et al.*, Vol. x (Minneapolis: University of Minnesota Press, 1986), pp. 215–242.

CHAPTER 2

The material world

God likes matter, He invented it.

C. S. Lewis[1]

Thus far we have worked with provisional concepts of the physical and mental. In order to further the case for dualism and to defend the intelligibility of theism, it is crucial to consider in greater detail the adequacy of these concepts. In turning to this project we meet with terrain that is inhospitable to dualism as materialists argue that there are good conceptual and linguistic grounds for concluding that the dualist notion of the mental is either empty or unintelligible. In this chapter I consider the general project of how we might attain a substantive, sharper notion of the mental and physical, and then address an important materialist challenge.

THE PHYSICAL, THE MENTAL, AND THE OSTENSIVE

Until now we have characterized the physical by offering what appear to be safe examples such as the human body as a whole, brain states, and H_2O, while the mental has been demarcated by examples like feeling pain, entertaining thoughts, having beliefs, desires, and so on. Reference to the physical world in more general terms has been secured by appealing to the content of contemporary natural sciences such as physics and neuroscience. The materialist and dualist strategies reviewed so

---

[1] C. S. Lewis, cited by Harold Ditmanson, *Grace in Experience and Theology* (Minneapolis: Augsburg, 1977), p. 76.

far amount to debate over whether our sample of mental items can fit into such a materialist schema with its sample of physical items. But how precise is our concept of the physical and the mental? Some materialists claim that the dualist use of phenomenology in identifying the mental is profoundly flawed and that our shared understanding of the physical is comparatively far more lucid and well grounded.

The phenomenological method employed in Chapter 1 capitalized on ostensive definitions, from the Latin *ostendere*, meaning to make manifest or to show. An ostensive definition succeeds to the extent that a term or phrase is defined by identifying what is manifested or disclosed in experience. Moritz Schlick characterizes a case of ostension as "a pointing gesture combined with the pronouncing of the word as when we teach a child the meaning of blue by showing him a blue object."[2] Without visual and auditory experiences, this gesture would have no purchase for a child. To some extent, mental terms can be defined by other mental terms, but if we are looking for a truly adequate conception of the mental, I believe it is difficult to avoid some ostensive reference to experience. From a dualist standpoint, ostensive reference to consciousness will wind up being quite different from pointing with one's finger at a blue ball in the middle of an otherwise empty room, partly because consciousness is so basic and constitutes the prerequisite for noticing anything at all, and partly because, if dualism is true, consciousness is not physical. Dualists face a serious conceptual challenge here in articulating just how the ostension of conscious experience can succeed, but before exploring these difficulties I consider the prospects of defining the physical. Can the analysis of physical objects and properties bypass some ostensive appeal to experience? My aim is to advance reasons why ostension appears to be required in order to conceptually ground our notion of the physical, and then to consider why ostension-on-behalf-of-dualism has met with such sustained, formidable criticism.

What are physical objects and properties? Obviously it

---

[2] Schlick, *Philosophical Papers* (Dordrecht: Reidel, 1979), p. 458.

would not do at the outset to reply "whatever exists," for that alone would not tell us anything distinctive about the physical. Consider, instead, the following seven characterizations of the physical, marked "a" through "g." Objections to some may seem contentious, but such digging around is important in order to see where the various accounts need supplementing and to build a case for what appears to be an important role of ostensive reference.

(a) A standard, current understanding of the physical is that *something is physical if it is posited and described in contemporary physics.*[3] As a rough account, this is certainly serviceable, but it is not altogether satisfactory as it fails to elucidate what it is that contemporary physics describes and postulates. What is involved in the practice of contemporary physics? It would be circular to analyze the physical as that which physics posits and describes and then to analyze physics as that which posits and describes what is physical. There are other problems with "a," as few contemporary physicists wish to claim that the current account of the cosmos is exhaustive or that it is correct in all points of detail. Too many theories of the physical world come in and out of fashion for us to believe confidently that our present theories are all we need for a final account of the material world. Thomas Nagel proposes the following way of opening up an analysis like "a." "New properties are counted as physical if they are discovered by explanatory inference from those already in the class of the concept of contemporary physics."[4] "New properties" apparently refers to properties the scientific community may come to recognize in expanding its theory of what exists from mass to force, kinetic energy, gravitational and electromagnetic fields, quantum states, and so on. Despite the fact that this clearly improves on "a", there

[3] J. J. C. Smart describes materialism as "The theory that there is nothing in the world over and above those entities which are postulated by physics." "Materialism," *Journal of Philosophy* 60 (1963), 651–652. Kathy Wilkes utilizes a similar thesis, but she is aware of the difficulties in doing so, "Mind and Body," in *Key Themes in Philosophy*, ed. Phillips Griffiths (Cambridge: Cambridge University Press, 1989), p. 74.
[4] Thomas Nagel, "Panpsychism," in *Mortal Questions* (New York: Cambridge University Press, 1980), p. 183.

is no obvious reason for ruling out physical properties that cannot be discovered through explanatory inference from currently known physical properties. This alone would not show that Nagel's stance is false, as he is advancing a sufficient, not a necessary, condition for being counted as physical, but it highlights the fact that his depiction of the physical is narrow and may not capture many physical properties. To avoid this latter problem the analysis may be reformulated.

(b) *A property or object is physical if it will be posited and described in physics in the future.* This allows for a revolution in science in which concepts are introduced that differ radically from our current repertoire. Unfortunately, this still needs to be supplemented. If physics as a science ceased to be, the physical world would not. As with Nagel's criterion, this would not show "b" to be mistaken, for accepting "b" does not commit one to believing the physical world exists only if posited by physics, but it underscores the fact that "b" does not identify a necessary feature of being physical. So, consider an adjustment in which we need not worry about the fate of physics as it is actually practiced.

(c) *A property or object is physical if it would be posited and described in a physics which is complete, exhaustive in all points of detail, and accurate.* This is better, but it rules out definitionally from the beginning that a complete and accurate physics would not posit nonphysical things, whether God or sensations (both construed along nonphysical lines). Some theoretical physicists believe there are scientific reasons for positing a God-like intelligence behind the material cosmos as its creator, and some neurophysicists, Wilder Penfield, John Eccles, and others, posit and describe the causal role of what they believe to be nonphysical in their account of neural activity. Even if these scientists are mistaken, why assume they are from the outset? Another reason for thinking "c" may be misguided is that it runs the risk of classifying abstract objects like numbers and sets as physical. The latter are routinely relied upon in physics, and yet it is difficult to construe such *abstracta* as good citizens of the physical domain. As William Lycan comments, "My appeal to sets ... is indeed an embarrassment to physicalism, since sets *et al* are nonspatiotemporal, acausal items ... eventually set theory will have to be either naturalised or rejected, if a thoroughgoing physicalism is to be maintained."[5] These problems to one side, none of the refinements of "a" avoid the problem of circularity. Art objects may be defined as that which artists make and artists may be defined as those who make art objects, but such circularity is not enlightening.[6] Consider, then, a different approach. The circularity emerges because the sciences are presumed to be identified in terms of disciplined inquiry into the physical. The following entry makes explicit a central feature of the scientific method.

(d) *A property or object is physical if it is in principle publicly observable.* This highlights what it is about the physical that leads many to believe that physics (along with the other physical sciences) can be employed in our demarcation of the physical. Physics is a theoretical and empirical science that insists upon the public, observable accessibility of its data and experiments. This construal of the material world is part and parcel of what is called the third-person character of the physical. "I declare my starting point to be the objective materialistic, third-person world of the physical sciences," writes Dennett. "This is the orthodox choice today in the English speaking world."[7]

Several problems beset this orthodox analysis, not the least of which is that there are items many classify as physical that cannot be observed, gravitational fields and subatomic particles, for example. Never mind the fact that cosmological theorizing in physics refers to events in the past that cannot be observed by us or our descendants. I believe these difficulties can be alleviated by relaxing the notion of public observability

---

[5] *Consciousness* (Cambridge, Mass.: MIT Press, 1987), p.90. For a compelling case for recognizing the existence of abstract objects see Michael Loux's *Substance and Attribute* (Dordrecht: Reidel, 1978).

[6] Such a depiction would not just be circular but unsatisfactory without specifying when it is that artists *qua* artists make objects, for artists make objects which are not art objects. For this reason "c" is couched in terms of what is posited and described *in physics* and not *by physicists*, for in their spare time physicists might posit and describe all kinds of things they would not when engaged in physics. I believe that the institutional theory of art and institutional theories of the physical and the ethical have similar limitations.

[7] Daniel Dennett, *The Intentional Stance* (Cambridge, Mass.: MIT Press, 1987), p. 5.

to include items that are observed indirectly and items that can be inferred on the basis of public observation. (This latter move would, however, confront us once again with the problem noted in "c": it rules out by definition the claims of those who believe that nonphysical phenomena should be posited to account for publicly observed data.) There may also be some legitimate worry that idealism allows for the public observability of various items whereby minds are observationally available to other minds. In idealism, the public observability of so-called physical objects can be analyzed in terms of observers possessing a complex array of mutually corroborating sense data. Perhaps this, too, may be set to one side. It is more important to note here that "d" employs the notion of observation. What is it to observe things? At least initially, this seems to involve conscious episodes and sensations, and it thereby seems to rest the notion of the physical upon some notion of consciousness, a notion that is ordinarily classified as mental. The idea of a public object as an object that can be observed involves a psychological notion and, as a result, the analysis of the physical is left dangling until we have some understanding of its nature. Far from the analysis of the physical being conceptually more basic or lucid than the mental, it seems the former cannot be any more basic and lucid than the latter. To claim otherwise would be equivalent to holding that we have a clearer conception of being tangible, visible, or witnessed than we do of touching, viewing, and witnessing. I am not arguing here that the *nonphysical* is more basic than the physical, but only that in characterizing the physical in ways like "d," the mental is presupposed. The same point would come out even more clearly if one were to follow some philosophers who delimit the physical as that which is "intersubjective." The notion of intersubjectivity explicitly builds upon the notion of the subjective, and the latter is a strong candidate for a mental activity or state.

One might try to recast "observation" in exclusively eliminative terms according to which visual observations become certain sorts of surface irritations on the retina and so on, but this leads to the counter-intuitive consequences chronicled in the last chapter. What is it that makes some physical irritations,

and not others, into what appear to be subjective observations?[8]
The same problem of presupposing an understanding of
conscious, psychological states attends the following analysis of
the physical.

(e) *Something is physical if no one subject is necessarily better placed
to know about it than any other subject.*[9] This continues to develop
what may be called the democracy of the physical. The physical
winds up being delimited by its excluding privileged cognitive
access. There are several limitations with "e." For a theist who
believes that God necessarily exists and is necessarily omniscient,
definition "e" leads to the conclusion that there are no physical
objects. Given the truth of this form of theism, God is a subject
who is necessarily better placed than any other subject to know
an object's mass, weight, shape, and size. As a result, an object's
mass, weight, shape, and size turn out to be nonphysical. This
reveals a real defect in "e" for theists who want to affirm the
existence of both a nonphysical God and a cosmos containing
physical elements. "E" may also be criticized on the grounds
that even if it correctly demarcates the physical, it does so on the
basis of something that is not constitutive of it. That is, the
criterion fails to illuminate what it is about the physical that
makes it such that it resists such ensured, direct epistemic access.
Criterion "e" winds up treating the physical principally in
epistemic, rather than in metaphysical, terms. But most
important to note here is that "e" presupposes the notion of
knowledge which, like observation, appears to be a mental
concept.

(f) In *Metaphysics and the Mind–Body Problem* Michael Levin
advances an analysis that is similar to "c," but with somewhat
more positive content. "A physical property is a property that
makes a difference in the motion of masses, a property that
figures in a (broadly) mechanistic explanation."[10] The physical
is thereby delimited in terms of our ability to explain the

---

[8] Quine makes a bid for talking about sensory experience in terms of surface irritations
in *Word and Object* (Cambridge, Mass.: MIT Press, 1960) p. 23.

[9] See, for example, Richard Swinburne, *The Evolution of the Soul* (Oxford: Clarendon
Press, 1986), p. 6.

[10] Michael Levin, *Metaphysics and the Mind–Body Problem* (Oxford: Clarendon Press,
1979), p. 63.

movement of masses. Like "d," this improves upon earlier entries that appeal to physics without specifying the distinctive features of physics as a practice. I think it is plausible to understand physics as principally explanatory in its aim, and not driven solely by the goals of prediction and control, and so "f" may be seen as a further explication of the characterizations "a" to "c." I shall assume that Levin's reference to our explaining the movement of mass is not limited to our current explanatory practice (as with "a"), but is more like "c." There are still at least four areas where Levin's analysis is in need of elucidation.

First, why could there not be physical properties that do not figure in any mechanistic explanations whatever (past, future, or under ideal circumstances)? Perhaps there can be physical properties, events, or objects that are idle from the standpoint of explanatory physics, or from the standpoint of explaining motion.

Second, Levin's account seems to commit him to the peculiar view that if all mass ceased to be in motion, its (formerly) physical properties would all cease to be physical.[11]

A third difficulty recalls a point made earlier under "c." According to dualist interactionism, a person's psychological desires, beliefs, and intentions are causally efficacious and, thus, should enter into explanations of human behavior and events in the physical world. If Levin's analysis of the physical is adopted, then these dualists are not really dualists, because what they characterize as nonphysical is thereby categorized as physical. Dualist interactionists are committed to holding that intentions have a role in explaining the location of at least some molecules; *ex hypothesi* my intending to write this sentence enters into the explanation of a host of moving molecules. If dualism is true, and intentions do enter into *bona fide* causal explanations of material change, then intending turns out to be physical. But this linguistic move seems vacuous and unhelpful. The great

---

[11] See Sydney Shoemaker's "Time Without Change," *Journal of Philosophy* 66 (June 1969), 363–381. J. L. Mackie has raised doubts about there being a necessary tie between physical things and causation in *The Cement of the Universe* (Oxford: Oxford University Press, 1974), p. 110.

archdualist René Descartes granted that if "corporeal" is defined as that which causally effects physical events, then the mind should be considered "corporeal."[12] But it would surely be disconcerting to have Descartes wind up a materialist, and, in the absence of decisive reasons for ruling out dualist interactionism, why build into one's very account of the physical a presupposition that it is false?

Fourth, what is mass? I am not sure how Levin wishes to analyze the notion of "mass," though I assume he believes that for an object to have mass is for it to have spatial extension, with volume, density, and weight as accompanying (perhaps non-essential) characteristics. If so, then Levin's account seems close to Descartes's, which we can now review as "g".

(g) Descartes advanced the thesis that *spatial extension is an essential characteristic of the material. If something is physical, it is spatially extended and vice versa.*

In my view, this account is among the most promising. Some objections to it seem to me to be misguided. For example, it has been objected that straightforward physical things such as objects with zero rest mass and fields lack spatial extension. If points exist, then they lack volume and shape, but they do not thereby lack location. Provided we understand Descartes's analysis so that spatial location suffices to secure spatial extension, "g" still seems acceptable. Fields and points (if there are points) have location, even if the location of the former lacks well-defined boundaries in terms of areas of operation, and the latter are virtually unobservable by us. So, Descartes's reading of what it is to be physical seems safe over against these problems as long as we do not assume that spatial extension must be voluminous and spatial objects must possess clearly demarcated surfaces.

Another apparent difficulty facing "g" can, I think, be met. Consider the following objection: If dualism is true and mental

---

[12] "If 'corporeal' is taken to mean anything which can in any way affect a body, then the mind too must be called corporeal in this sense," *Descartes, Philosophical Letters*, trans. and ed. Anthony Kenny (Oxford: Clarendon Press, 1970), p. 12. John Beloff is a dualist prepared to make a similar terminological adjustment, provided that "materialism" is defined with sufficient latitude, *The Existence of Mind* (London: MacGibbon and Kee, 1962).

properties that are nonphysical affect physical properties and events, do nonphysical properties wind up having spatial location? Thomas Aquinas held that "An incorporeal thing is said to be in a thing by contact of power."[13] On a full fledged dualist account like Descartes's the mind is nonphysical and yet located *in* the body in the sense that our personal life consists of mind–body interaction. Would that serve to make the mind physical? One way to settle this would be to contend that some object is physical only if no part of it lacks spatial location. From a dualist standpoint, the mind or person is manifested in bodily life (in ways discussed below), but this does not mean the mind is metaphysically the same thing as the physical body. Physical properties and objects on the other hand, are metaphysically the very same things as extended, located items. One result of this move would be that only thoroughly physical objects would count as physical objects, but this seems bearable. If one desires a more lax description of dualistically embodied minds, one could describe them as physical, but not only physical, without conjuring too much obscurity. Even so, "g" still does not seem to be entirely problem-free.

A more serious difficulty is that "g" would entail that a variety of objects often classified as nonphysical by some materialists as well as dualists turn out to be physical. The reason why some materialists deny the existence of dream images, hallucinations, and visual sense data is that these items seem to be spatially extended and yet nonphysical. If we grant that dream images and sense data are three-dimensional objects, they become very difficult to identify with specific brain states or other bodily processes. What are we to do with the visual denizens of luminous dreams? Are they some physical distance away from the rapid eye movement of the dreamer? Arthur Lovejoy once remarked that "if the dome at Washington is physical, it is a nonphysical and therefore another dome which the sleeper in Chicago entertains."[14] Of course, construing dream images as nonphysical does not commit one to believing

---

[13] Thomas Aquinas, *Summa Contra Gentiles*, trans. Joseph Rickaby (Westminster: The Carroll Press, 1950), chapter LXVIII.
[14] *The Revolt Against Dualism* (La Salle: Open Court, 1960), p. 89.

that the dream image of a dome is actually a dome (just as a
painting of a forest is not a forest), but the visual images are no
less spatial occupants on that account. Dualists like H. D.
Lewis, H. H. Price, and Howard Robinson recognize dream
objects and sense data in general, treating these as objects that
are not in the same domain as material things. Price makes the
following reply to a skeptic:

He is assuming that if an entity is somewhere it must be somewhere in
physical space. This is no doubt a logically possible assumption. It
might have happened to be true. But there is no sort of logical necessity
about it, and in fact it happens to be false. My visual image of the
Front Quadrangle is not anywhere in the physical world at all. It is
spatially extended. Its parts are spatially related to each other by
relations of location, and also by relations of larger and smaller.[15]

William Lycan is a materialist who appreciates the threat of
such visual sense data. He is pessimistic about whether sense
data can be absorbed in anything less than a fully developed
version of dualism or idealism. "We could not accept sense-data
and maintain that only physical objects exist; moreover we
would have to come up with some account of how human beings
are able to acquaint themselves with nonphysical individuals,
an account that would very likely entail that human beings are
not entirely physical individuals themselves."[16] On the face of
it, Lycan's worries seem well grounded. In the course of his own
resistance to dualism, Norman Malcolm took an eliminative
approach to dreams, denying that dreaming involves experiences.[17]

I think it is abundantly reasonable to believe dreams involve
visual images. There are, I think, good reasons to recognize

[15] *Thinking and Experience* (London: Hutchinson, 1969), p. 250.
[16] *Consciousness*, p. 88.
[17] Norman Malcolm, *Dreaming* (London: Routledge & Kegan Paul, 1989). Anthony
Quinton calls Malcolm's work The Light Brigade Charge in *The Nature of Things*
(London: Routledge & Kegan Paul, 1973), p. 325. Some dualists have treated
dream objects and other sensa as physical (Franz Brentano), whereas others
explicitly build into their account of the physical their immaterial character (G. E.
Moore). The positing of sense data is well criticized. An early, important paper
is G. A. Paul's "The Problem of Sense-Data," *Aristotelian Society Proceedings*,
supplement vol. 15 (1936).

sense data in general, but I do not want to harness the case for dualism here to making a case for such objects. Dualist interactionism can be true even if we do not have dream images and sense data. In this book I defend the reality of sensory experience, but, as I noted in Chapter 1, my aim is to remain neutral between the sense data and adverbial accounts of sensations. In arguing for dualism and for the coherence of classical theism here I do not want to take on board more theories than my project requires, especially when critics have independent reasons for objecting to them. So, I raise the problem of dream images as a challenge to criterion "g," not as a problem for materialism as a whole. If it is plausible to believe there are sense data, or even plausible to believe there could be sense data, whether or not there actually are any, we have reasons to conclude "g" does not state a sufficient condition for being physical.

If there are spatially extended objects that are nonphysical, must "g" be jettisoned altogether? Not entirely, for "g" may be altered to state a necessary, though not sufficient, condition for being physical. Consider g*: *If an object or property is physical it is spatially extended, but it is not necessarily true that if an object or property is spatially extended it is physical.*

The question I wish to raise now is whether the notion of spatial extension (or, going back an entry, Levin's notion of mass) can itself be spelled out without ostensive appeal. Even granting the limited acceptability of "g*," is our notion of the physical spelled out now in a way that does not require ostensive reference to experience?

What is space? How is it that we may conceptually grasp the notion of spatial objects without making use of ostensive reference? We may define in the abstract the idea of line, volume and subvolume, shape, points, proximity, and distance, but it is difficult to see how any of this can get started for us without our being apprised of spatial extension in the course of experiencing spatial objects. Once we have some conceptual fix on spatial dimensions, we may formalize their different relations, and argue about the nature of space, debating, say, whether space is indefinitely divisible, whether there can be points or unoccupied spatial regions, whether the relational or absolute theory of space is plausible, whether there is a fourth dimension (or there could be one, if there is not one), and so on. A number of phenomenologists and empiricists have recognized the need for ostension when it comes to identifying spatial extension ("We cannot here define visual or tactual depth otherwise than ostensively," writes A. J. Ayer), and I think the same point needs to be recognized when it comes to fixing our understanding of volume and its various dimensions in physical space.[18] I do not claim that it is metaphysically impossible for a being to understand spatial relations without ostension; God may well do so (in fact I believe God does), and possibly even we could have been made such that the notion of spatial extension was somehow innately built into us in a pre-experiential fashion. But none of these possibilities belie the legitimacy of our using ostension to form a conception of spatial extension and, given our actual constitution, the necessity of our doing so. Recall the discussion in the last chapter on Divine cousins. The possibility of alternative means of cognition does not demonstrate that there are defects in our own more humble ways of knowing.[19]

The import of the above observations on "a" through "g" is that these depictions of the physical require some grasp of the mental for them to be complete. I have not been assuming, however, that all our justified convictions about the physical world are built up in a hierarchical fashion, with each of them justified by prior convictions until we unearth an experientially confirmed foundational base. One can recognize the essential role of ostension in demarcating the physical, and also believe that our judgments are justified on the grounds of coherence, or that they form a holistic network that is mutually correcting and supporting. My remarks on "a" to "g" may give the impression that until the mental is grasped fully and in explicit, precise terms, the physical cannot be captured cognitively. Nothing so extreme is intended. I do hold that the mental must

[18] Ayer, *Philosophy in the Twentieth Century* (New York: Random House, 1982), p. 188.

[19] Kant held that our grasp of space is made possible by in-built forms of intuition, but he does not deny that experience is needed by us if we are to understand what it is to be spatial in the phenomenal world.

be recognized to be intelligible in order to philosophically ground our references to the physical world, but this is not to say our understanding of the mental must be fully articulated or analyzed prior to reaching justified beliefs about the material world. Recall Schlick's depiction of ostending color, pointing to a blue ball with one's finger, say. I do not think we can get such an ostensive project off the ground without being able to understand on some level that pointing with one's finger is an ostensive gesture; it is intended to pick something out, to direct one's attention to something. But consider how much of a detailed comprehension one must have of seeing a person's fingers and watching him point in order to comprehend the appropriate, ostending gesture. Very little. Similarly, our notion of the mental need not be explicitly analyzed to gain an understanding of physical objects. Children come to have the notion of enduring physical objects without possessing a philosophical concept of the mental. What I have been proposing thus far is that when our aim is to formulate an explicit, clear concept of the physical, we need some explicit, clear concept of the mental.

Many of the extant treatments of the mental in the literature today acknowledge the necessity of some kind of ostensive reference. Michael Pendlebury's comment about experience is representative. "It is not possible to define experience in an illuminating way. Readers, however, know what experiences are through acquaintance with some of their own, e.g. a visual experience of a green after-image, a feeling of physical nausea or a tactile experience of an abrasive surface"[20] Similar admissions are widespread, especially among dualist philosophers such as H. D. Lewis, A. C. Ewing, and C. A. Campbell. F. R. Tennant is not alone in holding that, as far as nonostensive depictions go, consciousness is "indescribable in terms other than synonyms for itself."[21]

---

[20] "Theories of Experience," *Companion to Epistemology*, ed. J. Dancy and E. Sosa (Oxford: Blackwell, 1992), p. 125.

[21] *Philosophical Theology* (Cambridge: Cambridge University Press, 1928), p. 15. I go on in this chapter to consider materialist, functional analyses that try to do better. Other depictions of the mental may be illuminating in different respects, but (I believe)

In turning to consider the materialist critique of dualist ostension, subsequent use of the term "physical" will be somewhat open ended to reflect the difficulties facing "a" to "g". By "physical" I will mean those things that are described and posited in mainstream current physics, or things like them, things that can be publicly observed, or things composing publicly observable objects, and things that are spatially located. If Descartes is right that there are nonphysical minds, these may be seen as truly nonphysical, for while they have location through causal embodiment, they are not metaphysically identical with that which is spatially located, the body. (More on this shortly.) I shall assume that things such as brains, nerves, photons, zinc, granite, baseballs, and their parts, are all safe examples of the physical. Decisions about the physical status of certain items may admit of negotiation, but there is not such a large penumbral region that the negotiation is *ad hoc*. Thus, imagine we possess good reasons to believe there are spatially extended sense data as conceived of by Lovejoy and Price. While these objects satisfy one condition for being physical, the fact (if it is a fact) that they do not satisfy others gives us reason enough for concluding they are nonphysical, for example they are significantly different from other, paradigm cases of the physical in that (by hypothesis) they are not composed of atomic and subatomic parts, or open to public observation at least under ordinary conditions, their behavior

none succeed in by-passing the need for ostension. Thus, depictions in terms of epistemic privilege and intentionality fall back on our experiential acquaintance with knowledge and other intentional states. Some philosophers depict the mental in a way that relies upon our understanding of consciousness – for example Fred Feldman in *A Cartesian Introduction to Philosophy* (New York: McGraw-Hill, 1986), p. 165 – or sentience – Frank Jackson in *Perception* (Cambridge: Cambridge University Press, 1977), p. 3. I think Tennant's thesis holds with sentience as much as it does with consciousness. Searle expresses the difficulty of measuring the appeal to experience. "How would one go about refuting the view that consciousness does not exist? Should I pinch its adherents to remind them that they are conscious? Should I pinch myself and report the results to the *Journal of Philosophy*?," *The Rediscovery of the Mind* (Cambridge, Mass.: MIT Press, 1992), p. 8. For an apt acknowledgment of the need to appeal to how things seem to us in such an analysis, see Edmund Husserl's *Ideas*, trans. W. R. Boyce-Gibson (New York, 1931), p. 76. Some critics complain that dualists propound a vacuous, solely negative treatment of nonphysical mental life, but I suggest that our notion of the nonphysical seems ill-defined largely because the notion of the physical has yet to be sharply delineated.

in dreams does not conform to laws governing the physical world like the law of gravity (though they may be correlated with brain processes that do), and so on. Later I discuss further the philosophical significance of our somewhat flexible conception of what counts as physical. At present, I think we have a sufficiently workable, albeit imperfect, understanding of the physical so that we can proceed with the materialist and dualist arguments in the offing.

THE PERILS OF OSTENSION AND THE PROMISE OF FUNCTIONALISM

Consciousness appears to be the last bastion of occult properties, epiphenomena, immeasurable subjective states – in short, the one area of mind left to the philosophers who are welcome to it. Let them make fools of themselves trying to corral the quicksilver of "phenomenology" into a respectable theory.[22]

Most of the problems with the dualist project of ostending consciousness stem from what critics take to be the dualist commitment to viewing the mental as obscurely private. It is the exclusive privacy of the mental, whereby it is supremely disclosed only to the subject in the given mental state, that creates such philosophical mayhem. Materialists argue that dualist ostension involves vicious circularity, a kind of contentless ineffability, and promotes a lethal form of skepticism. At best, the dualist construal of ostending consciousness is empty, at worst it is unintelligible. In its place, some critics advance functionalist theories of the mental that purport to accommodate a more stable, less obscure use of ostension, and provide a more unified characterization of personal and social life. I present the materialist attack on dualism first and then outline in more detail the version of dualism and ostensive reference I accept.

When it comes to ostending material objects, we employ a public convention involving observable behavior like pointing, and the objects we point to are themselves publicly observable.

[22] Daniel Dennett, *Brainstorms* (Cambridge, Mass.: MIT Press, 1978), p. 149.

Pointing to putatively immaterial items is another story and appears, on the face of it, to be absurd. How, for example, can I point to painful sensations? Do I point to a physical injury that gives rise to pain in myself or some other person? I certainly can try to do so, but, according to dualism, neither this nor pointing to sensory "pain centers" in the brain and nervous system would be to point to or directly identify the pain itself. And the problem is not just one of ostending a particular mental state as opposed to another. How is it that we can point to consciousness? In ostending consciousness, do I point to my body as a whole or draw your attention to my being awake, or to particular brain functions? The problem with the latter move is that, as Dennett observed in a spirit of uncharacteristic sympathy with dualism, brains look as though nobody is at home. There seems to be a considerable gulf between the myriad qualities of conscious life, with its colors, smells, sounds, tastes on the one side, and, on the other, the gray, comparatively more homogeneous, spongy matter inside the skull.[23] As we have seen, dualists capitalize on this apparent disparity in their case against Dennett *et al.*, but far from this conception of the mental serving dualism faithfully, such a relentlessly subjective outlook comes back to haunt dualism with a vengeance. Critics charge that the dualist view of subjectivity ultimately undermines the whole dualist project.

The problem with the dualist use of phenomenological ostension is that it promotes an austere, contentless depiction of mental references. If my aim is to pick out a given sensation like pain, without picking out the surrounding material conditions that cause the pain, or the material effects of the pain, I seem to be at a loss. To describe pain as painful appears to amount to no more than saying that pain is itself. How, then, is pain to be identified, or, putting the question in linguistic terms, how does the word "pain" come to have the meaning it has in our public language?

Michael Levin is representative of those materialists who underscore the public nature of our discourse about the mental.

[23] Daniel Dennett, *Consciousness Explained* (London: Allen Lane, 1991), p. 23.

On his view, we get along quite well with our mental terms because they are part and parcel of our materially grounded, public discourse.

A child first encounters "pain" when his parents notice that he is aware of some bodily damage. He impales himself on a splinter, and his mother commiserates: "Oh, how that must hurt." A child learns "pain" in terms of events involving bodily injury; the referential force of "pain" is closely tied initially to "what goes on when e," where e is some description of a public event.[24]

According to Levin and others, our mental language is couched in terms of such material observations. It is publicly formatted, as it were, as opposed to being constructed on the basis of the more mysterious machinations of dualistic introspection. There is an accessible, functional character to mental language insofar as the mental designates that which has an operative role in material, publicly observed relationships. Our mental terms do not have a meaning wholly cut off from the content they receive from the rich material circumstances in which such language is forged.

In Levin's view, the sharable, public nature of our language about the physical world is what allows us to have a language of the mental in the first place. In order to speak meaningfully of the mental, there must be ways in which our references can be publicly corrected and checked. If phenomenological ostension is our chief route to the mental, then each person seems to be locked into a peculiarly obscure privacy that threatens to make language between persons unintelligible. How can anyone other than myself know what it is that I am identifying by the term "pain"? If we banish, or treat as second-class, the material-object references in which talk of pain is founded, we seem to be saddled with obscurity and ineffability. It is ineffable in the sense that its intrinsic features seem to be incapable of informative description. This admission of ineffability may be begged off temporarily in analyzing mental terms when they are treated on a fairly abstract plane, but when the dualist tries to make fully explicit the content of mental discourse in a

---

[24] *Metaphysics and the Mind–Body Problem*, p. 103.

concrete fashion, this conclusion seems inescapable. How informative is it to describe "pain" as feeling "that way" in which I somehow point to the mental state I am in when injured?

Dualists face a dilemma. *Bona fide* description of the mental appears to land us in a thicket of rich references to material objects and relations, while to edge away from this toward the privileged vantage point of introspection increasingly diminishes the prospects of giving meaningful content to our shared mental discourse. The choice, then, is between extolling a purely ostensive method of identification which collapses into mystery and adopting a descriptive approach which is ultimately best underwritten by materialist assumptions. Levin sees the descriptive, and thus, by his lights, the materialist, account as the only promising one, supported by a general account of identifying objects.

Any robust identification of something must involve some level of description, identifying the thing or event or whatever as a certain sort or kind. Things are recognized by us as existing as something or other, possessing a nature or character, or being of a certain type. The categories we employ may be quite malleable, inchoate, and so pervasive that we fail to take explicit notice of them. Be that as it may, when I think of one of my mental states I do so in a way that construes it as a certain sort of state. To identify some state of mine as "pain" involves recognizing the feeling I have as fitting into a certain pattern of other mental and physical states. Recognizing this patterned character is already to load the dice in favor of a material, publicly accessible vantage point, for the materialist schema can appropriately ground our reference to the mental in which "pain" and other mental states fall into different types. In a dualist framework, it is unclear whether I can legitimately use the terms I do to refer even to my own mental states, let alone use public terms fittingly to describe others. If dualism is correct, how can I compare my own mental states with those of others? To suppose that I can telepathically inspect others' mental states will strike many as philosophically desperate. According to Levin, the most natural assumption to make is that our mental designations are fixed and adjudicated by behavioral, observable events. In a subjective world which others may access only indirectly, there can be no direct checking that I am appropriately following the rules of reference embedded in social practice.

In Levin's view, the material grounding of mental discourse provides us with a rich framework to decipher mental states.

A man may indeed have pains in his hand unlike those associated with lacerated skin. But how are such pains described if not as the sort of pain that comes from a pinch, or from gripping a tennis racket too long? These are all neutral descriptions, and reflection on how we communicate our pains to others provides endless examples of the aptness of such descriptions for fine discrimination. If anything, the variety of descriptions available in the public neutral vocabulary far outruns such a phenomenological vocabulary as we may have ... If rigid reference to sensations is secured by description at all, it is fixed by neutral descriptions even for the subject of sensation, since the only facts he knows about pains are circumstantial.[25]

This circumstantial awareness is not barren, taking notice of the mental only at its most outer parameter, because to know the mental circumstantially is to be aware of the mental's tangible, pervasive role in the public world. The dualist, phenomenological approach to language is not capable of trading upon such comparative, contextualized reference, without abandoning the claim that the mental has a rudimentary primacy of awareness over against our awareness of the physical.

Levin, like many other materialists, does not wish to deny the obvious fact that ostension has certain vital roles to play in the life of human discourse; he only wants to secure ostension as an activity that takes place within a thoroughly public world. Proper ostension takes place in the philosophical outdoors, and is not feasible as a means for linking together otherwise disparate, subjectively private worlds. To recognize an ostensive gesture as a gesture is already to be in a physical arena of references and checks. The problem with dualism is that it treats our convictions about material objects as something we each need to earn, whereas precisely the opposite is the case. Am I

[25] *Ibid.*, pp. 118, 119.

first aware of nonphysical, private, inner items, and then compelled to find my way out into awareness of the external world? No, we can avoid such an unpromising project of arguing our way out of a subjective world by realizing that we are out in the world from the beginning. The commonly accessible world is the real world.[26]

Dualists are advised not to resort to the peculiar supposition that the rules of mental discourse are themselves somehow revealed or authenticated subjectively. Rules are profoundly different from other dualistic posits of the mental world like sense data, sounds, smells, and so on. Arguably, a social rule cannot be something I introspect, as though it were a taste or flavor. Linguistic rules about how we use words are facets of the social, public world, not the fittings of our inner, mental life. The conventions of language are articulated in terms of social interaction, not hidden private acts.

According to some critics, the ostensive project as propounded by dualism is also plagued by a conceptual problem concerning its logical form. These critics argue that knowledge must always have a propositional structure. Knowledge involves knowing *that certain things are the case*, where this involves the mastery of various concepts, by which one can (at least in principle) affirm, deny, and communicate propositions. Dualists who rely on phenomenological ostension seem to be guilty of a category mistake. One cannot know mental states, strictly speaking: one can only know that certain propositions are true about mental states, and once we admit that propositions must be the instrument of reference, we are solidly in the realm of public discourse and away from the dualist world of hypersubjectivity. P. M. S. Hacker reproaches those who invoke claims to know mental states, without such conceptual, public wherewithal.

What is it to know what pain is like? Does the yelping dog whose paw has been trodden on know what pain is like? No, for whatever "knowing what pain is like" means, it does not mean the same as "being in pain." Is it to have "knowledge of certain kinds of

[26] Jonathan Dancy takes aim at dualist appeals to ostension in *Contemporary Epistemology* (Oxford: Basil Blackwell, 1985).

experience "? But what does that mean? I have a toothache, do I have knowledge of a toothache? Am I acquainted with toothache? Do I know nausea or cramp? These are slightly curious, quasi-poetic expressions. They are either philosophical nonsense, or they signify no more than having had the sensation ... The criteria for possession of a concept, for mastery of the use of a word, consist in one's correctly using and explaining an expression, not in one's medical history.[27]

The sort of arguments deployed by Hacker and Levin have had considerable representation in the contemporary philosophical literature, most famously in the so-called private-language argument of Ludwig Wittgenstein. Wittgenstein's work may be seen as providing one of the chief inspirations for the twentieth-century emphasis upon linking mental language with behavioral, observable conditions.[28]

The most widely accepted philosophy of mind today that builds upon the kind of considerations highlighted in the private-language argument is functionalism. Levin's account of the mental is very much in the functionalist school. According to functionalism, mental states are duly identified in terms of various causal relations, different in-put and out-put relations, that anchor our reference to the mental in publicly available circumstances. To be in pain is thus characterized as being in a state that is brought about in certain ways such as skin laceration and that gives rise to behavior like flight, yelling, avoidance behavior. As described, there is nothing about functionalism *per se* that requires one to assume that the different mental states are in fact physical. A dualist can, in principle, adopt a functionalist analysis of the mental and still contend that what satisfies the functional role for the mental is nonphysical. But most functionalists are materialists who see as one of the principal merits of functionalism the defusing of dualist appeal to phenomenological ostension.

At the end of this section, I want to emphasize a crucial strand in these antidualistic considerations. We have outlined the objections that dualism undermines intelligible language

---

[27] *Appearance and Reality* (Oxford: Basil Blackwell, 1987), pp. 146, 147.
[28] Wittgenstein's private-language argument is set forth in *Philosophical Investigations* (Oxford: Basil Blackwell, 1953). The status of sensations is not altogether clear in Wittgenstein's work: note paragraph 304, for example.

and reference to the mental. Let me also note how dualism is accused of inviting an intractable skepticism. All these objections taken together focus on the difficulty of harmonizing dualism with our ordinary understanding of persons and society.

Dualists face a lethal skeptical obstacle even if it is conceded that dualism can allow for a person making intelligible reference to his or her own mental states. For the sake of argument, imagine I can secure the references to my own sensory states. I am able to refer to my feeling pain as "pain," or "that way" as designated ostensively, in a noncircular fashion, without having to know about how others employ linguistic pain-references. But now, I face the so-called problem of other minds in a way, and with a force, that materialists do not. So long as we understand the mental in public terms that have materially confirmable references, we can secure our ordinary convictions about the way other people think and feel. To guarantee the truth of my belief that you are in pain I need only determine whether the relevant physical, criterial conditions are satisfied. But if I believe that being in pain involves something distinguishable from the satisfaction of such public conditions, I am in serious philosophical trouble. Could it be that what I assume to be other people are people in appearance only? Dualism seems to allow for the possibility that others who appear to be people (as they meet all the *physical* conditions for personhood) may yet wind up being shorn of consciousness. This could just as well be called the zombie problem as the problem of other minds. How do I know whether the people around me are not zombies? A suitably functionalist materialism does not seem to be faced with this problem, for if the mental is successfully defined or essentially characterized by public conditions, such conditions cannot obtain without the mental also obtaining.

As with the predicament concerning dualistic ostension, critics charge that each of the escape routes from the problem of other minds is perilous. Dualist philosophers have appealed to various strategies in order to redeem the belief in other minds which I address later. These include arguments that appeal to analogies drawn from a person's own mental–physical life, linguistic behavior, inferences to the best explanation, intuition, unique evidential relationships, and the goodness of God. Other dualists have given ground to the skeptic by conceding that we do not have knowledge of other minds, adding the caveat that the skeptic's point is moot because we simply *must* believe that others are conscious as part of our own biological necessity and animal faith. The point that materialists have pressed for here is that however dualists posture their justification for the belief in other minds (or the denial of zombies), their position will be comparatively more in jeopardy than the materialist account. Dualists have further to go than materialists.

Along these lines, materialists advance what may loosely be described as a phenomenological argument against dualism. Does it not seem that in our exchanges with other persons, we actually see, hear, touch the person himself or herself? We do not merely encounter clues as to what persons are thinking, mere signs or manifestations, but the persons themselves. In a comment that was aimed at unmasking the splintered character of dualism, Anthony Flew notes that we meet other people, not their containers.[29] Does dualism introduce a ponderous, convoluted inference here, when it seems none is called for?

If all these difficulties were not bad enough, some critics press skeptical objections against dualist phenomenology on its own terrain. Dennett and others protest that even if one permits the dualist sufficient leeway to play the phenomenological game, so to speak, it becomes increasingly murky and conceptually lame. Dennett reproaches those who aim at discovering intrinsic, mental states through introspection.

The final step [in a pro-*qualia* move at identifying our phenomenal states] presumes that we can isolate the *qualia* from everything else that is going on – at least in principle for the sake of argument. What counts as the way juice tastes to X can be distinguished, one supposes, from what is a mere accompaniment, contributory cause, or by-product of this "central" way. One dimly imagines taking such cases and stripping them down gradually to the essentials, leaving their common residuum, the way things look, sound, feel, taste, smell to

[29] See Flew's contribution to *Brain and Mind*, ed. J. Smythies (New York: Humanities Press, 1965), p. 26.

various individuals at various times, independently of how those individuals are stimulated or non-perceptually affected, and independently of how they are subsequently disposed to behave or believe. The mistake is not in supposing that we can in practice ever or always perform this act of purification with certainty, but the more fundamental mistake of supposing that there is a residual property to take seriously, however uncertain our actual attempts at isolation of instances might be.[30]

Instead, materialists counsel that we take very seriously the publicly available context in which we find ourselves, and leave behind the ineffable, contentless, circular, and virtually unknowable paraphernalia of dualism.

INTEGRATIVE DUALISM

I think we need to take seriously the public context of mental reference and the role of social norms in determining linguistic meaning, but I am convinced that this can be done without compromising the dualist emphasis on the subjectivity of the mental, and without any attrition in the phenomenological case for dualism launched in Chapter 1. A large portion of the objections to dualism reviewed above threaten only some, not all versions of dualism. In building a rejoinder to the spread of arguments above, I first outline the version of dualism I accept. This will then help in a defense of the phenomenological appeal I believe lends such weight to dualism. I accept what may be called "integrative dualism."

Integrative dualism goes substantially beyond the dual-aspect theory. Recall that according to the dual-aspect theory, mental properties are nonphysical, and yet there are only physical objects, and no immaterial persons, minds, souls, or selves. The person is conceived of as being a physical individual thing, with both physical and nonphysical properties. According to the version of dualism I accept, persons are themselves nonphysical individuals. As embodied beings, however, persons are not ghosts or mere accessories to their bodies.

[30] "Quining Qualia," in *Mind and Cognition*, ed. W. Lycan (Oxford: Basil Blackwell, 1990), p. 521.

Persons are integrally related to their bodies so that the person and his or her body function as a singular unit mentally and physically. The person and body are not, strictly speaking, metaphysically identical. They are separable individuals, but all this is in keeping with the proximate, materially conditioned, embodied nature of personal life.

Integrative dualism is juxtaposed to versions of dualism that depict the person and body as unduly remote and splintered. Of course, most materialist critics are convinced that *all* forms of dualism depict the person and body as remote and splintered, but my effort here is to articulate how a dualist may view the person and body as profoundly unified, while still remaining metaphysically distinct. What I take to be an excessively fragmented version of dualism is promoted chiefly by the critics of dualism. Consider, for example, the ways in which dualism is illustrated with the person (mind or soul) represented as a cloudy figure somehow floating on top of, or to one side of, the body. The immaterial aspect of the person is frequently pictured as an amorphous, quasi-material blob, as in Richard Taylor's introductory book *Metaphysics*.[31] Dennett caricatures the dualist notion of the person by reproducing in his book *Consciousness Explained* an image of Caspar the Friendly Ghost. Here the dualist view of the person (self, soul or whatever) is pictured as a floating, white marshmallow-like body.[32] This is all in the spirit of Gilbert Ryle, who lampooned the dualist as promoting a shadowy self behind the self we observe.

Some contemporary dualists do not stress their opposition to such splintered pictures. John Foster refers to subjects being "attached" to their bodies, Richard Swinburne writes about how "humans ... have to act and derive knowledge through one chunk of matter, their body," and W. D. Hart refers to "a person being 'lodged' in his or her body."[33] I agree that human persons are "attached" to their bodies, and that our bodies are

---

[31] *Metaphysics* (Englewood Cliffs: Prentice-Hall, 1974), p. 19. The illustration is by Roderick Chisholm.   [32] Dennett, *Consciousness Explained*, pp. 34–36.
[33] Foster, *The Immaterial Self* (London: Routledge, 1991), chapter 8; Swinburne, "Theism," in *A New Dictionary of Christian Theology*, ed. A. Richardson and J. Bowden (London: SCM, 1983), p. 563; Hart, *The Engines of the Soul* (Cambridge: Cambridge University Press, 1988), p. 1.

vehicles for our knowledge and activity, but these ways of casting the person–body relation can be misleading, prompting one to imagine the body is a mere domicile or a remote block of physical stuff to which one is hooked up or a thing one drives around. In fact, each of these dualist philosophers spells out in various places a unified understanding of the person–body relationship, and the version of dualism I adopt is articulated and defended in a way that is often, but not always, compatible with theirs. They are not *dis*integrative dualists! But what I hope to do is to take great care in developing a version of dualism that underscores the integrative, holist character of being an embodied person. It is to emphasize this point, and to guard against seeing the person–body relationship in terms of lodging or a *mere* attachment, that I have elected to employ the term "integrative dualism."

According to integrative dualism, the person and body differ metaphysically in the sense that they are separable individuals, and yet they function as a singular reality as an embodied person. The theme of separability will be central to a later section of this chapter, and a major concern of the next. In Chapter 3 I provide reasons for thinking it is metaphysically possible for the person and body to part company, as it were, but here my concern is to focus on the unity, not separability, involved with personal embodiment. The bare possibility of separability under exotic conditions does not cast a pall on their functional unity under ordinary conditions.

What it means for a person to be embodied is for a person to bear some of the following relations to his or her body, relations I characterize in the first person. I am sensorily bound up with my body in that I feel with these fingers and this skin, I see with these eyes, smell with this nose, eat and taste with this mouth, hear with these ears. I can have some sensory apprehension of the inside of my body, under the skin so to speak, as when I feel my heartbeat or have a stomach ache, feel thrills and internal pain. I also have what some have called proprioceptive awareness of my body, whereby I can be cognizant of the location of my body without my having to rely on eye-sight or touching with my hand or other bodily parts. Some have called this "knowledge without observation." I have the myriad of these sensory experiences as a result of my brain and spinal cord. The use of lungs, heart, and my other organs enables me to be conscious; damage to them can impair and imperil my conscious life.

I not only sense and perceive, but think and form judgments with my brain, not in the sense that my brain is a mere tool in these activities. I do not deliberately intend to move sections of my brain in order, say, to think mathematically or to move my fingers (not yet, anyway: I do not claim this is impossible), but my brain and other bodily parts are causally involved with my judging, perceiving, and so on. It is by means of my being embodied that I have the conscious life I have; it is by means of my body as a whole that I interact with other persons and material objects. In my acting in the world, my body is transparent to my intentions in the sense that I act in ways that are immediate, basic, or proximate. I can act on my body indirectly, as when I move my right arm by lifting it with my left hand, but I can also act in a basic, nonmediated fashion as well. In basic action, I act, but not in virtue of performing some other action. Dennett caricatures how a dualist might depict action as something involving ghostly processes, whereby a person moves a finger by moving a ghost finger first.[34] But none of this double-moving need be posited, any more than a dualist need posit a weird, infinite regress of acts to get an act going, so that, for example, for me to perform any act, moving my hand, say, I need to perform the act of acting to perform the act, which requires my performing the act of acting to act to perform the act, *ad infinitum*. The dualist is no more committed to such a regress than an identity materialist would be.

In integrative dualism, a person's physical movements may be seen as incorporating and realizing his or her intentions in materially conditioned forms. My body is not like a surrogate self in the world that I push around from a long distance away, but myself volitionally realized. An integrative dualist fully recognizes and insists that we can see people and their

[34] *Consciousness Explained*, part 1. The dual-aspect theorist Brian O'Shaughnessy adopts a view of agency that comes close to this depiction of agency.

intentions, desires, worries, sadness, pain, insofar as these mental events are integrally realized in bodily forms. H. H. Price embraced what I would call integrative dualism and recognized that "We think 'in' publicly uttered sound, public gestures, overt and publicly observable acts of writing or drawing"; and we do not just think, but we also have emotions and feelings as embodied beings.[35] What these will comprise, and thus how they will be seen, will depend, to some extent, upon the social context and the person's deliberate choice; sorrow will be expressed differently in accord with prevailing customs, a person's not disguising his or her feelings, and so on. My point is that integrative dualism places no serious philosophical obstacles here in describing our encounter with others. In an integrative scheme, it is not the case that our emotions and thoughts are *automatically* transparent and unmistakable to all other observers, but neither are they essentially obscure, and lodged in some foggy, ethereal cloud.

I believe the various embodying relations sketched so far articulate why we should treat the person and his or her body as a single unit in most moral, practical, emotional, scientific, and even religious contexts. In law, we rightly treat your assaulting my body as an assault on me: to touch my body is to touch me, to take my body to a political demonstration is to take me, to operate medically on my body is to operate on me. I address the specifically religious treatment of the singular unity of the embodied person in Chapter 4.

The term "integrative" comes from the Latin *integrare*, meaning to make up a whole, but in so using this term to describe "integrative dualism" I do not imply the view that a person's physical and psychological life is always in harmony and in good health. Obviously, heart failure, a broken leg, and so on can shatter one's mental life. No wonder such ills provide the basis for an experience that arises for some persons in terminal illness, that one is alienated from one's own body. One's body can seem, under certain circumstances, an enemy rather than a part of oneself as an embodied person. Consider,

[35] *Perception* (London: Methuen, 1954), p. 13.

for example, the case of the disembodied woman narrated by Oliver Sacks in *The Man who Mistook his Wife for a Hat*. Christina suffers severe sensory neuronopathies and comes to feel that her body is detached and unresponsive.[36] By "integrative" in the term "integrative dualism" I mean to designate the interwoven, functional unity or wholeness of embodiment whereby the welfare of person and body are profoundly linked, without suggesting that this relationship is always healthy or harmonious. There is, then, a sense in which integrative dualism is importantly different from the way Mary Daly has depicted Descartes's form of dualism: "modern philosophy's severed head."[37] Such accusations imply that dualism treats cases like Christina's as normative or, worse, that dualism treats persons like figures in the paintings by Magritte and Chagall in which heads are disconnected from their bodies and hover some distance away.[38] Because in integrative dualism there is an emphasis on the whole person and integral, physical realization, it is not committed to conceptually decapitating the embodied person or keeping the person sequestered in the head. Perhaps, as some materialists and dualists believe, the brain is the most crucial carrier of our personal identity (the person goes where the brain goes). Some are prepared to recognize the feasibility of persons switching bodies by switching brains. Integrative dualism need not deny this, but it is not committed at the outset to locating the person principally in the brain or head, and only intermingled or sporadically realized in the body as a whole. It is because of the pervasiveness of our sensory, perceptual, and agentive powers under ordinary, healthy conditions that integrative dualism sees the person as embodied, rather than merely embrained.

According to integrative dualism, then, the person is not contained in his or her body, as an inert physical object may be placed in a can or, to use one of Wittgenstein's illustrations, a beetle in a box. John Lucas embraces a version of dualism that ably brings this out by speaking of how the person is in space,

---

[36] Oliver Sacks, *The Man who Mistook his Wife for a Hat* (New York: Summit Books, 1985). [37] *Pure Lust* (London: The Women's Press, 1984), p. 253.
[38] See, for example, Chagall's *The Circus* or *To Russia, Asses and Others*.

but only contingently.[39] Embodied persons are indeed spatially located. The person is not *identical* with his or her spatial body in the strict sense that the person is incapable of surviving its demise, but the embodied person is indeed spatially realized, present and accounted for. From the standpoint of integrative dualism, it would be false to say the embodied person's body can only provide clues or hints about a person's identity, except, of course, when virtually all theories must acknowledge a person's ability to disguise his or her feelings, to be duplicitous, or, under conditions of severe impairment, the person has lost all motor control and yet remains conscious.

Integrative dualism does not lead us to the counter-intuitive conclusion that human beings lack physical properties. Dualist theories are sometimes characterized as denying that persons *qua* nonphysical beings have material attributes like being a certain size and weight. But in accord with integrative dualism, it is truly the case that I have the physical properties I believe I do, weighing so much, being a certain height, race, gender, and so on. What integrative dualism endeavors to do is to understand these properties as important features of what is involved with being embodied. Surely we are embodied, and integrative dualism advances this as its central claim in describing what it is to be the kind of physical animal that we are. Materialists may reply that dualists can only ascribe physical attributes to persons by courtesy, for example I only have the physical property of weighing so many pounds by virtue of my having various causal relations with a material object that has such a property. But this is to underrate the scope and character of the volitional, sensory, proprioceptive, and pervasive causally interwoven unity that marks integrative embodiment. Describing a person's body as his or hers by courtesy suggests that the body is like a guest, rather than that the body and person form a substantial unity.

Hacker and Kenny accuse dualists of what they call the homuncular fallacy, that of picturing the person as somehow behind the person we see. Hacker and Kenny envisage the

---

[39] J. R. Lucas holds that "minds are only contingently located in space, but necessarily 'located' in time." *A Treatise on Time and Space* (London: Methuen, 1973), p. 7.

person as a whole bearing the various attributes appropriate to persons, and for them this means seeing the person as a living, physical animal. It is due to this holism that Hacker and Kenny would object not just to dualism, but to some forms of materialism as well, for example Dennett's homuncular materialism with its top-down reduction of the person to hosts of smaller, subpersonal agents. Hacker writes:

> Descartes contravened the bounds of sense in claiming that it is the soul that sees, hears, tastes, smells and feels pains. Neither the soul or the mind can manifest visual discriminatory behaviour; the soul cannot look, peer, spot or glimpse and the mind cannot sniff, savour food upon the tongue, finger the soft texture of velvet. The "cannot" here is logical, signifying not inability, but senselessness, i.e. there is no such thing as a mind or soul acting thus. It is noteworthy that the homunculus fallacy is rife in the writings of contemporary psychologists and neurophysiologists who endeavour to explain the mechanisms of perception by attributing cognitive capacities and their exercise to the brain.[40]

I believe that the Hacker–Kenny criticism misses the mark at least as far as integrative dualism is concerned, as integrative dualism affirms that the embodied person thinks, sees, looks, glimpses, smells, tastes, touches, and so on, as truly embodied. It fully recognizes the united character of personal life, and does not leave the body and person dangling in scandalous disarray, picturing the person as inhabiting the brain or delivering commands to the brain from some remote, mental theatre. Embodied persons have a single history as integral unities, and are not locked into Ryle's caricature of dualism, according to which "a person lives through two collateral histories, one consisting of what happens in and to his body. The other consisting of what happens in and to his mind."[41] The integrated, embodied person does not lead such a double life. If it is a fact that a person and his or her body can have a double

[40] *Appearance and Reality*, p. 19.
[41] Gilbert Ryle, *The Concept of Mind* (London: Hutchinson, 1949), pp. 11, 12. Some of the animalists (or neo-Aristotelians) adopt this caricature. David Wiggins, Paul Snowdon, and Quassim Cassam seem to me to continue the Rylean tradition of underestimating the resources of dualism for providing an integral treatment of embodiment.

life, in that a person may survive the demise of the body and thus may eventually come to have a different history, this will not entail that he or she had a different history when an integral unity.

Has integrative dualism simply helped itself to the whole cache of materialism on the basis of coining a term? It is legitimate to raise a warning flag that I have not yet defended dualism from the objection that all physical–mental causal interaction is impossible. This is duly noted and will be addressed in the next chapter. Not all objections to dualism can be taken on all at once, and there is merit, I think, in laying out the version of dualism I believe to be best supported so that, at the very least, critics have a clear view of what amounts to their target. My plan is to defend this specific form of dualism against the linguistic, functionalist objections that were marshaled above, and then to provide more positive reasons for accepting integrative dualism. The person–body configuration I have been outlining does not, I submit, involve any obvious, internal incoherence, and my hope is that its strengths will become increasingly apparent.

I now turn to consider the problems with ostension and meaningful reference. Given an integrative dualist outlook, I believe we are able to develop what might be called integral ostension and to expose the shortcomings of functionalism.

ON BEHALF OF PHENOMENOLOGICAL OSTENSION

In mustering a reply to the objections facing dualistic ostension, it is important to appreciate the different ways in which ostension may be carried out and for what purposes, and to appreciate what integrative dualism is and is not committed to in this context. Ostension has been employed to support versions of foundationalism and radical empiricism. To some extent, Levin's objections, and those of other materialists, are aimed principally at dualistic uses of ostension that service these other theories as well. But the truth of integrative dualism and the phenomenological use of ostension are quite independent of the success of these other projects.

Foundationalism is the theory that all our justified beliefs can be ordered hierarchically, with each justified in terms of other, deeper levels of warrant. According to foundationalism, we require a basic level of evident beliefs or propositions on the basis of which we can properly justify other beliefs. Radical empiricism is a paradigm case of foundationalism in which the ground floor of all our beliefs is sensory experiences. According to a foundationalist empiricism, then, our most basic, evident ground floor consists of beliefs about sensations. A foundational schema was referred to at the outset of this chapter when I contended that philosophical depictions of the physical did not bypass the need of ostension and some grasp of the mental. I conceded, however, that we need not undertake an explicit philosophical inquiry into mental life to secure references to physical objects. Must dualists maintain that all our warranted beliefs about physical objects are hierarchically ordered and linked by evidential relations that are ultimately drawn from a base of sensory awareness or some privileged class of judgments or rational insights? There is nothing about dualism *per se*, let alone integrative dualism, that requires this. Dualists can allow that our various beliefs, including our beliefs that are founded upon the phenomenological appraisal of our mental life, are interlinked, mutually supported and holistically related. Integrative dualism can envisage our various justified beliefs as integrated with one another in a nonfoundationalist fashion. There is no need, then, for dualists to argue for the necessity of ostension to secure the meaningful content of *all* our terms and to defend a foundationalist version of justification. (Indeed, it would be challenging to defend the notion that the content of terms like "and" and "or" must be secured by ostension. What would one point to?) So, the dualist's ostensive appeal to phenomenologically evident features of our mental life is not *ipso facto* committed to the whole project of foundationalism.[42]

Once it is appreciated how dualism can be developed along integrative lines, and that it is not committed to foundationalism and radical empiricism, one can see how it may take on board

---

[42] Foundationalism is not without formidable support, in particular in the writings of Roderick Chisholm and Roderick Firth.

many of the points made by Levin and others about the public
character of our references to the mental. Given an integrative
dualist perspective, there seems little reason to deny a vital role
for interpersonal, social relations in shaping the language we use
to refer to our own and others' experience. The crucial points for
the dualist to emphasize are that it is our possession of mental
life in the first place that allows us to have social exchanges at
all, and that a large part of public discourse about the mental
amounts to identifying and communicating mental states of
which persons have experiential awareness. Consider, for
example, how Daniel Robinson and Geoffrey Madell have
responded to private-language types of argument on behalf of
dualism.

Robinson depicts the public sorting and correcting of mental
terms as ranging over sensations, where sensations are understood by him to be phenomenologically apparent, subjective
states.

If Tommy says (incorrectly), "This is a knife," we can supply the
corrective, "No, that is a spoon." The corrective is possible only if
each such noun is ostensively defined. But suppose Tommy comes in
clutching his stomach, crying and declaring, "I have a toothache!" If
we reply, "No, it must be a stomach ache because you're holding your
stomach," we have not corrected Tommy's ache but his vocabulary
or, more technically, his knowledge of human anatomy. Tommy has
learned nothing new about his sensations, only about how to signal
them and their location to others. He is learning how to answer the
question "where does it hurt?"[43]

This may not go quite far enough. For when we learn the source
of a sensation, we may be said to learn something about the
sensations themselves. Still, what Robinson has done is illustrate
how dualists can construe the social, public nature of discourse
as referring to, and incorporating, our experiential awareness of
pain and other mental states. There is something subjectively
felt when we feel pain and pleasure, and these are realized in
external behavior. Robinson does not treat sensations as
something that the one who has them knows only circum-

[43] Daniel Robinson, *Philosophy of Psychology* (New York: Columbia University Press, 1985), pp. 79, 80.

stantially or indirectly. Tommy has certain feelings that are phenomenologically apparent to him, and it is this level of awareness that fuels and informs the acquisition of mental discourse, grounding our recognition of the integral character of feelings and public conditions. It is not a case of positing an otherwise unknown X, lying some distance behind our behavior. Our awareness of mental states like pain are very much available and immediate, though the linguistic articulation of such an awareness involves guiding our references in light of public practices.

Madell adopts a similar stance. He insists that even if we concede a vital, central role for public language, there is a sense in which the legitimacy of public discourse must involve, rather than explain away, some role for subjectivity.

It may indeed be the case that to mean something by a word one must regard oneself as responsible to a norm, and that norm is a social one. But it remains the case that one's conscious entertainment of a thought, and one's impression that one is complying with the norms governing the use of the concepts involved in the thought, are matters of the psychology of the individual.[44]

Critics try to gain philosophical mileage out of the apparent disparity involved with introspecting social norms on the one hand and the putative introspective awareness of feelings, after-images, and the like. I see no real quandary here, though I do not think that "introspection" is the happiest term in this context. What Madell is pointing out is that the appeal to social norms does not displace the need to take into account the individual's subjective assumption of the norms, and this involves the person's looking outward, as it were, rather than looking inward.

If we do not follow Madell in recognizing an important role for consciousness, the very acquisition of language becomes puzzling indeed. How could public language get started without some conscious experience? I could not learn the meaning expressed by terms like "pain," "food," "mom," or "Tommy"

---

[44] Geoffrey Madell, *Mind and Materialism* (Edinburgh: Edinburgh University Press, 1988), p. 20.

without being able to consciously hear the relevant sounds or
see the relevant marks. Consciousness must come before
language practices. This may seem obvious, but it has certainly
been denied. Some materialists have even maintained that
consciousness only emerged when human organisms began
talking with themselves. Raymond Tallis' observation is on the
mark, in my view: "This seems to put the cart before the horse
in a rather spectacular fashion: one would have thought that
being conscious was the condition of overhearing oneself rather
than the consequence of it."[45] The resilience of subjectivity, and
the difficulty of eliminating it, is very much akin to a point made
on behalf of dualism in the last chapter in the section "Empirical
Evidence Revisited."

So, dualists can go at least part of the way to allow for the
public, operational role of language and reference. Mental
terms are integrally locked into the surrounding network of
material reference, but in pointing this out one has not made
any substantial headway in treating sensory states or subjective attitudes as physical. The materialist emphasis that our
identifying of objects pertains to types or kinds does not, alone,
support materialistic functionalism. Pain, pleasure, and the like
can all be recognized by dualists as bristling with distinctive
characteristics which make it false that pleasure is a kind of
pain, for example. The fact that we use material contexts to
communicate to others about our feelings does not diminish
their phenomenological status.

Is there a grammatical or conceptual error, as Hacker
suggests, at the very base of the dualist use of phenomenology,
whereby dualists do not adequately appreciate the propositional
character of knowledge? I do not think so. There is no oddity in
claiming that one is aware of certain sensory states where that is
understood along nonpropositional lines. Can't I be aware of
noise or heat or smells without knowing propositions that make
use of references to these states of awareness? Insofar as I know
propositions referring to them, such as "It is true that I hear a
loud noise," I think it is plausible to believe that I know it on the

[45] *The Explicit Animal* (London: Macmillian, 1991), p. 257.

basis (at least in part) of my awareness of the noise itself. Hacker's complaint, cited earlier, about the grammatical form of referring to our sensory awareness does reflect an important distinction; we can distinguish being in a given sensory state from conceptualizing that sensory state in propositional, communicable forms. But acknowledging that should not lead us to deny there is a *bona fide* subjective awareness of sensory states that we are phenomenologically apprised of quite independently of such communication-devices. Recall Hacker's parody of self-awareness: "Do I have knowledge of a toothache? Am I acquainted with toothache? Do I know nausea or cramp?" But the awkwardness involved is lessened when we rephrase this in terms of questions about whether you know what it is like to have a toothache (embellish this case somewhat: imagine this being asked of someone who has few nerve endings in his mouth), or imagine a woman asking a man whether he has any conception of the cramps and nausea involved with menstruation. Hacker places so much weight on the importance of public mastery of concepts that the vital role of subjective awareness (as well as medical history) drops into obscurity. If we wish to construe all our awareness as only awareness of the truth of propositions or truths about concepts, then surely such propositions and truths are precariously placed, for they at least appear to make reference to states and objects that are neither propositions nor concepts. To put the point simplistically, when I feel a toothache, I am not feeling a concept or proposition.

Once it is seen that integrative dualism can incorporate the tools of public reference, one can respond to Levin's complaint about the comparative poverty of the dualistic construal of reference to the mental. I think it is plausible to charge the materialistic functionalist with the poorer showing. Recall Levin's thesis that the dualist is locked into an ultimately contentless view of the mental, the mental winding up either as ineffable or descriptive in a fashion that can only be under-written by the truth of materialism. From the vantage point of integrative dualism, one can see how comparative, physically couched references to the mental are genuinely descriptive. The mental bathes the physical, so to speak, because the mental is integrally realized in public settings, but also because all our perceptual and conceptual taking in of physical items involves the exercise of subjective, mental capacities.[46] Dualists seem to me to be well placed here in claiming that theirs is the richer position vis-à-vis Levin's, for they can take on board whatever references to the mental are captured by the functionalist descriptions, *plus more*. Whereas the functionalist leaves the mental as something peculiarly bare as far as intrinsic phenomenologically evident features are concerned, the dualist upholds there being such abundant features *and* allows that these are typically picked out in publicly vindicated fashions. The plausibility of there being something more involved is considerable. Isn't it because of my subjective awareness of toothaches, nausea, and cramps, that I come to express myself the way I do when I tell others that I am hurt?

How should the dualist address all the skeptical worries reviewed earlier? One option would be to adopt what may be called *essential integrative dualism*. According to essential integrative dualism, there is a necessary correlation between the mental and physical matching all the functionalist configurations. On this account, the mental and physical are metaphysically distinct, but just as conjoined as Levin and other functionalists envisage. This necessary link is not due to the laws of nature, but to a deep metaphysical necessity.[47] If it is true that we know what others think and feel on the basis of public observation and language usage, then (it may be argued) this is because persons are necessarily such that they are physically realized as specified in essential integrative dualism. On this approach one can preserve the phenomenological plane of experience, and reap the benefits of those who insist upon the essential tie between behavior and the mental. It is not obvious that materialism does a better job against skepticism about other minds than this version of dualism.

---

[46] Contemporary antirealism testifies to the rich, portean character of the mental. While I am a realist, it is telling to consider the plausibility of claims by Nicholas Rescher, Hilary Putnam, and others who highlight our awareness that our conception of the physical is a conception, and that conceptions are mental.

[47] This necessary tie is often called supervenience. Those developing such accounts include J. Kim, E. Sosa, and M. DePaul.

Materialist functionalists may charge that their theory performs the anti-skeptical task much better as it involves positing only a singular kind of entity, as opposed to two, whether these be necessarily linked or not. But this does not strike me as an impressive advantage given the evident subjective character of experience, the difficulty of incorporating such subjectivity within materialism, and the prospects of positing a relation of supervenience. The anti-skeptical argument of materialism against dualism is built on the claim that we *do* know the mental life of others (when others are in pain, thoughtful, happy, angry). We know how other people use mental terms and we are able to correct their use of terms in referring to their own experiences, for example "No, the feeling you are now having is not pain." But it is one thing to claim we have such knowledge and another to claim that we know all the conditions that must be satisfied in order for us to be so knowledgeable. We may know certain things, and realize that this knowledge is made possible by more than one condition, A or B say, and yet not be certain whether our knowledge is due to A rather than B. To offer a trivial example of this imagine that I know you arrived in a building because I was told this by a reliable witness, but I cannot recall whether the person who told me was Stewart or Caroline or Nick or others whom I have reason to trust. I know the person who told me was trustworthy, but I do not know which person in particular provided the testimony. Similarly, I think essential integrative dualists are within their rights to charge that our knowledge of the mental life of others is underdetermined between their account and that of identity materialism. Just because we know of others' mental life, it does not follow that we thereby know that it is the truth of materialism as opposed to essential integrative dualism that enables us to have such knowledge. The mental–physical link is posited to be no less necessary than the formal identity relation of A is A. If I do know you are in pain when I see you injured, it is not at all clear that I thereby know that essential integrative dualism is false or that I am committed to believing that it is false.

Because essential integrative dualism retains the phenom-

enological character of experience, it is worth offering a
rejoinder here to the skepticism lodged by Dennett. The
essentialist stand is not an easy prey to skeptical worries either
from the outside, as it were, concerning our knowledge of other
minds, or from the inside, concerning the identification of our
experiential states.

Recall Dennett's charge that the phenomenological game
cannot be played effectively, for locating the relevant *qualia* is
nigh impossible. A reply may take two routes.

The first response is simply to hold the line and challenge
Dennett's claim that we suffer from confusing the intrinsic
features of our phenomenological states with our judging. Drink
coffee and note how it tastes to you. Do you like the taste? In
forming a judgment about whether you like the way coffee
tastes to you (the sensory experience), are you forming a
judgment about whether you like the coffee or are you making
judgments about judgments? At some further stage you might
be, but at the outset it certainly appears as though you are
judging the way something tastes, a sensory experience. I drink
the coffee as I am doing now and decide that I like it very much.
Is the taste itself a disposition to drink more coffee? This is
doubtful. Because I like the taste I may be disposed to drink
more, but the tastiness of the coffee itself is not that disposition,
or any kind of disposition at all. Dispositions do not taste a
certain way. Dennett complains of the difficulty of separating
qualia from how we "are stimulated or non-perceptually
affected," but it is not clear what this might mean. When I am
tasting coffee I may not be sure about how the physiological
causes operate in my mouth and eventually stimulate my brain.
I may not be sure whether my enjoyment of the taste is affected
by some hypnotic suggestion I have been subjected to. None of
this uncertainty lends any weight to supposing there is no
sensory state of tasting coffee such as I am enjoying now, nor do
these possibilities cause me to question whether I judge the
coffee to be enjoyable. Of course in learning that my enjoyment
is caused in part by posthypnotic suggestion, I shall learn to
question whether my judging coffee to be good is justified, but
this will cast no doubt on the fact that I did judge it enjoyable.

Tasting coffee under unfavorable conditions is still having certain sensations of taste.

Consider a second response. Even if there is no clear way to distinguish one's sensory state and one's judgment about the sensory state, have we eradicated phenomenological awareness? By no means. One has, rather, widened the arena of phenomenological appeal. Judging may not have a specific *quale* like a color, smell, taste, or temperature, but for all that, it is plausible to claim that there is a phenomenological character to making judgments. There is what we can refer to as the conscious experience of judging; we know in experience what it is like to entertain beliefs, to form judgments about what we desire and so on. Efforts to sever judgments from such surrounding feelings and experience strike me as strained. If you judge that some horrible fate awaits you and feel fear, is it the case that there is only an experience of the fear but none of the judgment? Arguably, feeling fear involves the relevant judgments about the threat as an integral part. The judging does not take place in a phenomenological sterile fashion with the experiential *quale* only emerging later. I believe that T. S. Eliot rightly drew attention to the experiential features involved with thinking in his work on the metaphysical poets. "A thought to Donne was an experience; it modified his sensibility."[48]

---

[48] Eliot, *Selected Essays* (London: Faber & Faber, 1932), pp. 287–288. Note also Swinburne, in *The Evolution of the Soul*, on the link between sensing and perceiving, and Colin McGinn on the consciousness-laden character of mental content in *The Problem of Consciousness* (Oxford: Basil Blackwell, 1990), p. 25. Someone may argue that judgments lack a *quale* or felt experience because, unlike sensations, they have content which is shareable and bears logical relations to other contents of judgments, they can be held irrationally, and we don't customarily associate a feeling character with beliefs (the bedrock of judgments). At best, such considerations only exhibit some of the ways in which sensations differ from judging. In recognizing that there is an experiential character to judging, one is not supposing that the object of judging is always an experience. I judge that a piano will fall on top of me in a few seconds. The object of my judgment bears logical relations to the content of other judgments (it entails that a musical instrument will fall on me) and can be held irrationally (I have a mild hunch that it will occur, but no real evidence), and the content of my judgment or belief is not itself a sensation (a piano is not a sensation). Even so, I know what it is like to make the judgment about the piano and there is, I believe, an evident experiential character involved. See also Richard Wollheim's "The Mind and the Mind's Image of Itself," in *On Art and the Mind* (Cambridge, Mass.: Harvard University Press, 1974).

Although I find essential integrative dualism plausible and I fully endorse the above reply to Dennett, I do not think the mental and physical are necessarily conjoined. I believe that the mental and physical are contingently related, and refer to this position as simply integrative dualism, without the additional gloss about essentiality. One way to make this contingency evident is by imagining the possibility that the physical and mental fail to be conjoined. Thomas Nagel, Howard Robinson, John Foster, and others each describe cases where the mental and physical come apart. Nagel writes: "I can conceive of my body doing precisely what it is doing now, inside and out, with complete physical causation of its behavior. But without any of the mental states which I am now experiencing, or any others for that matter."[49] Robinson makes a more global claim: "The mental might have been absent whilst the world remained physically the same expresses a metaphysical possibility," and John Foster couches his skeptical claim in terms of other persons: "I can acknowledge the possibility that the creatures which I have always assumed to be other persons like myself do not have minds at all."[50] Nagel introduces a case which strikes at the heart of the public-language argument, raising the question of how much we do know of the experience of others and their use of terms.

How much do you really know about what goes on in anyone else's mind?... How do you know, when you and a friend are eating chocolate ice cream, whether it tastes the same to him as it tastes to you? You can try a taste of his ice cream, but if it tastes the same as yours, that only means it tastes the same to you: you haven't experienced the way it tastes to him. There seems to be no way to compare the two flavors directly... Well, you might say that you're both human beings, and you can both distinguish among flavors of ice cream – for example you can both tell the difference between chocolate and vanilla with your eyes closed – it's likely that your flavor experiences are similar. But how do we know that? The only

[49] "Armstrong on the Mind," *Philosophical Review* 79 (1970), 402.
[50] *Matter and Sense* (Cambridge: Cambridge University Press, 1982), p. 23, 24, and *The Immaterial Self*, p. 21. See also Hilary Putnam's discussion of "super-spartans" in "Brain and Behavior," *Analytical Philosophy*, 2nd Series, ed. R. J. Butler (Oxford: Basil Blackwell, 1965).

connection you've ever observed between a type of ice cream and a flavor is in your own case; so what reason do you have to think that similar correlations hold for other human beings? Why isn't it just as consistent with all the evidence that chocolate tastes to him the way vanilla tastes to you, and vice versa?[51]

These cases highlight our phenomenological awareness of our own mental states and exhibit the difference between such awareness and the physical states accompanying it.

My aim in the rest of the chapter is to bolster the thesis that the mental and physical are contingently related and then to address further the implications of this for the problem of skepticism. In defending the intelligibility of cases like Nagel's above I use thought experiments. In Chapter 1 several thought experiments were considered, including Dennett's reductive strategy, Churchland's tales of creatures who can see temperatures, and finally the theistic thought experiment reversing Dennett's order of explanation. It will be useful here to gain a clearer idea of the limited but important role of this philosophical device before proceeding.

[51] Nagel, *What Does it all Mean?* (New York: Oxford University Press, 1987), pp. 19, 20. Common to much of the criticism of dualism is the charge that if we do use a common language then we must know precisely how others feel when they use mental terms. I address skeptical worries in what follows in the main text, but add here that it seems to me to be illicit to assume that sharing a language between persons requires the persons knowing in some indefeasible apodictic fashion that their words and phrases have precisely the meanings they take them to have. You and I can share a bus or sandwich without knowing about the other person; with language there must be more in the way of awareness of the other and *presumed sharing*, but why can't we share a language if we simply presume that the other shares the same meaning and is following similar linguistic rules? Imagine that you and I do share the same meanings and rules, and believe that we have good evidence for this, but would not claim to know it beyond all possibility of doubt (i.e. both of us think it is conceptually possible, however unlikely, that we do not share the meanings). I see no reason why we should refuse to consider this a case of sharing a language. In my view, sharing a language is more like sharing a friendship than sharing a bus. A friendship involves mutual recognition and presumed reciprocal attention. One of the risks of friendship is that it involves varying amounts of faith, and it would be an impoverished notion of friendship that insisted upon absolute epistemic certainty between partners.

THOUGHT EXPERIMENTS

A thought experiment, for our purposes, may be understood as a representation of what is purportedly a possible state of affairs. It might depict something that is actual, though typically in philosophical arguments that use them, it is not assumed at the outset that the state of affairs is already known to be actual. Thought experiments can range from the merely hypothetical to the conjectural development of an hypothesis that may turn out to be true. The appeal to thought experiments has, I believe, a well earned place in much philosophy, where different possibilities are imagined to test the adequacy of different theories in ethics, metaphysics, epistemology, and so on.

Thought experiments make explicit our conception of the nature of properties and objects, testing the adequacy of our conceptual schemes and enabling us to consider in what direction such schemes need to be enlarged, restricted, or abandoned altogether. If I am truly in possession of an adequate conception of pain or persons or material objects, then I must have some grasp of the boundaries and applications of such concepts. I do not have a clear, suitable understanding of personhood if, by my categories, a pencil turns out to be classified as a person and you do not. We witnessed some of the difficulties with analyzing the notion of material objects earlier, and thought experiments may be used to ensure that our identification of the physical is at least workable, even if imperfect. There is nothing awry about the technique of thought experiments *per se* that gives from the outset an advantage either to materialism or to dualism. Thought experiments can be marshaled from different vantage points, extending well beyond what is technologically possible or possible within the limits of the laws of nature as we know them. That is, in a thought experiment one might picture a state of affairs that is truly possible even though we ourselves have no means of bringing it about and, going further, even though it contravenes the laws of nature. Consider whether it is possible for a solid body to travel faster than the speed of light. None have been observed. Clearly we lack the technology of bringing about such a speedy projectile, and the possibility of there being such a thing seems ruled out by prevailing laws. Even so, one might still consider whether it is metaphysically possible for there to be such a solid body. Could God make it? A thought experiment would make explicit the nature of light, speed, solid objects, and the relevant conditions (as best we understand them) in describing the case.[52]

Despite the wide currency of thought experiments, there is some ambivalence about them. Principally philosophers worry that thought experiments are too easy to formulate, too random and unchecked. How do we *know* that what we describe as possible is indeed possible? Obviously the best test would consist of overwhelming evidence that the state of affairs is actual, but short of such evidence, a variety of factors may be involved, including our capacity to represent the state of affairs visually, to describe it in detail, and to consider whether its being actual is compatible with our background justified assumptions about the objects in questions. Some hold that the fact that some state of affairs seems to be possible only confers the smallest morsel of evidential justification for thinking it is genuinely possible. Margaret Wilson and Sydney Shoemaker construe some dualist thought experiments similar to Howard Robinson's and John Foster's as only establishing that the person making them has not noticed any contradiction in the description of the state of affairs. On this account, Robinson's picturing the material world shorn of mental life amounts to Robinson simply not detecting that a contradiction is involved with such a supposition. Margaret Wilson writes: "Thus, the fact that we can conceive that p does not entail that p is even possible: all that follows (at best) is that we have not yet noticed any contradiction in p."[53] And Sydney Shoemaker makes the same point. He holds that the purported conceivability of the mental in the

---

[52] Some philosophers introduce strictures here that I do not, whereby thought experiments are construed as describing states of affairs that are impossible in this world but true in some other possible world, or as states of affairs that are nonactual, impossible technically, but yet still possible. I mean none of these. Wilkes, for example, adopts a more restricted, and more skeptical, view of thought experiments than I do. *Real People* (Oxford: Clarendon Press, 1984).

[53] Wilson, *Descartes* (Boston, Mass.: Routledge & Kegan Paul, 1982), p. 191.

absence of the physical gives reason to believe that we have not
noticed an *a priori* entailment from mental predicates to physical
predicates.[54] This seems too weak in my view. Surely the
imagining of many states of affairs gives us more justification
than entitling us to conclude that no internal contradiction has
been noticed. To begin with some trivial, not very philosophically interesting examples, I think it is plausible to believe
that the state of affairs of there being a pyramid with a base of
100 miles or there being a restaurant with a counter 5 miles long
may both be assumed to be possibilities on the basis of their
descriptions in thought experiments. Surely these are *bona fide*
possibilities, and we may conclude this not just because no
contradiction was noticed in their imagining, or because no
entailments have been noticed that would expose some subtle
conceptual snag.

In the course of distancing myself from Wilson's and
Shoemaker's skepticism, I do not want to overstate the
evidential weight of thought experiments in terms of conferring
infallible guidance. David Hume went too far in his claim that
"nothing we imagine is absolutely impossible" without quali-
fying the limits surrounding this.[55] To conclude that some state
of affairs is truly possible we would need to know how carefully
the imagining of the state of affairs was carried out, whether the
person attended to the various properties involved, taking into
account independently justified theories. At the very least, we
need to construe the warrant of thought experiments as
principally conferring *prima facie* evidence. *Prima facie* literally
means at first glance, and refers here to an initial, presumptive
reason to believe something.

In an effort to bring to light varying degrees of conceivability,
I note the difference between what may be called weak and
strong conceivability. A state of affairs may be said to be weakly
conceivable for someone who reflects on it and believes it to be
possible on the grounds that she or he does not see that it is

[54] Shoemaker, "On an Argument for Dualism," in *Knowledge and Mind*, ed. Carl Ginet
and Shoemaker (New York: Oxford University Press, 1983), p. 248.
[55] Hume, *A Treatise of Human Nature*, ed. L. A. Selby-Bigge (Oxford: Oxford University
Press, 1965), p. 32.

impossible. For all the person knows, the state of affairs is possible. Strong conceivability involves a further claim, whereby the subject judges the state of affairs to be possible on the basis of a more positive grasp of the properties involved and the compatibility of its features with what the subject knows about the world and so on.[56] The two forms of conceivability may duly be termed weak and strong, as the strong conceivability entails weak conceivability but not *vice versa*. To use these terms, Wilson and Shoemaker seem to have identified only weak conceivability.

How might the epistemic weight of strong conceivability be measured? This is by no means easy to do. Some make recourse here to talk of strong and weak intuitions, though this alone does little work. I think we shall have to put up with an informal characterization of the difference between these forms of conceiving, which can be filled out with some illustrations in this and the next chapter. Strong conceivability involves a variety of factors, including forming a clear and distinct picture of the state of affairs or providing a detailed description of it and comparing this closely with one's picture and description of the world. I can strongly conceive of certain states of affairs like there being a hundred blue balls on a beach. At one stage of reflection I might weakly conceive of a state of affairs (there being spatial regions not spatially related to physical space) and then come to conceive strongly of it. In articulating a degreed notion of conceiving, I shall rely upon a somewhat rough grasp of intellectual vice and virtue. I propose the following principle for strong conceivability: *A subject, S, is justified in believing that a state of affairs is possible if the state of affairs seems possible to S and S is not intellectually negligent.*

It is notoriously difficult to give a satisfactory analysis of the concept of negligence and to specify the conditions under which accepting a belief is unjustifiably casual, as well as to analyze "attention words" in general, like *noticing*. It will suffice for my purposes here if we can simply characterize ordinary cases of

---

[56] This follows a distinction introduced by James Van Cleve, though I do not use his notion that we intuit propositions, "Conceivability and the Cartesian Argument for Dualism," *Pacific Philosophical Quarterly* 64 (1983), 38.

what I am terming intellectual negligence and not attempt a
strict philosophical analysis. To be negligent intellectually can
involve recklessness or carelessness, failing to attend to certain
important features of the matter at hand that would be apparent
after some further, *expected*, attention that is within the subject's
power. Intellectual negligence pertains to the care we take in
thinking. It does not, however, have obvious implications for
the *truth* of our beliefs, as it is possible to be intellectually
negligent in accepting some true belief and also possible to be
intellectually responsible in accepting a false belief. At first
glance, it might seem possible that there could be a barber who
shaves all and only those who do not shave themselves. But the
average person who reflects upon such a state would be
intellectually careless if she or he did not recognize the
problematic nature of such a supposition.[57]

Paul Snowdon criticizes the use of imagination in constructing thought experiments (his concern in this passage is with
imagining that a person could attain a new body as a result of
a brain transplant):

imaginability cannot be taken as a guide to possibility. Either it is
insisted that the objects of imagination must be possibilia, in which
case the claim to have imagined precisely what is at issue will simply
be disputed, and so, whether it is possible (and hence imaginable)
must be determined in some other way, or it is allowed that we can
imagine nonpossibilia, and then no-one need quarrel with the
theorist's claim to have imagined brain-transplants, but his achieve-
ment has no probative significance.[58]

At least in the thought experiments deployed in this book, the
use of imagination should not have these repercussions. Thought
experiments can certainly be advanced prior to anyone knowing
that they depict *bona fide* possibilities. There is no demand from
the outset that one accept thought experiments as truly possible.
One might begin by assuming that a state of affairs such as time
travel is possible, but on reflection come to see that it is

[57] I defend this depiction of responsible conceiving of possibilities in "A Modal
Argument for Dualism," *Southern Journal of Philosophy* 24:1 (1986), 95–108.
[58] "Personal Identity and Brain Transplants," in *Human Beings*, ed. David Cockburn
(Cambridge: Cambridge University Press, 1991).

impossible. As for imagining the impossible, I have explicitly admitted that one can imagine something is possible that turns out to be impossible. (One can also imagine that the impossible is impossible, as when one imagines that it is impossible for there to be more blue round balls than balls.)

Let us now consider thought experiments in philosophical action.

INVERSIONS

Spectrum-inversion thought experiments may be designed that exhibit functionalism's inability to account for the qualitative character of sensation terms. Consider, for example, a functionalist account of what it is like to see the color red. Functionalists may identify a host of factors involved about sensory receptors, lighting conditions, wave lengths, and the like. Is it possible that all these materially specified conditions be met and yet a person does not visually experience red but blue? Hilary Putnam advances a spectrum-inversion thought experiment as follows: "You wake up one morning and the sky looks red, and your red sweater appears to have turned blue, and all the faces are an awful color, as in a color negative."[59] Your visual field has become color inverted. Would you then call your red sweater blue? Probably, and probably this inversion would be detectable by you, for you would recall how things used to appear. Imagine, however, that you learn to adjust to the change linguistically, and in describing the world you call the sky, which now looks what you would have called red, blue. You then develop amnesia and forget that the inversion occurred.

In this case it would seem as if the sensation you are now calling a "sensation of blue" could have almost exactly the functional role that the sensation you used to call the "sensation of blue" used to have, while having a totally different character. But the quality has changed. The quality doesn't seem to be a functional state in this case.[60]

This thought experiment involves your coming to have a different color spectrum than you used to have (and thus

[59] Hilary Putnam, *Reason, Truth and History* (New York: Cambridge University Press, 1981), p. 80.   [60] *Ibid.*, p. 81.

involves what may be called intrasubjective inversion) and one different than color spectra of others (intersubjective inversion). Insofar as we can conceive of our phenomenal experiences becoming disjoined from their functional contexts, we come to recognize them as having a character that is more than their specified functional roles.

Does Putnam's thought experiment represent a *bona fide* possibility? I believe that it does, as does Nagel's, Foster's, and Robinson's. Putnam's is not advanced on the grounds that any such inversions have occurred or that the laws of nature allow for such shifts. The laws that govern these matters do not have the weight of absolute necessity like logical identity, say. A large number of functionalists themselves concede that the laws of nature are contingent and thus could have been otherwise. If we can sufficiently grasp a real difference in these thought experiments between visual experiences – the subjective under-goings – and the relevant functional roles, then we have some reason to differentiate them.

Thus far, Putnam's and Nagel's thought experiments may generate only weak conceivability, but, in my view, more credibility is in the offing as we consider the cases more closely and review some of the ways functionalists have sought to defeat these thought experiments (by showing that what appears to be possible is actually impossible).

One way of defending functionalism is to claim that it makes no sense to compare sensations between persons in the thought experiments of either inter- or intrasubjective inversion. This has been explored by Shoemaker and others, but has few adherents. To rule out on principle such comparisons would amount to adopting eliminativism (denying that there are any experiences to compare) or endorsing a very stern notion of verificationism, according to which if one cannot verify that a state of affairs obtains, one is entitled to conclude that the state of affairs is unintelligible, sheer nonsense. Verificationism is relevant here, as inverted-spectrum cases can cause worries that someone could have an inverted spectrum and yet no one could know it. But to rule out possibilities here because one could not come to know them seems desperate. A prior, more important concern should be: Can such states of affairs be consistently described and strongly conceived? If so, and it follows that something could obtain that was unverifiable, then so much the worse for verificationism.[61]

Shoemaker rejects thought experiments like those of Putnam, Nagel, *et al.* on the basis of his overriding functionalism, according to which the mental and physical cannot diverge. It is difficult to see, however, the independent rationale for his stance. That is, it seems as though he rejects these thought experiments principally because if they were true, his theory would be false. Consider, for example, his depiction of mental–physical correlation in a discussion of inverted spectra.

Shoemaker claims that if there is similarity between persons' sensory experience, this can only occur in virtue of physical similarities between the persons.

> The color experiences of two different creatures will be qualitatively comparable only if those creatures are capable of having states having the same qualia, and on my account this in turn will be true only if, for at least one color quale, both creatures are capable of having states that share at least some of the physical properties that are realizations of that quale.[62]

I think it is true that if all we know are the physical traits of different creatures it will be difficult indeed to compare their subjective experiences if they share few, if any material similarities. But granting this, why think it is impossible for there to be two creatures that have similar *qualia* or sensory experiences, but do not meet the requirement of possessing similar physical properties? Shoemaker sketches what it might be like to encounter a sentient creature who diverges from us physically. To ensure that the divergence is sufficiently radical, he imagines an extraterrestrial creature.

> Suppose, to invoke a favorite functionalist fantasy, that we come across a race of Martians who are behaviorally indistinguishable from us and have a "psychology" isomorphic with ours, but whose internal physical make up – their neurophysiology and biochemistry – is utterly different from ours. These Martians are to be creatures who share

---

[61] Sydney Shoemaker, "The Inverted Spectrum," *Journal of Philosophy* (July 1982), 365.　　[62] *Ibid.*, 373.

our mental states, at least on a functionalist view, but in whom the physical realizations of these states are as different as they could possibly be from their realizations in us.[63]

When terrestrial issues in the philosophy of mind include theories about would-be extra-terrestrials, patience may run thin. Conjuring up such cases, however, can highlight the broad ranging character of Shoemaker's theory. They also draw attention, I believe, to the fact that Shoemaker's theory is too extreme. On his view, these Martians would not have *qualia* similar to ours, and this seems unduly constrained. Perhaps they would, but maybe they would not. Shoemaker does not concede the latter possibility.

On my functionalist view of qualia, these Martians would have states having qualia – there would be something it would be like for them to have these states. But their experiences would not share any of the qualia our experiences have; for I am assuming that none of the properties that realize qualia in us could be instantiated in them. When it comes to comparing Martian experiences and ours ... their experiences and ours are not qualitatively comparable.[64]

Ruling out on principle different *qualia* because of different physico-chemical constitution seems to me implausible. It may be that under the conditions specified it would be difficult for us to "compare" our subjectivity with Martians', but it seems arbitrary to rule out that we might all see the same colors, have similar tastes, and the like, notwithstanding the possession of divergent material constitutions.

David Lewis' version of functionalism is subject to similar difficulties. Rather than analyze his view of Martians, however (Lewis denies the possibility of unique mad aliens), I focus on a point he raises common to most functionalist theories.[65] Functionalists typically undervalue the extent to which we are apprised of our subjective states. Consider Lewis' view of pain. On his theory, pain is identifiable in terms of its role in material causal relations. Over against the objection that it is conceivable that a state other than pain might have this role, Lewis is led to

[63] *Ibid.*, 373.   [64] *Ibid.*, 373.
[65] David Lewis, "Mad Pain and Martian Pain," in *Readings in Philosophy of Psychology*, ed. Ned Block (Cambridge, Mass.: Harvard University Press, 1980).

an entangled stance, i.e. that while it is necessarily the case that whatever plays the causal role in the functional analysis of pain is pain, it is not the case that such a state is necessarily such that it is pain. Lewis describes his thesis that pain might not have been pain as follows:

> If the concept of pain is the concept of a state that occupies a certain causal role, then whatever state does occupy that role is pain. If the state of having neurons hooked up in a certain pattern is the state properly apt for causing and being caused, as we materialists think, then that neural state is pain. But the concept of pain is not the concept of that neural state ... The concept of pain, unlike the concept of that neural state which in fact is pain, would have applied to some different state if the relevant causal relations had been different. Pain might have not been pain. The occupant of the role might have not occupied it. Some other state might have occupied it instead. Something that is not pain might have been pain. This is not to say, of course, that it might have been that pain was not pain and nonpain was pain; that is, that it might have been that the occupant of the role did not occupy it and some nonoccupant did. Compare: "The winner might have lost" (true) versus "It might have been that the winner lost" (false).[66]

This understanding of pain seems to me to be altogether counter-intuitive. It suggests that our subjective experience of pain is so thin that it could have been considered some other phenomenon if it were linked with different physical states and overt behavior. Consider the admittedly bizarre, yet still conceivable, possibility that the state we phenomenologically identify as feeling tickled had the causal role of being brought about by skin damage, and tending to make the subject groan and wince. According to Lewis' reading of the psychological, what we seem to identify in a direct fashion as feeling tickled must be classified as being in pain if it satisfies the relevant functional rules. On one day the phenomenological feeling of pain could satisfy Lewis' analysis of being in pain, and on the next day being tickled could do so, just as I might win a race today and you win it tomorrow. Surely this fails to do justice to our apprehension of being in pain and feeling tickled. As Tallis points out, the problem with functionalism is that it "denies, or

[66] *Ibid.*, p. 218.

overlooks, the primacy, the centrality, the all-pervading nature
of subjective experience, quite separate from its role in promoting action (or reaction).[67]

Michael Levin concedes that Lewis' view is implausible. But
rather than abandon materialistic functionalism, Levin seeks to
avoid Lewis' difficulties by using functionalist neutral descriptions to "fix the reference" of being in pain, as opposed to
serving as an account of the *meaning* of being in pain. Recall from
the exposition of Levin's position earlier that he allows for an
open-ended element in our mental discourse. Levin thereby
hopes to introduce a technical distinction between his and
Lewis' theories which will save functionalism. The advantage of
Levin's theory over Lewis' is not at all obvious, however.

Lewis analyzes pain as a nondirectly referring (or what is
called a nonrigid) concept, designating whatever occupies some
causal role. Levin agrees that Lewis' strategy fails to do justice
to the assurance we have of our subjective life. But Levin's
difficulty is that although he characterizes a psychological term
like being in pain as an indexical term, its reference is fixed by
the very same descriptions Lewis employs. If being in pain is the
referent, picked out by the functionalist descriptions, then
conceivably the psychological state of being pleased could be
picked out by the descriptions preserved for being in pain.
Levin's view does not seem better equipped to account for what
he concedes to be a contingent truth that pains, not tickles, play
the causal role they do. He agrees that "whatever would have
been (e.g.) the result of cutting my hand would have been pain"
is counter-intuitive because this could allow pain to be pleasure
but his own theory faces us with the very same problem, for
what the child first used his term "pain" to refer to when his
skin was lacerated could have been pleasure. What Lewis'
theory results in through specifying the meaning of psychological terms, Levin's results in through specifying the reference-
fixing of such terms.

While Levin's and Lewis' theories differ in detail, I think they
are both counter-intuitive in their attributing to persons only

the most attenuated awareness of what it is to be in pain. Levin grants that when I am in pain I can know that the hurting has the property of being wished absent by me, but his analysis seems to omit what makes us wish the hurting to be absent. Some functionalists do not hesitate to reject elements of the direct view such as our apparent immediate awareness of our desires, beliefs, and sensations. Lycan once remarked: "I am entirely willing to give up fairly large chunks of our common-sensical or platitudinous theory of beliefs and desires."[68]

---

[68] William Lycan, "Psychological Laws," in *Mind, Brain, and Function*, ed. J. J. Biro and R. W. Shahan (Norman: University of Oklahoma Press, 1982), p. 13. In the course of Lycan's insistence upon the open-ended character of our report of experiences he goes so far as to claim that events do not have individual essences. He offers the following case to illustrate his point:

You are sitting casually in an empty classroom, reading a book. Suddenly I burst in the door, holding a basketball, and proceed to bounce the basketball, very hard, on the floor. Then I leave. This episode was an event. What are its essential properties? That is, what are the properties in virtue of which it was the event it was rather than a numerically different event? That I was its protagonist? That a basketball was used rather than a soccerball? That the ball was bounced twice rather than three times, once, or not at all? That the episode took place in this classroom rather than the one next door? That it took place when it did instead of ten minutes earlier? None of these suggestions seems at all convincing, and I would maintain that events as such simply do not have individual essences unless their essences are very rarefied and elusive haecceities. If this is correct, then Kripke's claim that the phenomenal characters of pain-events (i.e., of episodes of hurting) are essential to those events is groundless or at least not in the least obvious – not nearly so obvious as it would be for Kripke's argument to succeed (dialectically speaking). (*Consciousness*, pp. 16, 17)

I think it is obvious that phenomenal feelings like being in pain have an essential character, and the expressive term "hurting" is an apt one for me to use in referring to the feeling of pain I underwent this morning as a result of an injury. I fail to see any force whatever in Lycan's analogy. Imagine the event occurs as Lycan described in which he enters the room you are in, bounces the ball, and so on. Now, what occurred had many features and involved many properties Lycan does not mention, nor could he. How could he hope to describe every property of his basketball or his left hand? The terms he employs designate general features of what occurred, for example he was holding the basketball, but in which way? But clearly it is essential that for an event to occur in which Lycan enters a classroom carrying a basketball, bouncing it and then leaving, it must involve essentially properties like being a basketball, being a classroom, being a person who enters a room, being a person holding a basketball, and so on. They are essential because without any one of them, e.g. there was nothing in the classroom ever having the property of being a basketball, the event would not occur. The fact that something in the room had the property of being a basketball is one of the features that are an essential element in virtue of which the event Lycan described occurred. It seems to me even more obvious that the experiential state of being in pain has an essential feel, "hurting," that is not at all rarefied or elusive.

Perhaps we should as well, but only, I think, if there are compelling reasons for doing so, and I regard the plausibility of the above thought experiments as exposing a real shortcoming in the functionalist program.

The central thesis of this section is that it is possible for there to be a divergence of the mental and physical in a way that is not permitted within the functionalist, materialist framework. Do these thought experiments only establish that an identification of the mental with either a functional state or a specific physical set of processes could be false? Many theories *could* be false that are in fact true. But here the possibility of there being the designated functional states without the requisite mental states and *vice versa* does establish that the psychological properties and physical properties are distinct. If they were identical then no occasion whatever could arise in which one obtained or was instantiated and the other was not. If your seeing red is the very same thing as the physical state plus the functional roles posited by Shoemaker, Lewis, Levin, *et al.*, then there could not be the inversions charted by Nagel, Putnam, myself, and others. Insofar as essential integrative dualism does not allow for such reconfiguring of the mental and physical, the above thought experiments also create a challenge to its outlook. But in arguing that our grasp of the subjective features of our experience is sufficiently informed that we can make sense of the strange options reviewed above, we must return to the problem of skepticism. Given that it is possible for the mental and physical to be reshuffled, as it were, so that the observable physical conditions do not by themselves give us an absolute guarantee as to the accompanying mental life, how can we be said to know about the subjective experience of others? The defense of integrative dualism can be read as a defense of skepticism.

On one level I am a skeptic. Insofar as knowing something involves absolute infallible knowing where I must rule out as absolutely metaphysically impossible that others are having certain experiences, I am not at all sure this can be done. Having said that, however, I think there is no reason to believe that any of us do have taste or visual inversion, or that any of us are zombies. Before proceeding in the next chapter to argue for a substantive dualist outlook, it will be useful to indicate in a little more detail how integrative dualism is not committed to an isolationist, excessively private notion of the mental. In the last two sections of this chapter I distinguish integrative dualism from a form of dualism that is, in my view, excessively private, and then suggest how integrative dualism treats the problem of other minds in light of a comprehensive theory of personal development in a public, intersubjective world. This will be done under the subheadings "The Private" and "God's Public."

THE PRIVATE

What I take to be an extreme dualist stand on privacy has been advanced by Geoffrey Madell. Madell deploys an important version of the argument against materialism based on the appeal to subjective experience, but he then, I believe, overstates its moral. I begin with a note on self-awareness and then turn to the details of his analysis.

In the various thought experiments above we have been considering the slippery nature of mental states, but we have not entertained cases where mental states are so slippery that we envision the possibility that these states are not states of some person, self, or subject of some sort. That is, in referring to pain, I have been assuming that we are referring to the pain of some being or other. In my having an experience of pain I am feeling not just pain construed as some kind of state that is "out there" I happen to link up with, but I am feeling a state of myself. I am the one who am in pain now. I was free from pain earlier and I hope to be free from pain later, but at this time I am hurting. The absurdity of supposing that a person's awareness of his or her own pain states is more circuitous is brought out in Charles Dickens' *Hard Times* when Mrs. Gradgrind says "I think there's a pain somewhere in the room, but I couldn't positively say that I have got it."[69] Madell's argument against materialism is not

---

[69] Cf. H. D. Lewis, *The Self and Immortality* (New York: Macmillan, 1973), pp. 79, 81, 82.

just that it cannot offer a credible account of subjective states themselves like pain, but that it cannot offer a credible account of one's self-identity.

The form of materialism targeted in Madell's argument holds that all truths about the world can be stated in physics, if not now, then as developed ideally over time, offering a complete account of all reality. Imagine that we have before us this account with its elaborate, sophisticated laws and such. No matter how well defined it is, physics will not include at least one fact. It will not inform us which person in the cosmos is me and which is you. Surely it is a fact that I am myself and I may grasp this in the course of my own self-awareness. As Madell states: "To put it bluntly, it is an objective fact about the world that one of the billions of people in it is me."[70] Madell reads this fact as indicating that we have a unique first-person access upon the world and ourselves, an access, and hence a truth, that is not captured by physics. A scientific description of you and me could tell us indefinitely many truths about us, but it could not tell us which person described is you and which is me. Madell writes:

How can one accommodate the existence of the first-person perspective in a wholly material world? A complete objective description of a particular person is one thing; the assertion, "the person thus described is me" is something in addition, and conveys more information. But this extra information isn't of a character which physical science could recognize. If reality comprises assemblies of physical entities only, it appears utterly mysterious that some arbitrary element of that objective order should be me.[71]

Does this line of argument succeed? I think it can be fashioned into an objection to materialism, though it requires elaboration and some revision of Madell's version of it is in order.

I agree that a depiction of the physical world cannot absorb without remainder the felt, phenomenologically apparent reality of the psychological. Our subjective states themselves are not neurophysiological patterns or other material occurrences, hence, *a fortiori*, our subjective states involved with self-awareness and self-reference are not either. But while Madell's

---

[70] *Mind and Materialism*, p. 119.   [71] *Ibid.*, p. 103.

reasoning seems plausible to me, I think it accomplishes less than he thinks it does.

Madell's thesis is that our self-awareness comprises a first-person point of view which cannot be captured from a third-person perspective. That is, he holds that my being me is something that can only be known from the inside, so to speak, and this represents an ultimate, private feature of reality. "The subjective cannot be included in any account of the reality which can be apprehended from more than one point of view."[72] An illustration may be of assistance. Imagine that we have a full account of the world's facts, not just about its physical features but psychological ones as well. In sum, imagine you have before you all the truths about the world except the truth about which person is you. The list may include: Arthur was born in 1957, he went to New York in the 1970s, he was happy in 1985, and so on. Could you know all the details of his life and many others and not know whether you are Arthur? I think this could occur under highly peculiar circumstances. After all, amnesia occurs and, perhaps, if you or I had amnesia and were given this exhaustive account of the world from a third person point of view we might not know who was Arthur and who was Charles, who went to New York in the 1970s, and so on. Madell reasons that this shortcoming is evidence that self-awareness expresses a special kind of fact, not captured by any outside analysis.

I agree that the case could occur as just stated, but I do not think this establishes Madell's strong views on privacy. Consider two statements, the first one uttered by you, Arthur:

(A) *I am in pain.*   (B) *Arthur is in pain.*

When someone else grasps "B," do they grasp something other than what is grasped by "A"? This seems wildly implausible. Clearly your state of self-awareness can be expressed by the first person pronoun "I" in a direct fashion, whereas I can only use the pronoun "I" to refer to you if I do so indirectly and

[72] *Ibid.*, p. 123.

awkwardly. I might do so in uttering: (C) *I think Arthur thinks "I am aware of being in pain."* But surely we are referring to the same thing when you utter "A" and someone else utters "B" or "C" (albeit "C" also includes explicit reference to the one who is, in turn, referring to you). I believe that the illustration given earlier and the quandary about knowing that you are Arthur is a function of the fact that both your self-awareness and the third person story of the world are incomplete. Imagine that the account of the world includes something like: (D) *Arthur is aware of himself* and, assuming recovery from amnesia, you grasp (E) *I am aware of myself.* Given that you are Arthur (a fact which seems to amount to you being you), "E" and "D" will always be co-instantiated in that when E occurs, D occurs. In the earlier, imaginary case we suppose from the very beginning that you do not know who you are (with amnesia), and presumably the list of world truths would include something like: "Arthur has amnesia. Arthur is reading a vast list of world truths. Arthur is not sure that the account of himself going to New York is about him or not," and so on.[73]

At this point it may seem as though I am siding too much with the materialist who insists upon the public intersubjective character of the world, especially the psychological. I am closer to some materialists than Madell on this point despite the radical gulf between the materialist and dualist outlook, but in my view there is no reason to accept an extreme insistence upon the privacy of the mental. In fact, such an insistence seems to run counter to the theistic notion that God knows of and has access to your internal, psychological life. The way God knows is different from mine, but I do not see any reason to think that a God's-eye point of view would have to leave out full knowledge of my self-awareness or yours.[74] But the intersubjective character of the mental here would not be due to the fact that the mental is really just a type of physical event, but to something altogether different: the nature of God. The materialist David

---

[73] For a good treatment of accessing propositions that contain ostensively private properties, see J. Kvanvig, *The Possibility of an All-knowing God* (London: Macmillan, 1986).

[74] Michael Beaty and I defend the coherence of God's knowing our psychological states in "God and Concept Empiricism," *Southwest Philosophy Review* 6:2 (July 1990).

Lewis would possibly be an ally in maintaining the conceivability of such high powered Divine access to distinct
mental states. He thinks it is possible for one person to know
what some sensory state is like without actually undergoing it.
Theists, too, would surely want to permit this, for otherwise one
faces the problem of accounting for how God can know about
sado-masochistic and other such feelings without having the
relevant feelings (and presumably having those feelings compromise Divine goodness). Lewis' case concerns the possibility
of grasping what it is like to smell a skunk without having the
experience of smelling it.

Having an experience is surely one good way, and surely the only
practical way, of coming to know what that experience is like. Can we
say, flatly, that it is the only possible way? Probably not. There is a
change that takes place in you when you have the experience and
thereby come to know what it's like. Perhaps the exact same change
could in principle be produced in you by precise neurosurgery, very
far beyond the limits of present-day technique. Or it could possibly be
produced in you by magic. If we ignore the laws of nature, which are
after all contingent, then there is no necessary connection between
cause and effect: anything could cause anything. For instance, the
casting of a spell could do to you exactly what your first smell of skunk
would do. We might quibble about whether a state produced in this
artificial fashion would deserve the name "knowing what it's like to
smell a skunk," but we can imagine that so far as what goes on within
you is concerned, it would differ not at all.[75]

Lewis' case recalls the discussion of kelvin and Divine cousins in
the first chapter and the possibility of different ways to access
sensory states. As I have suggested, my only caveat to what
Lewis says on this topic is that in the course of God's knowing,
or my knowing, what it is like for Arthur to smell skunks or be
self-aware, we are thereby grasping subjective states and, for all
the reasons given above, subjective states are not themselves
physical.

Madell's own attempt at securing his strict notion of privacy
seems problematic. He feels compelled to abandon a substantial
view of the self for reasons that take us back to his thought

[75] David Lewis, "What Experience Teaches" in *Mind and Cognition*, ed. William Lycan
(Oxford: Basil Blackwell, 1990), p. 500.

experiment. Imagine that the list of all world truths include
facts like: Arthur is an immaterial self or Arthur is nonphysical
but materially embodied or Arthur is a material substance.
Madell contends that you, Arthur, could know all such truths
about yourself as either a physical or a nonphysical substance
and yet not be sure which substance is you. He takes this as
indicating that your unique self-awareness and identity are not
a function of your being a particular substantive person, but a
function of your experiences being yours in an underived, not
further analyzable sense. To hypothesize that your identity is
ultimately grounded in being a substance, physical or nonphysical, is unmotivated.

If our question is "What makes a series of experiences over time all
mine?" then postulating an ego will not help, for this can only lead to
the further question "What is it for any particular ego to be mine?"
It looks as if the only answer we can give to this question, moreover,
is that an ego is mine if all the experiences had by it are mine; and that
is, of course, fatal to the attempt to explain what it is for these
experiences to be mine by postulating an ego. Experiences, it appears,
must be accepted as the fundamental bearer of subjectivity.[76]

If Madell is asked about how someone could know from a third
person point of view which stream of experiences are underivatively theirs, he would simply reply that they cannot, and such
an impossibility is precisely what his view of privacy insists
upon. "It is experiences themselves which are underivatively
mine, and these, though in the world, are not physical events in
the world ... The ultimate bearers of subjectivity are experiences, and experiences are mental particulars."[77]

I find Madell's stance here unconvincing for three related
reasons. First, he seems to be faced with intractable difficulties
in accounting for our personal identity over time. It seems
evident that we do endure over time notwithstanding our
constantly changing experiences. Moreover, it is also plausible
to believe that we may endure over time when we are without
any experiences whatever, as when I lose consciousness or am in
deep sleep. If Madell's theory is correct, how can he account for

[76] *The Identity of the Self* (Edinburgh: Edinburgh University Press, 1981), p. 135.
[77] *Mind and Materialism*, p. 123.

this continuity of identity? The philosophical and scientific analysis of this personal identity may not be obvious, but the fact of personal identity itself is so apparent in everyday life that, I think, it needs to be explained rather than explained away.

Second, his construal of experiences and mental particulars seems odd and his notion of the "ego" unnecessarily abstract. Experiences may include both passive and active states but in either event they are not particulars *qua* things but states of myself. My experiencing pain is, as I stressed earlier, my feeling a state of mine, just as my experience of actively being engaged in thinking is an experience of myself being a certain way. Madell seems to think that positing an "ego" involves positing some hidden thing in back of our experiences, veiled behind sensations and activity. But there is not, I think, any reason for us to embrace such views of a cognitively remote ego/self. The natural way to read our experience is that such experience is of and by a continuously existing, individual subject. Hence, Madell's whole way of articulating the issues at hand is open to question. We do not have to choose between treating my experiences or my self *qua* substantive ego as basic, because the former is a mode of the latter.[78]

Third, as I argued earlier, there is no reason to complain about the substance view leaving us conceptually in the dark with a rude, not further explained fact that you are you, I am I. I agree with Madell that self-awareness does cause a problem for materialism, but this is because subjectivity itself causes a problem for materialism and not because all third-person points of view must fail to capture the character and reality of our mental life.

Thus far I have held that there is insufficient reason to attribute to ourselves supremely private, exclusive access to our own mental states. This seems to be a mark against skepticism, just as the earlier material on our integrative, embodied life stands against making the person out to be a mysteriously hidden entity living, as it were, behind the mask of the body. However, I have also held that it is *possible* for the mental and

---

[78] Roderick Chisholm offers a superb treatment of self-awareness in *Person and Object* (La Salle: Open Court, 1976).

physical to be radically at odds, so that the functional realization of the mental is not captured publicly, and this offers some sustenance to the skeptic. How do we *know* that others do indeed have the subjective states that we assume them to have? Perhaps God has direct access of some kind to the subjective states of others, but we are less well off.

GOD'S PUBLIC

There are a number of options for the dualist in arguing for the legitimacy of our belief in other minds apart from adopting what we discussed earlier as essential integrative dualism. I shall outline three strategies, focusing upon the third.

The first concedes the most to the skeptic, and consists in locating one's justification for the belief in others' mental life in pragmatic terms. It is simply not possible to live without having such beliefs that others are what we assume them to be, conscious thinking persons. One may develop this line by offering some kind of overriding natural explanation of this need being wired-in biologically, but in doing so, one comes close to adopting the third alternative, "the appeal to the best explanation." Some materialists have taken this first approach, and dismissed the problem of other minds as simply boring or morbid. There are specific versions of this strategy in circulation, one of which is that a thorough skeptic cannot engage in the practice of philosophy, thus making the philosophical skeptic committed to an inconsistency of sorts.[79]

A second alternative offers ethical reasons for not being a skeptic. I have articulated a wager argument elsewhere to the effect that there are good ethical reasons why one ought to assume that other persons have the mental life that they appear to.[80] This second alternative might supplement the first. For those who can somehow live as skeptics about others' subjective life, it still can be argued that there are moral grounds why they ought not to. Perhaps this line of reasoning could be extended to argue that there are ethical considerations that should lead us to

[79] See Lycan, *Judgement and Justification* (Cambridge: Cambridge University Press, 1988), p. 195.
[80] "Imaginary Evil: A Skeptic's Wager," *Philosophia* 21:3–4 (April 1992), 221–233.

cultivate boredom with the whole skeptical enterprise here. While I think this way of addressing skepticism has merit, it would not satisfy a philosopher who is skeptical about both others' subjective life and the moral realm. A moral skeptic will be unmoved by this strategy.

A third alternative is to develop an anti-skeptical argument without begging the question against him or her. How difficult this will be depends upon what premises the skeptic will allow us in getting an argument started. If the skeptic will grant us that it appears as though there are other persons who have the subjective experiences we take them to have, *and* that we should accept things as they appear until we have positive reason for doing otherwise, then we are in good shape. But why should the skeptic grant us the first premise?

One reason for granting it is the so-called argument from analogy. It proceeds on the grounds that a person (the skeptic Eric, say) does know that he has subjective, mental states and that he also knows the link between such mental states and his physical body. He knows, for example, that when his skin is lacerated under certain conditions, he feels pain. He also realizes that other bodies are sometimes in circumstances similar to his own, as when George's skin is lacerated. He is then in a position to reason that when George is in a physical state analogous to his, it is plausible to assume that George is in a subjective, mental state analogous to his. The argument may be run rather modestly, only claiming that such an assumption is reasonable, not that it is incorrigible and infallibly known to be true.

The argument from analogy is probably among the least favored in the philosophy of mind literature. Descartes did not clearly advocate it, though Mill adopted it and one can find something like it in Malebranche. Objections to it include criticizing its proceeding on the basis of a sample of only one. Critics charge that it is unreasonable to advance a conclusion of such enormous scope (there are others who have subjective, mental states) on the basis of only a single case of mental–physical correlation. Critics have also questioned whether the argument can even get off the ground. Why should the skeptic grant that Eric is capable of distinguishing his own mental states from himself? Jonathan Dancy represents the skeptic's worry here:

The argument from analogy supposes that you can construct from your own case a concept of pains which can be felt by others rather than by you. But is it so easy to conceive of a pain which is not hurting you? You have to start from a pain of yours and conceive of there being something like this which hurts but which does not hurt you, and also that there could be something which is like you but not you for such pains to hurt. Both of these ideas are very dubious. How can you conceive of something as painful, as hurting, without conceiving of it as hurting you? Surely, in conceiving of something that hurts, you necessarily conceive of it as painful to you.[81]

In discussing Madell's treatment of self-awareness I defended the thesis that the awareness of our own subjective states and self-awareness are tightly bound together. It would be odd to suppose that there was extreme pain somewhere "out there" in a room and be unsure whether it was you who were feeling the pain. Is the connection so close that the argument from analogy would be rendered moot from the beginning?

I think that depends upon how much room the skeptic is prepared to give us. The skeptical move Dancy represents strikes me as extreme. We do, or so it appears, readily distinguish between pain as felt by others as opposed to pain as felt by oneself. On the inside, so to speak, it seems that we have some facility in seeing that pain and other sensations are accidental to who we are, for otherwise we would not be able to make sense of our being in pain at one time and not having such a sensation at another. One type of skeptic will concede these points, but press the case that while we can make these distinctions, we are not satisfactorily justified in believing that we are applying the distinctions properly. This form of skepticism seems far more plausible than one that questions whether we make any such conceptual distinction at all. If skepticism is directed upon calling into question whether we are capable of even such rudimentary distinguishing, then it is likely we have on our hands a radical skeptic of a high order, perhaps one who is

[81] *Contemporary Epistemology*, p. 70.

unsure about whether there is even an external world, or that memory is at all reliable, and so on. So, while I think the argument from analogy will be unsuccessful with the extreme skeptic, that is not to say that it lacks currency for the more modest one. A dualist may not be able to persuade a radical, Pyrrhonian skeptic that other persons exist as they appear to, but neither will the materialist or idealist.

I believe that the argument from analogy does have a proper place in guiding at least some of our beliefs about each other's subjective life. Surely it is a common practice to bring to bear our own first-person background of experience in coming to learn what others are thinking and feeling. Even so, my own preference is the so-called appeal to the best explanation approach, as standing for a wider umbrella of considerations that includes the argument from analogy.

What is the best explanation of what we all assume to be other persons? That they (or *we* as opposed to *you*) are cleverly designed automatons or person-like beings shorn of subjectivity and mentality? Is it likely that you are the only person with any subjective life? There is no evidence that you are, and a positive case against such a solitary metaphysic can be built on the basis of a myriad of considerations that includes the appeal to analogy, observed purposive behavior, language usage, genetic accounts offering an explanation for the emergence of sub-jective, conscious life, and so on. I think the appeal to the best-explanation strategy is best carried out when its net is cast widely, which is precisely what I want to do at various points in this book in filling out integrative dualism and a wider theistic vantage point. My aim is to return to the topic of the awareness we have of ourselves and of others in Chapter 6. My treatment will incorporate material from the next chapter on dualism as well as work in Chapters 4 and 5 on theism. Taking on such a wide purview is not itself exceptional. As has been well documented, materialists frequently advance their view of our knowledge of other persons (including whether they think there are persons) as well as their overriding metaphysic, on the basis of cumulative arguments. This stratagem can very well be labeled a cumulative best-explanation argument. I shall close

with some brief comments as to how theism might have a
bearing on our knowledge of other minds, and *vice versa*,
sketching a stance that I return to later. Descartes worried
about other minds and appealed to the goodness of God as part
of his escape route from skepticism. If God is all good, God will
not have made us such that our cognitive faculties will be
systematically misleading. Appeal to God's goodness is what
provides a warranty that our cognitive faculties, and one's own
and others' embodiment, are all functioning properly. Descartes
has been criticized on many fronts, not the least of which is that
his argument for God's existence is problematic and his
philosophical methodology is artificially ahistorical. On this
latter front, some philosophers have criticized both Descartes
and the modern skeptic on the grounds that they lose sight of
the contextualized, encumbered context in which we all find
ourselves. We do not begin our lives as little epistemologists but
as crying masses. Our mental world is built up slowly in terms
of felt needs, satisfied and frustrated desires, and appetite-
driven inference. Descartes and other theorists of the mental life
lose sight of the enmeshed, conditioned character of our life
from beginning to end. It is because we lose sight of this context
that theism seems like such an *ad hoc* hypothesis.

At various points in this book I have been anxious to distance
integrative dualism from Descartes's outlook. So, in this chapter
I have emphasized how integrative dualism can take the public
dimension of the mental quite seriously, more so than commonplace versions of Cartesianism. Along these lines, I think
that integrative dualism is well suited for fully recognizing the
historical, materially conditioned nature of meaning, though it
does allow (as the various thought experiments have illustrated)
that the mental is not reducible to a solely material base.
Notwithstanding this departure from the legacy of Cartesianism, I am in sympathy with Descartes's stress on the goodness of
God as providing a reasonable background metaphysic by
which to understand the cosmos as a whole, our integrative
embodiment, and our awareness of others. If there is an all-good
God, Descartes's conclusion seems quite plausible. I am not
proposing here that it is *essential* to adopt theism in order to trust

our cognitive equipment or to believe that integrative embodiment functions properly. I propose, rather, that in a theistic
outlook there is reason to have such trust.[82] Descartes' theistic
move is not, I think, at odds with appreciating the context and
historical setting of personal life, rather his viewpoint is
supported by a plausible account of personal development I
raise in Chapter 6. Briefly, one of the key tenets in some of the
recent psychoanalytic literature and in Attachment Theory is
that infants require that their care-giver be stable, nurturing,
and reliable. The care-giver may only need to be, in D. W.
Winnicott's phrase, "a good enough mother," rather than one
who is perfect, but without some goodness, the infant is unlikely
to develop any kind of stable personal identity and sense of
herself or himself in a public world.[83] Winnicott, Melanie Klein,
and others have defended accounts of personal development in
which the child trusts the goodness of the parent who alternatively identifies with the child's needs and yet draws the child to
higher levels of appreciation and affection. On this view, we
grow up as a mind within a mind, as the care-giver provides an
intentional, intersubjective world, assisting us in meeting our
needs, incorporating public language, and the like. Integrative
dualism is well suited to underwrite this picture of personal
interaction and growth, as it is not committed to the splintered
bifurcation that critics from Ryle and Hacker to Dennett accuse
it of.

Materialists can read this understanding of personal development as an interesting feature of the natural world,
whereas theists may see it as a clue (or reflection) of an
overriding theistic cosmos whereby we, and the cosmos as a
whole, have our being within an overriding Divine mind. In my
view, Descartes's philosophical theology, with a little help from
psychoanalysis and Attachment Theory, does not look so
conceptually bizarre.

[82] For a current treatment of epistemology from a theistic point of view, see Alvin
Plantinga's *Warrant and Proper Functioning* (Oxford: Oxford University Press, 1993).
[83] Relevant references are provided in Chapter 6. There are important respects in
which the proper functioning of the person–body relation from a theistic point of
view may be articulated in terms very much like Plantinga's account of the proper
functioning of cognitive faculties in *Warrant and Proper Functioning*.

All this is by way of sketching what I seek to fill out in the chapters ahead. We need to consider again the merits of integrative dualism. What further reasons can be given for adopting it, as opposed to a more modest dualistic theory? Certain materialist objections to dualism have yet to be fully addressed, and we will need to consider some fundamental aspects of the philosophy of God before we can debate what it might mean for there to be an incorporeal "good enough god" or a perfect one who sustains and pervades the cosmos.

CHAPTER 3

Persons and bodies

Miserably I tried to shut out the immensities by closing my eyes. But I had neither eyes nor eyelids. I was a disembodied, wandering view-point.

Olaf Stapleton, *Star Maker*[1]

In Chapter 2 I considered some of the difficulties with achieving a clear conception of the physical and mental. I argued that a philosophical conception of the physical cannot easily by-pass the need to articulate what is mental, or avoid the use of ostension. I then sought to develop a version of dualism that takes seriously the integral nature of personal embodiment. While integrative dualism upholds the contingent character of mental–physical interaction, it is not committed to the hyper-privacy and isolationism that makes it prey to the linguistic and conceptual objections raised by Levin and others. But why embrace integrative dualism, or any kind of substantial dichotomy between persons and bodies, rather than rely on a more temperate outlook like the dual-aspect theory? In this chapter I review six reasons why the dual-aspect theory is not sufficiently dualistic. The arguments may also be read as reasons for not being a materialist. The first five are considered only briefly, as the main work of the chapter defends the sixth, the modal argument for dualism. The earlier arguments have merit, but, in my view, the modal argument carries the greater weight. In addressing a series of objections, I offer a dualist rejoinder to the problems of individuation and interaction.

[1] Olaf Stapleton, *Last and First Men and Star Maker* (New York: Dover, 1968), p. 268.

FIVE REASONS TO MOVE FROM THE DUAL-ASPECT THEORY TO DUALISM

In this chapter the term "dualism" is used to designate the view that persons are nonphysical and hence not metaphysically identical with their bodies, without specifying integrative dualism in particular. This is partly because most of the arguments that follow support an overriding dualist outlook without exhibiting reasons why integrative dualism should be preferred to versions that place less stress on integral embodiment. Theological and ethical reasons for and against integrative dualism are taken up in the following chapter.

(1) *The primacy of the mental*

It has been argued that while the dual-aspect theory can accommodate the fact that the physical affects the mental, it cannot account adequately for the efficacy of the mental on the physical. Granted that there is two-way causal interaction, dualism is better positioned to account for it than the dual-aspect theory. The latter gives so much pride of place to the physical that it does not allow the mental sufficient independence for intentional self-determination.

Madell advances a version of this argument against a supervenient form of the dual-aspect theory. "Supervenience" specifies certain necessary relations between distinct properties. The property of being a figure may be said to supervene on the property of being a square because it is necessarily the case that when the second property is instantiated, so is the first. The relation here is not symmetrical, however, for if the property of being a figure is instantiated, it does not necessarily follow that the property of being a square is instantiated. Supervenient relations generate asymmetrical explanations: when property X supervenes on property Y, X is instantiated because of the instantiation of Y, not *vice versa*. If the mental and physical are harnessed together in this supervenient relation, then positing mutual mental–physical interaction is problematic. In a supervenient schema, just as an object's being square makes it a figure, not *vice versa*, it is the instantiation of various physical properties that brings about the instantiation of the mental properties involved, not *vice versa*. As Madell writes:

> Not only is talk of supervenience, and the discerning of some sort of necessary connection between the mental and the physical exceedingly unclear, but to suggest that the relation between the mental and physical is that the mental somehow supervenes on the physical is to fail to recognize that the determination often crucially runs the other way ... My physical behaviour is very often determined by my perceptions, judgements and decisions. This is something a dual aspect position seems incapable of recognizing; certainly, any position which sees the mental as supervening on, and thus in a sense determined by, the physical, can make nothing of it.[2]

Madell's argument may thus be represented as: the dual-aspect theory leads to epiphenomenalism, epiphenomenalism is implausible, hence the dual-aspect theory is implausible.

Materialists at this point might declare a plague on both houses and submit that neither version of dualism can account for causal traffic between the physical and mental, whether this be one-way or two-way. I address the problem of interaction below, and only comment here that while (in my view) Madell rightly criticizes *some* forms of the dual-aspect theory for their implausible epiphenomenalism, it is not clear that all dual-aspect theories have epiphenomenalist repercussions. Dual-aspect theorists can posit a contingent, but law-governed relation between the mental and physical, in which the relevant natural laws are themselves recognized as contingent, eschewing the structural confines of supervenience. Accepting the dual-aspect theory does not itself commit one to holding that the instantiation of the psychological is governed entirely from the physical upwards. There may be some motivation for analyzing macro-level causation in terms of micro-properties, if the object at hand is believed to be metaphysically homogeneous, so to speak. That is, in cases where an object is thoroughly physical, we may well set our sights on accounting for the molar behavior of some object like a protein in terms of its parts, its helices and

[2] Geoffrey Madell, *Mind and Materialism* (Edinburgh: Edinburgh University Press, 1988), p. 134.

sheets. The dual-aspect theory, however, posits a profound heterogeneity when it comes to persons: mental life is not just physical activity or a construct of material particles. The dual-aspect theory treats the mental as distinct and emergent. Given this demarcation, at least one of the motives for locating causal forces exclusively on the physical ground floor is diminished. Madell's warning about epiphenomenalism is judicious, but it is not clear that dual-aspect theorists are *ipso facto* committed to the same formal supervenient constraints that govern objects that are exclusively physical, shorn of any nonphysical, mental properties.

(2) *Empirical evidence for the primacy of the mental*

Empirical reasons have been offered in support of the thesis that physical processes are caused by psychological ones that are not themselves brought about by earlier physical processes. The scientific literature has focused on certain concrete cases involving the timing of neural events and reported mental reflection.[3] Even if successful in bolstering the claim for dualist interactionism, this line of argument would not compel us to move beyond the dual-aspect theory. If dual-aspect theorists can avoid epiphenomenalism as discussed above, then they may well be able to interpret the scientific data as evidence that a person *qua* material object with psychological properties can undertake some psychological activities in partial independence of physical processes.

By way of an overview of the first and second arguments, I want to underscore that theories which wind up on the epiphenomenalist side of the fence are at odds with our whole commonsense framework. It therefore seems to me that the underlying assumption in the first two arguments is sound. In ordinary life we certainly seem to act as though our beliefs and desires make a difference in what happens. In the course of reasoning with others, whether it be shop talk or legal debate, we presuppose that reasons and beliefs make a difference in each

---

[3] See John Eccles, *The Human Psyche* (London: Routledge, 1992) and the papers in *Mind and Brain*, ed. Eccles (Washington: Paragon House, 1982).

other's lives. If beliefs, intentions, and other psychological items are causally irrelevant, then our entire framework for thinking of each other as *bona fide* responsible agents is threatened. As Jaegewan Kim observes:

The intentional psychological scheme – that is, the framework of belief, desire and will – is one within which we deliberate about ends and means, and assess the rationality of actions and decisions. It is the framework that makes our normative and evaluative activities possible. No purely descriptive framework such as those of neurophysiology and physics, no matter how theoretically comprehensive and productively powerful, can replace it. As long as we think of ourselves as reflective agents capable of deliberation and evaluation ... we shall not be able to dispense with the intentional framework of beliefs, wants, and volitions.[4]

Those who deny the veracity of such a framework are faced with the awkward position of having to work within the very system (the system of accepting or rejecting beliefs based on reasons) they wish to repudiate.

(3) *Property problems*

Unfortunately, this rationale is not easy to formulate precisely. Roughly, the position is that person–body dualism is able to preserve a kind of ontological simplicity that the dual-aspect theory is not. We have little difficulty imagining how a physical object has physical properties, but it seems conceptually baffling to imagine how the very same object can have both physical *and* nonphysical properties. Talk of supervenience linking the two seems more of a way to label the conceptual difficulty of construing this hybrid than it does to explain it. Person–body dualism may itself have its conceptual peculiarities, but at least it does not assume that the physical has nonphysical properties. Instead, it delimits the self as a nonphysical individual having nonphysical properties and leaves the physical properties with the physical objects.

This line of reasoning has some intuitive force. Thomas Nagel acknowledges the puzzling nature of the dual-aspect theory,

---

[4] J. Kim, "Psychophysical Laws," in E. LePore and B. McLaughlin (eds.), *Actions and Events* (Oxford: Blackwell, 1985), pp. 369–396.

and Colin McGinn insists upon the irreducible mystery involved in its double-sided character. John Foster has emphasized the difficulty at issue here:

> The basic problem is ... understanding how it is possible for the same thing to possess two such different natures; how it is possible for something both to be a physical object and to have, in a way which is not amenable to conceptual or metaphysical reduction, additional intrinsic attributes which are extraneous to its physical character. If pain is a wholly non-physical state, how can we think of it as genuinely and irreducibly characterizing the very thing which is extended and material?[5]

While these considerations have real force, I do not think we have enough to go on here to justify moving beyond the dual-aspect theory.

It is not obvious why a physical object could not possess nonphysical properties. I have sought to articulate a version of dualism that permits us to affirm that the person *qua* nonphysical individual has physical properties in the course of being embodied. If you allow for a generous list of properties to be nonphysical, like being thought about by someone, then all dualists must grant that some physical objects have nonphysical properties. Some theists may want to allow that all the material constituents in the cosmos have properties like being created by God or being thought of by God and (perhaps) we should think of these properties as at least quasi-nonphysical. These cases may be dismissed as involving merely relational properties, not intrinsic psychological ones.[6] Still, I think we need further argument that the physical cannot have mental properties to conclude that the dual-aspect theory is in serious trouble here.

---

[5] *The Immaterial Self* (London: Routledge, 1991), p. 208.

[6] In Thomism the status of the God–creation relation is not altogether clear, nonetheless Thomists tend to recognize that there is a real relation between creatures and God, though the relation of God to creatures is another story. See the *Summa Theologiae* Ia.13.7, and C. F. J. Williams' "Is God Really Related to His Creatures?" for an analysis, *Sophia* 8 (1969), 1–10.

(4) *The mental subject*

John Foster has recently advanced an important argument for person–body dualism based on the view that a person is a basic subject. Foster's central claim is that each of us is a basic subject, and that we have this status in a fundamental, essential fashion. Being a self is something that does not admit of being conceptually broken down into more basic, subpersonal categories; it is underived and simple. Foster contends that a corporeal, physical object cannot have this foundational status. He advances this position in an imaginative fashion, arguing that if a subject, Jones, were physical, then his identity as a subject would be radically undermined.

Someone treads on Jones's foot – and, for the sake of an example, let us continue to think of Jones as a member of an animal species, with a corporeal nature. As a result of the stimulus, a neural event occurs in Jones's brain which directly causes a sensation of pain, and this sensation in turn (though only via some intervening neural process) causes, or in some way prompts, a certain vocal response. Our normal practice is to ascribe the pain-state to Jones himself, the corporeal being whose foot receives the pain-inducing stimulus and whose mouth emits the vocal response. But why not ascribe it instead to some corporeal part of Jones, e.g. to his brain, or to that part of his brain in which the relevant neural event occurs? Or alternatively, why not ascribe it instead to some larger corporeal object of which Jones is a part, e.g. to Jones together with the room in which he is currently located, or even to the whole physical world?[7]

Foster underscores the obvious fact that we do not indulge in such farfetched ascriptions, and there are reasons for it. However, he insists that no reasons about the material world suffice to provide a fully determinative answer to the question about the subject's essential identity.

Since the pain-state is non-physical, and thus not an aspect of the physical nature of the corporeal object to which we assign it, our conception of it does not force us to assign it to one kind of corporeal object rather than another. If we say that what is ultimately in pain is Jones's brain, or that it is the whole physical world, we do not seem to

[7] *The Immaterial Self*, p. 210.

be making an objective mistake, except insofar as there may be a general objective mistake in treating any corporeal object as a basic subject. But, presumably, if it were legitimate to treat corporeal objects as basic subjects, then the question of which objects qualified for this role would have an objective answer ... if we are free to assign the pain-state to Jones's brain or to the whole physical world, then we are equally free to assign it to the moon or to Mount Everest or to the dome of St. Paul's. And quite generally, we are free to select any material object which exists at every time at which Jones exists and re-assign the mental states and activities in Jones's supposed mental biography to this object.[8]

Foster finds such a laissez-faire status altogether unacceptable and, for this reason, rejects a corporeal view of persons and accepts person–body dualism instead. The latter can capture the identity of persons as a primitive, not further analyzable datum in a way the dual-aspect theory cannot.

To avoid some confusion, I note an important twist in Foster's position. Foster's philosophical profile is ultimately idealist, but in some of his work, especially *The Immaterial Mind*, he defends dualism. Foster is allied with dualists in believing the self to be nonphysical, though he later parts company over the status of the physical world. He has a stake, then, in the credibility of a key dualist tenet even if he does not eventually match the full dualist profile. While Foster's argument is impressive, I think it is unlikely to have the persuasive force he desires. His argument faces several obstacles.

Dual-aspect theorists will agree that the claim "Mt. Everest is in pain" is not false solely because Mt. Everest is a massive, physical object. Within their framework, being physical does not, of course, *ipso facto* disqualify some object from feeling pain, nor, presumably, should size. But dual-aspect theorists may go on to propose that the reason why some physical objects like Jones are subjects, and not others, is due to the prevailing laws of nature. The reason why Mt. Everest does not feel pain is that it lacks a brain and nervous system, and it could not feel pain unless it were so equipped. Foster himself insists upon certain ultimate, not further explicable, facts about persons and it is not

---

[8] *Ibid.*, pp. 210, 211.

obvious on the face of it why a dual-aspect theorist could not simply claim that there are certain ultimate facts true in this world about selves, psychology, and physiology. Some dual-aspect theorists contend that only certain sorts of biological animals can be persons. I think Foster would be correct to question whether the law-governed correlations between the brain and mental life are necessary, and thus whether the last claim can be vindicated. In Chapter 2 reasons were advanced for thinking the laws of mental–physical interaction are indeed contingent. But even if dual-aspect theorists concede that the laws of nature linking the mental and physical are contingent, are they in a philosophically embarrassing position? The answer is not a clear "yes."

Imagine they concede that there is a remote possibility that a mountain could be happy or pained, and allow that such a possibility is not conceptually absurd. Adherents of pan-psychism believe that all ultimate physical constituents of the cosmos have some modest level of psychic life. Perhaps their position could be spelled out in a generous way to give some sense to the claim of Mountain experiences.[9] As it happens, person–body dualists cannot easily rule out some of the puzzling features of Foster's case. Foster's example depicts a subject with a bizarre constitution, but the example could be reworked to describe a bizarre form of embodiment by a basic subject. Jonathan Harrison and H. H. Price are dualists who are prepared to countenance extended, bizarre forms of embodiment that rival the case of Jones. Consider Price's case:

There might conceivably be intelligent beings whose organisms are arranged quite differently, or who do not have organisms at all in the sense in which the human body is an organism, with a vast variety of organs all packed together in a clearly delimited region of physical space. The mind–matter linkage, whatever its nature is, might conceivably subsist not between a mind and a single compact piece of

---

[9] See Thomas Nagel, "Panpsychism". in *Mortal Questions* (New York: Cambridge University Press, 1980). Panpsychists tend to be reticent to attribute consciousness to things like mountains on the grounds that they do not embody sufficient coherence and unity. A panpsychist may believe that every fundamental entity in the cosmos has some rudimentary form of mental life, but that does not mean that everything (for example heaps, aggregates, collections) has mental life.

matter, but between a mind and many scattered bits of matter separated from each other by dozens of miles. Such a mind would have a kind of diffuse body without anything that could be called a shape. The question "where is it" would not have the same straightforward and unambiguous answer that it has when asked about a human being. All the same, if such an intelligence could control events in these scattered bits of matter in the kind of way we control our speech movements and finger movements and gestures, such events could be used by it as symbols.[10]

If we ensured that this defuse body had all the embodying relations we delimited in the last chapter, then I think a good case would be made for recognizing this as truly a defuse body.

(5) *The argument from divisibility*

This argument is similar to Foster's and can be developed in different ways. Consider one version: A person is not divisible. That is, a person cannot be broken into two or more separate things. Material objects are divisible, hence a person is not a material object.[11] My body may be cut in two, but, according to the argument here, this would not amount to dividing me. More than likely it would result in my perishing. Some initial objections to this argument are not decisive.

One obvious objection is that there is evidence from psychology that a person can be divided. Witness cases of multiple-personality disorder, in which a person seems to be divided into distinguishable personalities. But such phenomena do not, I think, discredit the argument. Cases of multiple personalities may plausibly be read as cases in which a single person has a host of separate personalities. Rather than undermine the thesis at stake here, such cases may bolster it. For it is due to the fact that we recognize a deeper unity involved with being a person

[10] Price, *Thinking and Experience* (London: Hutchinson, 1969), p. 213, and Harrison's "The Embodiment of Mind or What Use is Having a Body?," *Proceedings of the Aristotelian Society* (1973–74), 33–55.

[11] The divisibility argument is represented historically by a range of philosophers and often linked with arguments concerning personal identity over time. See *The Analogy of Religion* by Joseph Butler, first published in 1736, and *Essays on the Intellectual Powers of Man* by Thomas Reid, first published in 1785.

that we can say of a single person, Sybil, that she has multiple personalities. Otherwise we seem drawn in the direction of supposing that different persons share the same body. I do not rule this later possibility out as incoherent; I only note that the splintering involved in cases of multiple-personality disorder can be handled without discrediting the argument from divisibility.

What of the feasibility of dividing persons through brain bisection? In the brain, the two cerebral hemispheres have a functional duality which, when severed, appears to give rise to two centers of consciousness. There have not been any cases where brains have been fully severed with each cerebral hemisphere giving rise to a conscious life that is clearly distinguishable from the conscious life of the other hemisphere. Even so, critics may advance plausible thought experiments, in keeping with modern neuroscience, that outline how a single person might be subject to fission.[12] Imagine half your brain is transferred to another body lacking a brain, while the other half remains with your original body. Is it possible that such a split brain and body transfer would result in your becoming two persons? If so, it appears persons are not essentially indivisible. Proponents of the indivisibility argument may well simply deny that such brain transfers are (in principle) possible, but they could, I believe, allow that something that appears to be fission takes place while preserving their commitment to divisibility. Consider three ways of interpreting the split brain and transfer case.

(A) Given that there are indeed two persons, only one is the original, undivided person, the other being novel and emergent. The second self evolved or developed from the other. The original person never divided.

---

[12] A seminal paper on the scientific data is "Interhemispheric Relationships: The Neocortical Commissures: Syndromes of Hemispheric Disconnection" by R. Sperry, M. Gazzangia, and J. Bogen in *Handbook of Clinical Neurology*, vol. IV (1969). See the early important paper by Thomas Nagel, "Brain Bisection and the Unity of Consciousness," *Synthese* 22 (1971), 396–413. D. Robinson offers a balanced dualistic analysis of the relevant phenomena in "Cerebral Plurality and the Unity of Self," *American Psychologist* (August 1982), 904–910, and in "What Sort of Persons are Hemispheres?," *British Journal for the Philosophy of Science* 27 (1976), 73–78.

(B) Neither person after the split is the original, which ceased to exist at the splitting. In its place, two new persons emerged that bear a close similarity to the original. The original person was indivisible; it did not survive the brain split. Consider, finally, a more speculative option.

(C) Perhaps what appear to be two persons are actually two different ways the original person becomes embodied. Prior to the operation you have the unity of experience that typically attends your conscious life, but afterwards you have two distinguishable spheres of conscious experience and activity. Imagine that the post-operation "people" are to be called by your first and middle names, with Alice taking up residence in New York and Beatrice in London. What might it be like for you to have these two embodiments? Perhaps, as in Price's case of the scattered intelligence, you will find yourself looking out on the world from both places at once, fasting at one place while eating at the other, taking the tube in London while visiting the United Nations. Maybe your visual field would be like a divided movie screen. Now, I think a person may be able to be that spread out. If this is possible, we will be able to reinterpret cases of what seem to be outright divisibility in terms of different embodiments. If this scattered picture is too eerie, A or B may suffice.

Even if it were possible to defend the indivisibility of persons would we have good reasons for abandoning the dual-aspect theory? It is not clear that this is so. Consider a dual-aspect theory which holds that a person *qua* physical object is indivisible in the sense that were it to divide, the person would cease to be. This stand can be built on reasonable assumptions about the relationship between wholes and parts. Given any material thing that has parts, be it a car or island, and split it in two. Do you still have the same material object? Some might say you do, only adding that the object has now been shortened considerably, but, on the other side, it can be plausibly maintained that on a strict, precise notion of "sameness" you do not have exactly the same object. After all, the resulting object lacks half of what you had originally. Moreover, at least under standard conditions, a part of a car is not a car. In lieu of these considerations, it seems that dual-aspect theorists can defend the indivisibility of persons, should they choose to.[13]

It would be possible to distinguish at least three other arguments for dualism: the argument from disembodiment, the argument from doubt, and the argument from body switching, but I opt for bringing together aspects of each under a single heading below.

A MODAL ARGUMENT FOR DUALISM

The reasons I advance for person–body distinctiveness in the modal argument are analogous to those offered earlier for the distinction of mental and physical properties. My reasons for the latter involved various thought experiments in which mental and physical properties get reshuffled. I now want to consider amplified thought experiments that exhibit a sharper distinction between persons and bodies.

I believe it is possible for persons to exist without their bodies and *vice versa*. Our bodies may cease to be without our ceasing to be; we may perish and yet our bodies do not. The argument can be formalized in different ways. This version is cast in explicit opposition to the thesis that a person is his or her body. For ease of exposition I will employ the first person. Let "A" refer to me and "B" to my body.

(1) A is B (the hypothesis of the identity materialists).
(2) A cannot exist without B and B cannot exist without A.
(3) But A can exist without B and B can exist without A.
(4) Therefore premise "1" is false; it is not the case that A is B.

This reasoning may be termed the modal argument because of its concern with identifying what can and cannot occur; "modal" is a term many philosophers employ when referring to whether something is possible, necessary, or impossible, for example the proposition "$7 + 5 = 12$" enjoys a necessary

---

[13] Roderick Chisholm makes this move in various places, identifying the self with some "very small part of the body." Note his analysis of the most promising theories of the mind in "Keith Lehrer and Thomas Reid," *Philosophical Studies* 60:1, 2 (September–October 1990), 33–38.

modality, whereas the modal status of the proposition "There are nine planets" is contingent, for though it happens to be true, it might have been false. The modal argument here appeals to the apparent possibility of person and body separability. I review the argument by first providing a brief account of the premises.

Premise 1 is simply a bald statement of materialism. If I exist and materialism is true, then I am identical with my body. The force of the argument which follows is not altered if we restrict the scope of the materialist claim to my being identical with simply a part of my body, the brain, for example, or with some small object in the brain. Later I consider whether materialists need to be committed to such a strong identity statement.

Premise 2 is an instance of the indiscernibility of identicals principle that was introduced in Chapter 1. According to this principle if A is B, then whatever is true of A is true of B. At first glance, the principle seems unassailable. Surely if something is true of A, but not B, the two cannot be identical. Supposed counter-examples to it often stem from confusing ways of referring with the referent, failing to make clear what "A" and "B" stand for. Consider the objection: Red is *rouge* is *rot* is *ruber*. These are all identical color-adjectives, and yet it is not the case that what is true of each individually is true of the others. Two consist of three letters, and two of five. The problem here is readily alleviated once it is made clear that *if* our concern is with the identity of words as terms in a language, then we should not agree that "red" is *rouge*, and so on, for such an agreement would amount to asserting the evident falsehood that the English term is a French term which is the very same thing as the German and Latin terms. We should not agree with this because of the principle of the indiscernibility of identicals itself, for something is true of the term "red" which is not true of *rouge*. Were the two identical, whatever is true of the term "red" would be true of *rouge*. Once our concern is what "red" *et al.* refer to, we can agree that the referent of these terms is identical, and it is because only one thing is picked out that we may treat the terms as synonymous color-adjectives. In the modal argument, I am not proposing that "A" stand for the word "me" and "B" for the words "my body" to vindicate a peculiarly linguistic dualism (the term "me" differs from the term "my body" because the second has too many letters). Rather, the modal argument is concerned with the identity of myself and my body, the individuals (or individual) themselves (or itself).

Premise 3 does not assert that I ever have existed or will exist without my body, but simply that such separability is possible. A defender of the argument may believe that at no time have persons existed or will exist without their bodies. All the defender need claim is that it is *possible* that I can exist without this body or *vice versa*. The person may be envisaged as surviving the extinction of his or her body either in an altogether disembodied state or as reembodied. If it is possible for me to have a different body – body switching, as it were – then it follows that I am not identical with the body I have now. Of course, many people believe in the actual separation of the person and body at death, and some believe in a prenatal form of existence (most famously in western philosophy, Plato, but this is also widely subscribed to by believers in reincarnation in both East and West). Some believe that there is a kind of disembodiment immediately after death, while others believe in an afterlife in which persons receive new embodiment. This conviction is sometimes shaped by religious teaching, philosophical speculation, and cases in which persons report undergoing disembodiment. Frederick Holland has ably brought together literature from many disparate cultures that report cases of out-of-the-body experiences (often abbreviated to OBEs). There are recurring patterns in descriptions of OBEs taken from Chinese, Egyptian, Zoroastrian, Hindu, Jewish, and Islamic traditions. There are parallels, for example, in reports from the Indian tribes of the Argentine and Bolivian Chaco with *The Tibetan Book of the Dead*, the *Brhad Aranyaka Upanishad*, and the *Apocalypse of Abraham*.[14] Belief in the possibility of disembodiment and reembodiment is certainly not restricted to those in religious tradition. A. J. Ayer, who is not at all

[14] "Life Revisited: Parallels in Death Experiences," *Omega* 9:1 (1978–79), 1–11.

sympathetic with religious belief, concedes: "One can imagine oneself waking to find oneself deprived of any bodily feeling or any perception of one's own body; one can imagine oneself to wander round the world like a ghost, intangible to others and only occasionally visible."[15] And C. J. Ducasse, J. M. E. McTaggart and other nontheistic philosophers have similarly conceded that it is possible for persons to become disembodied. There are many documented cases in contemporary secular Europe and North America in which persons have reported what they take to be OBEs, some of which occurred after severe injury while others are reported under controlled circumstances.[16]

W. D. Hart provides a description of disembodiment worth citing here in which a person becomes disembodied in graduated, sensory stages.

> Imagine first that when you awake, your arm (only) is missing, but it feels (in your phantom arm) just as if your arm were there and against the bedclothes. Your phantom arm drifts through the mattress; but then it feels to you there (in your phantom arm) just as if your arm were there among the bits of stuffing in the mattress. Indeed, when your phantom hand drifts (drifts because we have not got as far as action yet) to the surface of your phantom shoulder, there is in each a feeling as if each were there touching the other. Now generalize; instead of a phantom arm, imagine you have a phantom body. The region at least over the surface of which you are sensitive is the relevant region. So the sense of touch could survive in a disembodied person.[17]

Hart goes on to describe ways in which the phantom body could become one's own volitionally, forming a point of reference with respect to material objects. The crucial step in the thought experiment is the separability from one's material body. As it happens, Hart does not think we ever will become disembodied, but he is convinced that such separation is *possible*, and can be imagined in detail.

[15] A. J. Ayer, *Central Questions of Philosophy* (London: Weidenfeld & Nicolson, 1973), p. 124. Ayer later reported having an OBE in "What I Saw When I was Dead," originally published in the *Sunday Telegraph*, 28 August 1988, but reprinted in Terry Miethe and Anthony Flew, *Does God Exist?* (San Francisco: HarperCollins, 1991), pp. 222–228.
[16] See, for example, R. A. Moody's *Life After Life* (New York: Bantam, 1976) and *Reflections on Life After Life* (New York: Bantam, 1978) and notes 40 and 41 below.
[17] *The Engines of the Soul* (Cambridge: Cambridge University Press, 1988), p. 141.

It is not that there is any special problem about whether disembodied people could engage in the higher mental functions. Indeed, belief and desire, thought and emotion, imagining and remembering, rage, envy, pride, and greed, and hope and love, dreaming and planning, and contemplation, musing and reasoning, and so on through the hard-to-survey canon of the higher faculties, the propositional attitudes, none of these seems to us who engage in them to make enough use of the body for there to be any obstacle whatsoever to our imagining ourselves engaging in them when disembodied.[18]

Hart conceives of a very robust personal continuity in this transition.

I note two further contexts which have a bearing on body switching and disembodiment. The first concerns philosophical idealism, the pro-consciousness thesis treated at the outset of Chapter 1. You may find yourself in the same position as many philosophers who reject idealism as a false view of this life and yet believe that it is only contingently, and therefore not necessarily, false. That is, idealism is not an incoherent philosophy even if, as it happens, material objects exist which are not themselves constituted by mental states and activities. If you think you could exist in an idealist universe (imagine that one day God made idealism correct), then you have reason to believe that you are not your material body, for no material object in this world, including your body, could exist under those conditions. Something would then be true of you which would be false of all material objects in our physical world. (If you follow this line of argument you can supply a rather full account of the character of a possible "next life" without having to involve a spooky realm of weird sorts of plasma. After all, you can claim that a "next life" could be just like this one, only as analyzed by idealists. "Could it be," asks H. H. Price, "that these idealist metaphysicians have given us a substantially correct picture of the next world, though a mistaken picture of this one?"[19] He thinks so.)

A second relevant area is ethics. In the course of ethical

---

[18] *Ibid.*, pp. 154, 155. I agree with Hart about the permissibility of there being such sensory life after the metamorphis.

[19] Price's "Survival and the Idea of 'Another World,'" in *Brain and Mind*, ed. John Smythies (New York: Humanities Press, 1965), p. 23.

reflection, we often seek to place ourselves imaginatively in the position of others, trying to imagine how they feel, act, and so on. We seem to be able to project our identity imaginatively in very different ways that require suspending awareness of our own social identities as well as our bodily life. This aspect of ethical reflection draws on something evident in literature: our ability (however imperfectly exercised) to begin at least to think of what it would be like to have been born under very different circumstances, perhaps to have been a different gender or race, to have had different sexual preferences. I do not suggest that the kinds of imaginative exercises here involve imagining actual body switching. If a white male sympathetically adopts the female narrator's point of view in, say, *The Women's Room*, and comes to rethink his patriarchal orientation as a result, has this involved his imagining he has switched bodies with the narrator? This is unlikely, but the ability persons have of identifying themselves with others' points of view, bodies, gender, race, does, I think, suggest (without proving) a contingent tie with our own material identity. The best way to clarify my point is through an illustration.

Consider how ethics and the conceivability of switching bodies are intertwined in Bernard Williams' book *The Problems of the Self*. Williams describes a case of body switching (inspired by a thought experiment of John Locke's) between an emperor and a peasant, but then concludes that such a switch would not be possible. He describes the switch in terms of the transfer of personalities, but this may be thought of as the transfer of persons, so that when the personality of the peasant is "with" (as Williams puts it) the body of the emperor, this amounts to the peasant's coming to have the emperor's body.[20] But however one wants to describe the precise details of body switching, notice the grounds offered by Williams for reaching a skeptical conclusion.

Suppose a magician is hired to perform the old trick of making the emperor and the peasant become each other. He gets the emperor and the peasant in one room, with the emperor on his throne and the

[20] John Locke, *An Essay Concerning Human Understanding*, ed. P. H. Nidditch (Oxford: Clarendon Press, 1975), originally published in 1690.

peasant in the corner, and then casts the spell. What will count as success? Clearly not that after the smoke has cleared the old emperor should be in the corner and the old peasant on the throne. That would be a rather boring trick. The requirement is presumably that the emperor's body, with the peasant's personality, should be on the throne, and the peasant's body with the emperor's personality, in the corner. What does this mean? In particular, what has happened to the voices? The voice presumably ought to count as a bodily function; yet how would the peasant's gruff blasphemies be uttered in the emperor's cultivated tones, or the emperor's witticisms in the peasant's growl? A similar point holds for the features; the emperor's body might include the sort of face that just could not express the peasant's morose suspiciousness, the peasant's a face no expression of which could be taken for one of fastidious arrogance. These "could"s are not just empirical – such expressions on these features might be unthinkable.[21]

The difficulty here seems to be that we cannot imagine a peasant speaking in a witty voice, smiling royally, being arrogant, and the like. But how serious are these barriers? Part of what motivates social change is imagining cases of role reversal in which the emperor and peasant do switch places, and one imagines what it would be like to speak with a different voice, to possess different features, to be less arrogant, and so on. Consider again the important role literature has played in effecting these changes when a colonialist contemplates the world from the standpoint of an indigenous people and the like. As C. S. Lewis writes in *An Experiment in Criticism*, one of the impulses to appreciate great literature is the fact that "we want to see with other eyes, to imagine with other imaginations, to feel with other hearts, as well as our own."[22]

If we are able to establish that 3 is indeed possible, then the conclusion, 4, follows from 1 to 3 taken together.

To clarify the nature of the argument further consider the following objection. Let A stand for Clinton and B for the 42nd President of the United States. Clinton is the 42nd President of the United States, yet it is possible for Clinton to exist and the 42nd President not exist. We can imagine that Clinton lost the election, for example, or we can imagine that the US govern-

---

[21] *Problems of the Self* (Cambridge: Cambridge University Press, 1973), pp. 11,12.
[22] In *An Experiment in Criticism* (Cambridge: Cambridge University Press, 1961), p. 137.

ment collapsed after the Bush administration and there is no 42nd President whatever. It appears, then, that the argument falters, for a case can arise in which A is B and yet it is possible for one to exist without the other. Could it also be the case that persons and bodies are identical and yet one exist without the other?

One way to avoid this difficulty involves the introduction of a distinction between direct and indirect reference. Roughly, an expression is used in a direct fashion when it is employed to assert of a particular thing that it has a given property. Thus if I point towards you and assert of you, " *That* person is the tallest spy," I am identifying you as a particular individual. Onlookers will still believe I am referring to you even if, as it happens, you are not the tallest spy because Boris in Istanbul is taller by an inch. This form of reference is sometimes called *de re* (literally: of the thing) reference, in contrast with what is called *de dicto* reference. *De dicto* reference is less direct. I refer to Boris *de dicto* or through a dictum, a proposition or descriptive sentence, when I report "The tallest spy is harder to hide than the shortest spy." Have I referred to Boris? Indirectly yes. But I may thereby refer to him without having any idea of where or who he is. If the title " 42nd President of the United States" is used in a *de dicto*, indirect fashion, then the critic is correct and the argument will need revision. But if employed in a direct *de re* fashion, the critic is mistaken. I say something false in claiming that Clinton can exist and that that person, the 42nd President, not, if by "the 42nd President" I designate the actual person "Bill Clinton" and not "whoever happened to be President after Bush." By construing our modal argument along direct-reference lines we avoid much of the criticism leveled against arguments like it.

Because of this, Sydney Shoemaker's criticism of a version of the modal argument similar to the one advanced here does not apply. Shoemaker concedes as a general truth (at least for the sake of argument) the thesis that a person can exist disembodied, but he insists that it does not follow "concerning any particular thing that it is possible that it should become disembodied. If it asserts any possibility at all, it asserts the possibility that there could be a person who undergoes disembodiment – and it is entirely compatible with the possibility of this that all actual persons should be essentially embodied and so incapable of becoming disembodied. "²³ To suppose otherwise is "like supposing that from the fact that there could be someone who could beat the current heavyweight boxing champion of the world it follows that I could beat the current heavyweight boxing champion of the world."²⁴

Shoemaker's point is well taken, but not as an objection to the *de re* or direct-reference form of the argument developed here. If it is true that I can exist and *this* body not exist, then it follows that I am not this body. The difference between this argument and the one Shoemaker criticizes is that it operates in terms of ascribing modal properties directly to me and this body. So, the modal argument does not go from:

(X) There could be someone who exists without any body
or
(X*) There could be someone who beats the current heavy-weight boxing champion
to
(Y) I can exist without a body
or
(Y*) I could beat the current heavyweight boxing champion.

Rather, the modal argument may be recast in the opposite direction. Because (Y) I can exist without a body, therefore (X) someone can exist without a body. Y entails X, just as Y* entails X*, but not *vice versa*.

The modal argument is therefore clearly distinguishable from versions of the so-called argument from doubt frequently criticized in introductory philosophy texts. Critics have argued that it does not follow from (L) I can doubt whether I am a material body, and (M) I cannot doubt that a material body is a material body, that (N) I am not a material body. These critics correctly point out that this is no more valid than the following parody: (L*) I can doubt whether you robbed the

²³ Sydney Shoemaker and Richard Swinburne, *Personal Identity* (Oxford: Basil Blackwell, 1984), pp. 142, 143.   ²⁴ *Ibid.*, p. 243.

bank, and (M*) I cannot doubt that the masked man robbed the bank, therefore (N*) you did not rob the bank. Sadly, unknown to me, you could still have committed the crime. Rather, the modal argument employs *de re* reference attributing to me certain properties (for example being able to exist without this body) that my body cannot have (for example surely this body cannot exist without this body).[25]

Having endorsed this direct-reference version, I note that the modal argument can be deployed without direct reference in a plausible fashion under one condition. If I am justified in believing that all material objects have some essential property and I can plausibly deny that I have such an essential property, I can plausibly distinguish myself from all material objects. In Chapter 2 I contended that the analysis of what it is to be a material object is by no means intuitively obvious, though I suggested that spatial extension was a reasonable candidate for an essential property of being physical. It may not be a sufficient characterization of being physical (dream images may be spatial and yet nonphysical), but spatial location or extension is a plausible necessary condition for being physical. This book, for example, is a material object, and it is spatially extended. It is also reasonable to believe that this book is essentially spatially extended. How could it exist and not be spatially extended at all? What would the difference be between annihilating the book and causing it to become spatially unextended? I can think of none. Mountains, stars, and human bodies are like this book in that it is not possible for them to exist and lack spatial location or extension. If I, on the other hand, can exist and not be spatially extended then it follows that I am not this book or any other material object that is essentially extended. Similarly, if one of the other depictions of material objects reviewed in

[25] I should add, however, that arguments for dualism can be developed which appeal to doubt and certainty. The case of the bankrobber would provide reason for thinking there is a distinction between the property being a bankrobber and your other properties, for it is possible to think of you without thinking of your being a bankrobber. Analogously, if I am certain that, say, I am in pain at a given time, and that I can doubt whether I am in any accompanying neural states, at that time, this provides some reason for thinking that being in pain is distinct from being in neural states as the former can be conceived without the latter.

Chapter 2 provides essential features of the physical (perhaps a disjunct like the object is posited by current physics or is publicly accessible or features in mechanistic explanations) and it is plausible that I am not so construed (I can exist even if all the objects posited by contemporary physics do not, and so on), then I can reasonably conclude that I am not a physical object.[26]

Assuming the evidential principle defended in Chapter 2 about strong conceivability, if it seems that one can exist without one's body (either acquiring a new one or becoming disembodied) and if one is not intellectually negligent, then one is *prima facie* justified in believing such a state of affairs to be possible. If the modal argument is successful in providing grounds for dualism when run in the first person, it can be extended to advance the same point with respect to others. It seems to me reasonable to believe that other persons can exist without their bodies (and *vice versa*), and thus it is reasonable to believe that others are not identical with their bodies.[27]

To elucidate the character and force of the modal argument, I critically assess Thomas Nagel's rejection of it. His work

[26] Descartes's argument for dualism involved such an appeal to essential properties. Because he was convinced that he could exist unextended and that extension was an essential property of material objects, he was entitled to conclude that he was not a material object. He did not have to settle the question of whether there really are material objects before concluding that he was not one. Hence, Descartes's argument is not defective through any difficulty with his having to fix *de re* reference to his body, as Bernard Williams seems to think. Cf. *Descartes, the Project of Pure Enquiry* (Harmondsworth: Penguin, 1978), p. 122.

[27] Cf. Shoemaker's comment: "There is no evident incoherence involved in holding that some persons have minimally dualistic natures while others are purely material creatures," in *Reason and Religion*, ed. S. Brown (Ithaca: Cornell University Press, 1977), p. 261. In my schema, if I were to suppose that you were fully and exclusively material, this would be tantamount to supposing that you lacked psychological properties and were not a person at all. Versions of the modal argument can be found in a number of sources. See, for example, Alvin Plantinga's *The Nature of Necessity* (Oxford: Clarendon Press, 1978), Richard Swinburne's *The Evolution of the Soul* (Oxford: Clarendon Press, 1986), Jonathan Harrison's "In Defense of the Demon," in *The Case for Dualism*, ed. J. R. Smythies and J. Beloff (Charlottesville: University of Virginia Press, 1989). See also Michael Slote's *Reason and Scepticism* (New York: Humanities Press, 1970), and George Bealer's "The Logical Status of Mind," in *Midwest Studies in Philosophy*, ed. P. French, T. Uehling, and H. Wettstein (Minneapolis: University of Minnesota Press, 1986). I developed an argument similar to the one developed in this chapter in "A Modal Argument for Dualism," *Southern Journal of Philosophy* 24:1 (1986), 95–108.

documents a peculiar resistance to employing dualist modal intuitions which is not uncommon. I argue that he has failed to appreciate fully the force of the modal argument. Nagel embraces a principle of evidence when it comes to judging what states of affairs are possible in his criticism of another theory, conceptual realism, a principle much like the one I defend in Chapter 2, but he does not appreciate the implications of this principle when it comes to assessing dualism.

Nagel's chief objection to the rationale for person–body dualism is that we have insufficient reason to trust our modal intuitions about persons existing without their bodies. He does not doubt that we do have dualistic intuitions, and he acknowledges the apparent conceivability of disembodiment and body switching. "The migration of the self from one body to another seems conceivable, even if it is not in fact possible"; "the truth of dualism of mind and body is conceivable."[28] But Nagel believes that reliance upon such subjectively apprised thought experiments is unwarranted. "What I imagine may be possible so far as what I know about my nature is concerned, but may not be possible as far as my actual nature is concerned. In that case I will not have imagined myself surviving the death of my brain, but will merely have confused epistemic with metaphysical possibility."[29] Nagel notes what I acknowledge at various points earlier, namely that it by no means follows that a given state of affairs is possible from its appearing to some subject to be possible. I admit that our judgments about what is possible are fallible in the sense of being capable of error, and corrigible in the sense that they are subject to correction. We often proceed philosophically, whether in ethics or metaphysics, with judgments that are by no means infallible or above adjustment in light of additional evidence, so the bare fact that the modal argument is based on corrigible grounds is no decisive mark against it. But at this stage in reviewing Nagel's work I simply underscore his worry that person–body modal thought experiments stem from "delusions of conceptual power."[30] "The apparent subjective conceivability of my moving to a

---

[28] Thomas Nagel, *The View from Nowhere* (New York: Oxford University Press, 1986), p. 33.   [29] *Ibid.*, p. 42.   [30] *Ibid.*, p. 35.

different brain ... seems conceivable, to the extent that it does, only so far as what my incomplete conception of myself tells me; and that isn't a reliable basis for deciding what is possible."[31]

Nagel does not offer a clear alternative to the person–body schema. He certainly does not advance any account of the psychological that would show it to be necessarily anchored physically, i.e. exhibiting a rationale for thinking there cannot be mental life independent of matter. "It may in fact be impossible for a mental event not to have physical properties as well, even though we cannot form a conception of such a necessary link."[32] Whether or not the psychological is anchored necessarily in the physical, Nagel preserves at least a modest dualism in which psychological properties are nonphysical. I argue that Nagel's resistance to modal intuitions is unacceptable given his employment of modal thought experiments in other contexts, chiefly in his argument against conceptual realism.

Nagel opposes a theory of conceptual realism, according to which there are no features of reality that extend beyond possible human conceivability. His principal rationale for rejecting this stance is a thought experiment involving creatures of different degrees of intelligence. He begins with the following observation:

There are plenty of ordinary human beings who constitutionally lack the capacity to conceive of some of the things that others know about. People blind or deaf from birth cannot understand colors or sounds. People with a permanent age of nine cannot come to understand Maxwell's equations or the general theory of relativity or Godel's theorem.[33]

I register a minor caveat before proceeding. I am not at all certain about the force of Nagel's claim about such a nine-year-old's incapacity. Surely nine-year-old Eric may be unable to grasp mathematical theories, to hear or see, given the laws governing our world, but is his inability one that is impossible in some absolute sense such that it is impossible to overcome? Couldn't God give Eric ears, eyes, and enhanced cognitive power? Certainly all sorts of barriers – neurological, anatom-

[31] *Ibid.*, p. 45.   [32] *Ibid.*, p. 47.   [33] *Ibid.*, p. 95.

ical, psychological, and social – may impede our cognitive and affective growth. But the evident reality or likelihood of these barriers would not show the thesis to be mistaken which held that there are no features of reality extending beyond (meta-physically) possible human thought. But placing this worry to one side, I cite the central passage in which Nagel proposes that it is possible we are in a position analogous to the nine-year-olds he envisioned earlier. Imagine:

There are higher beings, related to us as we are related to the nine-year-olds, and capable of understanding aspects of the world that are beyond our comprehension. Then they would be able to say of us, as we can say of the others, that there are certain things about the world that we cannot even conceive. And now we need only imagine that the world is just the same, except that these higher beings do not exist. Then what they could say if they did exist remains true. So it appears that the existence of unreachable aspects of reality is independent of their conceivability by any actual mind.[34]

Nagel defends his thought experiment against conceptual realism by appealing to a principle that if some state of affairs seems to be possible and we have no reason for thinking it impossible, then we are warranted in accepting it as truly possible. We may reasonably believe there can be features of reality extending beyond human intellection because this seems possible to us and we have not been "shown positively" that denial of this claim involves a contradiction. Nagel states his principle as follows: "Unless it has been shown positively that there cannot be such things – that the idea involves some kind of contradiction (like the idea of things that are not self-identical) – we are entitled to assume that it makes sense even if we can say nothing more about the members of the class and have never met one."[35] But if Nagel's argument against conceptual realism goes through, why not the dualist argument as well? In my view, the dualist is just as entitled to make an analogous claim about persons who can become disembodied or can switch bodies, for on Nagel's own admission, these seem to be possible and we have not been "shown positively" that such claims involve any contradiction. If there is any contradiction,

---

[34] *Ibid.*, p. 96.   [35] *Ibid.*, pp. 97, 98.

Nagel has not identified it. As for whether the dualist has confused epistemic and metaphysical possibility, the same charge can be leveled at Nagel's argument. In his own defense he writes: "Naturally the possibility of forming these ideas does not guarantee that anything corresponds to them. But in the nature of the case it is unlikely that we could ever have reason to believe that nothing does."[36] Dualists may assent to Nagel's dictum, merely applying it to their own case.

Let me review briefly how things stand in the argument for dualism. At various points I have drawn on the principle of the indiscernibility of identicals. If X is Y, whatever is true of X is true of Y. In the course of arguing for the distinction between mental and physical properties I employed the principle that: For any property X and any property Y, if I have reason to believe that I can conceive of X without conceiving of Y, I have reason to believe X and Y are not identical. Now, I am considering a specific case in which we are justified in believing something to be possible, a case when a person may exist without her or his body and *vice versa* which, if successful, will justify the belief that there is something true of the person, not true of her or his body, and thus warrant belief in the distinction between person and body. The outcome will amount to a dualism of person and body, not just a dualism of properties, or just a dualism of concepts. The argument has been run in a way that draws upon direct reference to persons themselves, though I have noted earlier how it can be construed in more general terms.

I now consider eight objections to the modal argument for dualism and to dualism itself. Any argument against dualism, to the effect that the theory is unintelligible or otherwise dubious on independent grounds, counts against the argument presented on its behalf. I have emphasized how modal judgments need to be informed by as much background information as we can canvas concerning the states of affairs involved in the thought experiment. Examination of these objections will serve to clarify the modal argument as well as to address some of the deep

---

[36] *Ibid.*, p. 98.

background objections to dualism. In the rest of this chapter I address the following points. (1) The problem of defeasibility and invincible ignorance: Under this heading I consider the limits of our modal intuitions and consider an argument to the effect that the modal argument is of no evidential worth whatever. (2) The modal argument begs the question. It cannot convince materialist philosophers, because they would not grant that persons can exist without their bodies. If they were to believe that they could exist without their bodies, they would not have to be convinced of the truth of dualism. Hence the modal argument does not provide any reason why materialists should abandon their position. (3) Certain conceptions of the person allow that persons are material objects now, but could become immaterial at some future time. Thus, it does not follow that I am nonphysical from the fact (if it is a fact) that I may come to exist without this body or any material body whatever. Materialists may object that I have not taken seriously enough the kind of self–body identity that makes persons material. This will include examining the claim that persons are not identical with their bodies, but composed by their bodies. (4) The thesis that persons are nonphysical leads to intractable problems of identity. After all, how can one individuate nonphysical persons if they lack bodies? (5) Antidualist thought experiments can be constructed with at least as much force as the modal argument favoring dualism. (6) The modal argument for dualism would establish that straightforward physical objects are actually nonphysical or contain nonphysical parts. Against one version of the modal argument, Peter Unger has maintained that it would establish that ships contain nonphysical parts. (7) Dualism conflicts with a coherent, unified theory of evolution. (8) Dualism cannot account for the causal interaction between persons and their bodies.

THE PROBLEM OF DEFEASIBILITY AND
INVINCIBLE IGNORANCE

This objection represents a challenge to what might be termed the optimism of the modal argument. It reiterates a concern expressed earlier (in Chapter 1), but deserves further investigation. In the modal argument we presume a satisfactory understanding of persons and material objects, but isn't our conception of our own identity too thin and fragile to support the weight placed upon it? Consider once again the case of water being H_2O. Surely many can doubt that this identity holds and thought experiments can be constructed in which it appears that water exists and yet H_2O does not. Do these thought experiments provide even a *prima facie* reason for believing that the two are distinct? No. We now know that the identity holds and that such purported imaginary conceiving is of no significance. In the case of arguments about the nature of persons, shouldn't we be more skeptical than ever about taking seriously such imaginary modal scenarios? Colin McGinn has recently advanced an argument to the effect that we should expect our understanding of consciousness and the self to be so limited that we are unable to grasp their connection with the body. In light of this cognitive closure to understanding our nature, modal intuitions are useless. After responding to the water analogy, I outline McGinn's position.

As for the water analogy, I suggest two responses. The first (and the one I prefer) is simply to "hold the line," so to speak. I think if you believe that you can conceive of water and not H_2O and have carefully reviewed the counter-evidence available to you, then you do possess *prima facie* warrant in believing there to be a distinction between the two. Presumably there could be stages in one's education when it seems unlikely that the liquidity of water is due to its micro particles and this initial judgment would not be unwarranted. The judgment is, of course, overridden by scientific findings, but the point is that there was some warrant to override. As I noted earlier, I believe that the apparent conceivability of non-H_2O water (if it is conceivable) may result from some important truths about water and aspects of the physical world. For example, it is possible, or so I believe, for us to experience many of the sights and sounds associated with water without water itself being present. There can be mirages, dreams, and hallucinations in which we may think water is present when it is not. Moreover, even when water is present it has effects which are not identical with its substantive H_2O structure. Consider the bluish appearance of a pool of water. Is the bluish sensory appearing itself H_2O? I do not think so.[37] So, while the thought experiment does not establish that water and H_2O are diverse or provide indefeasible evidence for such a thesis, it does bring to light the genuine fact that certain features we associate with water are not themselves identical with H_2O.

A second reply is more conciliatory. What is involved with conceiving of water without conceiving of H_2O? A hydrogen or oxygen atom hardly admits of easy visual detection, and if asked to imagine either, many people would probably draw a blank. Lacking such a conception, it is difficult for us to follow instructions asking us to imagine two cases, one in which water is composed of H_2O and another in which it is not. The two might be as indecipherable as two identical drawings of a house, one of which is said to be completely empty, while the other depicts a person in a back room which cannot be seen from outside. How would this difference be captured pictorially? Similarly, imagining we first have water *qua* H_2O and then have water *qua* some similar, real or imaginary, elements is nearly as or more difficult to do.[38]

Is the modal case of person and body analogous? I do not think so. In imagining that a person can exist disembodied or that my body could exist without me, I am not imagining some subtle alteration. It may make no difference which drawing of the house depicts which scenario because the presence or absence of the person in the back makes no difference as to how

---

[37] I believe that it is possible that we can be subjected to vast, systematic hallucinations offering as vivid a portrait of the world as we have under ordinary, veridical conditions. I explore the nature and implications of such a possibility in "Imaginary Evil: A Skeptic's Wager," *Philosophia* 21:3–4 (1992), 221–233.

[38] I discuss the difficulties of distinguishing cases in philosophy of mind later under the heading "Antidualist Modal Arguments."

each is drawn, but the possibility of my either receiving a new body or existing without a material body can be illustrated in more positive terms. My having a different body would consist in my ceasing to have the embodying relations I do with my present body and coming to have such integral, embodying relations with a different one. The difference between the water and person–body cases can be brought out by taking note of the enormous amount of parapsychical literature purporting to document cases of disembodiment and body switching. We do not have a similar class of reported incidents in which people claim to see and drink water, discovering that it is not H_2O but XYZ!

While the findings of parapsychology are not something I shall review in detail here, I note that some contemporary physicalists do take it quite seriously as a challenge to their position. D. M. Armstrong writes: "I think it is just possible that evidence from psychical research might be forthcoming that a physico-chemical view of man's brain could not accommodate."[39] And some investigators come close to claiming that the evidence is already in and weighted against physicalism.[40] Because reports of OBEs bring to light a sharp contrast between the house–water cases and the dualist one, I briefly note four ways in which OBE reports can be read and support dualist modal judgments. Putting the options in the first person, an OBE of my own may be read as: (i) I did leave my body *tout court*. My body had no substantial role at the time of my continuing identity and experience; (ii) I did leave my body, but only continued in existence and had the experiences I did because of my body's physiological processes, for example if the body were annihilated, I would not persist outside it; (iii) I

[39] Armstrong, "The Causal Theory of the Mind," reprinted in *Mind and Cognition*, ed. W. Lycan (Oxford: Basil Blackwell, 1990), p. 39.
[40] See John Beloff's "Dualism: A Parapsychological Perspective," in *The Case for Dualism*, ed. Smythies and Beloff and Pamela Huby's "Paranormal Phenomena," in *The Pursuit of Mind*, ed. R. Tallis and H. Robinson (Manchester: Carcanet, 1991). In his biography of Freud, Ernest Jones recalls his surprise to learn of Freud's interest in telepathy. "If we are prepared to consider the possibility of mental processes floating in the air, what is to stop us from believing in angels?," Jones asks, and Freud replies: "Quite so, and even *der Liebe Gott*." *Sigmund Freud, Life and Work* (London: Hogarth, 1952), vol. III, p. 408.

neither fully left the body nor remained integrally embodied but became partially extended, half in and half outside the body, so to speak; (iv) I did not leave the body at all, but only appeared to. I had visual and other sensory experience as if I were outside my body, even though I never budged. If we had evidence of i–iii I believe we would have empirical grounds supporting dualist modal judgments. But even if iv were the preferred way to receive OBE reports, this could still provide the dualist with some support in thinking that a person's existing independent of her or his body is something intelligible and possible. Conceiving of disembodiment is not like imagining there is a square circle or that something could be made up entirely of wood and not made of wood at the same time. Rather, it is something we may positively grasp, and not just weakly conceive.[41]

---

[41] Reports of OBEs are widespread and are often given in great detail, without any dream-like qualities being attributed to them. For a run-down on the literature, see Susan Blackmore's contribution, "Out-of-the-Body Experience," to *The Oxford Companion to the Mind*, ed. R. Gregory (Oxford: Oxford University Press, 1987). In a recent paper to be discussed further below, Dean Zimmerman disparaged the appeal to such OBE reports in support of dualism. "The conceivability of disembodied-seeming experience, is not at issue here, but rather the conceivability of my becoming disembodied. The experiences described as accompanying disembodiment are entirely irrelevant to this question. After all, someone else could have the experience of seeming to remember events in my life, seeming to see my body fall away, and so on, without having been me. Or I might survive as a disembodied amnesiac or perpetual dreamer who never has conscious recollection of events in my embodied life," "Two Cartesian Arguments for the Simplicity of the Soul," *American Philosophical Quarterly* 28:3 (1991), 223. But this seems an odd objection. The challenge of OBE reports is precisely that they do seem to make intelligible sense for the persons describing them, and they are described as occurring to themselves. In the course of my imagining myself to have a *bona fide* OBE, am I imagining myself having this or someone else? I would have thought it to be a case of imagining myself, just as when I imagine myself winning the lottery next year I am imagining myself and not someone who looks like me winning the prize. The fact that someone else might think they were me or that I might have amnesia at some point seems irrelevant. Zimmerman notes: "To really assess the conceivability of my disembodiment, I must consider the state of affairs itself, and not be distracted by the ease with which I can imagine disembodied-seeming experiences" (p. 223). I think the ease of conceiving such experience would not be distracting, but a helpful step in considering the state of affairs which, in first-person terms, would be the metaphysical possibility of my existing in a disembodied fashion. It is worth adding, too, that if I can survive the demise of my body as an amnesiac or perpetual dreamer this will serve to bolster the case for dualism, exhibiting a difference between the person and body. OBE literature does not just chronicle reports: some of it actually offers instructions on how to have OBEs, how to return to your body, and so on. Probably among the more bizarre, but quite detailed and amusing I have come across is *Astral*

Still, the defeasibility objection may not be put to rest, for Colin McGinn has recently advanced an important argument, one implication of which is that our modal intuitions should be discounted in our philosophical understanding of persons. His position can be represented as follows: If there is a necessary connection linking the person to his or her body we will not be able to detect it either through phenomenology or scientific inquiry. Hence the failure to detect it (a failure which Nagel seems to concede as well) should not count as evidence against there being such a necessary connection between person and body. What is the argument, and does it succeed in overturning dual thought experiments based on OBE reports or on other grounds?

McGinn's argument involves much that dualists will initially sympathize with. He opposes eliminativism and at various points underscores many of the reasons I also appeal to in arguing against physicalism. In *The Problem of Consciousness* McGinn writes:

The property of consciousness itself (or specific conscious states) is not an observable or perceptible property of the brain. You can stare into a living conscious brain, your own or someone else's, and see there a wide variety of instantiated properties – its shape, colour, texture, etc. – but you will not thereby see what the subject is experiencing, the conscious state itself.[42]

McGinn also claims that conscious states and brain states causally interact despite the fact that we cannot grasp how this takes place.

How is it possible for conscious states to depend upon brain states? How can technicolour phenomenology arise from soggy grey matter? ... How could the aggregation of millions of individually insentient neurones generate subjective awareness? We know that brains are the *de facto* causal basis of consciousness, but we have, it seems, no understanding of how this can be so. It strikes us as miraculous, eerie, even faintly comic.[43]

Projection: How to Achieve Out of Body Experiences, by J. H. Brennan (London: Aquarian/Thorsons, 1989).

[42] *The Problem of Consciousness* (Oxford: Basil Blackwell, 1990), pp. 10, 11.
[43] *Ibid.*, p. 1.

I address the problem of person–body interaction explicitly at
the close of this chapter where I shall maintain that person–body
interaction is no more or less miraculous and mysterious than
causal interaction between exclusively physical objects. But the
point McGinn goes on to make is that because we ourselves are
incapable of grasping how consciousness and brain interact, we
cannot place any confidence in modal thought experiments
which purport to characterize the relation between person and
body as contingent.

> Disembodiment is a dubious possibility at best ... The reason we feel
> the tug of contingency, pulling consciousness loose from its physical
> moorings, may be that we do not and cannot grasp the nature of the
> property that intelligibly links them. The brain has physical properties
> we can grasp, and variations in these correlate with changes in
> consciousness, but we cannot draw the veil that conceals the manner
> of their connection. Not grasping the nature of the connection, it
> strikes us as deeply contingent; we cannot make the assertion of a
> necessary connection intelligible to ourselves. There may then be a
> real necessary connection; it is just that it will always strike us as
> curiously brute and unperspicuous. We may thus, as upholders of
> intrinsic contingency, be the dupes of our own cognitive blindness.[44]

McGinn's final position is not agnostic but naturalistic, affirming that the person is a physical being.

  McGinn's position is one that is considerably more friendly to
dualism than many we have been examining in earlier chapters,
and, as I have often acknowledged, we do well to be warned
that modal intuitions are not infallible. Still, I think McGinn's
work has actually brought to light good reasons why we should
trust our modal intuitions rather than bury them. The effort he
makes to show that we will never penetrate the mystery of a
necessary relation between consciousness (or person) and brain
may be read as providing reasons for thinking there is no such
necessary connection. To posit such a connection, notwithstanding its being (on his hypothesis) unperceivable and even
inconceivable as necessarily linking consciousness and brain, is
to adopt a position which is, I think, in dire need of evidence. I

---

[44] *Ibid.*, p. 20.

believe McGinn to be correct in noting that "we find it taxing
to conceive of the existence of a real property, under our very
noses as it were, which we are built not to grasp – a property
that is responsible for phenomena that we observe in the most
direct way possible. "[45] I am in agreement with him that there
is a causal link between person and body, but what I want to
know is why we should think this link is noncontingent and
couldn't be otherwise. Isn't the simplest explanation of why we
feel the "tug of contingency," and even feel that there is a
"deep contingency" between person and body, that the relation
truly is contingent? The ground for thinking a relation is
contingent is typically the conceivability (or, ideally, the
actuality) of the relation failing to hold. We can, so I believe,
strongly conceive of the person–body relation being radically
altered, and, on this basis, I propose that the reason why we do
not grasp the necessary tie between person and body is that it is
not there. There *may* be matters that I (along with other dualists
like H. D. Lewis, Plantinga, Swinburne, Harrison *et al.*) am
overlooking in thinking persons and their bodies are contingently linked, but I see no reason McGinn has for thinking so.
If we do have solid independent reasons for believing that
persons are physical and all items in nature are causally linked
by necessary laws, our dualist modal intuitions may be
discredited. In the absence of those reasons, why "rest secure in
the knowledge that some (unknowable) property of the brain
makes everything fall into place"?[46] Hart puts the dualist
stance well in characterizing the defeasible, yet warranted use of
modal judgments when it comes to imagining disembodiment
and body–switching.

No matter what one imagines, there is no guarantee that one has not
overlooked some such important hitch; no matter how closely one
peers at an object, there is no guarantee that one has not succumbed
to some subtle optical illusion. But after a while the absence of
evidence for hitches becomes evidence for the absence of hitches; one
can only take one's best shot by inferring to the best explanation of
what one clearly and persistently seems to see or imagine, namely, that
it is actual or possible.[47]

[45] *Ibid.*, p. 21.   [46] *Ibid.*, p. 18.   [47] *The Engines of the Soul*, p. 29.

Before proceeding to the next objection, note the curious juxtaposition of the positions taken by Foster and McGinn. Both want to tie down the self, but in different ways. Foster holds that a physical self would be too ontologically promiscuous, able to link Mt. Everest and St. Paul's cathedral, while McGinn seems to think an immaterial self would be too cut off, floating recklessly, as it were, above the nexus of natural causes. I do not think either approach is fully satisfactory. I am not as reticent as Foster to recognize the conceivability of peculiar forms of embodiment, but I am more liberal than McGinn with his noncontingent cementing of consciousness among physical forces. As will become apparent in later discussion, I think contingency is something we must take seriously not just in the philosophy of mind but in understanding the cosmos as a whole.

BEGGING THE QUESTION AND NONDUALIST DISEMBODIMENT

I shall consider the second and third objections together. James Van Cleve advances the first objection. He holds that: "no one could be sure that his thinking did not entail his being extended unless he already knew that he was not a body. If so, Descartes' argument would be epistemically circular: it would contain a premise that he would not be in a position to affirm unless he already knew that the conclusion was true ... One must know whether he is extended before he can know whether his thinking entails his being extended."[48] Of course, the modest modal argument I defend would not be epistemically circular because a subject would first have to *know* that she is not extended in order to *know* that her thinking does not entail her being extended. The argument I present concerns *justified belief* and not knowledge claims. But does the modest modal argument require that a person be justified in believing she is nonphysical prior to justifiably believing she could be disembodied or switch bodies? I do not think so.

[48] "Conceivability and the Cartesian Argument for Dualism," *Pacific Philosophical Quarterly* 64 (1983), 41.

We may construct a number of cases in which Van Cleve's thesis is mistaken. A person may justifiably believe she can become disembodied or switch bodies on the basis of being told she can by someone she has found absolutely reliable in the past and has no reason to doubt. Prior to being told this, she may have had no beliefs at all with respect to person–body dualism. On the basis of what appears to be reliable testimony, she might justifiably attribute to herself the property of being possibly disembodied without speculating about its implications for the philosophy of mind. She could also be impressed by OBE reports. Evidence of a parapsychical sort of disembodiment can function as evidence for some dualist understanding of the person, without the person's having to be convinced of the prior truth of dualism.

These moves aside, a more accessible reply to Van Cleve can be mustered by addressing the following objection to the modal argument. Some philosophers hold that persons may become disembodied or spatially unextended notwithstanding the fact that persons are physical objects. D. M. Armstrong, David Lewis, Richard Boyd, and John Pollock have all endorsed the compatibility of dualist modal judgments about possible disembodiment and materialism. Certainly these philosophers do not hold that it is necessary to be dualists prior to accepting the premise that persons can be disembodied. Their thesis seems to belie Van Cleve's charge that someone must be epistemically justified in believing she is nonphysical prior to being justified in believing her thinking does not entail her being spatially extended. These nondualist philosophers who are friendly to dualist modal intuitions purport to harmonize such intuitions with materialism by treating self-reference in an indirect, *de dicto* fashion, by positing counterparts in possible worlds, and by embracing a liberal theory of identity over time. In each case, I think the dualist is warranted in rejecting the physicalist attempt at harmonization, while retaining strong modal convictions.

Armstrong concedes that "disembodied existence seems to be a perfectly intelligible supposition ... Consider the case where I am lying in bed at night thinking. Surely it is logically possible that I might be having just the same experiences and yet not have a body at all."[49] As a functionalist, Armstrong regards these thought experiments as offering good reason to believe that what satisfies the functionalist analysis of the mental might be a nonphysical self. At the beginning of his inquiry, for all Armstrong knows, he could be a nonphysical self that feels pain as a result of skin-tissue damage, which causes his body to withdraw from the source of the damage (i.e. fill the intermediary stage between the functionalist stipulation of the stimulus and response). As Armstrong goes on to argue for a materialist view of the person, he does not hold that what he in fact is (i.e. a material object) could exist in an immaterial fashion. Armstrong thinks that subsequent philosophical work defeats the plausibility such thought experiments might have for building a modal argument.

In reply, I contend that Armstrong's thought experiment admits of a plausible *de re* reading. I see no good reason to claim that in having the reflections Armstrong recounts, I am simply holding that whatever it is that occupies such-and-such a causal role among physical objects could become nonphysical or disembodied. Rather, it seems to me that *I* may exist spatially unextended. I believe with respect to myself that I could be disembodied and thereby attribute a modal property to myself in a *de re*, direct fashion. I do not simply subscribe to a *de dicto* proposition like "Whatever satisfies such-and-such functional analysis could be disembodied." In either case, Armstrong seems to be a philosopher who holds that he could be disembodied without believing that he is not a physical object.

David Lewis also holds that "persons and their bodies are identical" while granting that a person could become disembodied.[50] Lewis analyzes the claim that "a person could exist without his body" in accord with his elaborate metaphysics of possible worlds and his view of persons as aggregates of momentary stages. For Lewis, talk of possible worlds is not just

[49] D. M. Armstrong, *A Materialist Theory of Mind* (London: Routledge & Kegan Paul, 1968), p. 19.
[50] David Lewis, "Counterparts of Persons and their Bodies," *Journal of Philosophy* 68 (1971), 203.

an heuristic device to delineate ways-things-might-have-been or to describe a hypothetical state of affairs. Rather, Lewis believes there actually are possible worlds as spatio-temporal real objects, though none of them are spatially related to our world such that we will ever see them. To take the view that a person is an aggregate of stages is different from holding that a person is an individual who passes through stages. I adopt the latter view. I used to be an adolescent, a conservation aide, I am now an adult, a college professor. According to Lewis, however, I am not an enduring individual who travels from one stage to the next. His understanding of personal identity allows the possibility that the final stage of one's life may consist of a disembodied "ghostly" stage, notwithstanding one's being physical at an earlier time.

I do not think Lewis has successfully by-passed the dualist modal argument discussed here, though I note that he is another philosopher who belies the accusation that no one would believe in possible disembodiment without already presupposing the truth of dualism. The dualist claim as I have presented it, is that a person now has the modal property of being such that she can exist disembodied or switch bodies, whereas no physical object (or physical-object stage) has that property. To block this strategy, Lewis appeals to his possible-world metaphysics and his counterpart theory. He reads ordinary English locutions with ostensible, direct *de re* modal predication in terms of referring to a counterpart of the given object existing in a possible world. Thus, to claim that I could not possibly be a physical object is to claim that I have no counterparts which are physical objects in any possible world. To claim that I could exist without a body is to claim that I have a counterpart that is disembodied. This allows Lewis to acknowledge the ostensible intelligibility of possible disembodied life while all along maintaining that persons in this world are physical objects.

There are a number of difficulties with Lewis' analysis of modal statements. While it would be virtually impossible to do full justice to the sophisticated character of his system of possible worlds in this context, I draw attention to three problem areas.

I suggest that the more problematic the metaphysical equipment Lewis employs to accommodate modal intuitions, the more inviting the dualist interpretation of those intuitions.

(1) Lewis' postulation of possible worlds is at least *no less* puzzling than treating modal predicates of necessity and possibility as primitive features of objects and properties that exist. Why posit possible worlds to explain the existence of possibilities? Indeed, Lewis' positing indefinitely many possible worlds spatio-temporally distinct from ours seems wildly extravagant. Isn't it more reasonable (or at least just as reasonable) to believe that persons and objects have modal properties, like my having the property of being possibly a musician, without this requiring the invocation of Lewis' metaphysics? By suggesting that we treat modal properties as primitive, I do not mean that the possession of modal properties does not admit of *some* explanation. Thus, we could well say that my being possibly a musician is secured, in part, by my having certain other powers. But the fact that some things are possible which never occur does not require locating the possibility in some metaphysical region apart from this world.

(2) It is unclear that Lewis is able to capture what we mean in making modal claims or claims about what is and is not possible. The counterpart relation is not a straightforward identity relation. To say something about my counterpart is not, strictly speaking, to say something about me. When it is reported that I might have been a musician, according to Lewis' theory, I am reporting a truth about a counterpart in another world, not identical with me. This seems wrong-headed to me. Likewise, to say "I could be disembodied in another world" is not to say something true of me, namely that it is metaphysically possible that I could be disembodied, but to say of my counterpart, someone not identical with me, that he is disembodied.

(3) Consider a specific problem with the counterpart relation. This relation is based on resemblance. It becomes problematic for the counterpart theorist to understand satisfactorily what seem to be meaningful claims, such as, "It is possible that I could exemplify all (or most) of your properties, and you could

exemplify mine." The possibility I am imagining here is one in which I resemble you more closely than you resemble me. Conceivably, you could have had my schooling and my intuitions. You might have written this book and I might be reading it now for the first time. This would appear to be a genuine possibility, and yet the counterpart theorist would have a difficult time locating my counterpart as opposed to yours in the respective possible world. If the counterpart relation is all a matter of resemblances, it appears that Lewis could not recognize the possibility I have here identified.[51]

Lewis has sought to address the above problems, but none of the replies seem satisfactory to me. The more problems that arise from treating possible worlds along Lewis' lines, the more attractive it is simply to treat modal properties as primitive and basic, at least in the sense that their intelligibility does not rest upon any extensional treatment of the sort Lewis proposes. I think the dualist may plausibly regard its seeming to her that she can exist independently of her body as her attributing to herself the relevant modal property. She is not thereby referring to her counterpart.

Boyd and Pollock both adopt compositional theories of the person that purport to allow for personal disembodiment. Boyd accepts a physicalist ontology ("all events, processes, objects, and so forth are in fact material") in which persons are only accidentally composed of matter.[52] He admits "the possibility that certain kinds of actual world token mental events, states, or processes might be realized in some other possible world even if the body of the subject no longer exists."[53] He does not want to rule out there being a phenomenal *quale* to feelings that might be preserved for the subject during a radical shift of what constitutes or composes the subject. The so-called plasticity of mental events (the range of items that can compose a mental

---

[51] Kripke criticizes the counterpart theory succinctly in *Naming and Necessity* (Cambridge, Mass.: Harvard University Press, 1980), p. 45.

[52] Richard Boyd, "Materialism without Reductionism," in *Readings in Philosophy of Psychology*, ed. Ned Block (Cambridge, Mass.: Harvard University Press, 1980), p. 85.

[53] *Ibid.*, p. 101. Boyd envisions a physical person becoming nonphysical by having his parts systematically replaced by nonphysical parts (same page).

event) is supposed to be so flexible as to allow full disembodiment. Similarly, Pollock holds that persons are composed entirely of physical objects. While he believes persons are physical entities, he prefers to assert that persons are composed of physical objects rather than that persons are identical with physical objects. He insists that persons are only accidentally composed of physical objects. That is, "it is logically possible that persons might not have been composed of bodies."[54] He writes: "Ghosts and magnetic men are not logical absurdities; although they have no bodies, we would not find it impossible to reidentify them."[55] Neither Boyd nor Pollock analyzes his attribution of possible disembodiment to persons in terms of Lewis' counterpart theory.

My objections to the Pollock–Boyd theory concern two matters: the intelligibility of compositional relations and the identity of persons over time.

(1) The status of the person "entity" (as Pollock calls the person) is far from clear. Both philosophers insist that the person is not identical with his parts. If they did identify the person with his bodily parts, it would be puzzling indeed to believe that the person could survive the destruction of that with which he is identical. Furthermore, they are not committed to claiming that if a person comes to exist in a spatially unextended world, then, *ipso facto*, the person's earlier parts become unextended. That is, they are not committed to believing that if I became spatially unextended tomorrow then the heart, lungs and legs I have now will exist tomorrow as spatially unextended objects. But if the person is not identical with his parts, with what is he identical? Presumably if a person is a physical entity, he is somewhere. According to Pollock and Boyd, it is problematic to claim that I am identical with the physical entity sitting at my desk now. But then how many entities are at my desk? All the individual parts making up my body, plus the body as a whole which is identical with all parts, *plus* the person who is not identical with that whole, but some other thing?

---

[54] John Pollock, *Knowing and Justification* (Princeton: Princeton University Press, 1974), p. 290.   [55] *Ibid.*, p. 288.

It is worth pausing longer on this point. Could it be that persons themselves are not immaterial individuals, but at the same time not the collection of material parts making up their bodies? Perhaps the person may be viewed as a substantial whole in which the individual person is not identical with his fused-together parts. On this schema, the person would be thought of as possessing a unifying form without really possessing any parts at all.[56] If we look at a human as a "mere" parcel of matter, we can think of him as made up of parts. But that is not the only view to take, and if we think of a human being as a functioning living organism we are able to see him as something else. The Pollock–Boyd stance could be spelled out along these lines with the aim of arguing, ultimately, that persons are physical, though not essentially so. If they can secure a sufficiently flexible notion of personhood, perhaps they can have their physicalist view of persons now but allow for conceivable disembodiment later.

I am in complete agreement that the human body is no mere heap, pile, or aggregate of parts. This tenet is important to integrative dualism. I believe that the person and body are integrally related and thus that to view the body as an aggregate of physical objects is to have a partial view of personal identity. But while the dualist accounts for a unitary understanding of the person's bodily life in terms of continuing, integral causation with the person and body functioning as a single reality, how does the revised Pollock–Boyd scheme do so? What is the status of the unifying form that characterizes personal life? Persons are individuals, it would seem, and this is not the kind of being that can be identical with forms. I may be something formed, but how could I be the form itself? This seems as difficult to make out as the view that a person could be a set or process or property. I can be classified as a member of a set or be in process or be characterized by having a property, but it would be considerably more strained to think I as an individual could be the very same thing as a set, and so on.[57] The Pollock–Boyd

---

[56] This approach has historical roots in Aristotle.

[57] Cf. Roderick Chisholm's notes on the philosophy of mind in *Proceedings of the 9th Wittgenstein Symposium*, ed. Chisholm *et al.* (Vienna: Holder-Pichler-Tempsk, 1985).

revised thesis need not identify individual persons as forms, but if Pollock and Boyd see us as individuals with forms, they seem to leave us with an odd kind of dualism of their own. How are we to understand the relation between a person, you, as an individual with a form, and the body you have, conceived of as the material particles that make it up?

Further puzzles arise when we consider their account of continuity.

(2) Pollock and Boyd face difficulties in accounting for personal identity over time. It is, I think, implausible to construe our personal identity over time as something that is constituted differently by different objects. Roderick Chisholm puts the point well. If we accept the legitimacy of compositional relations involving physical bodies that conform to the Pollock–Boyd requirements, is it plausible to countenance this relation for persons? Chisholm thinks not.

The body that persists through time – the one I have been carrying with me, so to speak – is an *ens successivum*. That is to say, it is an entity made up of different things at different times. The set of things that make it up today is not identical with the set of things that made it up yesterday or with the set of things that made it up the day before. Now one could say that an *ens successivum* has different "stand-ins" at different times and that these stand-ins do duty for the successive entity at different times. Thus the thing that does duty for my body today is other than the thing that did duty for it yesterday and other than the thing that will do duty for it tomorrow. But what of me? Am I an entity such that different things do duty for me at different days? Is it one thing that does my feeling depressed for me today and another thing that did it yesterday and still another thing that will do it tomorrow? If I happen to be feeling sad, then, surely, there is no other thing that is doing my feeling sad for me. We must reject the view that persons are thus *entia successiva*.[58]

I believe it is this grasp we may have of our unity and identity that makes the compositional theory implausible. To hark back to our treatment of homunculi in the first chapter, it also brings to light why Dennett's schema is so implausible in which a person is conceptually broken down into varying teams of

---

[58] *On Metaphysics* (Minneapolis: University of Minnesota Press, 1989).

homunculi. Having defended the legitimacy of phenemeno-
logical self-awareness, we may now reinforce Ryle's criticism of
strategies like Dennett's.

Pollock and Boyd believe that persons are altogether physical
now with no immaterial parts and yet may become nonphysical.
It seems wildly implausible that some physical object, this book
or Michelangelo's statue the *Pietà*, could continue to exist if it
ceased to have any physical parts whatever. I myself do not
think it makes sense to suppose that an object like the *Pietà* with
size and shape can survive its loss of all physical parts. Is the case
of physical persons losing all physical parts any easier to
imagine? How is it that persons may survive the shedding of
physical parts unless persons are nonphysical?[59]

Apart from the sheer implausibility of supposing that a
physical object can become nonspatial, there is the problem of
how to account for the identity over time of the person before
and after the physical-to-nonphysical transformation. Let me
develop the point at issue by imagining that a person, Eric,
makes the transformation. There is no spatial continuity
between Eric-cum-physical entity (or Eric I) and post-trans-
formation Eric-cum-nonphysical entity (or Eric II). What
makes Eric II the same person, suitably transformed, as Eric I?
One could appeal to the psychological continuity between Eric
I and II and say that both share beliefs, memories, and the like.
But the psychological criterion of personal identity faces serious
problems that Pollock himself recognizes. For example, it seems
perfectly conceivable that I could lose all my memories and
personal beliefs, then gain new ones, and yet it still be the case
that I was the same person or subject through this change. It
was *I* who underwent this radical interruption of psychological
discontinuity. So what is it in virtue of which Eric II and Eric I
are the same? The dualist can claim that what makes the two
the same is that it is the same individual or concrete thing that
is first integrally embodied with such and such a body and then

[59] I discuss the possibility of physical objects becoming nonphysical again below.
Christopher Hughes has suggested that a coffee pot, a material object, could become
nonphysical in "Two Versions of Immortality," paper read to the Philosophical
Society, Oxford University, Fall 1991. Reasons below against Unger's ship becoming
nonphysical would apply against Hughes' coffee pot.

no longer in such embodiment. But the important point here is
that Pollock and Boyd deny that Eric I is some individual or
thing over and above his physical being and cannot ground the
claim of personal identity by which Eric I and II are linked on
the basis of Eric's being the same substance or concrete thing
throughout the transformation.

This problem is highlighted in Pollock's treatment of body
switching. He believes that it is possible for persons to switch
physical bodies under radical conditions in which no part of the
physical bodies is exchanged. But how could this be? Imagine
that there are twins Miriam and Miriam* who have the same
(twin) memories, beliefs, and desires. They have different
bodies, A and B. One day they switch bodies without any of the
parts (for example brains) of A and B being reshuffled. What is
it in virtue of which Miriam now has body B and Miriam* has
Miriam's former body A? Recall that Pollock avoids a
psychological-memory continuity criterion of personal identity
and, anyway, Miriam and Miriam* are imagined to have
qualitatively twin psychological lives. I believe that the dualist
is able to offer a better account that could differentiate between
a case in which Miriam and Miriam* exchange bodies and a
case in which they do not. The dualist contends that when they
switch, Miriam *qua* nonphysical individual ceases to be integrally embodied with A and comes to be integrally embodied
with B. When they do not exchange bodies, there is no causal
alteration between the individuals. But if we stay within
Pollock's parameters, there does not seem to be any way to
ground the difference between these cases. Note that I am not
claiming that dualism provides good evidential grounds by
which a third person could judge whether and when the
exchange occurs. I only claim that *if* such admittedly bizarre
body switching occurs, dualism can offer an account of what it
is for persons to exchange bodies, whereas it is far from clear
how Pollock's theory can.[60]

[60] For further discussion of such cases, see my paper "Pollock's Body Switching," in
Philosophical Quarterly 36:142 (January 1986), 57–61. A number of materialist
philosophers acknowledge the plausibility of body switching thought experiments,
even if they ultimately reject them as *bona fide* possibilities. Smith's and Jones'
comment is typical. "Consider too the familiar fantasy of finding oneself waking up

INDIVIDUATION

Critics of person–body dualism have held that nonphysical persons themselves cannot be properly individuated. These critics may well agree with me that Boyd and Pollock have an inadequate notion of personal identity when it comes to disembodiment, but disagree with me that the dualist's position provides anything like an acceptable alternative. The objection, then, is that if persons are nonphysical, there is no plausible account of what it is in virtue of which persons are distinct, whereas there is a plausible account of individuation if persons are material. For any concrete, distinct thing that exists, there must be grounds for its distinctness. Therefore there are no nonphysical persons and the dualist account of body switching and disembodiment above only appears to be more intelligible than Pollock's.

Several replies may be advanced. Some dualists try to solve this problem by proposing that nonphysical persons can be individuated on the basis of their causal relations to material bodies. Thus, the difference between two nonphysical persons is accountable on the grounds that they are affected by different physical objects. This may be of some limited help. Perhaps all nonphysical persons are causally linked up with distinct material objects, but of course this thesis leaves us with the

in someone else's body. It is very tempting to suppose that this idea of body-hopping makes sense; indeed, by science fiction standards, it is a very modest fantasy " (Ernest Jones and Peter Smith, *The Philosophy of Mind* (Cambridge: Cambridge University Press, 1986), p. 8). It is interesting to note how dualist accounts of body switching have a bearing in the current dispute between animalists, brain-identity theorists, and reductionists. Roughly, the animalists identify persons with the animal body, brain-identity theorists see persons as identical with their brains, and reductionists identify persons in terms of mental continuity. Reductionists tend to countenance all-out body switching, brain theorists will allow body switching only if it is effected by brain transplants, while animalists resist any such switching. For a look at the dispute, see Mark Johnston's "Human Beings," *Journal of Philosophy* 84:2 (1987), 59–83, and David Oderberg's "Johnston on Human Beings," *Journal of Philosophy* 86:3 (1989), 137–141. In my view, the reductionists are right to think that radical body switching is possible, but the animalists and brain theorists are right that such transfers are not feasible unless there is a substantial individual who continuously serves as the locus of identity. I agree that we need a substantial individual and I agree that body switching is possible; the substantial individual is the nonphysical person.

problem of accounting for how it is that particular material objects are causally linked with certain nonphysical persons. Besides, a Christian theist would be reticent to concede that all nonphysical objects are always causally related to material ones, for God is believed to be nonphysical and to have preexisted the physical cosmos.

Two other replies may seem more useful. One is to insist that all nonphysical objects will differ in terms of some qualitative property or other. A qualitative property is one that can be had by more than one object. So, being round is a qualitative property. Perhaps every nonphysical object is such that it differs from all others in terms of its qualitative properties. There is no person who has precisely the same set of qualitative properties as any other. Unfortunately, this is unlikely to appease the critic, for as our earlier case of Miriam and Miriam* illustrates, it seems possible that nonphysical persons could have identical qualitative properties, sharing indistinguishable beliefs, desires, hopes, and so on. The bare possibility of such duplication may not be worrisome in practice, but its conceivability means that the intelligibility of there being distinct nonphysical individuals depends upon there never being such a duplication.

A second reply would involve conceding that while non-physical persons can share qualitative properties, there will always be at least one nonqualitative property that will distinguish them, a property that philosophers call a haecceity. A property is an haecceity if it is such that only a single object can have it. According to this schema, I have the property of being me (or being Charles Taliaferro), whereas you have the property of being you. An haecceity is a necessary, essential feature of each object: you could not exist without having the property of being you. The existence of haecceities, which some philosophers have referred to as the thisness of objects, has had formidable defenders, most famously Duns Scotus in medieval philosophy; Roderick Chisholm and Baruch Brody have defended haecceities in the current literature. Madell's treatment of the first person point of view, as discussed in the last chapter, highlights some of the appeal in positing some basic private property like individual haecceities. We could accept

the existence of haecceities without going all the way with
Madell on his other points about the privacy of self-awareness.
If there are haecceities, then there will always be a way to
account for the individuation of nonphysical objects even if they
share all the same qualitative properties. Miriam will always
have the property of being Miriam, whereas Miriam* will
always have the property of being Miriam*. Other, outside
observers, may not be able to detect which Miriam has which
property, but this would not threaten the fact that each
individual was metaphysically distinct.

While some of these strategies are promising, I prefer a
slightly different tack. I think there are plausible grounds for
believing that there are haecceities, though these are not, in my
view, strong enough to carry the day fully against the antidualist
attack.[61] I shall argue that even if there are no haecceities, the
problem facing the dualist with individuating nonphysical
persons is no worse than the problem facing the materialist with
individuating material objects. How are two material objects
individuated? There are several possibilities, but here I focus
only upon the two most promising candidates.[62]

The first appeals to an absolute theory of space. According to
this theory, spatial coordinates are characterized as particular
things. Space is not analyzed in terms of material things and
their relations. This seems simply to shift the problem of
individuation from the domain of spatial objects to the domain
of spatial places, locations, coordinates. What makes one spatial
region of absolute space distinct from another? This proposal
does not provide any significant gain of intelligibility. It
ultimately forces the materialist to claim that the difference
between, or individuation of, coordinates is primitive, basic, not
further analyzable. Roughly, something is philosophically basic
if it cannot be analyzed in terms of some other type of entity or
property. If the materialist is compelled to believe that the
difference between spatial-ordinates is basic, I see no reason

[61] For a defense of haecceities, see Roderick Chisholm's *Person and Object* (La Salle:
Open Court, 1976) and Baruch Brody's *Identity and Essence* (Princeton: Princeton
University Press, 1980).
[62] For a fuller treatment of the problem of individuation see my paper "Dualism and
the Problem of Individuation," *Religious Studies* 22 (1986), 263–276.

why a dualist need be embarrassed by claiming that the distinctiveness of nonphysical persons is primitive, basic, not further analyzable. The dualist can elucidate part of what it means to be distinct (Miriam and Miriam* are distinct; that is, the one's thinking X does not *entail* the other's thinking X, the one's passing out of being does not entail the other's doing so) but this simply draws out the implications of being distinct rather than accounts for it. Why should the dualist be required to come up with a deeper account when the materialist lacks one?

Consider an alternate candidate for individuating material objects: spatial relations themselves. Material objects are distinct in virtue of their having certain spatial relations such as being several feet apart.

There are many objections to this thesis, some of which involve bizarre thought experiments in which two distinct material objects occupy the same space. I leave these to one side and press a deeper problem: spatial relations do not *account* for or explain the numerical difference of objects. Rather, it is in virtue of material objects being distinct that they bear spatial relations to one another. Edwin Allaire correctly observed, "Relations – I'll stick with spatial ones – presuppose numerical difference; they do not account for it. The thisness and the thatness of things is presupposed in saying the one is to the left of the other."[63] Obviously the spatial relation of being several feet apart does not have occult properties making the objects of the *relata* distinct. I conclude that this materialist proposal is no more helpful than the earlier one in individuating material objects. Far from accounting for material individuation, the relational theory presupposes it at the outset. Persons, like material spatial objects, can differ *solo numero*, or in number alone, without their distinctness being grounded in deeper facts about their properties or occupying units of space.

[63] Edwin Allaire, "Bare Particulars," in *Universals and Particulars*, ed. Michael Loux (Notre Dame: Notre Dame University Press, 1976), p. 300, and "Relations and the Problem of Individuation," *Philosophical Studies* 19:4, 61–63.

ANTIDUALIST MODAL ARGUMENTS

The dualist modal argument can be turned on its head. While my modal argument rests upon securing the possibility that persons can exist disembodied or switch bodies, some critics have argued that it is equally plausible to believe that it is possible persons are identical with their bodies. The evidential principle employed in my argument may be used in this antidualist argument. If it seems to a subject that he cannot exist without his body and he is not intellectually negligent, then he is *prima facie* justified in believing he cannot do so. An antidualist argument might then proceed: It is metaphysically impossible for a nonphysical thing to exist and there be no spatially unextended individual things. It is possible for me to exist and there be no spatially unextended individual things. Therefore I am not a nonphysical thing. Michael Hooker develops a related argument against Cartesian dualism based on what Hooker claims is Descartes's concession that it is possible that he is a physical object.[64] According to Hooker, Descartes allows that he could exist and no minds exist not identical with physical objects. If this is the case, then Descartes should conclude that he cannot be nonphysical, because a nonphysical thing is essentially nonphysical. Descartes's strategy can thereby be used against him. Dean Zimmerman adopts a similar antimodal stance. Against Swinburne's argument for dualism, which, like mine, subscribes to the possibility of disembodiment, Zimmerman writes: "It is conceivable that I be identical with my body, or some part of it – this is a state of affairs I can imagine easily enough, and with as much clarity and detail as Swinburne's favorite alternative."[65] Zimmerman thinks this renders benign the dualist modal argument. In reply, I make three observations.

First, as an historical *ad hominem* against Descartes, Hooker's argument is unsuccessful, for Descartes does not concede that he

---

[64] Michael Hooker, "Descartes' Denial of Mind–Body Identity," in *Descartes: Critical and Interpretive Essays* (Baltimore: The Johns Hopkins University Press, 1967), pp. 180–181.

[65] "Two Cartesian Arguments for the Simplicity of the Soul," 222.

could be physical. In the *Meditations* and elsewhere he does express uncertainty about whether he is a physical object, but this is different from holding that it is metaphysically possible that he is a physical object. At one point I may be unsure whether 1,567 + 134 is 1,901, but after reflection see it to be impossible. My initial uncertainty should not be read as a belief that it is metaphysically possible that such numbers do add up to 1,901.

Second, imagine that Hooker and Zimmerman are correct and the epistemic principle I have identified can support either dualist or antidualist conclusions. I do not think this removes the warrant a subject may have either in believing she can exist and there be no unextended objects or in believing she cannot do so. The same principle, such as the principle of charity (believe the testimony of others until you have good reason to disbelieve it), can lead different persons to radically different conclusions depending upon who offers them testimony. If I have very good reason to believe that I can exist without this body and even without any physical body whatever (I see nothing contradictory about it, it does not breach any evident philosophical or scientific truth, and I can positively conceive it: perhaps I have even had an OBE, or I have read about others who seem otherwise trustworthy and they report such experiences), then I have good reason to believe that I am not this body or any physical body. If I am in this position, then I am warranted in believing that I could not exist if there were no nonphysical things, for I am myself nonphysical.

Third, I am not sure that the antidualist argument is as easily constructed as critics suppose. Is it the case that, as Zimmerman claims, one can easily conceive of person–body identity? I do not think so. The problem lies in the difficulty of distinguishing a case of identity from a case of integrated dualism.

What is it to imagine (picture, conceive, think) that I am identical with my body or brain as opposed to imagining that I am integrally embodied? At first glance, it seems easy enough. The way to think of yourself as the very same thing as your body is simply to look at your body and think of it as you. Alternatively, you might do the same thing with your brain. It is not clear, however, whether this is enough to secure imagining person–body identity as opposed to integrative embodiment. According to integrative dualism, you constitute a unity such that under almost all conditions you and your body should not be treated differently. To imagine that you are your body will have to involve more than imagining that you are volitionally, sensorily, and proprioceptively embodied. Distinguishing identity from integrative cases will also have to involve more than imagining that if your body perishes you do, for it is perfectly compatible with integrative dualism that persons do not survive the demise of their body. I believe that to picture the person–body identity relation successfully, one must imagine that something could not be the case, namely that it is impossible that the person can become disembodied or switch bodies. It is the identity of person and body that would make it impossible for these to occur. This involves a negative existential proposition of a high order. Now, we can in many instances easily justify our commitment to negative existentials, as when I justify my belief that there are no elephants in the train car which I am riding in now. Given what I know of elephants, I seem to be fully warranted in believing that what I see in the train car excludes any elephants being present. The case is not akin to the house illustration earlier, in which we are unsure which illustration is supposed to represent a house with a person inside. In my view, the dualist modal thought experiments are closer to the elephant ones, while the identity theorists are much closer to the house illustrations. Let me explain.

In the dualist modal thought experiment I imagine existing disembodied or switching bodies, and this involves imagining that something is present and that something is absent. I am present and my former body is not, or at least it has ceased being my body and has become a corpse, for example. Such a state of affairs is not indeterminate between dualism and physicalism; the burden of this chapter has been to argue that it is not compatible with physicalism. To imagine such a state of affairs is to imagine something positive, clear, and determinate, and one which we can specify in terms that exclude the presence of my former body. This is a case more like the elephant. The materialist's imagining his body and the falsehood of dualism is more problematic. How are we to picture the absence of a nonphysical being? On an integrative dualist schema, my existing as a nonphysical individual is compatible with the most thorough embodiment. For the materialist to describe fully a state of affairs which is on a par with the dualist's, the materialist must imagine that what the dualist proposes is impossible.[66]

Is the dualist really at an advantage here? The advantage I propose is that the identity theorist's modal experiment is underdescribed unless it ranges over imagining a host of cases that must be judged impossible, while the dualist advances a positively described state of affairs which requires that we judge it to be possible. If we must weigh with Zimmerman which seems "easier" to imagine, I propose the latter. Consider two objections.

Objection 1: Materialists may protest that dualists are committed to a negative existential judgment of the same magnitude as they are, namely the impossibility of persons existing and there being only physical individuals.

Reply: There is a difference between what is entailed by dualism and what arguments are advanced to support dualism. Obviously, many things can be entailed by the conclusion of an argument which are not part of the body of evidence which lends support to the conclusion. This is what is happening with the dualist argument. If it is true that nonphysical individuals cannot be physical ones, the dualist thesis that persons are nonphysical entails that persons cannot exist when there are only physical individuals. But is the reason why someone accepts the dualist thesis about persons that they see that this is so? Not necessarily. I may be unsure about such a broader issue, but convinced that persons can exist disembodied (switch bodies, etc.). It is because I believe this is possible that I may come to believe something else is impossible. The identity theorist is saddled with a bigger task, for his imagining that he

---

[66] Zimmerman treats the dualist modal thought experiment in a way that collapses the important difference between imagining oneself to be capable of disembodiment and imagining oneself to be nonphysical, p. 223. As I argued in response to Van Cleve, one can well consider and be justified in believing in possible disembodiment without realizing (or even while denying) the link with dualism.

is his body must involve his imagining that the dualist views are impossible, for otherwise he is not imagining a state of affairs that excludes dualism.

Objection 2: The critic may offer the following analogy and line of argument. "In order to know that this page is this page, must I grasp that it could not exist without itself?" The absurdity of answering "yes" brings out the absurdity of the constraints you propose that the materialist must labor under. If materialism is true, then the terms "person" and "body" pick out the very same individual. Surely I do not need to see the claim that I am my body as amounting to the more cumbersome thesis that I cannot imagine my not being my body.

Reply: The analogy with the page needs to be adjusted if it is to fit the case at hand. The way it is described in the objection makes it seem as though I am introducing a complex account of identity statements, as though I claim that it is puzzling to charge that the page is self-identical. I am convinced that there is no reasonable doubt that what I identify as this page is this page. But the case can be altered to bring it somewhat closer to the case for and against dualism. Consider the question of whether "this page" – construed ostensively as designating the specific material object in front of us – is "this page" in which the latter designates something which various philosophers have been disposed to think is distinct, for example: the page as it appears to one in sensory experience or a page time-slice or the proper parts of the page as distinct from the page as a whole. I have not been arguing that to entertain the truth of person–body identity, one must explicitly consider the merits of person–body dualism, as though dualism enjoys an across the board conceptual primacy. A thoroughgoing materialist who thinks dualism is an obvious absurdity may not give dualism any real notice, just as someone who is not tempted by idealism will fail to worry about whether what she takes to be a straightforward physical object is actually a bundle of sense perceptions. Rather, I contend that *if* you grant integrative dualism some initial plausibility as making sense *and then* try to conceive of a case of person–body identity that clearly rules it out, this is not at all easy to do.

NONPHYSICAL SHIPS

Peter Unger has recently criticized a version of the modal argument on the grounds that it generates the absurd conclusion that straightforward physical objects have nonphysical parts.

   Unger's philosophy of persons and consciousness has elements that are somewhat hospitable to dualism. He does not rule out dualism on conceptual grounds, and seems suspicious of there being necessary links between the mental and the physical that are somehow discerned *a posteriori* or by experience. "The physical approach," he writes, "is not offered as any sort of analytic or conceptual truth ... I see no conceptual necessity about our being physical at all."[67] If Unger is hereby making a substantial concession about possible disembodiment or body switching, the modal argument can get off the ground. But he construes the modal argument in the way I represent below as (1a) to (1c), and then objects to it on the grounds that it would also vindicate the argument (2a) to (2c).

(1a) It's not analytically true that I'm a physical entity. So,
(1b) it's not necessarily true that I'm a physical entity. So,
(1c) I have, as an essential part, something not physical.

(2a) It's not analytically true that my ship is a physical entity.
(2b) It's not necessarily true that my ship is a physical entity.
(2c) My ship has, as an essential part, something not physical.[68]

Unger concludes "Like you, I'm ever so confident that (2c) is false, that no ship on earth has any part, essential or not, that's non-physical."[69]

   Unger's argument does not impinge on the modal argument defended here. I have sought to develop the modal argument employing direct reference as opposed to relying on bare analytical, conceptual assumptions. This is a point I raised earlier in replying to Shoemaker's objection to the modal

---

[67] See Unger's "Précis of 'Identity, Consciousness and Value'" and "Reply to Reviewers," *Philosophy and Phenomenological Research* 52:1 (March 1992), 150. Although I do not accept Unger's gradualism, there is nothing about integrative dualism *per se* that rules it out.   [68] *Ibid.*, 170, 171.   [69] *Ibid.*, 171.

argument. The modal argument focuses on whether certain persons have certain capacities; is it possible that I could be disembodied? This concerns more than asking whether it is analytically true that I am physical. I have been contending that this seems to be possible, and Unger does not, as I noted, appear to rule this out on grounds of conceptual necessity ("I'm not that confident that I myself have only physical parts") – or on grounds that dualism is otherwise demonstratively false.

With the modal argument revised to a *de re* form, have we succeeded in escaping Unger's charge of absurdity? I have held above in discussion of the *Pietà* that it is implausible to believe that a physical thing can become nonphysical. Given what we know of ships, does it seem plausible that any of them could be physical and then become nonphysical? I do not think so. In support of the premise that it is not analytically true that his ship is a physical entity, Unger notes there would be ships in an idealist cosmos. In such a cosmos, ships would consist in an array of sensory experiences. I agree, and so I agree that it is not necessarily true that if there is a ship then it is a physical entity. That said, consider a material ship in our world. Is it possible for that ship to become nonphysical, to become an array of sensory experiences? I do not think so. Imagine the first stage of transition in which the physical mast is "replaced" by sensory experience. Imagine that the ship otherwise looks the same as before. The sailors still see what seems like a thirty foot wooden mast. I would say that at this initial stage the ship has lost its mast and the sailors are hallucinating one in its stead. How are we to picture coherently the sailors hoisting a material sail up a nonphysical, sense experience? Even if you think the ship survived this mast episode, it would be difficult to imagine that the original material mast could survive a metamorphosis to immaterial yachting.[70]

---

[70] *Ibid.*, 171. My thanks to Peter Unger for discussing these possibilities with me.

EVOLUTION

Does dualism run aground on the shoals of established views of evolution? William Lycan thinks so, and puts his objections as follows:

Evolutionary theory impugns Dualism in reminding us that humans are at least animals, a biological species descended from monimids and from even earlier ape-like creatures by the usual dance of random variation and natural selection. The evolutionary process has proceeded in all other known species by increasingly complex configurations of molecules, grouping them into organs and then into organ systems including brains supporting psychologies however primitive. Our human psychologies are admittedly more advanced, and breathtakingly so, but they are undeniably continuous with those of lower animals (a human infant must grow to mature adulthood by slow degrees), and we have no biological or other scientific reason to suspect that Mother Nature (as subserved by population genetics) somewhere, somehow created immaterial Cartesian egos in addition to all her cells, organs, organ systems, and organisms.[71]

Much of the force of Lycan's objection stems from saddling dualism with the view that only humans have psychological life. As noted in the Introduction, Descartes thought nonhuman animals were shorn of conscious, subjective experience and therefore were not selves ("Cartesian egos"). Interestingly enough, Descartes would have agreed whole-heartedly with Lycan that there was little evidence of any nonphysical ego or self among sub-human organisms.

Because of our close bodily similarity and natural bond with other animals and organisms, it would indeed be peculiar if only we had a psychological life whereas our biological kin did not. Most contemporary dualists resoundingly reject such a constrictive viewpoint. Descartes's stance is seen to be especially

[71] Lycan, p. 3. Smith and Jones also write as though dualists are committed to believe humans "are marked off from the rest of nature by possessing an extra non-physical component," *The Philosophy of Mind*, p. 4. M. Bunge, too, assumes that dualists are in trouble when it comes to evolution. "Dualists do not accept materialistic (biological) explanations in the matter of mind: they cannot admit that molecular changes and environmental factors can act on minds." *Brain and Mind*. Ciba Foundation Symposium chaired by J. Searle (Oxford: Excerpta Medica, 1979), p. 58.

loathsome by animal rights activists. Most dualists today argue for animal, mental life on the basis of our own experience (it is evident that we ourselves have feelings like pain) and the close analogy between our physical constitution and those of other animals. We know that in our own case we are more than physically observable states, the carbon, hydrogen, and so on making up our cellular life. We thereby have sufficient grounds for believing that creatures who are similar to us in constitution and behavior have more as well.[72] Philosophers and environmentalists will differ as to the scope of intelligence and sentience they recognize among nonhumans (it is evident that dolphins, whales, horses, cattle, pigs experience pain, but less obvious whether shrimp do), but they are certainly not committed to believing "Mother Nature" only threw in mental states and selves with the evolving of *homo sapiens*. So, I conclude that dualism is not saddled with conceiving humans as altogether disparate and set apart from natural processes.

As an aside, I note that the evidence for recognizing the full-blooded personhood of some nonhuman animals, cetaceans, for example, is very strong. This is not just a matter of having evidence that they can experience rudimentary mental states like pleasure and pain, but they can love, grieve, envy, and undergo other such feelings and make judgments that comprise being a person.[73]

Lycan's objection from evolution does not, then, effect a non-Cartesian, more robust affirmation of the dualist character of animal life. Still, Lycan's point may be redeployed along different lines. Does dualism falter because the causal mechanisms of evolution cannot produce nonphysical life? Well, what reason is there for thinking that the mental and physical cannot effect each other? Some dualists accept a version of emergent evolution, according to which the creation of certain physical organic stuff brings about the relevant nonphysical life. Some dualists will construe this in naturalistic terms, while

---

[72] Some arguments for nonhuman animal mental life seem to presuppose a dual-aspect theory. This is certainly true of the writings of Peter Singer and Tom Regan. Regan's *In Defense of Animals* (Oxford: Basil Blackwell, 1985) is representative.

[73] See, for example, Peter Dobra's "Cetaceans: A Litany of Cain," *Boston College Environmental Affairs Law Review* 7:1 (1978).

others will make appeal to Divine creativity in bringing about consciousness, but in either case Lycan's revised objection only has force to the degree that we think mental–physical interaction is philosophically suspect.[74] If we have no reason to reject such interaction, it is difficult to see how the current evolutionary accounts must militate against dualism.

INTERACTION

How can something nonphysical causally interact with something physical?

Those who endorse the thesis of person–body interaction customarily reply to this query with a simple response, namely that it is a fact that the mental and physical *do* causally effect each other and this fact is no more or less mysterious than the causal relations we find in other, exclusively physical, contexts. This has been the approach of C. J. Ducasse, H. D. Lewis, A. C. Ewing, Richard Swinburne, and John Foster, among others, and it is one I shall follow.[75] The physicalist critic is somewhat hard pressed, I think, to provide evidence that the only causal relations possible are among physical objects. I am not aware of any compelling reason for thinking that nonphysical objects cannot have causal powers; certainly the fact that nonphysical objects like numbers (if they exist and are nonphysical) cannot causally effect material things is no reason to believe that persons (as conceived by dualists) cannot. Numbers are abstract objects, whereas persons are concrete individuals. Some reasons advanced by physicalists to identify necessary features of causal relations do seem successful at identifying what is essential to physical-to-physical relations. Thus, thoroughly physical interaction is marked by all the causal *relata* having some spatial

[74] See *The Self and its Brain* by Karl Popper and John Eccles for discussion on the origin and evolution of consciousness (London: Springer International, 1977).

[75] H. D. Lewis, *The Elusive Self* (Philadelphia: Westminster Press, 1982), C. J. Ducasse, *Nature, Mind, and Death* (La Salle: Open Court, 1951), and A. C. Ewing, *Non-Linguistic Philosophy* (London: Allen & Unwin, 1968). See also C. A. Campbell's *On Selfhood and Godhood* (London: Allen & Unwin, 1957) and Stephen Evans' "Separable Souls," *Southern Journal of Philosophy* 19:3 (1981), 313–331. Kant also held that the mind–body relation was no more mysterious than physical–physical interaction, as did Martin Knutzen before him.

location. But what further reasons are offered for thinking this is an essential feature of all causal relations whatever? The materialist cannot simply charge that evidence is completely lacking for mental–physical interaction, as the weight of this and the earlier chapters has identified some reason for thinking the mental and physical are distinct and, if we follow the precept of trusting appearances until we have strong reason otherwise, it seems that the mental and physical do interact.

Objecting to dualist interaction on the grounds of a closed, deterministic science is less and less plausible given the shift in the scientific community toward quantum theory. Quantum theory insists that atomic and subatomic particles are not deterministically fixed. The interplay of particles is such that more than one possible outcome, motion or event, is possible. Where is the problem, then, in allowing that I as a nonphysical person can bring it about that certain possible, material outcomes occur as opposed to others? Patrick Sherry has recently objected to Richard Swinburne's version of person–body dualism because he feels that Swinburne left it "unclear how human freedom 'plugs into' random movements at the subatomic level."[76] I do not think the fact that there are nondeterministic layers to the physical world illustrates how person–body interaction or human freedom takes place. Rather, the point is that this level of indeterminism recognized by many scientists shows that mental–physical interaction (as well as freedom) cannot be ruled out in the name of an established, deterministic science. We experience ourselves as very much "plugged into" the physical world, and what quantum theory does is to dispel picturing the material world as hermetically sealed off from "outside" forces. We simply do not have decisive reasons for thinking no "outside force" can effect the physical world. I therefore think David Lewis and others are misguided in their strong antidualist orientation.

But if something non-physical sometimes makes a difference to the motions of physical particles, then physics as we know it is wrong. Not just silent, not just incomplete – wrong. Either the particles are caused

[76] Patrick Sherry, review of Swinburne's *The Evolution of the Soul*, *Philosophy* 63 (April 1988), 283.

to change their motion without benefit of any force, or else there is some extra force that works very differently from the usual four. To believe in the phenomenal aspect of the world, but deny that it is epiphenomenal is to bet against the truth of physics.[77]

Compare work by Henry Margenau which does not at all play into Lewis' corner. Margenau's concern here is with the brain but he believes that such indeterminacy is a feature not limited to neural systems.

The physical organ is always poised for a multitude of possible changes, each with a definite probability; if one change takes place that requires energy, or more or less energy than another, the intricate organ furnishes it automatically. Hence, if there is a mind–body interaction, the mind would not be called upon to furnish energy.[78]

John Eccles and others have adopted a similar stance. Of course if physics is explicitly conceived of as providing (ideally) exhaustive descriptions and explanations of all reality, then it is at loggerheads with dualism. But this conception seems to be an articulation of physical*ism*, a philosophical theory (or one version of it) and not an account of physics itself.

Are there features of physical-to-physical interaction which makes it less mysterious or conceptually puzzling than mental to physical interaction? Well, as just indicated, in physical interaction both *relata* have spatial location, and perhaps this provides an important aspect to causal exchange. After all, isn't it clear that the reason why certain material objects affect others (baseballs breaking windows) is material contact? In reply it may first be noted that material contact is not a universally recognized feature of all physical interaction. Indeed the causal effect of some objects on others, the effects of gravitational fields, for example, does not seem to involve material contact in an obvious way. Second, why should spatial contact have causal repercussions? The fact that spatial objects coming in contact

---

[77] D. Lewis, "What Experience Teaches," *Mind and Cognition*, ed. Lycan, p. 513.
[78] Henry Margenau, quoted by Eccles in "Brain and Mind: Two or One?," in *Mindwaves*, ed. C. Blakemore and S. Greenfield (Oxford: Basil Blackwell, 1987), p. 301. See also *Mind, Brain, and the Quantum* by Michael Lockwood (Oxford: Basil Blackwell, 1989), and *The Emperor's New Mind* by Roger Penrose (New York: Oxford University Press, 1989), along with the discussion of the latter book and Penrose's response in *Behavior and Brain Sciences* 13:4 (1990), 643–705.

routinely generates (or constitutes) causal exchange is obvious enough, but why does it do so? Is it because of the objects' mass or volume? If so, why do mass or volume have the causal liabilities and powers they do? Perhaps the materialist may count herself to be in better conceptual shape than the dualist in that the causal powers and liabilities of physical objects are had in virtue of the parts making up the objects. It is problematic to use an analogous appeal to parts in an account of the powers and liabilities of nonphysical persons. As Hilary Putnam once commented: "By virtue of what properties that it possesses is 'consciousness' able to effect Nature in this peculiar way (reducing wave lengths)? ... no answer is forthcoming."[79] But how many answers are forthcoming from the materialist? Salt may have the powers and liabilities it has in virtue of its parts A, B, and C. But what is it in virtue of which A, B, and C have the powers and liabilities they have? Either we shall have to rest with A, B, and C simply having those powers as a brute, not further explainable fact, or we shall have to go deeper by speculating that A has its properties because of its parts D and E, and so on. Eventually all disputants will have to come to a point of claiming that things have certain powers without being able to offer a deeper account or that the physical interaction we observe is accounted for by a mysterious causal chain, containing infinitely many parts, each part of which requires its parts, in turn, to account for its peculiar causal powers. Rom Harré speculates that the terminus of inquiry into the physical world may have to appeal to a "species of entity whose powers are its very nature."[80] None of these options seems demonstrably better than the dualist's positing person–body interaction.

Fortunately, from my point of view, it is no longer quite as fashionable to decree as a matter of conceptual necessity that if something is causally efficacious with respect to the physical world, then that thing is *ipso facto* physical. Douglas Long endorsed such a stand. "If the presence of a conscious entity could so much as deflect the pointer needle of a meter, we could no longer pretend that we understood what was meant by

[79] Hilary Putnam, *Mathematics, Matter, and Method* (Cambridge: Cambridge University Press, 1979), p. 165. [80] "Surrogates for Necessity," *Mind* (July 1973), 375.

denying that such an entity was a species of physical phenomena."[81] The question-begging character of such a position is
now less easy to disguise. The materialist Quine has recently
noted that "the science game is not committed to the physical,
whatever that means," and speculated that explaining certain
events could, in principle, radically widen the margins of what
science is prepared to discuss.[82] "In that extremity, it might
indeed be well to modify the game itself and take on as further
checkpoints the predictions of telepathic and divine in-put as
well as of sensory in-put."[83]

H. D. Lewis ably summarizes the strategy I endorse in his
response to Bernard Williams' criticism of dualism because of its
positing mind–body interaction.

We may indeed admit that there is "something deeply mysterious
about the interaction which Descartes' theory requires between two
items of totally disparate natures, the immaterial soul and ... part of
an extended body" (B. Williams). But it is no more mysterious than
many other things which we find in fact to be the case, and it is
somewhat unfair for this reason to speak of "the obscurity of the idea
that immaterial mind could move any physical thing" (Williams).
"Obscurity" is a mildly reprobative term, and suggests that there is
something which should be made plain. But there is a limit to
explanation and a point where we just have to accept things as we find
them to be. No explanation of ours is exhaustive, and if the world is in
some ways very remarkable, we must accept that too.[84]

More will be said about mental–physical interaction and the
relationship of personal activity and the laws of nature in the
next two chapters. But enough ground has been covered by this
and the first two chapters, I hope, to show that dualism has
considerably greater strength than many of its critics suppose. I
think that none of the eight objections overturn the modal
argument or, more generally, show dualism to be false or
philosophically inferior to materialism.

[81] "Disembodied Existence, Physicalism and the Mind–Body Problem," *Philosophical Studies* 31 (1977), 310.
[82] *The Pursuit of Truth* (Cambridge, Mass.: Harvard University Press, 1990), p. 20.
[83] *Ibid.*, p. 21.
[84] H. D. Lewis, *The Elusive Self*, p. 38. See also John Foster's ingenious case in *The Immaterial Self*, pp. 170, 171.

CHAPTER 4

God and the world

Some claim that God is incorporeal, others that He is
corporeal.

Tertullian[1]

In the first three chapters I argued against a materialist theory
of persons. If successful, this removes an important obstacle to
theistic belief. Jonathan Barnes points out that adopting a
materialist account of persons and retaining a conventional
understanding of the Divine, compels one to conclude that
neither monotheism nor polytheism is true. "If Gods are
persons, then Gods are corporeal. Allow this, and it is reasonable
to assert as an empirical truth that no Gods exist."[2] In arguing
against materialism, I advanced reasons for not dismissing
theism on these grounds. If integrative dualism is plausible,
there is reason to resist the skepticism of Nielsen, Edwards,
Daher, Flew, MacPherson, Rorty, Miles, Kenny, and others
who, like Barnes, link their reservations about the existence of
God with their reservations about dualism. More needs to be
said, however, about theological and ethical reasons for
rejecting dualism and overturning an incorporeal view of God
as a person or person-like reality. It may well be that while
integrative dualism is philosophically defensible, it is religiously
indefensible. Some theologians, convinced of the inadequacy of
dualism, have articulated physicalist notions of both God and
human persons.

---

[1] Tertullian, *Apologeticus*, cited by Stanislaus Grabowski, *The All-Present God* (London: B. Herber, 1954).
[2] Jonathan Barnes, *The Ontological Argument* (London: Macmillian, 1972), p. 84, 85.

I begin with comments on the theological context of this debate.

Christian theological tradition is not uniform in its theory of human nature. There is widespread belief that human persons are made in the image of God, but there is no clear consensus about how this should be analyzed. Dualist anthropologies are well represented, though not always in the form of *integrative* dualism. There are dualist elements, both explicit and implicit, in early Jewish religious literature, but one can also find there and in early Christian theology materialistic notions of the self as well. Some scholars insist that Jewish tradition and primitive Christianity were thoroughly materialist and that any dualist elements are an undesirable import from Greek philosophy, especially Platonism. Some early Christian apologists adopted a corporeal view of persons, as did Tertullian (second to third century), Faustus of Riez (fifth century), and others.[3] The Creeds of the Church can be read as presupposing dualism, but dualism is certainly not an article of faith. The Chalcedonian Creed, for example, uses dualistic language in describing the person of Christ (who is said to consist of soul and body), but, like much credal language, this can be conceptually unpacked in a variety of ways as metaphorical or as culturally bound formulas of what could be explicated in materialist terms, or as "religious" as opposed to metaphysical truths. The Creeds of the Church, then, can be interpreted in ways that do not *explicitly* require their adherents to adopt dualism.

The historical debate in theology over human nature often touches on the same issues that occupy modern philosophy. Medieval theologians worried about individuating immaterial souls, the intelligibility of mind–body interaction, the conceivability of an immaterial reality, and so on. A problem for

[3] David Paulsen builds a case for construing a corporealist understanding of God as very primitive in Christian tradition, *Harvard Theological Review* 83:2 (1990), 105–116.

dualists in the early Christian era and subsequent medieval thought was the arduous task of distinguishing their view from Platonic dualism, a theory closely linked with an array of positions at odds with classical Christianity, including beliefs in the innate immortality of the soul, prenatal existence, and a network of reincarnations according to which souls transmigrate through successive generations. Platonism was also harnessed with belief in a demiurgic, finite deity, the denial of *ex nihilo* creation of the cosmos, and a proud view of philosophy that leaves little room for revelation. Of greatest importance here is the fact that Platonism seemed to vindicate a low view of the body, depicting it as a prison and an impediment to illumination. In contemporary theology and philosophy, many Christian dualists have a similar task of disentangling their stance from a family of views linked with Descartes, including belief in a mechanistic view of nature, a low view of nonhuman animals as machines lacking consciousness, belief in the soul's innate immortality (as in Platonism), and a denigrated view of the body. The dualism that has taken shape in Christian tradition has not always remained free of Platonism and Cartesianism. Because of this, it is easy to sympathize with its critics. Who would not want some alternative anthropology given dualism's occasional role in excessive ascetic theology, Gnostic religious practice, and other-worldly theology with its neglect of this-worldly ethical and political obligations? But while I have sympathies with materialism, my concern is to show how integrative dualism does not fall prey to such theologically unacceptable practices and world-denigrating beliefs.

Historically, Christian tradition has always offered some resistance to the negative aspects of what may be called Platonic Cartesianism. Such resistance has been more pro-matter than pro-materialism. The goodness of the immaterial does not preclude the goodness of the matter. It is common to the vast majority of theologians in the Christian tradition to affirm both the goodness of God and the fundamental goodness of the physical world and material, embodied life. The goodness of matter is often treated as a revealed theological truth (in

Genesis the creation is deemed good) as well as an entailment
from belief in a supremely good God who would not have
created matter if it were of its very nature evil. Witness St. John
of Damascus' injunction: "Do not blame matter, for it is not
dishonorable. Nothing is dishonorable which was brought into
being by God."[4] Belief in the goodness of the material world is
also thought to be secured by the doctrine of the incarnation. As
a perfect being, God could not have assumed a nature that is
inherently evil.[5] Some theologians insist upon the inherent
goodness of matter based on the fundamental precept that all is
good, *omne est bonum*.[6] My aim is not to chart all the details of
these theological projects. To do that would mean including
an examination of the extent to which theologians have
disagreed about the effects of moral evil (especially "the fall")
and sought to reconcile belief in the goodness of matter with an
equally strong conviction that matter can be a vehicle of
destruction.[7] My aim is to observe here that much Christian
theology has historically been opposed to theological and
philosophical systems which construe matter *qua* matter as
inherently evil without embracing a version of materialism
according to which persons are exclusively material. Witness
Irenaeus *contra* the Gnostics in the second century, Augustine
contra the Manicheans in the third and fourth centuries, or,
jumping ahead, William Temple *contra* what he took to be the
excesses of Cartesianism in the twentieth.

Among those typically classified as dualists in Christian
tradition, there are varying degrees of explicit advocacy of a
kind of integrative dualism. Augustine (who followed Plato in
thinking of humans as rational souls using bodies) is often
considered insufficiently integrative, with Boethius doing only a
little better. Athenagoras and Irenaeus understood soul and

[4] Cited in *Deification in Christ* by P. Nellas (Crestwood, N.Y.: St. Vladimir's Seminary
Press, 1987).
[5] There is a good discussion of this and related issues in Etienne Gilson's *History of
Christian Philosophy in the Middle Ages* (New York: Random House, 1955).
[6] See *Being and Goodness*, ed. Scott MacDonald (Ithaca: Cornell University Press,
1991).
[7] For a helpful anthology of some of the more important contributions on the problem
of evil see *The Problem of Evil*, ed. M. McCord Adams and R. M. Adams (Oxford:
Oxford University Press, 1990).

mind to be so interwoven with the body as to place their dualism very close to the dual-aspect theory, though neither was a thoroughgoing materialist. Of the early Christian theologians, perhaps Gregory of Nyssa, Nemesius, Claudianus Mamertus (fourth and fifth centuries), and St. Gregory the theologian (in the seventh century) are among the clearer advocates of an integrative dualism.[8] It may even be queried whether Descartes was as thoroughly non-integrative a dualist as he is made out. Despite the real differences between integrative dualism and Descartes's theory of the mind, he did not utterly forsake the profound unity between soul (mind or person) and body. Commenting on the union of mind and body, he wrote that "to conceive the union between two things is to conceive them as one single thing."[9] Descartes did not want to construe embodiment with the crude analogy of the mind being in the body as a captain is in a ship.[10] So, even if we part company with Descartes, as I believe we should, because of his view of nonhuman animals and so on, he did not utterly ignore the integral unity of personal, bodily life.

Even a brief overview of theological reflection on persons must note the vexed question of where Thomas Aquinas fits into the dualism debate. At many places he may be read as a dual-aspect theorist, but no more. While Augustine fashioned his anthropology in generally Platonic terms, adopting an explicit mind–body dualism, Aquinas fashioned his treatment of persons in extended Aristotelian categories. Aristotle's anthropology was naturalistic and, while one can detect hints of dualism in his philosophy, it was certainly anti-Platonic. Aristotle viewed the soul as the form of the body, and, because the form of the body is neither an individual nor substance, this would seem to clinch a nondualist stance. Where Aquinas parts company from Aristotle, and where I believe he comes closer to integrative dualism, is in contending that "The human soul retains its own

[8] A helpful review of the literature may be found in Margaret Miles' *Fullness of Life: Historical Foundations for a New Asceticism* (Philadelphia: Westminster Press, 1981).

[9] *Descartes, Philosophical Letters*, trans. and ed. A. Kenny (Oxford: Clarendon Press, 1970), p. 141.

[10] See "The 'Scandal' of Cartesian Interactionism" by R. C. Richardson for a helpful analysis of Descartes's position here, *Mind* 91 (1982), 20–37.

being after the dissolution of the body. "[11] The soul "has its own mode of existing superior to that of the body and not dependent upon it. "[12] This represents a departure from Aristotle's schema. It is, rather, in accord with the modal argument presented in Chapter 3 above, for it is partly due to the conceivable separability of soul and body that Aquinas thinks of a human being as "composed of a spiritual and of a corporeal substance. "[13] In effect, Aquinas views our souls as subsistent and intrinsically independent of matter. There is no doubt, however, that Aquinas' strong Aristotelian orientation led him to emphasize that it is the union of soul and body in this life which has sensations, passions, and acts. In Aquinas' view the soul without the body and the body without the soul is not a fully human being. If for Augustine it was vital to impress on his contemporaries that we are more than physical, for Aquinas it was vital to stress our physical reality and the fact that we are not entirely immaterial. Still, Aquinas sought to strike a balance. On my reading, he could follow neither Aristotelianism nor Platonism without serious qualifications about both. Human beings are not exclusively matter, but neither are we exclusively form or soul, taken alone. In all, I believe Aquinas' philosophy of mind is somewhere in the neighborhood of integrative dualism.

Because integrative dualism places such weight on the functional unity of person and body, a decision between dualism and the dual-aspect theory will not affect one's decisions in law, aesthetics, ethics and in a vast majority of cases. In theology, too, I do not think accepting a dual-aspect theory rather than integrative dualism will alter one's views on, for example, Christ's ethic of compassion, the relation between mercy and justice, and many other vital religious teachings. For some theologians, the distinction between dual-aspect and more

---

[11] *Summa Theologica* I. 76. 1.   [12] *Disputed Questions of the Soul*, 14.

[13] *Summa Theologica* I. 75. Aquinas was not alone in this insistence upon the soul as constituting only a part of what it is to be human. Pseudo-Justin Martyr advances a related point. See *The Ante-Nicene Fathers* (New York: Charles Scribner's Sons, 1899), pp. 297–8. I note that Aquinas' insistence upon the soul's survival of biological death puts him somewhat close to the modal-minded dualist, but he would not accept the version of the modal argument as developed in the last chapter.

developed dualist theories is only important when it comes either to articulating a theology of the Divine nature analogous to our own, according to which God and created persons are both regarded as nonphysical, or to defending a conception of the afterlife. On the latter front, witness John Calvin's work *An excellent treatise of the Immortalytie of the soule, by which is proved that the soules, after their departure out of bodies, are aware and doe lyve, contrary to that erroneous opinion of certain ignorant persons who thinke them to lye a sleape until the day of Judgement* (1581). Integrative dualism is well placed to defend the intelligibility of Calvin's view of the afterlife. As A. J. Lyon puts it: "If a 'disembodied soul' is a logical impossibility, then not even God could have 'disembodied souls' 'in' His heaven. Saying this is not denying His omnipotence, any more than saying that He cannot create a circle with the same area as a square."[14]

While dualism has a healthy (though by no means exclusive) representation among Catholics, the Orthodox, and Protestants, it has serious contemporary theological critics, some of whom are prepared to accept exclusively materialist theories of both ourselves and God. In some theological circles, being labeled a "dualist" is almost as bad as being branded a "fundamentalist."

POSTDUALIST THEOLOGY OF HUMAN NATURE

Adrian Thatcher is a representative critic who draws upon both theological ethics and religious doctrine in his case against dualism. This passage ably launches some of his complaints against dualism:

In mind–body dualism, the human body is easily disparaged, because it is inessential to mind and to personal identity. Since, for Descartes, only the mind is conscious, the body is no more than an object, a machine governed by mechanical laws. Deprived of its soul, it is without religious significance. It is often blamed for being the source of sin, without regard for the fact that sins such as pride, malice, uncharity, and so on, if we are to assign sins to the different substances of the person, would have to be assigned to the non-bodily side. In

[14] A. J. Lyon, "Problems of Personal Identity," in *The Handbook of Western Philosophy*, ed. E. H. R. Parkinson (New York: Macmillian, 1988).

Descartes' own method for establishing the certainty of his own existence, other people have no part, self-identity and self-certainty being established in isolation. Our feelings and emotions, essential ingredients of our moral and aesthetic awareness, are untrustworthy because of their bodily origins and are of no philosophical interest. Since only persons have an additional immaterial substance, the rest of creation is void of religious significance.[15]

Thatcher charges that the shift in contemporary scientific theory about matter has opened the door for a religiously healthier, nonmechanical but holist understanding of the person.

First, a brief observation on the significance of scientific theorizing. Like Thatcher, I welcome elements in contemporary scientific theory, and I agree with Thatcher about the importance of recent work in quantum mechanics. However, whereas Thatcher assumes that a mechanist view of matter makes dualism appear plausible, I think a mechanist view of matter has been the reason why many have rejected dualism. It has been the background assumption to the charge that dualism is unable to account for nonphysical mental events (persons, souls, minds) causally interacting with the physical world. Once mechanism is given up, dualism is somewhat less easy to reject out of hand, for it becomes more difficult to insist that the physical world forms a fully determined, closed system.

Thatcher's more important criticism of dualism focuses on ethical, social, and religious values at stake and can, I believe, be met only by distinguishing different versions of dualism. It is surely possible to be a dualist and to disparage the body, to distrust our emotional and aesthetic sensibilities, to treat the nonhuman natural world as having no religious worth, and to promote an isolated conception of selfhood void of social dimensions. Indeed, historically Gnosticism and Manicheanism represent movements which are subject to some of Thatcher's critique. There have been dualists who shunned bodily life, as did the third-century philosopher Plotinus. The historian Porphyry records that Plotinus never celebrated his birthday

[15] Adrian Thatcher, "Christian Theism and the Concept of a Person," in *Persons and Personality*, ed. A. Peacocke and G. Gillett (Oxford: Basil Blackwell, 1987), p. 185.

because he regretted the joining together of his soul with a material body! Epictetus so denigrated the body that he depicted the human person as a small soul carrying around a cadaver. Theologians who inherited a body-denigrating dualism seem to warrant the charge of somatophobia (fear of the body). Clement of Alexandria (d. 213) had such difficulty reconciling a negative view of the body with belief in the incarnation that he denied that Christ digested food and defecated! Because of such vexed aberrations, it is not surprising that critics of dualism often suppose that it is twisted, ethically and metaphysically. Fergus Kerr's account of dualism, like Thatcher's, portrays the dualist as enwrapped in epistemological solitude and treating living bodies as though they were mere masks. In *Theology after Wittgenstein* Kerr bids theologians to abandon dualistic theories which construe the body as something manipulated from behind.

Despite its checkered history, I want to emphasize that not all forms of dualism fit the Thatcher–Kerr model. Certainly integrative dualism as developed here affirms that, as an embodied being, the person and body function as a single unit. Because the person and body form a unity, it is mistaken to think of the body as "no more than a mere object." The body is an object, but it is an object that constitutes, in part, the embodiment of a person. The integrative dualist needs to eschew all suggestions that the person is a "mere" attachment to an object, as though one's body were an accessory.[16]

I believe critics like Thatcher, Kerr, and Jantzen saddle the dualist with an unduly bifurcated view of what is involved in human embodiment. In the course of Jantzen's sketch of what is amiss with dualist anthropology she maintains that dualism implies it is false, strictly speaking, to claim that you or I do such things as walk or eat apples. Dualism implies that "My body did these things, moved to do them, somehow, by my incorporeal mind."[17] Must dualism have this implication? I

[16] Some of the dangers that arise from seeing the person as an attachment are reviewed by Johanna Hodge in "The Exclusion of Women from Philosophy," in *Feminist Perspectives in Philosophy*, ed. M. Griffiths and M. Whitford (London: Macmillan, 1988).
[17] Grace Jantzen, "Reply to Taliaferro," *Modern Theology* 3:2 (January 1987), 191.

think not. My walking deliberately to buy and eat apples involves more than bodily movement, but surely the dualist does not thereby sever the respective movement from the psychological. Walking deliberately is a psycho-physical event. When I eat an apple, the advocate of integrative dualism can soberly claim that it is I who eat the apple. There is no more reason for the dualist to be bound to disclaim this than for the materialist to be bound to disclaim it on the grounds that, strictly speaking, I did not eat the apple but my teeth did. To isolate the psychological as my contribution is no more plausible than isolating some minute part of the bodily motion involved.

I see no reason why integrative dualism should in any way lead us to disparage the body ethically. Apropos Thatcher's comments, dualists may think of bodily life (and psychological life, too) as a source of sin, but so of course can materialists. If a Cartesian were to blame the body for sin itself, this would seem to rest on a conceptual confusion. If the body itself does not think, how can it have a vain, pompous self-image? It is far more reasonable for a certain type of materialist rather than a dualist to blame his body for pride because, *ex hypothesi*, he *is* his body, and to blame his body is to blame himself.

Must integrative dualism lead to distrusting or denigrating our aesthetic, moral, and emotional lives? Certainly no more so than materialism. According to integrative dualism, aesthetic, moral, and emotional life is integrally bound up with our physical constitution. I assume that if there were any reason to distrust our physical constitution, these reasons would plague materialism as well. Happily, I think there is no serious reason for either dualist or materialist to fall into deep skepticism at this juncture.

Does dualism necessarily promote an inferior social philosophy? Here Thatcher is backed up by other critics of dualism who associate it with an excessive individualism. Frederick Stoutland supports Thatcher's judgment.

It [dualism] puts the human world in individual consciousness, leaving the rest of reality, stripped of its meaning and significance, to the natural sciences. To do this is to conceive of the human world as a collection of individual minds and their experiences, and thus to force a conception of social reality as only a collection of individual minds. No room is left for a genuinely social conception of the social world.[18]

Here, as elsewhere, the chief enemy of many antidualists is a specific form of dualism, in this case Descartes's more than Plato's dualism. Descartes constructed his case for dualism, in part, on the foundation of self-knowledge, and some critics have seen this to have been at once philosophically and politically disastrous.

Does *integrative* dualism underwrite the legacy of individualism and undermine the social world? I do not see why it should. One can be a dualist and readily recognize the ways in which social relations and institutions shape and constitute our self-awareness. In Chapter 2 I argued that dualists can go a long way toward joining the materialist in emphasizing the importance of public language and social setting. There is no incompatibility here, or with dualism and recognizing the existence of social entities such as nations and corporations. In our philosophy of the social sciences I think we need to guard against assuming that to recognize the mental as a distinctive nonphysical realm always leads to individualism and the equally implausible thesis that to reject the nonphysical status of the mental always leads to collectivism and anti-individualism.[19]

The discussion of the public nature of the mental in Chapter 2 has already indicated respects in which dualists can treat the mental (and the person himself or herself) as publicly observable and available to others. They are sometimes accused of being fixed with only a very narrow notion of social meaning. Dualists are supposed to be able to grant only the existence of narrow content for word meaning. A broad view of content in linguistic meaning sees that the meaning of our terms is partly determined by the way the world is; the term "oak" as I use it, for example,

[18] Frederick Stoutland, "Self and Society in the Claims of Individualism," *Studies in Philosophy and Education*, 10 (1990), 108.

[19] See, for example, David-Hillel Ruben's *The Metaphysics of the Social World* (London: Routledge & Kegan Paul, 1985). He employs an argument for social entities analogous in some respects to the modal argument for dualism.

depends on the nature of oak trees and the common pool of knowledge about it. Narrow content concerns only what may be known internally with respect to what we know independently of the world. On this account, the term "oak" used by me would have the same meaning even if there were no oak trees. I sought to show earlier that dualism is not forbidden from taking seriously the public orientation of language. I believe that the most promising direction for dualists in the philosophy of language is to conceive of linguistic meaning as integrating our social *and* individual lives. Michael Polanyi rightly observed how linguistic meaning is cut from the same cloth as our integral psychophysical life. "To use language is a performance of the same kind as our integration of visual clues for perceiving an object … or our integration of muscular contractions in walking or driving a motor car."[20]

The dualist who is also a theist would not buy Stoutland's splintered picture, because if theism is true then the natural world is the result of conscious life in the form of Divine creative agency. The natural world is not "stripped of its meaning and significance" (as though it had both until dualism came around) but recognized as richly valued. The natural world can be recognized as valuable both because of its being the result of God's activity and the Divine omnipresence, *and also for its own sake*. The inherent value of the nonhuman world may reside in the fact that there are many forms of consciousness and sentience other than human as well as in the value of living, nonsentient things like plants or entire ecosystems like a rain forest. The truth of dualism does not entail that these are of no moral, aesthetic, or religious interest.[21]

The recurring problem with adopting dualism is the assumption that to adopt a dualism between person and body commits one to other positions quite distinct from it, almost as

[20] *Knowing and Being* (London: Routledge & Kegan Paul, 1969), p. 193. Because integrative dualism can take on board a public dimension of linguistic meaning it is not prey to Lynne Baker's anti-Cartesian mediation in *Saving Belief* (Princeton: Princeton University Press, 1987).

[21] A dualist could well accept Robin Attfield's view of the inherent value of nonsentient life forms. See his "The Good of Trees," *Journal of Value Inquiry* 15 (1981), 35–54, as representative.

though if you adopt a dualism between person and body, then *ipso facto* you are committed to accepting a host of other views, including "dualisms" between humans and nature, reason and emotion, fact and value. Carolyn Merchant explicitly ties mind–body dualism in with the project of dominating nature, capitalism, the maximization of self-interest, environmental exploitation, and the denigration of women.[22] On the contrary, I believe that one can adopt integrative dualism and reject all these associates and adopt socialism, an environmental ethic that insists upon biospherical equality, and uphold the unity of fact and value, reason and emotion, humans and nature. It is telling that the outlook of many indigenous peoples who are applauded as having environmentally friendly outlooks as opposed to more western dominance–submission hierarchies did distinguish between persons (or spirits, minds, souls) and bodies. One can make a case that a form of integrative dualism has been held in Native American religions that many in the environmental movement applaud.[23] In brief, you can be an integrative dualist and adopt versions of Marxist, radical, or liberal feminism depending upon your theory of value and gender. As for the ethics and politics of gender, there is nothing essentially patriarchal about integrative dualism.[24] One may hold that there is a radical difference between male and female that is biologically constituted, as some feminists wish to do, or construe the distinction as entirely socially constructed, or reject it as having no currency, upholding ideals of androgyny in its stead.

Before turning to Thatcher's additional theological objections, consider the complaint lodged earlier that dualism treats the body as a mask. It is worth noting that some materialistic identity and dual-aspect theorists may meet up with a similar

---

[22] See Merchant's contribution to *Radical Environmentalism*, ed. Peter List (Belmont: Wadsworth, 1993).

[23] See J. B. Callicott, *In Defense of the Land Ethic* (Albany: State University of New York Press, 1989) in his defense of Native American ecologically sensitive ethics over against criticism by Tom Regan and others.

[24] In the language of ecofeminist Karen Warren, my thesis is that the distinction between person and body can be made in "non-oppressive contexts," "The Power and Promise of Ecological Feminism," *Environmental Ethics* 12 (1990), 125–146.

complaint insofar as they identify the person as part of the brain. Be that as it may, I think the dualist can account for the fact that the body is not a mask, but that it can function as one. Masks may serve to disguise our true feelings, hiding from others our shame or pleasure. Some persons are able to turn their faces into a kind of veil that effectively camouflages their emotions. A mask can also serve to accentuate and express one's true feelings, as when I don a cheerful mask at your party when I am, indeed, feeling cheered. Perhaps it is no wonder that our English word "person" is derived from the Latin *persona*, meaning a mask used by a player. But the integrative dualist will want to insist that we can distinguish a mask from a person's body. Masks do not admit of the kind of sensory and volitional immediacy that marks the embodying relations mapped out earlier. To wear a typical mask is to cover one's face, using a physical covering which is not part of one's sensory, proprioceptive, emotional, or volitional embodiment. Thus, when I feel shame the mask does not turn red, though my face will; when I smile the mask's expression does not change; the mask is not sensitized like my skin, for when I feel the heat of a flame with my skin, I do not feel it with my mask, and so on. Things may get trickier if we imagine technologically sophisticated masks. Imagine I have severely burned my face and a mask is surgically implanted, providing me with a full layer of skin to which my nerve endings are attached, allowing me to feel with this "mask," and have all the other embodying relations. Under such conditions, I think we should hesitate to call this new addition a mask and instead think of it as my having a new face.

Of course in raising the mask objection critics like Kerr are not supposing that dualists cannot tell the difference between their faces and the masks you buy in a store. Their worry is that dualists make the body into something *much more like* a mask than it actually is. Some hyper-Cartesian dualists do wind up with a problem here in which the body seems altogether remote from one's personal identity. If dualism can fall foul here, so can materialism. Different forms of materialism may also be used in alienating the individual from her body. Consider, for example, a collectivist political culture which construes your body as being owned by the state or tribe, all of this being founded on a materialist understanding of human nature. I believe that, in part, whether a person treats his body as a mask or something alien can be more a matter of ethics and psychology than metaphysics. Consider, for example, Gilbert Ryle's description of the dualist predicament. An integrative dualist will reject this as a metaphysical portrait of the person–body relation, but recognize cases in which persons, either through mental illness or choice or persecution, live as though they are their own prisoners, cut off from the world around them.

> There is immured in a windowless cell, a prisoner who has lived there in solitary confinement since birth. All that comes to him from the outside world is flickers of light thrown upon his cell walls and tappings heard through the stones.[25]

Accepting materialism (of whatever stripe) is no guarantee that one can avoid Ryle's prison.

Consider now some of Thatcher's more specific religious objections to dualism. He charges that "The doctrines of creation, incarnation, resurrection and ascension all favor the nondualist view" of the person.[26] Thatcher argues along two fronts when it comes to creation, one of which involves the appeal to specific Biblical passages which purportedly entail that dualism is false. To investigate the matter responsibly would take us too deeply into an historical study outside the boundaries of this project. I offer only three brief observations: First, Thatcher himself admits that the Biblical testimony is not decisively antidualist. Second, there are Biblical scholars who argue forcefully that a dualist anthropology is assumed in major portions of the Old and New Testaments.[27] Third, Thatcher may be correct that Biblical tradition militates against an extreme dualism of person and body (one involving degradation

---

[25] *The Concept of Mind* (London: Hutchinson, 1949), p. 223.
[26] Thatcher, "Christian Theism," 183, 184.
[27] See, for example, John Cooper's *Body, Soul, and Life Everlasting: Biblical Anthropology and the Monism–Dualism Debate* (Grand Rapids: Eerdmans, 1989). Cooper defends what he calls holist dualism. Essentially this is the view I defend under the title "integrated dualism." I review Cooper's work in the *International Journal for Philosophy of Religion* 35 (1994), 57–59.

of bodily life) and draw the unwarranted conclusion that
Biblical testimony is therefore against all forms of dualism. I
believe that Biblical testimony is compatible with integrative
dualism, though not the somatophobia of some ancient philosophy. Compare the Biblical description of the body as a temple
as opposed to thinking of it as a prison, as did the ancient
Pythagoreans.

Thatcher's main creation-oriented objection against dualism
is that it unduly blurs the distinction between God and creation.
Dualism presumes that the soul is immortal.

> To say that our souls are immortal is to blur the distinction between
> Creator and creature. What is created, as the biblical passages just
> quoted clearly show (Genesis 3:19, Isaiah 40:6–8, James 4:14), has an
> end as well as a beginning: indeed, the whole point of these images in
> these verses is to draw attention to the brevity of human life, especially
> when compared with the eternal life of God.[28]

As an aside, it is ironic Thatcher complains here about blurring
the distinction between God and created persons, whereas he
elsewhere welcomes a God–world or spirit–matter blurring.
"The blurring of the distinction between spirit and matter also
blurs the distinction between God and the world ... theology is
the better for it."[29] Not all blurring is objectionable, so let us
concentrate on the kind he finds problematic.

It is clear, I think, that Thatcher's criticism, if successful, only
works against forms of dualism which entail that the person (or
soul) is immortal. There is nothing about integrative dualism
per se which entails that persons will survive the death of their
bodies. There are dualists who deny that persons survive bodily
death and others who are agnostic about the afterlife. I subscribe
to the central Christian conviction that there is an afterlife, but
do not see this as unduly deflating a God-creature distinction.
At this juncture perhaps Thatcher is presuming a sharper
dualism between God and creature than I do.[30]

---

[28] Thatcher, "Christian Theism," p. 183.   [29] *Ibid.*, p. 187.
[30] I defend some of the ethical and theological motivations for believing in an afterlife
in "Why We Need Immortaility," *Modern Theology* 6:4 (1990), 367–379. For a
recent, fine treatment of Christian perspectives on the afterlife, see Stephen T. Davis'
Risen Indeed (Grand Rapids, Eerdmans, 1993).

In the final analysis, however, Thatcher's worry does not seem to be that if dualism is true, persons survive death. It turns out that he himself wants to allow for the resurrection of embodied persons, at least in the case of Christ. Thatcher's worry, then, seems to be that characterizing the person or soul as immortal amounts to attributing to it an intrinsic power of surviving death so that death is not survived because of the grace of God operating externally on the soul but because of its innate constitution. Creatures, then, would be immortal on their own steam and not require the grace of God. Such a high view of the soul's (or person's) nature is foreign to classical Christianity and not mandated by integrative dualism. Even when some Christian philosophers have developed theories of the person which characterize survival of bodily dissolution as natural, this is rarely thought of as possible without the accompanying agency and goodness of God.[31]

Thatcher believes that the Christian understanding of the incarnation, Christ's death, resurrection and ascension forms a cumulative case against dualism.

The incarnation of God in Christ is a profoundly materialistic affair which allows the human nature of Christ in its totality – not merely Christ's human soul – to be taken up into the perfect unity of his single Divine Person. Moreover, the resurrection and ascension of Christ seem clearly to exclude dualistic accounts of the human person. The death of Christ was a real and total death, not merely the death of his mortal body. The miracle of the resurrection is precisely that God raises Jesus from the dead, not that he raises Jesus' mortal body and reunites it with his immortal soul. What purpose does the resurrection of Jesus serve, we may ask, if Jesus was not really dead? Was it just to convince the disciples that the bonds of death were forever loosened? Hardly, for if the disciples had believed in immortal souls they would not have required assurance on that point; and if they had needed such assurance, a resurrection miracle would not have provided it; it would merely have created confusion. The ascension of Christ is also rendered superfluous by a dualist account of the person; for the soul of

---

[31] This is certainly true for Leibniz and Thomas Reid. Even Plato in the *Timaeus* refers to the immortality of the soul as something bestowed by God. Bishop Butler's defense of the afterlife may suggest that he attributed undue independence to the soul, but this impression is only sustained if one ignores Butler's overriding treatment of the contingency of the cosmos and God's creative conservation of all that exists.

Christ, being alive after his physical death, would presumably have been capable of returning to the Father without its body. What then is the ascension? A highly visual way of saying cheerio? It is, rather, the return of the transformed, transfigured, glorified, yet still embodied, Christ to the Father... The point is that the theological convictions expressed by the resurrection and ascension narratives make much better sense on the assumption that all men and women are essentially bodily unities, after, as well as before, their bodily deaths.[32]

Non-Christian theists would not be swayed by these considerations, but do these considerations provide Christian philosophers and theologians with overriding reasons to dispense with dualism?

If so, I fail to see that Thatcher has established this. Consider the incarnation first. In treating the incarnation, Thatcher focuses upon its role of uniting the human and divine. This is appropriate, though I assume that any construal of this God–human unity similar to the classical doctrinal picture must preserve some sense in which Christ as the second member of the Trinity preexisted the incarnation. The very term "incarnation," which means to become infleshed, is traditionally employed to refer to the belief that God became embodied as a human being, Christ being both true human and true God. I agree that the incarnation is "profoundly materialistic" in that Christ had a real material body and underwent a thoroughly physical life, albeit this was not an exclusively physical affair. If the person Jesus Christ was exclusively physical and he was identical with the material body he had in the first century, then believing in Christ's preexisting his first-century life would amount to believing that those molecules and their various parts constituting his body preexisted the first century. Presumably the Biblical and the subsequent traditional understanding of Christ's preexistence involves something altogether different.

Some popular nontraditional accounts of the incarnation will not have the burden of making such claims of preexistence intelligible. Thus, if one interprets the incarnation along metaphorical lines (Christ was a living metaphor of God, or an

[32] Thatcher, "Christian Theism," p. 184.

icon of the Divinity) or accepts an adoptionist outlook (Christ was fully human and adopted by God as the person in whom and by whom God would be revealed through the unity of will and purpose), there need be no supposition that Christ as a person predated the first century. Theologians adopting such positions may have other motives for accepting integrative dualism, of course, but will not need to draw on it in their philosophical Christology. It is a different story for defenders of a Christology in keeping with the Nicene and Chalcedonian Creeds.

If we embrace integrative dualism, we do not face at least one obstacle in the way of traditional, Christian views of the incarnation. How is it that God as an incorporeal being could become the very same thing as an exclusively material entity? In the last chapter we discussed the counter-intuitive character of supposing that the physical can become nonphysical. Similar difficulties face supposing that something nonphysical can become physical. If integrative dualism is true and we are nonphysical, albeit physically embodied, the incarnation can be understood as a nonphysical God becoming physically embodied, not God becoming metaphysically identical with a physical object.[33] I fill this out further in the course of considering Thatcher's thesis that religious convictions about the death, resurrection, and ascension of Christ are antithetical to dualism.

Thatcher's comments highlight the fact that a Christian anthropology must, at the very least, embrace integrative dualism as opposed to a more disparate dualism, deprecating the body. Integrative dualism, as I have been developing it here, is in no danger of a cheap view of the body and it can well be employed to elucidate aspects of the incarnation. What it means for Christ to have his incarnate body is for there to be

[33] For a recent treatment of the incarnation, see Thomas Morris' *The Logic of God Incarnate* (Ithaca: Cornell University Press, 1986). It seems to me that dualism best serves Morris' account, providing a basis for him to respond to some critics. Note P. Quinn's review of Morris' *Understanding Identity Statements* (Aberdeen: Aberdeen University Press, 1984) in *Faith and Philosophy* 3 (1986), 471. Patrick Richmond and I offer a defense of the Chalcedonian view of the incarnation in "Language, Truth, and Logos", a book-length manuscript in preparation.

relations much like those we bear to our bodies: Christ's sensory experience and proprioceptive awareness are a function of his bodily organs, nervous system and brain, Christ acts with his hands, and so on. Christ's life is everywhere in Scripture understood as a pyschophysical unity, for Christ experienced the world and acted in and through his body. Viewed in this way, it is natural to see the resurrection and ascension as bodily as well as spiritual events. Christ's physical reality allowed for a personal exchange and contact before and after his death which was continuous, intelligible, and human. Theological dualists who stress mental–physical integration are as well placed as anyone to appreciate Christ's physical presence; they simply insist that Christ's presence was not *exclusively* physical.

There is a tendency in some theological literature to assume that if Christ was embodied, he could not have been incorporeal. Witness David Paulsen's comment: "For if God must be incorporeal, then the resurrected Christ cannot be God."[34] But this collapses the thesis that Christ is incorporeal with the claim that he is disembodied. If integrative dualism is tenable, the resurrected, embodied life of Christ is not at all incompatible with believing Christ to be incorporeal. In light of integrative dualism, one can see that traditional Christianity is not committed to what David Paulsen describes as an incompatible triad (three propositions that cannot all be true), which he represents as:

(i) Jesus of Nazareth exists everlastingly with a resurrected body.
(ii) Jesus of Nazareth is God.
(iii) N (if x is God, then x is incorporeal).[35]

Integrative dualists would not construe the incorporeality of God in a way that entails the conceptual absurdity of God's having a body (whether temporally or everlastingly), any more than they would construe ourselves as nonphysical in a way that would make it conceptually absurd for us to have bodies.

Thatcher's understanding of Christ's death is somewhat puzzling. He insists that this death was "not merely the death of

[34] David Paulsen, "Must God Be Incorporeal?," *Faith and Philosophy* 6 (1989), 76.
[35] *Ibid.*, 76.

his mortal body."[36] Of course, if materialism is true, that is precisely what death will be. Thatcher notes that Christ's death was real and total. Does Christian tradition uphold the view that at the crucifixion Christ's death was total in the sense that Christ was annihilated and ceased to be? Given one form of materialism, the death would not have involved such absolute annihilation because the body did not cease existing absolutely, and, *ex hypothesi*, Christ is his body.[37] I think it unwise to see Christ's death as annihilation for several reasons. Not only is it not mandated by Scripture, but it seems incompatible with the general understanding of death in the contemporary Hebrew culture, which envisioned the person as having some, shadowy, post-mortem existence. Explicit scriptural testimony has it that Christ was not annihilated at death (I Peter). Finally, if Christ is God and God exists necessarily, Christ could not have been annihilated. A necessary being cannot cease to be.

In general, I think the Christian understanding of the afterlife is best served by assuming a dualist view of human nature. It is widely believed in the Christian tradition that persons exist after the destruction of their body and that, at the resurrection, they will receive either a new embodiment or an embodiment that is constituted by their reconfigured, transformed earlier body. The personal life between death and resurrection is often thought of as either disembodied or as some intermediary embodiment (think of Dante's portrayal of the latter in the *Divine Comedy*). These scenarios all assume some form of dualism, for if materialism is true and the person is her body, then the annihilation of the body entails the annihilation of the person. Even if my body is not annihilated, but simply dispersed, it is hard for a Christian materialist to embrace the notion that at biological death individuals exist in personal communion and exchange with God. Imagine that I am this body and that at death my body is scattered throughout the world, perhaps some of it eaten by cannibals who are eaten by other cannibals and who, in turn, are consumed by sharks, and so on. How can it be

---

[36] Thatcher, "Christian Theism," p. 184.
[37] For a review of how materialists conceive of corpses, see *Confrontations with the Reaper* by Fred Feldman (New York: Oxford University Press, 1992).

that I am that dispersed material object that was once my relatively unified body and I am simultaneously in conscious fellowship with God? This would certainly require an imaginative stretch beyond some of the configurations John Foster spells out that we discussed in the last chapter.

Those who believe in an afterlife and adopt a materialist understanding of the person sometimes wind up denying that individuals have any conscious life after death prior to the reconstituting of their original body at the resurrection. Other materialistically minded theists have sought to avoid the latter position (often called mortalism) as well as the difficulties facing a corporeal resurrection (God's having to sort out the molecular constitution of bodies who have died millions of years ago) by maintaining that God recreates persons in a different material form after their original earthly body dies. It is very difficult to embrace this last scenario without being committed to some residual dualism, however, for the scenario supposes that certain things are possible for persons which are not possible for their bodies.[38] My goal is not to rule out all materialist notions of an afterlife: I have been more interested in the prior task of arguing against materialism in general. Still, I believe that materialist treatments of the afterlife face some difficulties, and I have argued that an integrative dualist can believe in an afterlife without at all viewing the body as religiously, aesthetically, and ethically insignificant. Recall that Dante had an exalted view of the body which he hailed as holy and glorious (*la carne gloriosa e santa*), notwithstanding his firm conviction that at death persons receive a different form of embodiment. There is no place in integrative dualism for the supposition that embodiment is *per se*

---

[38] Thus, if one allows that a person may be recreated after passing out of existence, but his original body not, then one is committed to the nonidentity of the person and his body. Perhaps the best-known defense of the afterlife involving a material reconstruction of the body is Peter Geach's *God and the Soul* (London: Routledge & Kegan Paul, 1969). The desirability of dualism as a framework for believing in the afterlife is brought out by the following writers: Jonathan Harrison, "In Defense of the Demon," in *The Case for Dualism* ed. J. R. Smythies and John Beloff (Charlottesville: University of Virginia Press, 1989), p. 59; the exchange between Sydney Shoemaker and H. D. Lewis in *Reason and Religion*, ed. R. Bambrough (Ithaca: Cornell University Press, 1977); Thomas Nagel, *What Does it all Mean?* (New York: Oxford University Press, 1987), the chapter "Death."

somehow religiously unacceptable or of marginal value. Integrative dualists may deem some forms of embodiment better than others, but this is no more amiss than a materialist granting that some material bodies are better than others.

I shall now consider important theological reasons that are raised for rejecting the belief that God is immaterial. P. W. Gooch aptly points out the tension created by rejecting a nonphysicalist view of created persons while preserving a nonphysicalist view of God.

There seems in those who press for materialism a blindness to the implications of their views for the nature of God. They speak sometimes disparagingly of "nonmaterial ethereal substance," as though immateriality were to be unquestionably linked with a vague dissipation of identity and reality, but for them God himself is spirit, supremely real without occupying space.[39]

Something like the quandary Gooch describes may be lurking in the following passage from McGinn's *The Problem of Consciousness*. "God, knowing the details of the hidden structure, can see quite plainly that there are no immaterial substances and the like, and He fully appreciates the nature of the necessities that link consciousness to the body."[40] Well, if God knows there are no immaterial substances, one is left wondering what God could be. Is God a material substance or perhaps some nonsubstance, either material or immaterial? Is the Divine consciousness (if there is one) somehow necessarily linked to a body?

POSTDUALIST THEOLOGY OF GOD

A chief religious objection to the classical portrait of God as an immaterial reality is that it leads to an excessively transcendent view of him. Here and in subsequent chapters I seek to articulate a version of classical Christian theism which takes God's

---

[39] "On Disembodied Resurrected Persons: A Study in the Logic of Christian Eschatology," *Religious Studies* 17 (1981), 211. Note Hilary Putnam's admission in *Renewing Philosophy* (Cambridge, Mass.: Harvard University Press, 1992), p. 1.
[40] *The Problem of Consciousness* (Oxford: Basil Blackwell, 1990), pp. 107, 108. It isn't clear to me that McGinn intends this passage and many other references to God to be taken as making serious ontological claims; theism may be involved here and elsewhere as an heuristic device.

transcendence seriously and yet also insists upon his proximate
indwelling in the world. At the outset I note that classical theists
can go so far as to maintain that the world is very much like
God's body, even though this analogy must be very carefully
hedged.

According to classical theism, the world as a whole is
volitionally and cognitively open to God. God knows of the
cosmos with supreme clarity and can exercise supreme power in
it. As discussed in various places above, embodiment involves a
variety of psychophysical relations including volition and
cognition. The body I have is mine (in part) because of its being
volitionally and cognitively bound up with me. Hence, there is
some analogy between the person–body and God–world relations, an analogy endorsed by many theologians from Augustine
to William of Auvergne. The God–world relationship as
envisioned by Christian theism will not, of course, amount to
being exactly like our relationship to our bodies, because other
embodying relations such as proprioception and reliance upon
sense organs do not obtain in God's relation to the cosmos as a
whole. These do not come into play with God's relation to the
whole cosmos, though they do for the incarnation. So, while
God *qua* the embodied Jesus had eyes, nose, ears, heart, lungs,
and the like, God, apart from this specific incarnation, does not
possess such bodily parts. God does not need to use any parts of
the world as sense organs, limbs, and brain, and God does not
respond to the world in the way we do, with our bodily nerve
endings and spinal cord. Moreover, classical Christian theists
wish to preserve a sense in which creatures act in relative
independence and freedom from God's control. I am not acting
as God's hand or whatnot when I wrongfully assault someone.
These reasons, among others, are sufficient to caution classical
theists about making any unqualified claims that the world is
God's body. Also by way of disanalogy between God and the
world, person and body, the world and God are altogether
disparate insofar as God exists necessarily and the world only
contingently. The very existence of the world is dependent upon
God's conserving creativity. Even granting all this, however,
classical theists may still see the world as constituting a partial

Divine embodiment. The cosmos is expressive of God's creative, conserving agency and is present to God's mind insofar as God knows of its aspects. I therefore do not think it is at all inappropriate to see Divine agency and awareness as constituting a kind of partial embodiment, and I will try to amplify and defend this understanding of God in the chapters that follow, sometimes using the term "integrative theism" to distinguish the version of classical theism I am principally concerned with. Integrative theism is essentially classical theism with an emphasis upon the immanent, ultimately passionate presence of God in the cosmos.

Some recent theology has failed to appreciate how the classical theistic tradition can countenance thinking of the world as the partial embodiment of God. Thus, Grace Jantzen criticizes the classical model on the grounds that "An incorporeal being would be limited to those sorts of activity which do not require a body for their performance."[41] This is an odd qualification. If the reasoning of the last chapter is viable, you and I are incorporeal beings who are integrally embodied. I may be capable of existing without my body, but it does not follow from this that I am limited to acting under such disembodied conditions only. Analogously, why would God's incorporeality prohibit him from using (or having) a body under certain circumstances? It will be useful to lay out in further detail the postdualist theology which critics of the incorporeal view of God have advanced.

I focus first on Grace Jantzen's holism, according to which God and the world are a single reality, and Thatcher's God-as-Being theology. Both align themselves with Christian tradition, though each is critical of the classical God–world relation in which God is envisioned as an incorporeal person-like reality. Consider Jantzen first.

It is difficult to assess what she calls holism, in part because it is not well developed in the literature. It seems closest to what

---

[41] Jantzen, *God's World, God's Body*, p. 106. Jantzen notes in "Reply to Taliaferro" that her intent was not to discredit a nonphysical view of God and humans, but to explore the holist theological alternative, p. 189. Still, it is difficult to read her *God's World, God's Body* without encountering many objections to the nonphysicalist, classical theology: see, e.g., pp. 74, 75, 80–82 especially.

we have been calling the dual-aspect theory. Jantzen wants a material picture of humans and God without outright reduction of the psychological to the material the way eliminative materialists like Churchland envision. Jantzen's philosophy of mind is neither a form of dualism between person and body nor unqualified physicalism. Although she maintains that a person is neither a nonphysical thing nor a whole consisting of a nonphysical thing and a physical thing, Jantzen also states that "it is a mistake to say that a person is nothing but his or her body."[42] Evidently Jantzen holds that persons have both physical and psychological properties. She writes that human consciousness, personality, and feelings "transcend the material world."[43] "A person's thoughts are more than his or her brain processes, and human loves and hatreds more than chemical balances."[44] Persons "cannot be fully described or understood in strictly physiological or mechanical terms."[45] Having secured a dualism of properties here with respect to human nature, she endorses a similar position in her theology of God. She writes that "God is not reducible to the physical universe."[46] In rejecting reductionism, she insists that although God is not incorporeal, God has nonphysical, psychological properties like being loving, being omniscient, being omnipotent, being able to respond to prayers, and so on. Just as my being in pain is not identical with a particular brain fiber firing, God's being in pain is not identical with a particular earth tremor.

Jantzen claims that the parts of the universe are parts of God. Because the universe is composed of matter and energy, God is composed of matter and energy. Unfortunately the precise nature of this divine part–whole relationship is not altogether clear. She denies that it can be understood either in terms of physical laws or solely on the basis of formal mereological (part–whole) relations. Thus she maintains that it is unacceptable "to appeal to materialistic mechanism in giving an account of the transcendence of God."[47] Presumably, then, we cannot account for God's knowledge and love in virtue of some physical, material law of nature. The scientific inquiry that

---

[42] *Ibid.*, p. 142.   [43] *Ibid.*, p. 125.   [44] *Ibid.*, p. 125.   [45] *Ibid.*, p. 125.
[46] *Ibid.*, p. 127.   [47] *Ibid.*, p. 129.

leads us to understand the behavior of macroscopic physical objects in terms of its microstructure will not lead us to account fully for the behavior of God. She likewise does not develop her theology of God by appealing solely to formal mereological relations. She remarks that "it is false that a thing can be no more than the sum of its parts," but this sheds no light upon how it is that God *qua* corporeal reality with divine properties of power and knowledge is related to the corporeal parts making up that corporeal reality.[48] Some mereological relations are straightforward, such as the size and shape of a whole being a function of the size and shape of its parts, but the Divine part–whole relation creates a number of puzzles which Jantzen does not consider, two of which I cite briefly.

Jantzen wishes to avoid a view which identifies God with a finite deity like Zeus. Moreover she claims "Nothing on earth is God or could be God."[49] A serious problem arises for Jantzen as she seems to accept the following two points. (A) The universe, and thus God, can be finite. "If the universe is God's body, then, if the universe is not spatially infinite, God is not spatially infinite."[50] (B) "God could change the shape and contents of the universe in any way he chose."[51] God "can, if he chooses, change his shape and size."[52] If A and B are correct, could not God eliminate all physical objects except this page? If God did this and God is identical with the physical universe, God would be identical with this page. Of course, according to Jantzen's theory, God would not be nothing but this page in a reductionist sense. But this page would be God.

Another puzzle arises about understanding God's identity over time if God and the universe are "one reality" and yet God can radically alter the contents of the universe. If God replaced every object in the universe with distinct physical objects all at once, would God still be the same? Would this involve one God ceasing to be and another coming into being, or would there still be the same God notwithstanding the replacement of all God's parts? Jantzen does not satisfactorily clarify the God–world relation to handle these and other puzzles. The relation of

[48] *Ibid.*, p. 147.   [49] *Ibid.*, p. 12.   [50] *Ibid.*, p. 106.   [51] *Ibid.*, p. 106.
[52] *Ibid.*, p. 107.

God and the parts making up God in Jantzen's theology seem to me at least as mysterious, or more so, than the classical Christian treatment of God and the world. Her repeated appeal to the notion that a thing can be greater than the sum of its parts does nothing to elucidate the problem of identity over time, nor to lend any plausibility to her notion that the world can have the Divine properties she imagines. Surely we would not wish to hold that some statue made up entirely of marble parts (as a whole) could be thoroughly wooden on the grounds that wholes are greater than their parts summed.[53]

A central reason for not identifying God and the world stems from the conviction that the world itself, whether made up of just physical things or mental objects as well, does not exist of necessity. It is this contingency that fuels theistic cosmological arguments. The contingent character of the world has been widely recognized in philosophy, science, and the arts. Early on, William James observed: "The unrest which keeps the never stopping clock of metaphysics going is the thought that the nonexistence of the world is just as possible as its existence."[54] One might well add that it also keeps going much novel writing, music, poetry, and film that explores our contingent character. The contingent status of the cosmos can be brought to light by way of thought experiments, imagining the great realm of mass and energy ceasing to be *in nihilum*. Some contemporary physicists have supposed that mass and energy can and do pass out of existence at certain times. They may be mistaken, but I believe they are depicting something which is logically (or, broadly, metaphysically) possible.[55]

[53] See Bruce Reichenbach's useful discussion of the fallacy of composition in *The Cosmological Argument* (Springfield, Ill.: Charles C. Thomas, 1972).

[54] Cited by J. D. Barrow and F. J. Tipler in *The Anthropic Cosmological Principle* (Oxford: Oxford University Press, 1986), p. 103.

[55] On the contingency of this world, note David Lewis in *On the Plurality of Worlds* (Oxford: Basil Blackwell, 1986), pp. 1, 2. I articulate a version of the cosmological argument in *Contemporary Philosophy of Religion* (Oxford: Basil Blackwell, forthcoming). Versions of the argument are developed by Richard Taylor in *Metaphysics* (Englewood Cliffs: Prentice-Hall, 1974), William Rowe in *The Cosmological Argument* (Princeton: Princeton University Press, 1975), Hugo Meynell's *The Intelligible Universe* (Totowa: Barnes and Noble, 1982), Bruce Reichenbach in *The Cosmological Argument* (Springfield, Ill: Thomas Press, 1972), William Craig in *The Cosmological Argument from Plato to Leibniz* (New York: Barnes and Noble, 1980) and in *The Kalam*

If it is plausible to think of the cosmos as contingent and God as necessary, there are further grounds for rejecting God's identity with the world. Jantzen appears to recognize the contingent character of (at least) much of the cosmos, namely that God can change God's constituent parts of mass and energy. If God is wholly made up of contingent parts, the supposition that God as a whole is necessary or noncontingent strikes me as conceptually strained. Wholes can have properties not possessed by parts, as when a table as a whole weighs fifty pounds whereas none of its parts taken individually does. But this alone cannot license attributing to wholes radically divergent properties not found among their parts. Obviously a whole made up of nothing but wooden parts cannot be nonwood as a whole. It is not at all clear that a world-God can be necessary if all God's constituents are contingent.

Thatcher does not deny God's necessary nature, but his distrust of dualism leads him to distrust the construal of God as a person. Thatcher believes Christianity is best served religiously and philosophically by understanding God as Being, not " a " being and hence not a person. In part this represents a recovery of a rich tradition within Christian theism shared by important figures in traditional Judaism and Islam.[56] Identifying God as *Being* as opposed to a being is intended to underscore God's uniqueness; God is not a member of a species or one of many possible gods. A recent defense of this view by Gary Legenhausen, like Thatcher's, leans heavily on the repudiation of Cartesianism and the supposed implausibility of thinking there can be a nonphysical person.[57] Thatcher employs the Being tradition in his articulation of a Christian theology, insisting that God is not a person and yet God is the ground or cause of the created world including persons.

The Being tradition is complex and impossible to weigh fully in passing. I focus some brief comments principally on Thatcher's version of it. I contend that Thatcher's theology involves

---

Cosmological Argument (New York: Barnes and Noble, 1979) and Richard Swinburne in *The Existence of God* (Oxford: Clarendon Press, 1979).

[56] Philosophers have developed alternative conceptions of Being, from Parmenides and Plato to Aquinas to Heidegger.
[57] " Is God a Person?," *Religious Studies* 22 (1986), 307–323.

its own dichotomy which is at least as puzzling as person–body dualism and conceiving of God as an incorporeal person-like being. In fact, there are reasons for thinking it even more puzzling. Serious doubts can be raised as to whether Thatcher can consistently embrace his Being theology and Christianity.

Thatcher writes: "Although not a being, he [God] is still identifiable, for he can be contrasted with all that he has made."[58] How are the two related? At least with respect to the classical God–world relation we may have some analogy of how God relates to the world in our appreciation of ourselves as nonphysical persons in causal relation with a physical world. There is no comparable analogy with respect to the Being–being relation. What is Being as opposed to beings? How does Being make beings? It is difficult to see one's way clearly in responding to either question. The classical model again has available an analogy in ourselves when we create works of art. Even if the analogy is based on a weak resemblance (God creates *ex nihilo*, but we do not), there is still personal agency involved in both cases. By contrast, there are no unproblematic cases in which we observe Being creating beings. One aspect of the Being–being distinction Thatcher specifies is a respect in which Being *qua* God exists necessarily, whereas beings *qua* you and I exist contingently. "The contrast between necessary being and contingent being is well expressed by the contrast between 'being' and 'a being.'"[59] If the material world is contingent, then God *qua* necessarily existing reality must be distinct from the material world. The same thing cannot exist both necessarily and contingently in the same respects. Thatcher seems to reject one kind of dualism while introducing another.

The questions raised here do not constitute anything like decisive problems with the God as Being tradition, though I think they do exhibit some of the formidable obstacles facing Thatcher's understanding of God. It is puzzling, too, how Thatcher can believe that God is not a person and endorse many traditional claims about God's creativity, love, and so on. Thus, Thatcher believes that: "The fundamental attribute of

[58] Thatcher, "Christian Theism," p. 188.   [59] *Ibid.*, p. 188.

divine existence is love. Divine existence brings into being and nurtures an object for its love in creation, and unites it with itself in redemption."[60] Thatcher is also wont to think of Christian theism as substantiating belief in a personal God even though he thinks God is not a person (the latter claim is part of what he calls the "personalist consensus"). But surely nurturing, loving, and creating are preeminently personal attributes. If these attributes are applicable to God in any substantive sense, we seem far more in line with the "personalist consensus" than the impersonal alternative.

At various points in the literature the debate over whether God is a person is more of a terminological dispute than a substantive one. If you build into your definition of "person" that to qualify as a person one must be contingent, fallible, finite, and the like, then it follows that God (as envisioned in classical theism) is not a person. In this book, I have not been bent on analyzing all the necessary and sufficient conditions for personhood, partly because I do not think that the boundary of the concept is sufficiently sharp. I have assumed, rather, that you and I are persons and am working from there to defend a nonmaterialist reading of subjectivity and selfhood in the course of articulating a theistic world-view.[61] So, I will not try to press Thatcher's thesis too hard by arguing that God is indeed a person, though I do want to preserve the notion that God as traditionally conceived is at least person-like. As noted above, it is not clear to me whether Thatcher can dismiss this person-like character of God to the extent that he does and yet retain much of the core of Christian theism. Having identified this theological concern, I want to adopt a conciliatory stance. I propose that if the Being tradition is vindicated and one wants to hold on to the

[60] *Ibid.*, p. 188. In support of understanding God as a person, see Karl Rahner, *Foundations of Christian Faith*, trans. William V. Dyck (New York: Seabury Press, 1978), p. 73.
[61] The debate over the scope of personhood often takes place on either an abstract or a concrete level. On the abstract side, some philosophers introduce purely conceptual strictures as to what counts as a person (e.g. possessing self-awareness over time, rationality, sensations) while others begin with concrete cases of what they think are clear persons and nonpersons (e.g. competent adult humans yes, snails no) and then devise a theory to handle puzzle cases (e.g. robots). Ideally, I think a methodology that balances each is in order.

metaphorical (analogical) attribution of personal characteristics of God, there is still a role for articulating the coherence of
referring to God as a nonphysical person-like being. If the
metaphorical reference to God as a person-like reality is utterly
unintelligible, it is hard to see how it can be of much use,
however attenuated.

In my judgment classical theism can preserve the insight that
God is a necessarily existing reality and the world contingent
and yet give pride of place to Thatcher's insistence upon the
uniqueness and proximity of God. Because of the contingency of
the cosmos we have reason to believe that God is not identical
with it. But the cosmos can still be understood to be, in
Thatcher's terms, lodged in God's infinite being. Before we seek
to spell out more fully how classical theism can accommodate
such a view, attention needs to be given to a series of additional
arguments against the classical understanding of God as an
immaterial reality. I review five such arguments, the first two
stemming from Jantzen and Gaskin.

THE ARGUMENT FROM DIVINE KNOWLEDGE

Jantzen argues that it is an essential tenet of Christian theism
that God's knowledge of the world be direct and unmediated.
An incorporeal person cannot have direct knowledge of the
external world, states other than himself or herself. "A
disembodied spirit could have direct knowledge only of his or
her own thoughts and feelings; all knowledge of the world
external to him – or herself – would be mediated."[62] Hence,
God cannot be an incorporeal, disembodied person. In contrast,
an embodied, corporeal being may be understood as having
direct acquaintance with her bodily states. "An ordinary
human being has, in addition to direct knowledge of his or her
mental states, direct knowledge of his or her body."[63] By
imagining God to be embodied in the whole universe, she claims
that the theist has a plausible model to understand God's grasp
of the world's states. God's powers of acquaintance are
extraordinarily more powerful than our powers of acquaint-

---

[62] Jantzen, *God's World, God's Body*, p. 80.   [63] *Ibid.*, p. 81.

ance, but God's power is similar in kind to our own. On the other hand, the incorporealist theologian must attribute to God faculties entirely disanalogous with our own and in the face of the counter-intuitive notion that a nonphysical being can grasp what it is to see, feel, smell, and so on, without having sense organs. "Without sensory apparatus, how can he [God] hear our prayers?"[64]

In the whole of our experience, eyes are necessary for sight (materially, if not logically), ears for hearing, a body for touching. Although we are not compelled by strictly logical considerations to say that this must be the case universally, we have no grounds within our experience for thinking that it is not.[65]

Although Jantzen does not herself attribute sense organs to God, she claims that her model of a person's direct acquaintance with bodily states effectively captures what is involved in the Divine direct acquaintance with the world. The ostensibly direct acquaintance we have of the location of our bodily parts does not seem to be mediated by sensory organs like the ears and nose. In response, I note three points.

(A) It is not obvious that Jantzen is correct in claiming that we are directly acquainted with our bodily states. She appeals to the awareness each of us can have concerning the location of our bodies: "I know where my left hand is without looking for it, even if you have blindfolded me and then moved my hand."[66] This seems most plausibly read as mediated by sensory awareness, namely proprioception.

(B) Even if our access to our bodies is direct, why think this means that we are identical with our bodies or that this rules out our incorporeality? There is nothing about dualism *per se* that excludes our having direct access to states other than ourselves. As an aside, it would be strained to hold that if we are directly aquainted with something (X), then X is ourselves or part of ourselves. (Some philosophers claim that we can be directly acquainted with abstract, mathematical propositions without adopting the view that these are somehow part of themselves.)

(C) Jantzen herself admits that God does not have ears, eyes, and other sense organs. Why think, then, that her position has

---

[64] *Ibid.*, p. 73.   [65] *Ibid.*, p. 76.   [66] *Ibid.*, p. 81.

an advantage over the classical one in terms of God's knowledge? She concedes that perception does not logically require any physical organ (hence she does not think God has spatial eyes located around the world). My question is: if a physical organ is not necessary for perception, why think having a physical body itself is necessary? The answer is not clear.

Before considering Gaskin's version of the Divine-knowledge objection, I briefly consider Jantzen's point about sense organs. I agree with her that there are no compelling reasons to believe that sense organs are necessary for God's grasping truths about the world's sensible states. Anthony Kenny offers the following standard analysis of an organ of perception: "A part of the body which can be moved at will in ways which affect the efficiency of the sense in question."[67] What overriding reason is there to suppose that it is absolutely necessary that a person must have a mobile bodily part to have a full range of sensations? Consider one proposal according to which sense organs are necessary because otherwise we would be unable to account for a person's sensations of this room being of this room. It has been argued that for the sensations to truly be of the room there must be causal interaction between the room and resultant sensations. Physical sense organs are the locus for such interaction. If God does have sensations of the world's states, but lacks sense organs, God's sensations of the room are not derived from the causal links that engender the appropriate sensations such as we endure in which light rays hit the retina, and so on. If you add to this the view that sensing is itself a corporeal activity, then we seem bound to recognize that there must be some corporeal object which functions as the vehicle for sensing, hence a sense organ.

I do not find these reasons compelling. Part of the burden of the early chapters was to argue that our sensory experiences themselves, along with other psychological states, are not physical. On this view, the bare fact that there are sensations does not itself require that there be physical objects or processes. Sensory perception is, of course, typically analyzed as involving

[67] Anthony Kenny, *Action, Emotion and Will* (London: Routledge & Kegan Paul, 1963), p. 57.

more than there being sensations and there being an object sensed: there is said to be some causal connection between the two. Could this causal connection hold between God *qua* nonphysical being and objects like this room? Well, reverting again to our earlier arguments over dualism, I have defended the view that *qua* nonphysical beings we can causally interact with our bodies, and if this physical–nonphysical interaction is to be countenanced, why reject out of hand the supposition that God and the world interact? God's sensing of the room could still satisfy all the requisite conditional or counterfactual conditions that typify our own sensory perceiving, i.e. God's sensory representation of the room is such that, necessarily, if there is a motion in the room, there is a mapped isomorphic motion in the Divine sensory representation. As for causal connections, what could be more so than the theistic account of God's causally creating and sustaining in existence all features of the room? (See the next chapter for more on this.)

Gaskin offers an objection similar to Jantzen's against the notion of there being a "dispersed" incorporeal knower of the world. His argument proceeds from the notion that having perceptual or sensory access to the world must always be from a particular point of view. There cannot be any nonperspectival, nonview seeing. Gaskin charges that it therefore makes no sense to see or perceive something from all perspectives at once. He takes the classical theist to be committed to holding that God does have this puzzling, all-perceiving ability, what is sometimes called omnipercipience. Gaskin charges that this objection works equally well against the notion that God can act at any point in the universe. Acting, like seeing, must be from particular points of view. Although I address the problem of Divine action in the next section, it will be useful at this point to see how Gaskin links the problems of action and knowledge.

I do not think it is merely a failure of my anthropocentric imagination that I cannot grasp what it would be like to be a conscious agent everywhere at once. Conscious agents (men, cats, dogs, ghosts and Greek Gods) act from a point of view of the universe. They even have a point of view of their own bodies where a body is present. God, *ex hypothesi*, does not. If I imagine myself able, as a basic act, to turn the moon round on its axis so that you could see the other side of it from earth, I would inevitably conceive of myself seeing the moon from some point of view. The supposition of a sight, or an awareness, which embraces all points of view, is not just omniscience, it is dispersal of the agent. It might be like seeing myself from my own fingertip and from everywhere else on my own body simultaneously. I cannot make much sense of even that degree of dispersal of my centre of consciousness, let alone understand a dispersal which embraces every view of everything in the universe.[68]

An incorporeal, omniscient being would thus be supposed to have absurdly dispersed, multitudinous perspectives, taking up remote points of view simultaneously.

Gaskin charges that he cannot make much sense of there being "a sight, or an awareness which embraces all points of view." One reason why it is difficult to assess the force of this objection is that Gaskin does not state what he means by "a point of view." Can one have a point of view or an awareness that embraces other points of view? Presumably my visual field may be larger at one time than it is at another. Perhaps this involves my latter point of view encompassing my former point of view; the former point of view being a part of the latter, so to speak. Another example in which a subject seems to enjoy a variety of views simultaneously occurs when a subject looks at several television screens or mirrors. If Gaskin allows that a point of view, or a person's awareness, may embrace any more than one point of view, what reason is there for believing there could not be an overarching conscious awareness encompassing all points of view? In the passage cited above, Gaskin suggests that the problem with such an omniperceiver hypothesis is that it requires conceiving of a perceiver inordinately dispersed about the cosmos.

At the outset I note that classical theologians have been careful to avoid using terms like "dispersal" to characterize Divine omnipresence because of its suggestion of God being a material thing scattered or spread out over the cosmos. It would be less misleading to refer to God's omipresence or ubiquitous perception, but for present purposes we may retain the term

[68] J. C. A. Gaskin, *The Quest for Eternity* (Harmondsworth, Middlesex: Penguin, 1984), p. 112.

"dispersed." Gaskin refers to degrees of dispersal, and his analogy with his fingertips and other bodily parts suggests that he does not think of himself as dispersed throughout even his own body. Where is Gaskin's center of consciousness, then, if anywhere? If he allows for any dispersal at all, say a cubic millimeter, what convincing philosophical reason is there to believe that it is impossible for there to be a person with a greater degree of dispersal, one that is a cubic centimeter, a kilometer, or the size of a galaxy? Perhaps Gaskin does not think his center of consciousness is dispersed over any spatially extended region at all. Be that as it may, Gaskin has causal and cognitive powers with respect to his whole body. He has the power to move a macroscopic physical object, even if this is only part of his brain. Moreover, he can feel remote parts of his body simultaneously, a pain in his back and a pain in the fingertips. He correctly observes that he does not see himself from his own fingertips and from anywhere else on his body simultaneously. (Does Gaskin suppose that to be dispersed over his bodily surface he would have to be covered with eyes? If he had such eyes, what would the eyes on his fingertips look at to see Gaskin?) But is it metaphysically impossible for there to be an observer enjoying indefinitely many distinct perceptual experiences of her body from different angles? I know of no evident philosophical obstacles to imagining a creature which could enjoy such distinct visual experiences simultaneously. We do not need to appeal to any outlandish science-fiction thought experiment to claim that it is coherent to suppose a person's causal power can extend over a certain area. We find this in our own case. If the argument of Chapter 3 is sound, we enjoy this range of causal power without being identical with our bodies. Perhaps the objection to the dualist thesis of mental–physical interaction would bolster Gaskin's case, for then the theist would have difficulty supposing that God can affect the world or know of it without God being a material object, spatially present in the world. But we have seen that the problem of interaction is not at all decisive.[69]

---

[69] Some of the objections Terence Penelhum raises against disembodiment seem to be grounded upon the objection from interaction and individuation reviewed in

It may be objected that imagining God sees the same object from a variety of perspectives raises the following logical problem. How something looks depends upon the conditions under which it is observed. Thus, you and I may see the same object, but I see it as blue and you green. If a super observer is imagined to see an object from all conceivable viewpoints under all conceivable conditions, perhaps the observer would see the same object as both entirely blue and entirely green at the same time. The latter seems impossible: the same region cannot be both blue and green in the same respect, and thus the notion of a super observer seems impossible. But why think it necessary that a being having indefinitely many perceptual experiences should have these in an overlapping fashion so that its perceptual experience would require incompatible colors to cover the same region? Gaskin does not provide us with any argument here. Those who have speculatively attributed omniperceptual or omnivoyant powers to God, such as Nicholas of Cusa in the fifteenth century, did not see any difficulties with God's keeping the viewpoints distinct.[70]

THE ACTION OF GOD OBJECTION

I consider now a second Jantzen–Gaskin objection to Divine incorporeality. Both correctly maintain that God's action on the world is what some philosophers have called basic. An agent performs a basic act when she performs the act and its performance did not involve doing some other act. Basic acts are unmediated. Both Gaskin and Jantzen suppose that if God's acts in the universe are basic, then God cannot be a nonphysical thing, distinct from the world. Rather, the universe must be God's body. Gaskin states the argument succinctly.

The basic acts which a person can perform are movements of his own body. Now if God is an omnipresent spirit which moves any part of the universe as a basic act, this must surely mean, if the analogy with a human agent is to hold in any way at all, that the universe is identical

Chapter 3. See his *Survival and Disembodied Existence* (New York: Humanities Press, 1973).
[70] Nicholas of Cusa, *The Vision of God*, trans. E. Salter (New York: Frederick Ungar, 1960).

with God's body ... If God's embodiment is the universe itself and its movements are his basic acts, then it would appear to be absurd to speak of God creating heaven and earth. Heaven and earth *are* God.[71]

Both in Gaskin's criticism above and throughout Jantzen's important book *God's World, God's Body*, in which she proposes her postdualist view of God, there is the recurring problem of failing to distinguish carefully between the thesis that God is nonphysical and the view that God has no body. To repeat, classical theism holds that God is continuously causally involved in the world, conserving it in being, knowing it, and able to exercise omnipotent power with respect to it. According to certain theories of embodiment such a comprehensive causal relation amounts to treating the universe as a partial Divine embodiment, albeit subject to all the qualifications discussed earlier. This embodiment does not entail that God is identical with the universe, heaven, and earth. At one place in *God's World, God's Body* Jantzen notes the difference between the thesis that God is embodied and God is corporeal, but the distinction is otherwise ignored. She writes: "An incorporeal being, for instance, would be limited to those sorts of activity which do not require a body for their performance."[72] Why assume that an incorporeal being does not or cannot have some embodiment? If integrative dualism is correct, then I am incorporeal and have a physical body. Jantzen mistakenly equates being incorporeal with being disembodied. "Now, a disembodied being would not have a body to move, and therefore could perform no basic actions. But how can he get any action on the world started?"[73] The important issue here is whether a nonphysical being could perform basic actions in bringing about physical and non-physical events and, as far as I can tell, neither Gaskin nor Jantzen provides any argument for thinking a nonphysical being could not do so. A classical theist can grant that if a subject is able to bring about certain physical changes in a

[71] Gaskin, *The Quest for Eternity*, pp. 112, 113. For a similar objection to God based on agency, see chapter 2 of *Atheism* by M. Martin (Philadelphia: Temple University Press, 1990).
[72] Jantzen, *God's World, God's Body*, p. 85. Martin also sometimes collapses the thesis that God is incorporeal with the view that God cannot have a body, e.g. p. 313.
[73] Jantzen, *God's World, God's Body*, p. 85.

direct, unmediated fashion, then certain physical objects are (at least part of) its body. This would not itself entail that the subject is physical.

Finally, I note that Jantzen's own theistic perspective faces a problem similar to the one she attributes to the classical theist. As she does not identify God's mental life with the world, God's willing or intending that, say, some physical movement occurs is distinct from the physical movement itself. Even though, according to Jantzen's thesis, the physical movement is part of God (or in God), it is distinct from the Divine intention or willing. There remains a recalcitrant puzzle then in Jantzen's theology of God about psychophysical interaction. She avoids the dualist quandary of accounting for the interaction between two radically different substances, but there is still the fact of interaction involving radically different properties.[74]

THE FRANKENSTEIN OBJECTION

In this and the next section the objections to dualistically motivated philosophies of God are religious. It has been argued that to conceive of God along personal lines fails to do justice to the religious experience of God as truly other. God, rather, begins to look like a human artifact. It is not possible to consider this objection in light of a fully articulated theory of religious experience, but I briefly respond to Patrick Sherry's version of it here. Sherry takes special aim at Richard Swinburne's philosophy of God. Sherry writes that this God is "more like a

---

[74] Ishtiyaque Haji follows Jantzen in conceiving of God as a spatial being he calls a superbody which "could be something like an electrical field," "God and Omnispatiality," *International Journal for Philosophy of Religion* 25 (1989), 107. Insofar as Haji conceives of God as possessing psychological attributes which are not themselves physical, he will also have a residual dualism like Jantzen. In "Reply to Taliaferro" Jantzen freely acknowledges the recalcitrant mystery in her theological model. Referring to God's omniscient knowledge of the world, Jantzen writes "How God does this is a mystery, on any theological model, just as how physical states are or give rise to conscious states is a mystery on any theological model" (p. 191). My aim in this chapter has been to establish that the classical model is no more mysterious than Jantzen's holism, a claim she seemed reticent to accept in *God's World, God's Body*, where she writes: "The route I plan to follow, is to question the doctrine of divine incorporeality, and to show that a much less mystifying doctrine of divine perception can be offered on a revised model of the God-world relationship," p. 7.

super-Frankenstein than the God of Abraham, Isaac and Jacob."[75] Continuing the Frankenstein theme of sorts, Sherry contends that envisaging God as a nonphysical person (as Swinburne does) leads theists to seek unhealthy analogies in parapsychology for ways of spelling out our relationship with God.

It is unfortunate ... that so many philosophers of religion look to parapsychology for parallels ... Since telepathy is normally used to refer to intuitive communication between people distant from each other, this is surely precisely the wrong model for God "in whom we live and move and have our being." Similarly with the other commonly used parallel, that of theoretical entities in scientific explanations. The parallel is useful in giving us the idea of an invisible and independent agent, but it misses the characteristic of personal agency. And again, more seriously, it misses ... the link between spirit and spirituality.[76]

Sherry's scruples have merit, but do not, I believe, expose decisive problems for envisaging God as nonphysical and person-like. When would the difficulties be so serious as to call into jeopardy the philosophy of God defended here? Frankenstein's monster was crudely man-made, cruel, murderous, vengeful, finite, ignorant, and not a creator of any kind. If a philosophy of God collapses into this quagmire, so much the worse for the philosophy of God. But conceiving of God as a person or person-like reality need not oblige us to imagine any of these qualities, nor does Sherry offer us any reason for thinking that if our concept of God as a person-like reality is human-fashioned, that is all it is. The parallel with Frankenstein's monster may have *some* inviting features for our conceiving of God (he wanted friendship; he was an outcast despite his initial good-hearted attempt at making friends, and so on), yet the disanalogies are so gargantuan that I see no danger of a slippery slope from a person concept of God to a gothic horror show.

Would it be so awful to use telepathy as a model for understanding God's awareness and communication with us in

[75] *Spirits, Saints, and Immortality* (Albany: State University of New York Press, 1984), p. 13. [76] *Ibid.*, pp. 16, 17.

religious experience? Perhaps if that were the only model, and
clearly using it would be off the mark insofar as it carried with
it the assumption that God is metaphysically remote, ghoulish,
dead, ethically iffy, and finite. But telepathy stands for a kind of
awareness that does not rely upon sensations, and it seems that
if one made the suitable adjustments, there would be no danger
of noting that God's awareness of the cosmos may well be like
that. Sherry's own preferred construal of God's nonphysical
presence in the cosmos leans heavily on the notion of awareness
and communication. These have promise, in my view, but do
not supplant the need for taking on board a nonphysical person-
like conception of God.

Sherry draws on the notion of communication in general as a
way in which to begin thinking about God as a nonphysical
power.

Communication gives us a good starting-point for trying to grasp the
idea of a non-physical power, one that is as good as that from
parapsychology and better than that from theoretical entities in
science, for it gives us the concept of an interaction which is not a crude
"spanner in the works" process.[77]

But how can we introduce the concept of communication
without invoking some notion of a person or thing doing the
communicating? Indeed, the notion of communication in such
a religious context seems to bring us closer than ever to
understanding God as a person or person-like being. From the
standpoint of integrative dualism communication is not a sore
subject, for communication involves mental–physical interaction in which the physical and nonphysical are profoundly
interwoven.

Sherry's effort to avoid drawing on something like dualism
(integrative or not) leads him to see God as analogous to words,
books, and films.

It [Sherry's approach] enables us to meet Paul Edwards' objection
about the propriety of applying predicates like "wise," "good,"
"just" and "powerful" to an incorporeal spirit. For we already use
such terms of human expressions and creations which communicate
meanings, as when we speak of a "powerful argument," "moving

[77] *Ibid.*, p. 24.

words," "a thoughtful book" or "an intelligent film." It may be replied that these are analogical uses: I am not sure that all of them are, but even if they are, this is sufficient to refute the objection that they may be used only of bodily organisms.[78]

I think that strict materialists do need to worry about positing immaterial objects. If they do wind up acknowledging films, words, arguments, and books as nonbodily things, then a radical antitheistic argument to the effect that there cannot be anything nonbodily, God included, has been challenged. But on all fronts, I suggest that it is integrative dualism and the notion that God is indeed a person, or person-like being, that can give these other analogies some kind of grounding. In Christian religious tradition, is God conceived to be more like a book or an author, one who argues or what is argued, one who speaks or what is spoken? Waxing anachronistic, we might well ask, too, whether God is more like a film maker or a film. The problem with linking God with the second of each pair is that none of them is capable of thinking, knowing, acting with its own purposes, loving, listening to prayer, and so on. Sherry may have avoided the danger of conceiving of God like Franken-stein's monster, but at the risk of making God out to be like Mary Shelley's book *Frankenstein*.

I suggest that Sherry has not raised a decisive difficulty with conceiving of God along personal lines, or shown there to be deep problems with drawing upon dualism in one's philo-sophical theism.

GHOST OR IDEA?

I will only note and address this objection very briefly. Nicholas Lash holds that dualistically motivated forms of theism have the following implications:

It implies that God is either a kind of mental event, a thought rather than a thinker, or that he is of the same order as the entities investigated by students of the paranormal. For the consistent dualist, God is either an idea or a ghost.[79]

[78] *Ibid.*, p. 24.
[79] "Materialism," in *A New Dictionary of Christian Theology*, ed. A. Richardson and J. Bowden (London: SCM, 1983), p. 353.

Lash's thesis is plausible so long as dualism is formulated in a hopelessly obscure form. But if the case for integrative dualism holds up, then we may envisage ourselves as nonphysical and yet neither ideas nor ghosts. Why should God wind up in either camp in virtue of being nonphysical? Integrative dualism has also been cast so as not to construe persons as mental events or thoughts. Rather, persons are individuals. It is worth underscoring the disanalogy with Lash's idea or ghost dilemma posed against dualists. On any customary treatment, ideas are inert, not capable of knowing things, powerfully creating a cosmos, and so on. The notion of a ghost comes a little closer, in that ghosts are assumed to have quasi-immaterial status and are capable of knowledge and agency. But in folklore and the popular imagination, they are finite in power and knowledge, former human beings, contingent, and ethically uneven. Only if we carefully revise the notion of "ghost" so that the object of our reference is believed to have the array of Divine attributes that are at the heart of theism, and remote from Dennett's Casper the Friendly Ghost, do we get on track and move from the realm of poltergeists to the notion of the "Holy Ghost."

THE UNIQUENESS OF GOD

Consider, finally, an objection lodged by Brian Davies. Davies objects to conceiving of God as a nonphysical person on the grounds that this would unduly place God among the creaturely categories of genus and species. Central to Davies' philosophy of God is God's unparalleled uniqueness. God does not belong to a particular class of objects, whereas cats and human persons do. God cannot be a person, then, because that would make God into a creaturely individual. I consider briefly several tiers in Davies' argument.

Davies is strongly committed to God's distinction from the creation.

God cannot be comprehensible in terms of what Aristotle meant by "genus" and "species." God cannot be classified as a member of the world; he will be no possible object of research for biologists, zoologists, physicists and chemists. Nor can he share with things in the world certain of their essential features ... We can also deny that God is an individual. By this I do not mean that God is in no sense a subject or an agent. I am not denying the reality of God. But suppose one concentrates on the sense of individual (arguably its most common sense) according to which to call something an individual is to imply that there could always be another of the same kind. In that case, so I am arguing, we would be right to deny that God is an individual. We can deny that he can be thought of as sharing a nature with other things.[80]

Is it essential to Christian theism that one embrace such a conclusion?

Earlier I noted that some of the disputes over whether to call the God of Christian theism a person are sometimes terminological. At this point I think we may come very close to making a choice of terminology rather than substantial metaphysics. If by "individual" one means that the object is one among many of the same sort or a particular vegetable, animal, or mineral, then denying that God is an individual makes sense. But if one refers to God as an individual and adds all the qualifications of God's unique reality (the supremely good, omnipotent, omniscient, sole Creator of the cosmos *ex nihilo*, and so on), are we in theological or philosophical trouble? Davies seems prepared to think of God as, in some sense, *like* a subject or agent, so a strict, radical separation of God and cosmos does not seem easily ruled out.

One argument that Davies offers to supplement his non-individual strategy seems to me to be unsatisfactory given the defense of integrative dualism in the last chapter. Davies argues for the nonindividuality of God based on the thesis that individuation involves materiality and God is immaterial.

We distinguish between individuals in the world because they are material or because they exist in a context of materiality. In this sense to understand something as an individual is to understand it as part of the material world. And in this sense we can deny that God is an individual. For if God is the Creator ex nihilo, then, as we have seen, he cannot be anything material.[81]

---

[80] Davies, "Classical Theism and the Doctrine of Divine Simplicity," in *Language, Meaning and God*, ed. Davies (London: Geoffrey Chapman, 1987).

[81] Ibid., p. 62.

If the problem of individuation investigated in Chapter 3 has been successfully overturned, then we can see that being an individual does not entail being material. Of course, Davies is free to specify that in some specific sense or respect God is not an individual, i.e. God is not a physical individual, but the point remains that this is not the only sense that "individual" and "individuation" have. There are nonphysical individuals as well as physical ones.

Davies lists a host of other reasons why we should resist thinking of God as a person:

People are also commonly associated with, for example, bodies and parents and food and drink and sex and society and death. Yet God is said to be above such things. He is said to be bodiless and immortal or eternal. So it also seems appropriate to deny that God is a person. If people are our models for persons, then in an obvious sense God, it would seem, is not a person ... Or consider the question of space. People are in space. So they are here and not there, there and not here. Yet God is supposed to be everywhere, which can be taken to mean that he is also nowhere. So again the point can be pressed. If people are our models for persons, and if this implies that God is what people are, then God is not a person. For God is not anywhere, while people are always somewhere.[82]

If integrative dualism is assumed, we do not have such a long list of disanalogies. Human persons are nonphysical, though physically embodied. I have suggested earlier ways in which God may be understood to be present to this spatio-temporal world that are analogous to our relationship with our bodies. Further development of this thesis will be a chief concern in what is to come.

I have been arguing that there are theological reasons for taking integrative dualism seriously as an account of the unified character of our embodied life and a framework within which to understand specific Christian theological beliefs like the incarnation and the afterlife. I then went on to defend the notion that God may be viewed as a nonphysical, knowing agent who is not identical with the material cosmos. It is now my aim to articulate in more specific terms the God–world relation and to

[82] Ibid., p. 65.

see if it can be developed along the lines of what may be called integrative theism. All I have said about integrative theism so far is that it is a form of theism that emphasizes the close, embodying relation between God and the world notwithstanding the fact that God and the world are not metaphysically identical. How this is to be developed, and what its bearing is on integrative dualism, will be the project of the remaining two chapters.

CHAPTER 5

The omnipresence of God

What about God? Is it easy to grasp how he lives without
a body?

Lactantius (third century)[1]

According to classical theism, God is incorporeal and yet
everywhere present throughout the cosmos. There is no place
where God is not. What could be meant by such a claim? The
aim of the first three chapters has been to address a series of
philosophical objections against dualism, while the goal of
Chapter 4 has been to explore theological and ethical reasons
for rejecting dualism and an incorporeal view of God. Having
set forth an integrative understanding of the person–body
relationship, I now wish to consider the respects in which theism
can envisage an integral relationship between God and the
cosmos. In this chapter I develop a preliminary depiction of
God's omnipresence and then provide an overview of the link
between the case for theism and the case for dualism.

Part of what it means for theists to claim that God is
everywhere present in the cosmos is for God to know all parts
and aspects of the cosmos, and to be able to exercise omnipotent
power with respect to all such parts and aspects. Moreover,
God's omnipresence is a function of the cosmos as a whole and
all its constituents being such that they exist in virtue of God's
causal, conserving power. Were it not for God's conserving
power, the cosmos would not exist. In elucidating this understanding of omnipresence, I focus first on the nature of Divine
agency and then on the nature of Divine knowledge.

[1] From "The Blessed Life," in *Apocalyptic Spirituality*, trans. B. McGinn (New York:
Paulist Press, 1979), p. 45.

DIVINE AGENCY

Theists in the classical tradition have helped themselves to
substantial features of folk psychology in their various accounts
of Divine activity, referring to God's purposes, knowledge, love,
and creativity. If the arguments of the earlier chapters have
credibility, this recourse will not seem wrongheaded, at least
from the very outset. Theists who subscribe to dualism have
tended not to be given over to the doubt-ridden skepticism some
attribute to them. Thatcher has characterized dualists as
promoting skeptical worries about our place in the world. In the
last chapter I maintained, *contra* Thatcher, that the dualist has
no more reason to be skeptical about the reliability of our
cognitive faculties than a materialist has. Indeed, I think
proponents of integrative dualism and classical theism have less
reason to be skeptical about our commonsense convictions than
at least some of their opponents. It would be puzzling to suppose
that an all-good God constructs creatures with cognitive
faculties designed only to mislead and generate systematically
mistaken views. It would be less odd, I think, for us to be
in such a sorry state of cognitive failure if the world were the
outcome of mere chance or the outcome of natural laws which
do not themselves reflect the intelligence of a good agent or, to
wax fantastic, the outcome of a malign agent.[2] In discussing the
problem of other minds earlier I noted how dualists have
appealed to the goodness of God in underwriting their confidence in perception and judgment, and this is something I
return to in the last chapter.

Classical theists, especially in Judaic and Christian traditions,
have generally assumed that our experience of ourselves as
agents is reliable. We are what we seem to be, agents who make
a difference causally in what occurs. Our self-knowledge may be
imperfect, but we may be sure that we are not mere patients.
Obviously our causal contribution in conscious activity is
sometimes meager, and sometimes altogether absent, yet I
believe we do experience ourselves deliberately acting to bring

[2] See the discussion of cognitive development in Chapter 6.

about changes. I join a number of philosophers and psychologists who believe that we experience ourselves not only as causally effective, but as effective as voluntary agents. According to what is called libertarianism we voluntarily perform an act when we act and yet could have refrained from doing so, given all the same prevailing conditions. Freedom involves the ability to do otherwise, not simply the freedom from external constraints like chains. I freely give you a gift when I make the offer and yet could have refrained from doing so, all other conditions being constant.[3] Determinism is the philosophical position denying this phenomenologically based view of freedom. According to determinism, all events that ever occur are such that they are causally necessitated to do so given the laws of nature and all the antecedent and accompanying conditions. If determinism were true, then, strictly speaking, my giving you a gift would not be free in the sense that I had the power to do otherwise, given the laws of nature and so on. The thesis that determinism and freedom are incompatible is called incompatibilism. The view that determinism may be true and yet it may still be the case that people act freely is called compatibilism.

I believe that the best case favoring libertarianism along incompatibilist lines rests in appealing to the phenomenological character of agency and in showing that none of the positive arguments for determinism succeed. Many, though by no means all, determinists admit that we at least appear to have the radical, voluntary ability identified by libertarians.[4] They correctly point out that our assumption of free agency is fallible. I think it proper to concede this point. Obviously I may assume that I am free to leave a room whereas, unknown to me, all the

[3] I adopt the libertarian outlook of Peter Van Inwagen as laid out in his *An Essay on Free Will* (Oxford: Clarendon Press, 1983), John Foster in *The Immaterial Self* and Roderick Chisholm in *Person and Object* (La Salle: Open Court, 1976). For an important defense of the view that causation need not always be understood deterministically see G. E. M. Anscombe's *Causality and Determinism* (London: Cambridge University Press, 1971).

[4] Thomas Nagel seems to concede that we at least appear to have free agency. See his *The View from Nowhere* (New York: Oxford University Press, 1986), p. 113. He goes on to raise doubts about whether such appearances have any validity. I address his stance in "Nagel's Vista: Taking Subjectivity Seriously."

doors are locked and I cannot escape. But I do not think the bare possibility of error here is sufficient to overturn its being reasonable to trust appearances until we have positive reasons for doubting them. One of the most powerful reasons determinists have employed to discount a libertarian view of agency has, I believe, been defused. It is argued that determinism is a required presupposition of scientific inquiry and thus that the success of such inquiry establishes the truth of determinism. Given the acceptability of quantum theory by many in the scientific community this argument has lost the prestige it once enjoyed. In a sense we have already indirectly covered a range of arguments employed by determinists, chiefly the arguments for eliminative and identity materialism. Dualism does not entail libertarianism, nor does materialism entail determinism. Still, we have seen the way different materialist schemas tend to treat phenomenology with suspicion, and it is therefore not surprising that this leads to various reservations over arguments for libertarianism based on first person reports. I think the failure of these deterministic arguments, coupled with the fact that there are reasons for believing that compatibilism is not able to do justice to what we mean by "freedom" in our commonsense convictions about action and responsibility, makes libertarianism the philosophy of choice.

Despite the adoption of libertarianism in what follows, theistic determinists may still sympathize with the account of omnipresence below for two reasons.

First, some theistic determinists make an exception when it comes to God: they believe that while the cosmos is thoroughly determined, God is not. They therefore have a stake in the intelligibility of a libertarian account of God, even if they believe that the need for such an account drops out when it comes to events within the cosmos.

The second reason may be described as an *a fortiori* one. In some respects, theistic libertarians have a more difficult time than determinists when it comes to characterizing God's omnipresence. If theistic determinism is true, everything that occurs in the cosmos may be seen as stemming either directly or indirectly from God's will. There will be no volitional barriers between what has, is, and will occur and what God has decreed. This is a stern notion of omnipresence in which God's ubiquity is not compromised by agents who can act in ways that are other than God has elected, hence the role of theistic determinism and the teaching of predestination in either its singular form (God predestines the elect to salvation) or its double form (God both predestines the elect and predestines others to reprobation and damnation). There is no puzzle for the theistic determinist concerning God's knowing future "free" acts when it comes to creatures' ability to do otherwise. Libertarians (such as myself) worry whether God's knowing how a person will freely act is internally consistent. Can I be said to have it in my power to do some act or refrain from it if God has prior knowledge about what I will actually do? It is because I doubt whether liberty can be preserved under such conditions that I develop a view of God's omniscience below that does not require God to know all future free activity. The point I am making here is that theistic determinists will not have to hedge any such positions, and they may thereby claim to have a more robust account of God's presence than libertarians. Given this ostensible advantage, why would a theistic determinist have an interest in the success of a libertarian account of Divine omnipresence? I suggest that a theistic determinist may have sympathy with the alternative account below on the grounds that if a libertarian model can succeed in grounding claims of God's omnipresence, then, *a fortiori*, so can a deterministic one. If God may be understood as fully present to a cosmos in which there are libertarian agents, then it will be all the more evident that God may be understood as omnipresent in a determinist cosmos.[5]

I consider three areas in which classical theists draw upon and refine views about our own agency in articulating the philosophy of God.

First, classical theists have outlined ways in which Divine action is more voluntary than our own. Arguably, voluntary action is vitiated by ignorance and volitional impairment like

[5] One of the best current defenses of theological determinism is "Predestination Defended" by Patrick Richmond (Green College, Oxford), presented to the Joseph Butler Society, Oxford University, Fall 1992.

loss of motor control. Thus, if I am ignorant about whether my pressing a button will cause an electric fire, I cannot be said to cause a fire voluntarily when a fire breaks out as a result of my act. Similarly my voluntariness is diminished to the degree that my volition is impaired. Imagine that when I deliberately intend to do something like lift my hand, something else occurs, my left foot moves, for example. I cannot be said to have moved my foot voluntarily under those conditions. As God is thought of as maximally knowledgeable and not subject to such peculiar volitional impairment, God is believed to act with greater voluntariness than we do.[6]

Second, theists have understood God's agency to be unmediated. While we can perform basic acts, these can involve highly complex physical factors. The deliberate raising of a hand involves many neural events and muscle movements, whereas with God there is no such physical complexity. This immediacy of God's activity highlights a respect in which the world does not function as God's body the way material bodies function as our own. Such a freedom from bodily control represents an important respect in which God's agency is less bounded than our own.[7]

Our self-awareness is fallible, and occasions may arise when what we take to be a voluntary act is not so, but brought about instead by factors we have no control over or for reasons we would repudiate were we fully conscious of them. With God there is no such fallibility, nor is there a physiological base to undermine Divine freedom. God does not have a body that could preempt, control, or otherwise physiologically anticipate voluntary intentions.

Third, and in some ways most important, classical theists assume that the scope of Divine agency is infinitely larger than our own. God's omnipotence has been variously analyzed. Some characterize omnipotence as the ability to do anything logically possible or to bring about any consistently describable

---

[6] For a defense of the view that ignorance reduces voluntariness see Aristotle's *Ethics III*. Joel Feinberg defends this notion in *Harm to Self* (Oxford: Oxford University Press, 1986).

[7] David Brown, *Continental Philosophy and Modern Theology* (Oxford: Basil Blackwell, 1987), p. 51.

state of affairs. For reasons I have spelled out elsewhere, I maintain that for God to be omnipotent amounts to God being such that it is impossible for there to be a being with greater power. I understand greatness of power in terms of both the scope of activities which can be performed and the way these are performed. This latter specification is important, for imagine two beings, A and B, who are capable of bringing about an equally large scope of states of affairs, but A can do so immediately without any assistance, whereas B can do so only with A's help. I am inclined to see A as more powerful than B even if A always must help B in performing any act B undertakes.[8]

Given the magnitude of omnipotence, how are theists to understand God's creative conservation of the cosmos? Must his conserving of the cosmos be understood in terms of his making indefinitely many discrete acts of the will? If so, this would seem to conjure up what Richard Gale in another context called a chatter-box God. Is theism, then, committed to the view that with respect to each individual and property of the cosmos God must at each time will that individual or property to exist? I do not think so. Singular intentions can be highly determinative and complex. In writing this sentence, for example, I intend to write the sentence as a whole and I am not engaged in hundreds of discrete volitional acts to write each letter, and each part of each letter. Nonetheless, in writing a sentence I intend each letter to be in a certain order. Similarly, God's conserving of the cosmos may be thought of as a singular, enduring intention to sustain the entire cosmos replete with all its individuals and aspects. Theistic determinists will envisage God's intention here as omni-determining, whereas libertarians will see this as God conserving in existence a cosmos in which some creatures have powers of agency. In the latter scheme, God is the underlying cause that endows created individuals with powers of self-

---

[8] This represents a modest extension of my position as laid out in "The Magnitude of Omnipotence," *International Journal for Philosophy of Religion* 14 (1983), 99–106.

authorship.[9] Both libertarian and deterministic theists face a problem, however, in attributing absolute omnipotence to God.

Some philosophers, most recently Donald Davidson, have maintained that without laws of nature there can be no causality. "Where there is causality, there must be a law."[10] If this is assumed, then we are stuck with the peculiar view that if God is a causally effective agent, then this agency must be in virtue of some law of nature. God's being omnipresent throughout nature is thereby seen as due to a law of nature. Gilbert Fulmer has sought to turn this into an argument against the very existence of God. Fulmer argues:

For if the god can impose his will on the world, it is a natural law that whatever he wills, occurs. That is, it is a fact of the universe that if god wills X, then X is the case; for example, if he wills that $e = MC^2$, it is so. And this fact cannot itself be the product of the god's will; for if it were not a fact, his will could produce no effects whatever – and to make his will effective would be to produce an effect. The fact that events occur as he wills them cannot be the result of his will. Thus this fact is logically more fundamental than the god's choices: his acts presuppose this fact, but not the converse.[11]

Fulmer argues that if God exists, God is the author of all the laws of nature. But God cannot be the author of all the laws of nature, because God cannot account for the law "Whatever God wills, occurs." This law is a law of nature, for it cannot be produced by God without already preexisting. Theism is false, because God is imagined to be above the laws of nature, whereas it is impossible for any being to occupy such a place.

It is logically impossible that any agent could stand above and control the whole of nature, because his very power to act would be a fact which was not the result of personal agency, and hence natural. Therefore the being himself would be a part of nature: he would be

[9] In "The Art of Creation and Conservation" I argue for a cognitive component in the analysis of God's singular action of creatively conserving the cosmos, *New Blackfriars* (July/August 1986), 315–323.

[10] Davidson, "Mental Events," in *Experience and Theory*, ed. J. Foster and Swanson (Amherst: University of Massachussetts Press, 1987), p. 208.

[11] Fulmer, "The Concept of the Supernatural," *Analysis* 37 (March 1977), 114.

subject, as are we all, to natural law. Thus the animistic belief that nature could be the work of a supernatural creator cannot be correct; the concept of such a being is incoherent.[12]

Thus, Fulmer concludes, God cannot exist.

In the present context, it will not do to fall back on a conciliatory stance, conceding that there cannot be any ultimate agent responsible for all of nature, while holding out for the coherence of a God so powerful as to be the cause of all natural laws except one, "Whatever God wills, occurs." There is no need for this fallback, however, for classical theists can agree with Fulmer that "Whatever God wills, occurs" is not a product of God's will but insist that this fails to yield Fulmer's conclusion that "Whatever God wills, occurs" is a law of nature.

What we ordinarily classify as laws of nature pertain to events and objects within nature. This talk of nature may obscure matters, however, for classical theists acknowledge the un-created nature of God as well as created nature. When classical theists refer to nature, then, two things may be referred to: (a) nature as the created cosmos, distinct from God, where God may be thought of as above or below nature, a supernatural, extramundane reality, or (b) nature as the essential character of something. For example, many classical theists consider God's being omniscient as an essential property of the Divine nature. God could not exist and fail to be omniscient. Now, if "Whatever God wills, occurs" is a law of nature in accord with the first meaning of nature, Fulmer's point has force, for there would then be a sense in which God has power in virtue of the laws of the cosmos. But why not assume that "Whatever God wills, occurs" is simply a fact about the Divine nature, a fact that is true in virtue of God's innate, inherent power? In other words, why not think of this so-called law as an implication of nature in the second, "b," sense as opposed to being a law independent of God?[13]

---

[12] *Ibid.*, 115, 116.
[13] Richard Taylor refers to nature in the "a" sense in his *Metaphysics* (Englewood Cliffs: Prentice-Hall, 1974); so does Emil Brunner in *Christianity and Civilisation* (London: Nisbet), p. 27. J. S. Mill employs the term in a way closer to "b" in *Three*

An analogy may be useful. As it happens, I can build boats. I believe that this fact is best thought of as being true because I have the relevant ability and power. It is a true fact about boats that they can be built by me, but surely this fact does not explain why I can do it; the fact that I can do it is what accounts for its being true of boats that I can construct them. Analogously, if there is a powerful Creator able to bring about this cosmos, why think the explanation of this resides with the cosmos or a law of the cosmos? It seems far more reasonable to think of God's power as inherent and intrinsically residing in God rather than obtained in virtue of something external to God.

This approach receives some support in some branches of contemporary philosophy of science in which laws of nature are not themselves considered genuinely explanatory of events. Laws are regarded as merely abstract descriptions of how things occur. The real explanation (as opposed to bare description) of events rests in the powers and liabilities of the concrete objects involved.[14] Oxygen behaves as it does because of its constituent parts and other particles, remote and proximate. It does not behave the way it does because of higher laws which are derived from still higher laws, and so on. According to this scheme, Davidson might be correct that if there is causality, there are laws, but laws exist only as descriptions of the causal power of concrete things which are not themselves laws. Oxygen itself is not a law, and its peculiar properties are what justify the descriptions which function as laws. Similarly, the classical theist may hold that it is God's intrinsic power which explains the truth of the so-called law "Whatever God wills, occurs" rather than *vice versa*.

Fulmer offers a sketchy argument for his law, namely that if the law "If God wills X, X" did not obtain, God's willing could not produce any effects. But alter his argument slightly. If it

Essays on Religion (1874) when he takes nature to be a name for all facts, actual and possible.

[14] See, for example, R. Harré's and E. H. Madden's work on the notion of powerful particulars in their *Causal Powers* (Totowa, N. J.: Rowman and Littlefield, 1975), and Barry Cohen's and James Humber's "Sterling Lamprecht's Critique of Causality," *Transactions of the Charles S. Peirce Society* 9 (1973), 41–54.

were not a fact that I exist, then it would not be the case that I exist. Does this mean that my existence is somehow due to the *fact* that I exist? This is doubtful. If this reasoning were sound, it would give rise to a causal theory of facts which would be altogether mysterious and metaphysically extravagant. There is no evident absurdity in positing the existence of a being who has certain intrinsic causal powers not derived from or possessed in virtue of Fulmer-like laws.

Fulmer's argument does bring to light the fact that God cannot take credit for bestowing upon Godself all God's creative power. God would have to have power in order to do any bestowing or creating at all. God cannot get all power by simultaneously bestowing all power and receiving all power, nor do I see how even an infinite series of God's giving power to give power ... can pull off the self-creating or self-sustaining feat. No being can be that powerful. But the fact that God cannot create God's creativity in some absolute sense need not lead us to look outside of God for an account of why or how God has power. It follows analytically that if X is not created by God, then X is not the creation of God. But it does not follow that if X is not created by God, then X is not God or X is not a property of God. God may not have created God's being omnipotent. But God's being omnipotent, if true, seems more a matter of God's being subject to God's own nature, which is to say it is a matter of God being God, rather than it being the case that God is subject to some created or uncreated law of Fulmer's natural world. Thomas Tracy ably summarizes the self-determining character of God: "His intentions, including his commitment to unity of action, are not the result of causally sufficient conditions rooted in a sub-intentional basic life pattern. Insofar as his intentions are necessitated, they are necessitated by his own nature, by what it is to be God."[15]

---

[15] Thomas Tracy, *God, Action, and Embodiment* (Grand Rapids: Eerdmans, 1984), p. 139. Thomas Morris and Christopher Menzel have advanced an argument to the effect that God can create himself, an argument that has a bearing on Fulmer's atheological position. See "Absolute Creation," in *Anselmian Explorations* (Notre Dame: University of Notre Dame Press, 1987). I take issue with them in "The Limits of Power," *Philosophy and Theology* 5:2 (Winter 1990), 115–124. I believe that the stance I adopt

DIVINE KNOWLEDGE

God's being omnipresent involves more than God being able to exercise causal power at all points of the cosmos. It involves God's exercise of knowledge as well, God's exercise of cognitive power. A person's presence at a given place is realized in part by her awareness of what occurs around her. In ordinary contexts, we may well talk of someone being more or less present in a given place than another insofar as she is more or less attentive. God's presence in the cosmos is realized, in part, by God's being supremely attentive, grasping what occurs at every place in the cosmos. In this section I seek to develop an understanding of God's omniscience at odds with the standard accounts. Standard analyses of omniscience are advanced in terms of God's knowing the truth values of propositions. For example, Kenny writes that "The doctrine of omniscience is easy to formulate precisely: it is the doctrine that for all p, then God knows that p."[16] Richard Swinburne proposes that "To say of a person P that he is omniscient at time t is to say that at t P knows of every true proposition that it is true."[17] Sometimes standard accounts are modified to avoid the problem of supposing that a being knows future contingencies, namely propositions concerning what a free being will do in the future. As I noted earlier, some libertarians believe that if God knows that you will freely do some act tomorrow, then you cannot have real freedom, for it must be the case that what God knows will occur and this is difficult to reconcile with the notion that you could do otherwise. To avoid such problems Swinburne identifies limited or modified omniscience as: "A person P is omniscient at time t if and only if he knows of every true proposition about t or an earlier time that it is true and also he knows of every true proposition about a time later than t, such that what it reports is physically necessitated by some cause at t or earlier, that it is true."[18] One also finds modified accounts of omniscience which

in this section is compatible with affirming the simplicity of God, but does not require it.

[16] Anthony Kenny, *The God of the Philosophers* (Oxford: Clarendon Press, 1979), p. 10.
[17] Swinburne, *The Coherence of Theism* (Oxford: Clarendon Press, 1977), p. 162.
[18] *Ibid.*, p. 175.

avoid claiming that God knows the truth values of propositions containing indexical properties like "now" or "being me" as used by a different subject. In Chapter 2 I noted, and found unsuccessful, one attempt to secure an ultimately private treatment of self-awareness that precluded external access. At this point, I shall argue that none of the standard analyses of omniscience, with or without these modifications, identify sufficient conditions for being omniscient. Some version of the standard account may be essential to identify the scope of an omniscient being's knowledge, but I believe that standard accounts fail because they do not identify the requisite cognitive power involved with omniscience.

I suggest that the classical theistic claim that God is omniscient should be conceptually analyzed as the claim that it is impossible for there to be a being with greater cognitive power. The notion of cognitive power can be readily illustrated. When I know certain things to be the case, that I now see something green or that I hear music, I am exercising cognitive power or ability. When I know $2 + 2 = 4$ I am exercising my cognitive power to grasp the truth value of a necessary proposition. I consider the capacity to know about the world to be a cognitive virtue, the word virtue being derived from the Latin *virtus*, meaning power. I believe that the traditional theistic understanding of God's omniscience includes attributing to God unsurpassable cognitive power: God's omniscience is composed of God's exemplifying supreme cognitive virtue. The disparity between standard analyses of omniscience and the view I am defending can be brought out in the following thought experiment. For ease of exposition, I identify the standard view as claiming that a being is omniscient if and only if it knows the truth values of all propositions. The force of the thought experiment is not diminished by substituting other versions of the standard view.

Imagine that there are two subjects, Miriam and Eric. Both know the truth values of all propositions, but they differ in the following respect. The truth value of all propositions is directly evident to Miriam in virtue of exercising her own cognitive power. She knows all true propositions incorrigibly and infallibly. In order for Miriam to know that it is snowing in Chicago she does not need to undertake numerous observations, examining cloud formations and atmospheric conditions from a variety of angles. Eric, on the other hand, only knows the truth value of all propositions by virtue of Miriam's informing him of their truth values: he must rely upon evidential mediation across the board. Miriam informs him, for example, whether my thesis is correct, but Eric does not know this because of an ability to discover the truth of the matter on his own. Imagine that Eric is even essentially such that he could not have Miriam's extraordinary cognitive power. Eric is epistemically dependent in that he must rely on another being's epistemic work if he is to have knowledge of the world. Eric does not lack all cognitive power, for he can appropriately grasp Miriam's instructions and know them to be reliable, but his knowledge of the world is invariably mediated by Miriam. Were Miriam to be less courteous or well disposed, Eric would be completely ignorant of the world.

In the above thought experiment Miriam possesses unsurpassable cognitive power. Such an upper limit is absolute and, I think, altogether intelligible; it is not analogous to identifying some greatest possible number. There are always numbers greater than any particular number, but a being could not have greater cognitive power than to be such that it knows the truth values of all propositions without evidential mediation. To expect further cognitive advances would be like expecting someone to travel faster than instantaneously in between two distant points. Eric may not be epistemically tarnished in his failing to know the truth value of any proposition, but he lacks the maximally excellent cognitive power attributed to Miriam. Far from being on a par epistemically, Eric lacks the supreme cognitive virtue or perfection which Miriam enjoys.

The standard analyses of omniscience are unable to identify satisfactorily the epistemically important difference between Miriam and Eric. According to the standard views, both subjects are omniscient. Proponents of the standard view may differentiate Miriam and Eric by claiming that while both are omniscient, they attain this omniscience in different ways.

While this is not *obviously* wrong, I find it ultimately un-satisfactory as it ignores the classic notion that knowledge involves a kind of power and it is possible to distinguish degrees of such power. While the standard analyses emphasize an omniscient being's *knowing all* where the concern is to identify the scope of a being's knowing, I do not wish to ignore what it means to claim that a being is *all-knowing*, taking into account the scope of a being's cognitive power. The old maxim "Knowledge is power" is right according to my view, not just because a knower tends to use knowledge in life's practical affairs, but because knowing something to be the case itself involves the exercise of cognitive power. When attributing knowledge to any subject, we attribute to it a certain power. A being whose knowledge of the world must be derived and gleaned from the work of another epistemic agent is surely less powerful cognitively than a being whose knowledge of the world is underived and direct. Evidential doglegging is not the equivalent of direct access. Just as it is counter-intuitive to suppose that a being is omnipotent and yet there could be a being with greater power, I believe that it is counter-intuitive to suppose there is an omniscient being and yet there could be a being with greater cognitive power. I propose that Miriam is omniscient and Eric is not.

If we allow the condition I have identified to serve as a necessary condition for being omniscient we are able to distinguish readily the epistemically important difference be-tween Miriam and Eric. To put my view in the form of a maxim, when it comes to omniscience, it is not just a matter of *what* a subject knows, but *how* a subject knows it. In contrast, the standard views have no obvious way to preclude there being an indefinite series of epistemically dependent beings like Eric. Imagine that the first Eric derives all his knowledge from Miriam and then passes on the appropriate information to the second Eric, and so on to the thousandth Eric. The standard views entail that so long as the thousandth Eric is such that he knows the truth values of all propositions he is omniscient. *Ex hypothesi*, Miriam does not know the truth values of any proposition that the thousandth Eric does not know.

Even if I am incorrect in claiming that the standard view fails to characterize sufficient conditions for being omniscient *per se*, I believe that the above thought experiments bring to light the inadequacy of the standard views in characterizing the cognitive power classical theists have wished to attribute to God. The additional condition I have sought to identify is in accord with an Anselmian conception of God. In the *Proslogium* vi Anselm notes that God cognizes all things to the highest degree, a claim which is akin to maintaining that the cognitive power of an omniscient being is such that a being with greater cognitive power cannot be conceived. Anselmians focus on the supreme excellence or perfection of God, and in thinking about omniscience in particular I propose that we take into account cognitive excellence and perfection. We often in practice recognize different degrees of intellectual excellence. Why not incorporate such judgments about excellence into thinking of omniscience as supremely excellent cognitively?

Could it be that the standard view of omniscience is not even a necessary condition for omniscience? Perhaps, though I believe that something like the standard view is required for us to identify the full exercise of an omniscient being's cognitive power. If we held simply that a being is omniscient if and only if it is impossible for there to be a being with greater cognitive power then the following problem would arise. Perhaps Miriam could have unsurpassable cognitive power and yet refuse to exercise it for any but the most trivial purposes, say only in her knowing general propositions about her epistemic ability; or maybe she decides not to use her power at all and she knows no propositions whatever. I do not think Miriam can then be properly regarded as omniscient. I believe that to attribute omniscience to a subject includes attributing unsurpassable cognitive power as well as attributing the exercise of such power so that some version of the standard view is also satisfied. I suggest the following necessary and sufficient conditions for being omniscient. *X is omniscient if and only if it is impossible for there to be a being with greater cognitive power and this power is fully exercised.* This account may be adopted by theistic determinists, but it will be especially valuable for libertarians as it leaves open the extent of God's knowledge of the future. Imagine that neither God, nor any being, can know future free action. On the account of omniscience advanced here, so long as God's cognitive power is unsurpassable, and it is fully exercised, God's not knowing future free acts does not compromise God being omniscient.[19]

Having set forth the rudiments of an account of God's presence in and to the cosmos, I consider its bearing on the case for dualism. This provides an opportunity to advance the strategy introduced at the close of Chapter 1, in which theism and dualism are developed in partnership.

THEISM AND DUALISM

Materialists claim that they possess a stringently simple philosophy, eschewing the comparatively more complex, disparate character of dualism. Thus, some materialists may well complain about integrative dualism and the accompanying treat-

---

[19] I first developed an analysis of omniscience like the one here in "Divine Cognitive Power," *International Journal for Philosophy of Religion* 18 (1985), 133–140. This is criticized by J. Kvanvig in "Unknowable Truths and the Doctrine of Omniscience," *Journal of the American Academy of Religion* 58 (1989), 485–507, to whom I respond in "Reply to Kvanvig: Omniscience and Unknowable Truths," *JAAR* 61: 3 (1993), 553–566. Kvanvig construes my theory of omniscience as supposing that for a being to be omniscient it must be omniscient essentially (p. 489). While I do think God is essentially omniscient, the focus of my analysis is on viewing omniscience as the exercise of supreme cognitive power or virtue, whether or not this power is possessed essentially by its bearer. Those who construe omniscience as pertaining only to the scope of truths grasped may wind up committed to a view like mine if they have an extremely strict view of knowledge, according to which we only know things which we grasp directly, incorrigibly, and infallibly, without evidential mediation. This identifies a supreme upper limit epistemically, and omniscience would then involve the exercise of such power in knowing the scope of truths grasped. Those with a considerably weaker notion of knowledge, according to which one may know things and yet not be absolutely certain (failing to have knowledge infallibly and incorrigibly) may face the odd possibility that a being could be omniscient and not very intelligent. Imagine that without Miriam Eric is gullible and epistemically incompetent in every way. All the others in his world think of him as stupid, and with some justification, even if this is rather unkind. Eric is constantly accepting false beliefs until Miriam assists him in identifying which beliefs are true and which are false. Eric is enabled to acquire the scope of knowledge satisfying the standard analyses of omniscience with only the barest, minimum warrant compatible with knowledge. The standard views would not discriminate between awarding "omniscience" to Miriam and Eric, albeit he got there by the skin of his epistemic teeth, so to speak.

ments of causal interaction and individuation: "I may have to accept certain features of the cosmos as basic in my world-view, basic in the sense that I make no appeal to some other reality which is ostensibly 'deeper' to account for there being a world at all or for there being the kind of world that there is. If you are correct, I may have to accept that physical objects can differ *solo numero* and, granting some of your assumptions about contingent relations, that dualistically conceived mental–physical causal interaction is not, in principle, impossible. Even so, you wind up positing twice the mystery and complexity I do, for you believe that it is the case that physical beings can differ *solo numero*, causally interact, and so on, *and* you believe that nonphysical beings can differ *solo numero*, causally interact, and so on." Anchoring the complexity of the cosmos in God's creative intention has struck some critics as simply introducing a whole new range of factors which then need to be explained. J. J. C. Smart comments that "if God invented the laws of nature there must have been complexity in him. So there would be as much need to explain the complexity of God as that of the universe."[20]

If the work of this and earlier chapters is successful, then theism may be seen to provide dualism with a profoundly unified account of the cosmos, understanding the laws of nature, and nature itself, as stemming from a singular, Divine reality. If classical theism is true, then the explanation of why there are physical and nonphysical beings, why physical and nonphysical beings exist that may differ *solo numero* and interact causally, is the underlying powerful agency of God. A theist will look to the singular reality of God as part of the account of both the physical and the nonphysical. Does this compound the mysteries at hand or simplify them? In one sense, the theistic dualist will always have a more complex world-view than materialism, as it will be more complex than idealism, but in another sense theistic dualism will provide an important overarching simplicity. According to classical theism, in back of the complex character of the cosmos, there is an intelligent, value-directed motive, one that is singular, and from which are derived ever

[20] J. J. C. Smart, *Our Place in the Universe* (Oxford: Basil Blackwell, 1989).

more determinate intentions. Traditional theologians have identified the overriding reason for God's intent to create and conserve the cosmos in terms of goodness. God creatively conserves the cosmos because it is good to do so. It is because of this unified intent that there is a problem of evil for theism. How is it that the parts of the cosmos fit together so that the creation as a whole is indeed good? Do we have reason to believe that the cosmos is such that it is better that it exist than not? Even if the whole cosmos is more good than ill, what of the cost to individual creatures in it? The problem of evil would not emerge in a theistic philosophy if God were conceived of as an amoral reality or attributed with conflicting, incoherent drives. Shortly we will discuss in more detail God's responsiveness to the evil in creation; the point I am seeking to highlight here is that the controversy over the problem of evil illustrates the theistic commitment to a unified understanding of the cosmos. If theism is true, then there is a unity behind the diversity of the cosmos because, to use Dennett's phrase for describing the dualist notion of a conscious subject, there is a Divine Subject where "it all comes together."[21]

In my view, theism provides not so much a compounding complexity as a grounding as to why there is a complex cosmos at all. Recall the point made earlier that, in creating, God is not saddled with carrying out infinitely many discrete acts of the will. Theism would seem to double the complexity if we had to assume that for every particular feature of the cosmos, God has

---

[21] Daniel Dennett, *Consciousness Explained* (London: Allen Lane, 1991), p. 39. The unified drive of theism may be fruitfully compared with Plato's notion of the good. He saw the form of the Good as ultimately explaining the existence of other forms and, through varying agencies, of the cosmos itself. At this juncture, Christian theism has some Platonic elements without Plato's accompanying degradation of the material world, without the demiurgic notion of God as finite artifact of preexisting matter, and so on. For a recent Platonic account of cosmology friendly to theism, see John Leslie, *Value and Existence* (Oxford: Basil Blackwell, 1979). For an analogy of the way in which more specific intentions follow from the general intention to do good, compare the natural-law tradition, which sees the highest law as "pursue good, avoid evil," from which other laws take shape. By understanding God's aim as directed upon the good, I am not making any explicit claim as to whether all goods are commensurable. I have, elsewhere, sought to articulate a theistic framework within which to assess competing goods, "The View from Above and Below," *Heythrop Journal* 30:4 (1989), 385–402.

a different, unrelated motive for making it, and has to perform infinitely many discrete acts of the will to create and conserve it in existence from instant to instant. There would also be a doubling of complexity if we introduced a layer of theistic metaphysics on top of natural, physical processes without supposing there to be an explanatory relation between them. But in proposing that the complex character of the cosmos is derived from God's overriding intention to bring about something good, we subsume (without replacing or eliminating) our various scientific and psychological explanations in terms of something we take to be deeper and simpler.

A theistic dualist will understand the emergence of consciousness and the organic from a nonconscious and inorganic world as stemming from an abiding, intelligent agency. Causal interaction between person and body will therefore not seem like a Pickwickian anomaly that has been accidentally thrown up by the physicist's world of blind forces. Our capacity for free choices can likewise be seen as stemming from a deeper free choice. This comes to the fore with special clarity in the theology of Gregory of Nyssa in the fourth century, expressing views widely shared in Christian tradition. "The fact that our nature is an image of the Nature which rules over all things means nothing else than this, that from the start our nature was created sovereign... In the self-determination of free choice he [the human being] possessed the likeness of the sovereign of all."[22]

To appreciate further the strength of theism here, consider the work of Raymond Tallis, who has sought to offer a unified picture of consciousness and the physical world without invoking theism or an underlying metaphysics of materialism or of dualism. Tallis insists that states of consciousness are not identical with physical states and that there is a causal interplay between mental and physical. Thus far, it seems that Tallis subscribes either to a dual-aspect theory or to outright dualism,

[22] Cited from *On the Creation of Man* and *On Virginity* in *Deification in Christ* by Panayiotis Nellas (Crestwood, N. Y.: St. Vladimir's Seminary Press, 1987), p. 26. For a modern view linking the conception of Divine and human agency, see R. Swinburne, "The Limits of Explanation," in *Explanation and its Limits* ed. D. Knowles (Cambridge: Cambridge University Press, 1990). "He [God] acts directly on the universe, as we act directly on our brains, guiding them to move our limbs," p. 191.

but in the final analysis neither seems satisfactory to him. He thinks that causal interaction between the disparate realities of the mental and physical is left as too mysterious on any form of dualism, and that all forms of materialism falter because they do not take subjective phenomenology with sufficient seriousness. Instead of electing one of these alternatives, Tallis opts for a middle path, according to which both mind and matter are manifestations of a singular reality he calls "presence."

> It may be better not to begin with either mind or matter since both starting points lead to insuperable problems as to how the one gains access to, or interacts with, the other. If primacy is granted to material objects, there seems to be no basis for the way one material object becomes present to another, as when I am aware of something ... And the problems that result when one begins with mind seem even more acute ... In short, if one starts either from mind or from matter, there is no basis for the presence of one object to another. Presence, the inter-relation between subject and object, cannot be derived from either matter or mind; it must therefore be primary. It is the subject and object, mind and matter that are derived or secondary substances ... Presence is the underived, and underivable, condition of the possibility of individual relations, of the presence of one thing to another, or of the object–subject interaction.[23]

Mind and matter are thus viewed as aspects that emerge or stem from a metaphysically prior or deeper reality.

I fully endorse Tallis' concern to locate a unitary account that sees the mental and physical as bound together, manifesting something singular. Unfortunately, as he himself admits, the notion of presence he invokes is not abundantly clear. He acknowledges "the difficulty of characterizing the stuff that exists prior to mind and matter and of conceiving any kind of research program to cast light on this stuff."[24] I would go further in underscoring the difficulties here. What can "presence" mean? If "presence" names an internal relationship consisting of a subject and object, what sort of relation is it? Is it simply spatial or psychological or causal or some combination

---

[23] *The Explicit Animal* (London: Macmillian, 1991), pp. 246, 248. Tallis' perspective here is in the tradition of neutral monism, which is represented by Bain, James, and Russell, going back to Spinoza.　　　[24] *Ibid.*, p. 247.

of these? To speak of the presence of a subject to an object sounds suspiciously like speaking of them existing together and, thus, more description (or naming) of subject–object relations than explanation. If "presence" is a "stuff," what kind of stuff is it? Does it admit of quantification or degrees of intensity? Tallis gives us very little lead here on how to address such questions. I believe that the notion of "presence" is more at home when we speak of some person being present to another, and this, I think, is a rich notion with many nuances involving degrees of attentiveness, depth of affection, and responsiveness. I may be said to be more present to you to the extent that I am attentive, caring, responsive, and so on. But if by "presence" we mean the presence of persons, then what persons are being alluded to?

Essentially, Tallis' notion is in accord with a philosophy of mind that is not widely represented in western philosophy, but has been articulated by William James and Bertrand Russell earlier in this century, called neutral monism. According to this theory, mind and matter are not substantially real, inimical realities, but manifestations of some other, deeper reality that is neither mental nor material. This third thing is what gets siphoned off in either metaphysical conduit when we approach it under the guise or description of mental and physical. In a sense, the mental and physical are this third thing seen from two different angles. The appeal of neutral monism rested, partly, on the fact that both Russell and James were dealing with what is now seen to be an outmoded concept of matter. Once the notion of the physical has been expanded to include energy, it becomes somewhat less motivated. Contemporary materialists now freely admit the existence of more than matter in the sense that they recognize the existence of energy. On this front, it is interesting to note that the terms "materialism" and "physicalism" are now typically used interchangeably (a practice I have followed in this book), despite the fact that if materialism were interpreted as meaning that there is only matter, most of those who call themselves materialists would hold that such a theory is false. In practice, neutral monism has not proved to be a stable alternative to the standard array of options in the philosophy of mind, collapsing either into materialism, idealism or some form of dualism.[25] Still, I suggest that neutral monism, and specifically Tallis' notion of presence, does have great appeal from the standpoint of achieving a deep connection between the mental and physical.

I believe that Tallis' fascinating proposal may be respected, and the neutral monist drive for unity incorporated, within a theistic view of the cosmos which accounts for mental–physical life as itself the outcome of a presence, the presence of God. God's presence is constituted by the relations picked out earlier in this chapter in terms of knowledge, power, and creative conservation.

By way of underscoring the link between theism and dualism, I consider what mutual support dualism and theism can lend each other. It will not be very impressive if we argue for theism on the basis of dualism and then argue for dualism on the basis of theism. I am not endorsing such circular reasoning, but in noting and rejecting this type of circularity we should be careful not to obscure some of the legitimate ways in which dualism and theism can provide mutual support. How might this mutual support be realized?

I have been maintaining that the plausibility of dualism provides reasons for not rejecting theism on the basis of reasons advanced by Jonathan Barnes and many other philosophers. But imagine that you are *not* fully convinced by earlier chapters that dualism is true though you now think it is theoretically coherent, and not nonsense. That is, the notion that we ourselves are immaterial but physically embodied does not seem impossible to you, though you are not prepared to endorse the modal argument for dualism. Given that you believe it is not incoherent for a person or intentional agent to be nonphysical, a hurdle placed by Barnes in his treatment of the ontological argument for God's existence has been lifted. And a principal objection (it is incoherent to suppose that there could be an

---

[25] Armstrong reports that "all dualisms are inherently unstable, with a tendency to collapse one way or the other," but the opposite could be said about monistic schemes like neutral monism. They have a tendency to "collapse" into distinguishable categories. *Brain and Mind* (New York: Excerpta Medica, 1979) p. 33.

incorporeal person) raised by Kenny with the argument from design and by Miles with the argument from religious experience has been overturned. The way is cleared to some extent for reexamining these arguments, which could ultimately have an evidential bearing as to whether a dualist view of persons is (after all) reasonable to accept. The reasoning here could take different forms, only one of which would be along the lines I have been suggesting. Imagine that a principal reason you have had for thinking dualism is false (even though coherent) is that this seems to commit you to viewing the emergence of consciousness from nonconscious matter as anomalous in an otherwise uniformly material cosmos. Other things being equal, you take simplicity to be a mark of the true (*simplex sigillum veri*) and this tips the scales against dualism. Imagine, however, that you come to believe theism is plausible in the way we have recounted, perhaps by way of accepting a version of the ontological or cosmological arguments. This would then give you reason to see the emergence of consciousness over against a very different background of assumptions: consciousness as a nonphysical reality would not be anomalous, but would figure in the account of the cosmos as a whole. A reason you had for rejecting dualism would then be removed.

We can also imagine the line of reasoning here taking an opposite course. Imagine that you think there is some reason for accepting dualism, but not one strong enough to outweigh the reasons you have for adopting a fundamentally unified worldview, once again following the *simplex sigillum veri* dictum. Now, imagine you find theism to be implausible and have no reason to accept a cosmology or theory of ultimate reality which is intentionalistic. Under such conditions, the implausibility of theism may well prompt a rejection of dualism.

In all such reflection, it is of great importance to balance one's view of particular matters in light of a comprehensive conception of reality. Too often philosophical problems are dealt with in a piecemeal fashion, and it is forgotten how they may relate to other, seemingly remote concerns. Stephen Pepper aptly observed how we sometimes forget the role that a world-hypothesis can serve.

For we all have and use world hypotheses, just as we have animal bodies, have perceptions, and move within geometrical relations. It is just because world hypotheses are so intimate and persuasive that we do not easily look at them from a distance, so to speak, or as if we saw them in a mirror.[26]

By holding a mirror up to both dualism and theism I hope to draw attention to how the two can be part of a coherent comprehensive understanding of ourselves and God. In the last chapter I focus on the nature of personal life and the integral nature of God's presence to the cosmos.

[26] *World Hypotheses* (Berkeley: University of California Press, 1942), p. 2.

CHAPTER 6

Integrative theism

God is closer to me than I am to myself.

Meister Eckhart[1]

In the last two chapters I defended the intelligibility of understanding God as a powerful Creator, present in the cosmos as an incorporeal being with supreme cognitive power. In this chapter I consider in more detail the nature of personal life and explore the philosophical opportunities for understanding what theists describe as God's interior presence. I seek to chart the different respects in which the development of personal life requires a kind of shifting attachment and detachment. Integrative dualism places great emphasis on the holist, unitary nature of embodied life, while it also allows that relations with one's body, oneself, and others can be unduly absorbed or detached. The account of attachment and detachment outlined in the first section of the chapter will serve as a basis upon which to examine Eckhart's claim, a claim that echoes Augustine's prayer, "Thou [God] wert more inward to me than my most inward part; and higher than my highest."[2] The chapter concludes with articulating integrative theism, which is essentially classical theism, and the thesis that God's love of creation is to be understood in affective, passionate terms.

---

[1] German Sermon 69 (trans. M.O'C. Walshe, *Meister Eckhart: Sermons & Treatises*, vol. II (London: Watkins, 1981)), p. 165.

[2] Augustine, *Confessions*, *iii*, 6, 11.

DIMENSIONS OF PERSONAL IDENTITY

I submit that the development of our personal lives involves a series of attachments and detachments whereby the boundaries of our lives are constantly having to be drawn and redrawn. To achieve a sense of our personal identity requires our identifying certain states and objects as ourselves, or as only part of ourselves, and identifying states and objects as other than ourselves. I consider the respective acts of identity involving attachment and detachment in light of integrative dualism.

At the most fundamental level, our possessing a determinate notion of our own identity is grounded in our capacity to identify states of ourselves in contrast to the states of other persons and things. I only secure a conception of myself in an environment that is not myself to the extent that I realize the objects making up my environment have a reality not constituted by my own states of awareness or by my activities. For example, I realize that the tree I am sitting under is not itself one of my perceptual states and that it is not volitionally dependent on me. The tree is not one of my actions, as if I were somehow "treeing" or otherwise constituting it. My sitting beneath the tree is not sitting beneath a part of myself, or beneath an act of my will. How the tree looks to me depends, in part, on my sensory faculties, but the tree itself exists independently of my eyes and the functioning of my other cognitive faculties.[3] I doubt that the growth of our personal life involves a neat process

---

[3] It is worth considering whether some kind of cognitive detachability would have a role for the idealist or antirealist. I think it can. The power of detachment as I outline it in the text is not the power to conceive of an object one does not conceive of (at the same time), or objects not conceived of by some mind. Rather, it is the power to conceive of objects or states of the world which do not themselves depend for their existence upon one's own cognitive and ontological powers. Idealism is not solipsism. So long as idealism makes some distinction between selves or selves and their sensory states, it can provide a role for cognitive detachment as a virtue. Antirealism may seem the least amenable to recognizing cognitive detachment as virtuous. Michael Dummett, Nelson Goodman, and Hilary Putnam have advanced in different forms the thesis that the world is partly our construction. Even so, these anti-realists can still allow a role for detachment relative to the world-view we have constructed and embraced. Thus, they could allow that it would be a mistake for you and me, given our shared "way of world making," to think the trees in the yard are entirely our construction.

whereby we first secure a robust sense of self and then formulate a clear demarcation of what is "out there." Social psychology has well documented how our development is a mixed affair in which boundaries are not at all neat.[4] But clearly, for me to secure a sense of myself as possessing some identity as an individual distinct from the identity of the tree *et al.*, I must be able to conceive of its life as having some reality independent of me. Attendant on this demarcation is the awareness of the fact that my beliefs about the tree are not just beliefs about my own states, but beliefs about something which is not me. What I want to underscore here is that in personal development a crucial role is played by our exercising a power which we may term the power of detachment. It could just as well be called the power of identity: the ability to identify oneself involves the capacity to recognize both what is and what is not oneself. By the power of detachment I mean our ability to identify ourselves as either independent of or more than some state or object. It is exercised in the case of external objects like the tree, but also in ways more internal to our conception of ourselves.

In order to appreciate my identity over extant periods of time I must realize that I am not composed solely of the sensory (and other mental) states I am in at any given instant. If I were identical with my current sensory states, then the instant these ceased to be, I would cease to be. I only see myself as a self existing over time to the extent that I realize I am more than these states; I am the one who am having these experiences, a person who may come to have different ones.

In the course of seeing myself as someone who has a future and is able to act voluntarily I must also be able to appreciate a further balance between attachment and detachment. Consider a case of making a decision about whether to make a donation to Oxfam for famine relief or spend the money on dinner. I contemplate two (ostensibly) possible futures, weighing reasons for and against each. In contemplating one option

---

[4] For a review of this literature see Rom Harré's *Social Being* (Oxford: Basil Blackwell, 1993). I do not go as far as Harré in his view that persons are social constructs, but I believe that he has properly drawn attention to ways in which social settings have a forceful role in our self-development.

as an option, I exercise the ability to see myself as doing an act while all along appreciating that I may not do it. I might well hold before my mind two outcomes, imagining that in one I make the Oxfam contribution and in the other I have eaten well but feel a gnawing guilt. My capacity here can be thought of as a power to balance a sort of attachment and detachment. I remain sufficiently attached, as it were, in contemplating these conceivable outcomes, realizing that in each I am contemplating what *I* would do, and not the undertakings of some counterpart of myself or a clone. There is detachment insofar as I realize that neither future state and action is inevitable. I am not bound to wind up being well-fed and feeling guilty.

Another region of personal identity requiring a balanced detachment and attachment has to do with coming to terms with the unconscious. Assuming the existence of the unconscious, I believe that a vital aspect of our personal identity is realized when we come to see ourselves as more than our conscious life. Occasions may arise when I must detach myself from an overly narrow view of my identity in order to appreciate my possessing beliefs and desires on an unconscious level. Detachment here is not by way of realizing that I am different from my conscious self, but by realizing that there is more to myself than what I am aware of consciously. Are dualists in any kind of philosophical danger in positing an unconscious? They need not be, though some versions of dualism may be.

Some dualists contend that consciousness is an essential feature of all mental states, thus making it impossible for a subject to possess mental states that one is not conscious of. On this reading, it is problematic to assume that a subject can have unconscious beliefs and desires. The prohibition against the unconscious becomes even graver when dualists insist that consciousness is an essential feature of being a person, thus making it impossible for a person to exist and not be conscious. In response to this stricture, Peter Carruthers poses the following dilemma: "The dualist will either have to deny that we are ever really unconscious, or deny that our existence is continuous throughout our lives. "[5] I do not think that either denial is very inviting, though each has been attempted by able philosophers.[6] Fortunately, nothing in the articulation and defense of integrative dualism lands one with the above difficulties. It is nowhere claimed that persons cease to be when they are unconscious, nor is this entailed by the modal argument of Chapter 3 or the appeal to subjective experience in Chapters 1 and 2. (I assume, however, that there is some plausibility in holding that under most conditions the *irreversible* loss of consciousness by a person would be a mark of death. In such cases, I think we would tend to describe the person in terms other than of being unconscious, i.e. of failing to be either conscious or unconscious.)

The unconscious can be variously analyzed. A chief dispute is whether to treat the unconscious as a dispositional or categorical state. According to the former, Miriam's having unconscious ill-will toward her mother means she would have such ill-will consciously under certain conditions. The categorical thesis is that Miriam has ill-will toward her mother, and this is a *bona fide* mental state of hers, though she is not conscious of it. The dispositional theory has the advantage of being somewhat simpler, in that it does not posit actual beliefs and desires that have a submerged life of their own. The categorical school has the advantage of being able to draw on unconscious beliefs *qua* beliefs in their explanation of human behavior. Dispositions do not cause things to occur, so the dispositional school will have to read the causal role of unconscious beliefs in terms of whatever mental or physical basis gives rise to them. Given a robust integrative understanding of the person–body relationship, it is not philosophically hazardous to recognize a physical categorical base for the unconscious in the sense that it enables the subject to have the appropriate conscious beliefs and desires.

The truth of integrative dualism does not require adopting either the categorical or the dispositional account. Fortunately,

---

[5] Carruthers, *Introducing Persons* (Albany: State University of New York Press, 1986).
[6] See the treatment on selves enduring over periods of unconsciousness by H. D. Lewis in *The Elusive Self* (Philadelphia: Westminster Press, 1982) and Richard Swinburne in *The Evolution of the Soul* (Oxford: Clarendon Press, 1986).

too, it is not committed to the hyper-private view of subjectivity associated with Cartesianism or a neatly delineated picture of the stages of personal identity. The truth of integrative dualism is compatible with recognizing that our earliest level of consciousness may be remarkably similar to Tallis' notion of presence, reviewed in the last chapter, in which subject and object are not clearly differentiated. I do not think Freud was off the mark when he observed the way in which we only gradually come to differentiate ourselves from the world, and this often involves the interplay of fantasy, projection, and identification. Freud noted: "Originally, the I includes everything, later it separates off an external world from itself."[7] Following Freud, Jonathan Lear has recently observed that "The I is what emerges from this differentiation. What we have is mind spread out over a relatively undifferentiated field: that from which I and world will emerge."[8] On this account, our mental life is recognized as protean and malleable, taking shape gradually through the exercise of our powers of projection, identification, and separation.

Because integrative dualism is not disadvantaged by an excessively private notion of the mental, it need not ignore the role of others in the emergence of our personal identity that has been duly recognized in psycho-analytic literature. I am very much drawn to the Attachment Theory of John Bowlby and Mary Ainsworth and impressed by aspects of the thought of some of those who have refined Freudian models of consciousness like D. W. Winnicott, Melanie Klein, and Wilfred Bion.[9] Each develops a different account of consciousness. There is not enough space here to articulate these and indicate

---

[7] Freud, *Civilization and its Discontents*, cited by Jonathan Lear, *Love and its Place in Nature* (London: Faber & Faber, 1990), pp. 149, 150.

[8] *Love and its Place in Nature*, p. 199.

[9] I record my debt here to the Philosophy and Psychoanalysis Reading Group at Oxford University, 1992–1993, and especially to Dan Isaakson, for helping me see the importance of this literature. There are crucial differences between these writers; I am capitalizing on the fact that each has tried to articulate different respects in which mental development occurs in a shared identity with the care-giver in a way that involves introjection and projection. I do not accept, for example, Winnicott's more Humean notion of the self. A good overview of some of the literature is Inge Bretherton's "The Origins of Attachment Theory: P. John Bowlby and Mary Ainsworth," *Developmental Psychology* 28:5 (1992), 759–775. See Melanie Klein's *Love,*

specifically what aspects of each are best supported, though for present purposes this is (fortunately) unnecessary. Here I simply wish to underscore how integrative dualism can take on board more specific theories of personal development that bring to light the intersubjective, shared dimension of personal identity. Winnicott has, I believe, correctly grasped the role of the caregiver in infancy, noting how the varying degrees of care, attention, and need-satisfaction create natural stages by which an infant comes to realize her independent identity.

The need for a good environment, which is absolute at first, rapidly becomes relative. The ordinary good mother is good enough ... What releases the mother from her need to be near-perfect is the infant's understanding. In the ordinary course of events the mother tries not to introduce complications beyond those which the infant can understand and allow for ... In infant care it is vitally important that mothers, at first physically, and soon also imaginatively, can start off by supplying this active adaption, but also it is a characteristic maternal function to provide graduated failure of adaption, according to the growing ability of the individual infant to allow for relative failure by mental activity, or by understanding.[10]

Integrative dualism can allow for Winnicott's contribution, and even go further by recognizing the different ways in which infants come to internalize imaginatively their experience of the care-giver. There is no reason why the work of Melanie Klein, Wilfred Bion, and others who have capitalized on the infant's tendency to form a vital, imaginative tie with the care-giver cannot be taken up by the dualist.

The psychoanalyst Jonathan Lear has drawn on Freud's conception of the role of love in the early stages of mental development, and used this in his conception of how we variously take shape as subjects through attachment and detachment.

The original identification is rather an initial differentiation by which some of the qualities of the loving mother, the loving world, are taken

Guilt and Reparation and Other Works, 1921–1945 and *Envy and Gratitude and Other Works*, 1946–1963, both published by Delta (New York, 1975).
[10] D. W. Winnicott, "Mind and its Relation to the Psyche–Soma," in *Collected Papers* (New York: Basic Books, 1958), p. 245. I part company with Winnicott on his more Humean notion of the self.

to exist on this side of the emerging boundary. This isn't just a mistaken drawing of the boundary by a little cartographer; it is an active taking in. The infant takes in his mother along with his mother's milk ... It is through love that the boundaries of the soul are redrawn ... For Freud, love is manifested in human life in the process of individuation. It is in response to a loving world that a human is able to distinguish himself from it. By internalizing that love, the human establishes himself as an individual I, a locus of activity distinct from the rest of nature. The process by which the human soul comes to be is a lifetime activity.[11]

This outlook closely accords with Klein's view that the mother (care-giver) functions as a container for the infant. We grow up, as it were, as a mind within a mind. Ideally this is through the loving identification of the mother, and the reciprocal identifying and detaching of the infant in the course of developing as a person. Recognizing what Klein and Lear have documented as our growing up in intersubjective ways is, in part, unsurprising if integrative dualism is true. John Bowlby has ably construed this intersubjective life between care-giver and child in which the child recognizes itself as an individual through attentive regard and guidance. Commenting on the mother–infant relationship, Bowlby writes: "She orients him in space and time, provides his environment, permits the satisfaction of some impulses, restricts others. She is his ego and super-ego."[12]

In the treatment of the problem of other minds in Chapter 2 I noted the importance of placing the problem in light of one's comprehensive world-view. Objections to dualism are often based on the supposition that dualists must begin their quest to secure access to the external world from an isolated mental world, radically cut off from others. My proposal is that dualists need not do so and, set over against a theistic cosmos, there is reason to expect that we have the faculties of imagination, projection, and apprehension of the world we do enabling us to live intersubjectively. In my view, those philosophers who either deny subjectivity outright or who link it with public discourse so that prelinguistic infancy is shorn of mental life are in greater

---

[11] Lear, *Love and its Place in Nature*, pp. 161, 177.
[12] "Maternal Care and Mental Health," *World Health Organization Monograph*, Serial 2 (1951), p. 53.

trouble than dualists. I believe that such materialist alternatives are more prone to characterize personal development in sterile, zombie-like ways than your average form of dualism, let alone integrative dualism.[13]

The power of detachment and the various attendant forms of identification I have drawn on have a positive, essential role in our personal development, but they can also play a crucial role in our fragmentation and disintegration.

HUMAN ABSENCE AND DIVINE PRESENCE

The power of detachment as exercised in personal development may be thought of along the lines of Aristotle's treatment of the virtues as properly proportionate means between the defects of excess and deficiency. On the positive side, the power or virtue of detachment is properly exercised in my realization that external persons and objects are indeed distinct from myself, when I realize that there is more to myself than a given occurrent sensory state, my conscious desires, and, in some contexts, more than one inevitable future. Presumably such detachment has a vital role to play in ethics when I appreciate that there are persons other than myself who have legitimate claims on my life, and a vital role in emotional maturation. It can also have a reparative role in moral reformation. Under conditions in which I have acted wrongly with ill motives, part of the reformation of my character must take the form of my detaching myself from these motives and acts as I renounce these as unfitting, and no longer expressing my designs.[14] The term "detachment" may suggest *ennui* and listlessness, a boring, sterile, melancholic state, but the way I am using the term here as a virtue, detachment is a power that enables us to live passionately and actively. In loving another person, I must be able to exercise some of what may be called detachment in the

---

[13] Witness, for example, the stark picture of infancy in "The Subject of Mind" by Marcia Cavell, *International Journal of Psycho-Analysis* 72 (1991), p. 148.

[14] Behind this construal of detachment is my view that there is a close relation between epistemic and moral virtues. Just as there is an essential detachment in our cognitive life in recognizing others as others, I believe that there is an ethical detachment we need to take seriously as well. See my "Relativizing the Ideal Observer Theory," *Philosophy and Phenomenological Research* 49:1 (September 1988), 123–138.

realization that my beloved is not me and that when she loves me, this is not simply me loving myself. However, on either side of what marks proportional, "virtuous" detachment and attachment lie problems, and in what follows I want to identify different areas in which things go awry. My purpose will be to give some sense to the notion that a person may be distant from himself through misguided detachment and attachment, and then to go on to defend the Eckhart–Augustine notion I cited earlier that God is closer to ourselves than we are.

(1) *Detached self-assessment*

Imagine that I have a wildly distorted view of myself and think I am the greatest pianist in the world. When I look in the mirror, I think to myself: "Ah, the greatest pianist in the world is wearing a green tie today." Little do I know that I am actually one of the world's worst pianists and that the greatest pianist in the world is currently in Vienna and has never worn a green tie. There is a rather large gap between my beliefs about myself and who and what I am; one might well say there is a great distance.

The popular phrase "to be out of touch with oneself" expresses this rather well. In the case imagined, I fail to be in touch with myself. Paradigm physical objects like stones and trees cannot do this. Whenever and wherever a stone touches the ground, it is touching the ground. By way of contrast, whenever and wherever I believe I am looking at the greatest person on earth (me), it by no means follows that I am truly doing so. Just as a correct view of my powers and liabilities signals a kind of proximity to myself, false beliefs illustrate well a sense in which I fail to be present to who I am.

This distance from oneself can occur in cases like the pianist example or in deeper, philosophical terrain as well. To the extent that I adopt a false metaphysical picture of my place in the cosmos, there is a sense in which I may be said to distance myself from myself. The truth of the matter admits of many gradations and legitimate interpretations, but some examples may firm up the idea. If I take myself to be the reincarnation of

Plato, a Berkeleian spirit, the embodiment of Kant's "good will," the voice and consciousness of Hegel's Absolute or a Nietzschean superman above the herd of humanity when I am not such a reincarnation, there is no Berkleian spirit, Kantian good will, or Hegelian Absolute, and Nietzsche's scheme of superman and herd rests on conceptual and ethical errors, then there is a sense in which I have become detached from who I truly am. We will differ in how seriously we measure this detachment based on how much of our sense of who we are is bound up with such grandiose philosophical viewpoints. In the case of deeply held convictions as with religious theism, I believe the stakes are higher than, say, convictions about more abstract philosophical matters (the conviction that sets are not properties or that propositions are timeless). Thus, if theism is false and yet I live my life consciously in light of what I believe is God's will, then there is a sense in which I am detached from myself. The opposite may well be the case for someone who resolutely lives a self-conscious atheism if it should turn out that he is mistaken and he is made in the image of God.

The kind of detachment I sketched so far involves falsely held convictions, but I think detachment may also occur in cases where we fail to have convictions. If I fail to have any deep conception about my identity, unsure whether I am part of a naturalistic or theistic cosmos, for example, there is a sense in which my grasp of myself will be partial. This is not necessarily a defect. Indeed, if the evidence does not lead us to adopt any position at all, perhaps rushing ahead to form a conviction (even if true) would be intellectually negligent. But defect or not, there is a sense in which agnosticism about the philosophy of human nature will be an agnosticism about (and therefore, in a sense, a failure to connect with) ourselves.

(2) *Detached goals*

I believe that our identity is partly constituted by what we choose to pursue, our central projects. This is made possible by our capacity to realize that there is more to ourselves than being mere patients who enjoy a bare momentary existence. Consider a case in which I may desire and even endeavor to be the greatest pianist in the world. To the extent that I am alive to this project, one that I am deeply committed to, I am close to myself or who I am. But imagine that there are times when I am overcome with weariness or hysterically out of joint in terms of my long term motives and goals. Now, it could be that this failure to be enchanted by, or psychologically attentive to, my project discloses a very real and legitimate reassessment of my commitments. Nonetheless, there may be occasions when my commitment remains constant and yet my attentiveness and spirit temporarily wane. I can become detached from the goals I have set for myself. Imagine that during an episode of *ennui* I sell my piano for a song and afterwards declare my act to be idiotic, pointless, mad. We may plausibly take certain cases like this as instances of my temporarily losing touch with my settled, central drives or projects. I thereby fail to be present to myself insofar as I fail fully to appreciate my central goals.

Consider the kind of closeness that typically characterizes friendship. A friend may not sympathize with all (or even most) of one's goals. Nonetheless, a salient feature of much friendship involves more than acquaintance with at least some of our central commitments. We expect friends not to be bored by the goals that shape our lives. A best friend may try desperately to get me to stop my piano-playing or perhaps prevent me from destroying pianos. She remains distant from me insofar as she finds my projects and goals to be of little interest, neither delighting in my success nor grieving over my ills.

There is some popular literature that commends persons to be their own best friends. At first, this literature may seem conceptually awry. Being a friend might well appear to be a dyadic relation like being a sibling and hence not something that can have a role in one's relationship with oneself. It makes little sense to claim that a person is her own sister. Yet there is some sense in speaking about being one's own good friend, just as there is sense to claiming that someone cares about themselves. In the *Laws*, Plato suggested that we are (or can be) friends with ourselves. What this may amount to is that one cares about one's own goals and projects, one takes interest in one's own welfare, one avoids self-destruction (presumably self-destruction may amount to a case in which one is one's own enemy). It seems to me that insofar as we fail to give sufficient concerned attention to ourselves, we fail to be fully present to ourselves. Those who fail to be their own friends (or even interested in themselves) fail to be close to themselves.

Our projects can serve to cement the detachment outlined under self-assessment. When I act on the basis of a profoundly false understanding of myself I can become further estranged and disengaged from who I am. Thus, imagine I wrongly believe that the nonhuman environment is placed here entirely for us humans to use however we please regardless of the impact on nonhuman animals, creatures whom I decide to treat as nonsentient machines. Further, imagine that I wrongly assume the female gender to be biologically, emotionally, and intellectually inferior to males, and so treat women in the condescending, patronizing fashion in which a superior talks to underlings. All such action may be seen as driving a wedge between who I am (a person whose gender is not superior and whose species shares this planet with other sentient, conscious nonhuman animals who deserve respect) and who I take myself to be. In this schema, vanity and other vices may be seen, in part, as cutting ourselves off from others as well as ourselves.

Through adopting certain projects that might otherwise be healthy I can secure a certain narrowness of pursuit and excessive preoccupation that serves to cut myself off from myself. In cases of obsession I may cease to retain a grip on the rest of my life which falls into obscurity. By way of a reckless, dogged pursuit of one thing, I lose out on other regions of my being. Examples from literature can bring this home. Witness the growing obsession of Jarvet, the police inspector, in Hugo's *Les Misérables*, an obsession which ultimately consumes him, as realized in his final act of suicide.[15]

---

[15] Amélie Rorty's notion of character is relevant here, *Mind in Action* (Boston: Beacon Press, 1988), chapter 4. We can become unduly identified with a fixed set of dispositions that don't permit needed transformation and reform; we can be "characters" rather than selves, souls, or persons. See Rorty's taxonomy here.

(3) *A detached unconscious*

Earlier I noted how an important step in our personal identity involves realizing that there is more to ourselves than our conscious life. This requires a certain measure of detachment as we appreciably realize this extension of ourselves: I cannot legitimately identify myself exclusively by my conscious states. The realm of the unconscious stands for an aspect of our personal life which (under present conditions) we will rarely, if ever, be able to fully integrate consciously. Whether the unconscious is treated along categorical or dispositional lines, it is an area of personal life which may be quite alien from who we think we are. From the standpoint of the categorical theory, this may involve my unconsciously having beliefs and desires that conflict with my conscious beliefs and desires, whereas for the dispositionalist this will amount to my having dispositions to have beliefs and desires in conflict with those I have consciously. The complex character of conscious and unconscious life gives ample room for us to become estranged from ourselves.

(4) *A detached past*

Insofar as persons have a past they know little about, they can be detached from who they are. Detachment from one's past is not always unhealthy. There is an important role in moral reflection for detaching oneself from past wrongdoing in the course of renouncing one's former, evil intentions, and resolving on new courses of action. But detachment can be overplayed even here, if it leads someone to deny any continuity of identity with their past. One's personality or character is largely constituted by what one assumes to be reliable memories of one's past. Insofar as my memories are distorted or lost altogether, I believe that I am less present to who I am. I can endure over time as a self despite vast changes, but who I am is, in a sense, inseparable from who I have been. I am the person who used to do such and such and who suffered this and that in the past.[16]

[16] In *An Essay on Human Understanding* John Locke developed a theory of personal identity that gives pride of place to memory claims. While I do not think he

(5) *A detached future*

Aristotle once wrote that we should call no one happy until they are dead. Aristotle believed that a person's happiness, flourishing, or fortune involve matters stretching beyond the person's individual, current states. Roughly, whether or not one has truly flourished, and may be justly considered to be happy in the full sense, depends, in part, upon the eventual success of one's projects, the results of one's life, perhaps the well-being of one's children, and the like. We may not subscribe to Aristotle's dictum or his rationale, but I believe that there is an important insight in his view. Imagine that I have every reason to expect to live many years but have no conception of what will happen to me in that time. Perhaps I am like Søren Kierkegaard's aesthete, who lives only for and in the pleasure of the moment. If so, my life will be truncated in an important respect. We are creatures who live in time and, while there may come a last moment to our lives (if there is no afterlife), arguably this only occurs once. We have probably all been guilty of living in and for the future and neglecting the importance of the present moment. In so doing we wind up being remote, inattentive, or even oblivious to who we are. But I also believe that insofar as we are inattentive or completely ignorant of what is to come, or what we may reasonably anticipate, we are also remote from who we are. I do not suggest that we are remote from ourselves to the extent that we fail to know precisely in every point of detail what will take place. Clearly the future is not wholly written out for us, the rest of our lives stretched out in fixed pattern. More modestly, I suggest that if we utterly disregard or even suppress all anticipation of what we will be like, we are not close to who we are.[17]

These may not be the only respects in which human beings may be said to be distant from themselves. Surely each of the above cases could be brought about in many different ways, and

succeeds, this should not lead us to ignore the enormous role that memory has in our identity.

[17] I believe that there is some insight behind Heidegger's notion in *Being and Time* that human being or *Dasein* includes an orientation toward the future.

in different combinations, but they will serve here to bring to light some of the ways in which God may be proximate to each of us.

Could God fail to be close to Godself in any of the ways just outlined? In the incarnation there may be a sense in which God was distant from Godself in the human life of Christ, the second person of the Trinity. Perhaps God *qua* Jesus Christ did not always know his nature (1), his Messianic mission (2), his unconscious (3), his past (4), or his future (5). By envisioning this lack of unity with who he is as the Divine, second person of the Trinity, the incarnation may be understood as a profound self-limitation allowing God to be subject to many of the fragmenting conditions we are susceptible to. I will not try to develop these implications here.[18] Instead, consider whether God *qua* omniscient, omnipotent, loving Creator could be somehow remote from Godself.

As an essentially omniscient being, God could not have a false self-understanding (1). Insofar as God is envisioned as truly omniscient, God may be assumed not to have an unconscious. God knows all; there could not be facts about Godself of which God has no consciousness (3). God must likewise be conceived of as being alive to God's projects (2). Some religious literature abounds with pleas that God be less relentless in bringing about God's revealed will concerning human history. Philosophical theists are divided on the matter of whether God has a memory. If God is outside time, God has no past to remember. But if God

---

[18] Cf. Thomas Morris' *The Logic of God Incarnate* (Ithaca: Cornell University Press, 1986). I believe that the considerations I have cited here can be accommodated within Morris' two minds theory of the incarnation. Morris contends that within the single, expansive consciousness of God as second member of the Trinity, there was (and is) a distinct conscious life, the life of Jesus of Nazareth. Jesus, the God-man, was limited in ways in which Jesus as God is not. Thus, the God-man was not omniscient during earthly life, he could be tempted by sin, and so on, whereas God as unincarnate supremely perfect being was (and is) omniscient, cannot be tempted, and the like. Morris describes his theory as the two minds theory as he posits a mind (incarnate Jesus consciousness) within a mind (broader God consciousness) which includes incarnate Jesus (consciousness as a subset or proper part). What I have proposed in the text is that the mind of the incarnate Jesus may have undergone a time when he was not close to himself in the psychological respects delineated. I seek to develop a traditional account of the incarnation in "Language Truth, and Logos", a book-length manuscript in preparation with Patrick Richmond.

is in time, God has a past and future to remember and foreknow respectively. Given either theological understanding of God's relationship to time, I believe that God *qua* omnipotent, omniscient being could not undergo a remoteness from Godself. If God has memories, these may be presumed to be exact and true. If God has a future, God may be presumed to know this with the greatest precision that maximal cognitive power allows. What if theological libertarianism is assumed, and God cannot (in principle) know future free acts of creatures or of God's own? Even here, if omniscience is read as maximal cognitive power, as presented in Chapter 5, God knows all that it is metaphysically possible to know about the future. Thus, he knows all conceivable outcomes of creaturely free action, albeit God he does not know which of the myriad of choices may be selected. Still, the divine predictions are conceived of as being unsurpassably great, as exact as is metaphysically or logically possible. God knows all that may be possibly known about the future; God is cognizant of God's own temporality (if God is temporal) and does not live in the present moment without forethought about what is to come. I conclude that an omniscient, omnipotent God cannot be remote from Godself with respect to God's past (4) or future (5).

How close can God get to you? Very. First note the way in which we may believe that God is close to a world of inanimate objects. In accord with the account of Chapter 5 the classic tenet that God is omnipresent amounts (in part) to the claim that for any object that exists, God knows the object exhaustively, God can exercise omnipotent power with respect to the object, and God creates and conserves it in existence. There is no spatial intermediary that obtrudes between God and the object, prohibiting God from acting upon or knowing about the object. God may be understood to be present to us in these respects and others as well. Consider the closeness of God to created persons in relation to their remoteness from themselves.

God knows my lack of piano skills, my thoughts, feelings, yearnings. God knows the truth and falsity of my different conceptions of human nature. God is aware of my jealousy and Freudian impulses; indeed, every feature of my life is transparent to the omniscient God. No matter how well I know myself, the scope and precision of God's knowledge of me is unsurpassed. God will have a deeper, clearer grasp of my unconscious than I do (and know whether the categorical, dispositional, or some other theory of the unconscious is correct!). My plans, projects, and goals cannot escape the attention of an omniscient God. Depending upon one's theology, one may suppose that God knows our future precisely in every detail or, short of that, that the knowledge God does have of our future is unsurpassable. I conclude that in all these respects God may be understood to be profoundly present to our lives.

If theological determinism is true, then God's presence in one's life will be more thorough than libertarianism, for all one's actions will be seen as ultimately determined by God. It is here that I think libertarianism has the advantage, for it will decidedly not count the free agency of creatures as always a reflection of God's intentions. Whether theists are libertarian or not, adherents of classical monotheism in Jewish, Christian, and Islamic traditions will recognize an ethical dimension to God's omnipresence.

I believe that in ethical monotheism, the omnipresence of God is to be understood in terms of God addressing the goods and ills of the cosmos. In part, this involves God's judging the goods of the cosmos to be truly good and the ills to be truly ill. It also means that when created persons act justly they are thereby in closer proximity to God in the sense that there is Divine–human accord, as opposed to when persons act unjustly and are thereby remote from God's purposes. I want to explore an additional affective dimension to this understanding of God's presence. I believe that part of what it means for God to be present to the cosmos is for God to be affectively responsive to its states, feeling sorrow for its ills, and taking pleasure in its goods. This stance has been widely held. Witness, for example, Bertrand Brasnett's comment some seventy years ago: "When a good man turns to evil and a bad man turns to good, these facts are not without significance for the life of God. To suppose that they are is to write God down as indifferent to good or evil ...

But if God rejoices over the conversion of the evil-doer and sorrows over the good man who goes astray, his happiness and sorrow must vary in some degree as good or evil predominate upon the earth ... So far as we can see, sin must cause God an everlasting pain. "[19] Is it permissible to describe God in such affective terms, feeling pleasure or grief? I believe that it is and that there are sound religious reasons for thinking God is affectively responsive to the world and its creatures. This touches on a key component of integrative theism, distinguishing it from other versions of classical theism. Not all forms of traditional theism have welcomed belief in God's affective presence.

DIVINE PASSIBILISM AND IMPASSIBILISM

Traditional impassibilists maintain that God is without passions (the literal meaning of *impassibilis*), while passibilists attribute to God passions like sorrow and pleasure. I adopt a version of passibilism which sees this sorrow and pleasure as part of what is involved in God's loving creation. Before advancing a rationale for embracing passibilism, I offer an overview of some of the relevant concerns.

According to Divine impassibilism, God is not subject to the defects of pain and suffering. This seems like a foregone conclusion to some traditionalists on the grounds that God is eternal, immutable, and incorporeal. Being subject to passions like sorrow appears to require being temporal, subject to change, and corporeal. Since God is none of these, impassibilism seems to follow naturally. It is now apparent, however, that such considerations are not sufficient to secure the case for impassibilism.

The belief that God is eternal in the sense of being outside of time and that God is immutable has been under serious attack in recent years, with the result that many theists now conclude that the notion of Divine eternity is itself unintelligible or, if intelligible, incompatible with God being an all-knowing, intentional agent. For some Christian theists the portrait of God

[19] Brasnett, *The Suffering of the Impassible God* (London: SPCK, 1928), p. 74.

as an immutable Creator of a changing world which God
entered as Christ has likewise appeared incredible. It is partly
because I am impressed by these considerations that I articulate
and defend a philosophy of God not committed to the tenets of
eternity and immutability. The widespread adoption of a
similar posture among contemporary theists is some indication
that traditionalists cannot rule out passibilism on the basis of
assumptions shared by all theists. Furthermore, it is not obvious
that traditionalists can altogether exclude passibilism even
given their understanding of the Divine.

Traditionalists argue, against their critics, that an eternal,
immutable God can know about the world's temporal states,
judge the world's goods and ills, and act in the world. If they are
right here, why cannot an eternal, immutable God sorrow and
delight over the world's states as well? My point is not to argue
for the coherence of supposing that an eternal, immutable being
can do what the traditionalists claim, but to propose that the
prospects for arguing that God can judge, know, and act
atemporally seems no more promising than arguing that God
may have affective sorrow and pleasure atemporally. Does the
notion of a being who knows something nondurationally make
more sense than that of a being who feels something nondurationally? I do not see that one has a clear advantage over the
other.[20]

Does the incorporeality of God rule out passibilism? This
question speaks more to the heart of this book's project. What if
pleasure and sorrow are the very same thing as bodily
phenomena and, thus, having emotions requires having a
body? The burden of Chapters 1 and 2 was to argue, *contra*
materialism, that sensations are not themselves bodily, physical
states. If the arguments were successful, the objection at hand
fails. But perhaps the objection may be reformulated as the
thesis that emotions like compassionate sorrow are bodily
informed, even if they are not themselves physical states. That

---

[20] Reasons for thinking knowledge states are not essentially temporally extended trade
on thinking of these states as dispositions which are only part of the story. Note Gale's
discussion of the nondurational present. Vernon White has some discussion of how an
eternal God might be credited with feeling, *The Fall of a Sparrow: A Concept of Special
Divine Action* (Exeter: Paternoster Press, 1985).

is, for a person to feel sorrow involves feeling a kind of bodily fatigue or physical heaviness. If that is plausible, it can still be argued that without a physical body, it is difficult to make sense of possessing such feelings as compassion. This may be even more apparent in the case of other emotions, such as anger. We readily associate being angry with physiologically inferred sensations like feeling the rush of adrenaline, the flushed face, the tightening of muscles, and so on. As God lacks muscles, adrenaline, and so on, it seems as though God cannot have anger, compassion, jealousy, and other emotions.

I believe that this defense of traditionalism has some plausibility, for we do associate the emotions with various sensations that are shaped by our embodied life. A passibilist might make the desperate move of granting the bodily informed character of emotions and yet conclude that all this shows is that God must have a body-image of some sort. A material body is not required. It is evident that persons can have "phantom pains," feelings that appear to be in body parts that no longer exist: for example pins and needles "in" an amputated leg are often reported.[21] Perhaps God only requires a sort of bodily surrogate, like these phantom limbs, to feel the requisite emotions. Fortunately, I do not think we need to attribute speculatively such a phantom status to God in order to ascribe emotions intelligibly. Consider, first, the complex character of emotions, and the reasons for thinking that emotions involve more than sensations.

Emotions must involve more than sensations in order to distinguish them from bare sensory undergoings. What makes an emotion compassion is not simply the sensing of bodily fatigue, physical heaviness, or some such similar sensory state. These could just as well be the result of a heavy meal and thought of as mildly unpleasant. To have compassion is to care about someone or something, and this is constituted, in part, by a cluster of judgments. Thus, it makes little sense for me to be said to have compassion for you unless I judge that you are the bearer of some misfortune, even if only the misfortune of failing

---

[21] According to Brian O'Shaughnessy there is a wide role played by the body-image, *The Will* (Cambridge: Cambridge University Press, 1980).

to receive something good that you did not expect. Are emotions, then, simply judgments and not sensations at all? I think a middle course is in order here. Emotions involve judgments as well as some felt quality of consciousness such as sorrow. To construe emotions as entirely constituted by judgments misses out on the evident feelings that are involved here, but having said that much, I want to insist that emotions like compassion and anger need not be thought of as grounded in an actual body or body-image phenomenology. Couldn't you feel angry with me without feeling displeasure at any specific bodily location? Imagine that you judge me to have wronged you in some way and, upon seeing me, you feel enormous displeasure and perhaps even have a felt urge to harm me. It is not at all obvious that such displeasure and desire require bodily phenomenology.[22]

If we can make sense of a being who feels pleasure or compassionate sorrow without these being grounded in a bodily informed phenomenology, then it need not worry us if there are other states psychologists want to classify as emotions that do have bodily grounding. The "logic" of feeling compassion does not seem to fit other feelings, like feeling a pin prick in one's foot or an itch in the arm. Feeling compassion for a friend's injury or pleasure in a friend's visit do not require someone's having these feelings "at" any specific bodily region in the way that feeling a toothache does. Feeling emotions does not take place through a material sense organ the way seeing shapes occurs on account, in part, of one's eyes. In light of the case against materialism above, I conclude that God's incorporeality need not stand in the way of ascribing emotions to God.

At this juncture, one may well wonder what could be the appeal of impassibilism. Why not allow that God's care for creation is also manifested by God's compassionate sorrow for those who suffer injustice? Impassibilism is difficult to reconcile with the Christian theistic conviction that God became incar-

---

[22] For a vigorous analysis of the cognitive content of various emotions, including compassion, see R. Solomon's *The Emotions* (Notre Dame: University of Notre Dame Press, 1983). In effect, I stand in between Solomon's purely cognitive account on the one side and the various sensory, anticognitive ones on the other.

nate as Jesus Christ and suffered. Indeed, the Apostles' and Nicene Creeds both bring together in single documents the declaration of Christ's Divinity and suffering. Why hold to such a declaration while accepting Augustine's warning: "Far be it from us to imagine that the impassible nature of God suffers any vexation. For as He is jealous without any envy, is angry without any perturbation, is pitiful without any grief, repents without having any evil in Him to correct, so He is patient without any suffering"?[23] Augustine's stance seems uninviting when one appreciates that attributing an emotion like compassion to God does not amount to thinking God has a vice like envy or a sort of subethical vexation like feeling annoyed over something trivial.

Despite this appeal, passibilism has been severely criticized of late, with Richard Creel mounting a sustained, formidable case for impassibilism based on ethical and religious grounds. I now review Creel's rationale for impassibilism in some detail before developing a response.[24]

A CASE FOR IMPASSIBILISM

To understand Creel's case for impassibilism, it is important to note a significant dimension in his philosophy of creation and values.

Creel contends that a principal reason for God's creation is the significant exercise of creaturely freedom. This is not to say that all the rest of creation exists solely for the sake of autonomous agents, but that a chief end or purpose of the existence of autonomous beings is their exercise of freedom. This may be accomplished by creatures either freely electing a just,

[23] Cited by J. K. Mozley, *The Impassible God* (Cambridge: Cambridge University Press, 1926), p. 107.
[24] When it comes to mounting a positive case for passibilism, I will not appeal to specific theological teachings about Christ. Traditionalists have not denied that Christ suffered, but they have argued that this suffering was due to Christ's human nature as opposed to the Divine nature, which is impassible. This seems inadequate to me, as a nature cannot suffer (literally) though a person can, but I will not explore the incarnational implications of this further here. See *Summa Theologiae* I a. 46. 12. For traditional theism in the Thomist school, part of the problem with passibilism is that it seems to commit us to believing that there are real relations between God and the world. Cf. I a. 13. 7.

Godward life or by electing destructively cruel ends. Thus, God
did not bring about creatures solely (or supremely) for their
exercise of freedom toward the good, but for their exercise of
freedom toward either good or evil. The import of this position
may be brought to light in considering how Creel would reply
to the question "When, if ever, would God's creation of the
world be a failure?" As far as God's purposes are concerned, the
world would be a failure only if there failed to be significant
exercise of creaturely freedom. Unlike John Hick, who would
count creation a failure from a God's eye point of view if a single
creature remained forever out of harmony with Divine–human
fellowship, Creel holds that the crucial element is the creatures'
deciding and acting either for or against this harmony.[25] Once
that element is secured, creation is not a failure. The wrongful
exercise of free will is not a proper object of Divine sorrow. The
existence of an afterlife creates an additional arena for free
choices, so those not given an opportunity to act freely in this
world do not escape freedom in an afterlife. Creel goes on to
develop a wide understanding of creation and its variety of
goods, but the point to emphasize is that Creel attaches great
importance to autonomous freedom and he believes that God
takes such freedom very seriously.

I now turn to consider Creel's six chief arguments for denying
that God suffers. The majority of these arguments are aimed at
bringing to light moral and conceptual problems with Divine
passibility.

  1. Creel rejects as wrong-headed any argument for Divine
suffering on the grounds that it is only on the basis of such a
passibilist theology that we can appreciate the evil and ill that

[25] Hick has laid out and defended his view of freedom and creation in a number of
places, preeminently in *Evil and the God of Love* (New York: Harper & Row, 1978).
Both Hick and Creel are libertarians. In part, it is out of this high view of freedom
that Creel departs from one aspect of traditional impassibilism in allowing that God
does not know which of many future free acts a creature may perform, *Divine
Impassibility* (Cambridge: Cambridge University Press, 1986). Creel nonetheless
insists that God does not undergo substantial volitional alteration in the course of
God's relationship with creatures, because God knows all acts we could do (the so-
called conditionals of freedom) and has never not known and willed precisely how to
respond to each at the appropriate times. God's actions unfold in the world as
eternally willed, but which of the Divine acts are realized depends upon which free
acts creatures perform.

befalls creatures. He contends that the horror of Auschwitz is not contingent upon whether God is grieved by it. The crimes of Auschwitz are profound moral wrongs and may be recognized as outrageous without supposing that God sorrows over the horrors. Indeed, a mark of a mature person is judging Auschwitz evil for its crimes without making reference to the response of an outside observer.

2. Following upon the heels of the first objection, Creel questions whether the passibilist's attribution of suffering to God serves any purpose. As a supremely good being, God's sorrowing should in no way be required to aid God's acting justly, goading God on, so to speak. It is no mark against an agent who works tirelessly in, say, relief efforts for refugees or distributing food to urban indigents that he is not emotionally sorrowful. Presumably God may act out of love and justice without being motivated by sorrow. Likewise, Creel suggests that from the standpoint of the victim, it is surely suspect if she demands or desires that the one helping her feel sorrow. To wish that others share one's sorrow may be understandable under certain circumstances, but it is hardly praiseworthy. When one is raped or robbed, say, surely one should not desire or wish that those aiding one be raped and robbed. Better to wish that no one had to suffer these ills. Similarly, there is something dubious about wishing God to suffer. Why not simply wish God to bring healing and redemption in this life and the next?

3. If God is supposed to be sorrowing, our worship of God may come dangerously close to pity. Surely pity and worship are worlds apart and Christian Scripture and tradition hardly give any place for pitying our Maker. Passibilism is in danger of promoting pity over worship.

4. Creel offers an intriguing objection to a passibilist conception of God which may be termed the argument from revenge. Passibilism allows for creatures to take revenge upon God, or to inflict considerable harm upon the Creator. He advances the objection in the form of a speech by a Nietzschean figure.

I may not be able to kill him [God], but I can make him damn well sorry he ever created me. He will be like a vampire who cannot die though over and over I pound a stake into his heart! Sometimes I will curse him; other times I will ignore him; then when he thinks his heart must absolutely break because of my bad manners, I will create yet more effective ways of distressing his stupid sentiments. What if he casts me in hell for my mockery? If he does, then he will know that he has lost and I have won; remember, he loves me and must eternally grieve for me in my eternal damnation. And I in hell will continue with words and gestures of contempt and obscenity to remind him that he has lost and therefore is contemptible – that he could neither win my heart nor subdue my disdain. Of course, if he is too weak to force the prospect of such everlasting insolence, he might instead consign me to oblivion, snuff me out – but even then I shall have won. The only way he can win is to grant me heaven because of my courage and cleverness.[26]

Such Divine vulnerability to continuous harm seems pointless at best, while at worst it reflects a maudlin sentimentalism.

5. Creel's fifth rationale in opposing passibilism lies in his concern for hope. Other things being equal, we have a *prima facie* obligation at least to hope that other beings are not in pain or suffering or (alternatively) that if they are suffering, this suffering may be redeemed or amended. This is like a cosmic principle of charity. One application of it is that we should hope God is not suffering or in pain. The argument here is not a straightforward metaphysical one. It might better be construed in the spirit of William James as bringing to light what Creel believes is the greater attractiveness or appeal of impassibilism. This argument from hope may be construed as offering a moral or axiological reason for preferring that the impassibilist be right and the passibilist wrong.

6. Finally, Creel advances what may be called the problem of percentages. Process theologians and even some neoscholastics have contended that while there is some sorrow in God, this is not God's dominant emotion. Happily, the sorrow is encompassed by a greater joy or bliss. Such a position might appear to preserve a robust view of Divine vulnerability without falling prey to the fourth Nietzschean objection above. The problem with this lies in accounting for the relationship of joy and sorrow

[26] Creel, *Divine Impassibility*, 125, 126.

in the life of God. Are we to believe that God feels 5 percent or
10 percent sorrow and 95 percent or 90 percent joy? All of this
seems to house a conceptual absurdity, supposing that the
Divine psychology is in constant emotional flux and instability.

Behind the problem of percentages lies a more general worry,
I think, about the problems involved with an anthropo-
morphizing of God. If we think of God alternatively in sorrow
over ill and pleased with the good, don't we wind up with a view
of God in storm and stress or euphoria, ever adjusting to the
unstable currents of the world? Does God, then, have moods
which are ever changing? Can God be irritated or annoyed or
giddy? These questions bring out the baffling, if not completely
illicit, notion of a God of emotions. Add to this the problem of
even stating the passibilist position with precision. Passibilists
speak of God sometimes feeling pain over evil or sorrow or
suffering. Are all these equivalent? Passibilist theology would
seem to rest on a crude, confused anthropomorphism.

A PASSIBILIST RESPONSE

I take Creel's points to expose serious problems with an
unreflective passibilism. Are all forms of passibilism unacceptable? I do not think so. First, I consider the general
rationale why I am not persuaded by Creel.

I believe theistic passibilism is defensible insofar as we can
understand God's sorrow, not as an imperfection, but an aspect
of what it is for God to be supremely good. The supreme
goodness of God at issue here is God's possessing an ethical
nature whereby God approves of the good and disapproves of
the evil in creation, and, most poignant and central to underscore, God's loving creation. In light of God's all-good nature,
I think theists must see God's judgments as ranging over more
than whether autonomous choices occur. If the goodness of God
is to be understood in terms that are intelligible to our moral
experience, surely murderous torture, rape, spite, and so on
must be seen as something God disapproves of in the profoundest
terms, and where any of this evil is inflicted out of autonomous
choice, I believe we must understand God as profoundly

disapproving such an exercise. This concession alone would be enough to secure a passibilist foothold, given a sensory treatment of judgment advanced by David Hume. Hume argued in his *Treatise of Human Nature* that disapproval consists in a feeling of pain, while approval consists in a feeling of pleasure. This seems to me to be wrong as an analysis of approval and disapproval, but I think Hume's move here forces us to see the close proximation or conjoined nature of disapproval and an affective response.[27] What I think is proper is to follow Hume's line not in bare approval and disapproval, but in loving approval and disapproval. When we bring in the tenet that God is loving – something attested to in the Torah, Biblical, and other traditional sources – a passibilist philosophy of God seems virtually unavoidable. I develop two thought experiments in support of this stance.

Imagine that Miriam and Eric both work with indigents in a soup kitchen. Each works with the same diligence and resilience. Both are attentive to those around them, outgoing, humorous, and successful at getting people clothed and housed. Imagine that each disapproves of the ills that have befallen the homeless, the result, say, of malignant social forces set in motion by a growing affluent business. Each approves of the good of each person they see, approving the preciousness of being alive and the courage of their fellow workers. Now imagine that there is only this one difference. Miriam affectively sorrows over the ills that have befallen the innocent, but Eric does not. Miriam feels sorrow in the course of her caring disapprobation of the wrongs that have been done to some individual. Eric disapproves just as strongly and acts just as carefully as Miriam in assisting the person, but he feels no sorrow.

In this thought experiment I think Miriam has a good or excellence that Eric lacks, the good of affective love. I am not sure Eric could properly be said to love Jones and the others without having such an affective response. We may say that he acts out of care and perhaps even that he does a loving act, but it is not at all obvious that he truly is loving.

---

[27] I try to link pleasure and approval, displeasure and disapproval in "The Ideal Aesthetic Observer," *British Journal of Aesthetics* 30:1 (1990), 1–13.

To support this, imagine a different case from the other side of the moral landscape. Lucifer X and Lucifer Y are fiendish agents in the world. Each approves of torturous killing of innocent persons, the destruction of wildlife, and so on. Each disapproves of compassion and justice. At the sight of Hitler, both nod in approval, whereas the sight of Mother Teresa makes them shake their heads in disapprobation. Imagine now that Lucifer X not only approves of Hitler but feels a great pleasure in thinking of Hitler's "great work." Lucifer X enjoys Hitler's work and is always glad when the innocent are destroyed, and saddened when they escape. Lucifer Y is the very same as Lucifer X but without these additional affective responses. He does his work no more or less effectively, but without any accompanying pleasure or sorrow. When Lucifer X spies an innocent person in pain he approves of this and feels great pleasure that it is occurring. Lucifer Y spies the same thing but only approves of it.

I believe that our judgment of this case should be parallel with the earlier one. Lucifer X and Y are profoundly evil, but Lucifer X has managed to achieve a distinctive, additional evil Lucifer Y lacks. Lucifer X has an odious affective hate and love which the other devil lacks. Lucifer X hates Jones, but one might wonder whether Lucifer Y does. Perhaps Lucifer X simply proceeds in a bloodless, bureaucratic fashion with his respective judgments.

Franz Brentano, the Austrian phenomenologist, was so impressed by the role of love and hate in moral experience that he sought to define good and evil in terms of correct love and hate. Good is something which is correctly loved, while evil is something correctly hated.[28] Whether or not his theory succeeds as an analysis, I think his point about the fittingness or appropriateness of such affective responses is readily apparent and comes to the fore in the two thought experiments above. Miriam correctly loves, whereas Eric only correctly judges. Lucifer X's loves and hates are incorrect, while Lucifer Y is

---

[28] An excellent introduction to Brentano and defense of some of his main notions is Roderick Chisholm's *Brentano and Intrinsic Value* (Cambridge: Cambridge University Press, 1986).

faulted for incorrect judgments. The close fit between moral judgment and emotion is brought out by the eighteenth century British philosopher Richard Price.

> I cannot perceive an action to be wrong, without disapproving it; or disapprove it, without being displeased with it ... To behold a virtue is to admire it. To behold it in its intrinsic and complete importance, dignity and excellence, is to possess supreme affection for it. On the contrary, to perceive vice is the very same as to blame and condemn. To perceive it in its naked form and malignity, is to dread and detest it above all things.[29]

Max Scheler in this century adopted a similar outlook, articulating in a nuanced form the idea of there being a normative order of love (*ordo amoris*). The moral life consists, in part, of affective responsiveness. This idea can also be found in Pascal's work in his description of the order of the heart, *l'ordre du coeur*.

Why attribute sorrow to God? Because sorrow seems to be an essential component of what is involved with loving compassion for the enormous numbers of creatures who are unjustly marred. God is a supremely good, loving Creator and it is therefore appropriate to think of God as having compassionate sorrow over the ills that afflict creatures. In my view, to suppose that God sorrows in this way is not to suppose that God has any inherent imperfection or defect. True, it is to suppose that God is subject to what we may well characterize as an ill – sorrow taken by itself is not good nor desirable – and we may well ask whether this is not a defect even if it cannot ultimately destroy God. My reply is that such sorrow is not an imperfection, when the ill stems from a supreme excellence such as the great excellence of God's loving creation. God's compassionate, sorrowful love is a reflection of perfection, not an imperfection. I seek to clarify and bolster this thesis in the course of replying to Creel's objections point by point.

1'. I agree with Creel's thesis that our sense of the horror of Auschwitz should not rest entirely upon our sense of how God responds to it. The account of Divine suffering above is not

---

[29] *A Review of the Principal Questions in Morals*, ed. D. D. Raphael (Oxford: Oxford University Press, 1948).

committed to the view that an appreciation of Divine sorrow is essential to our sense of the horror of Auschwitz. I do not think it is implausible, however, to contend that an appreciation of the horror of Auschwitz can rightly lead to an appreciation of the magnitude of Divine sorrow. More on this below.

2′. While I believe that Creel is correct that we should not think God requires us to be goaded to act justly by sentimentality or maudlin emotions, I think God's just action in the world may be understood as stemming from God's loving approval and disapproval (and, therefore, his joy and sorrow) over the world's states. God's sorrow is not something over and above God's love for creatures. Rather, it is a constituent of this love. One does not so much love the person's good because one sorrows over her obstruction or joys over her development, but one's love consists at least in part in this joy and sorrow. The felt joy and sorrow are a part of what is involved in our love, rather than extraneous attachments.

Creel's observation about the victim's point of view is apt. On reflection, I do not think we should find admirable the desire of a victim that others meet the same fate as her. In believing that God sorrows, are we in the same boat as this victim, a victim who wants not only others to suffer, but even the one who is resolved to come to her rescue? Not necessarily. It is not inappropriate to desire that your rescuer or savior love you. If an essential component of concerned love is to feel sorrow over harm, you may rightfully expect and hope the rescuer will have some sadness over your ill fate. This is not the same as being a patient with AIDS who hopes that the attending physician also contracts the virus.

3′. I do not think that construing God's disapproval of creaturely harm and cruelty as sorrow need collapse the worship of God into pity. When one pities another being, one supposes oneself to be in a comparatively superior state. It is difficult to think of ourselves being superior to the supreme Deity who, if God sorrows, does so as part of a holy love for creation. Surely it would be odd for us to think a Being whose perfect love of the world includes grieving over its ills is inferior to ourselves. See also replies 4′ and 6′.

4′. Is a theology allowing for Divine sorrow as I have articulated it here a Nietzschean dream come true? Yes and no. I think that if God does grieve over the world's ills there is a sense in which a wrongdoer winds up producing greater ill than if God were indifferent to the world or did not exist at all. If the passibilist God exists, the horror of the Holocaust brought about suffering not just to the human victims, but to God as well. So, passibilism does lead us to understand the world's ills in a magnified or intensified fashion. That said, however, recall that the suffering or sorrow of God is articulated here as a manifestation of a supreme excellence of God, God's moral, loving nature. Thus, there is a disjointed sense in which Creel's rebel is enabled to do more ill, given passibilism, but the rebel also thereby creates occasions for the manifestation of a Divine excellence.

How are the good and ill to be balanced or calculated? This is a difficult matter to address, but it may not be necessary to answer it in a precise way to defend passibilism. For now I note that the passibilist can object on various grounds to comparing God with a vampire (God does not haunt castles, biting the necks of victims, and so on), but own up to thinking that God is subject to genuine ills. Christ, after all, did have nails thrust into him. The passibilist can hold that it is open to God (a) to allow the rebel to continue endlessly and for God to sorrow with ever deepening intensity, (b) to allow endless rebellion but limit the sorrow God undergoes, (c) to offer heaven by way of the Beatific Vision, (d) to allow the rebel to perish and God to have endless sorrow, or (e) to allow the perishing and God only limited sorrow. Option "c" names the option that Christian tradition has identified as the salvific efficacy of an ultimate religious experience. Thomas Aquinas and others have believed that there can be a high religious experience which will overcome all resistance to God among creatures. This is the "grant me heaven" option Creel's rebel speaks about, but with this rider: the granting of heaven is not something which will leave our rebel capable of continuing with contempt and horror. The granting of heaven here would involve moral transfiguration, detachment from past wrongdoing and a radical embracing of an altered life. If option "c" seems like an impermissible overriding of the rebel's freedom, any of the other four possibilities could be taken up and spelled out. Options "a" and "b" at least have the advantage of keeping open the possibility of the rebel's free repentance. If the rebel's case is so described that free repentance is impossible, "c" and "d" begin to seem less and less repellent. There may be no moral duty for God to keep in existence creatures who resolutely refuse to act justly. Even if we propose "e" as a possible response to Creel's objection, the theist may still envision God's love to be displayed as very great compassionate sorrow and grief.

In assessing these cases, it is important to see that they raise only some issues that pertain especially to the passibilist theist. The impassibilist who believes God to be good will face related puzzles as well, such as will God ever override the ultimate free choices of creatures? Will God allow for an endless hell of malice and spite? Would God's moral nature allow God to permit certain creatures to cease existing? and so on.

By way of illustrating the character of theistic passibilism consider a contrasting case involving the now familiar passibilist devil Lucifer X. Let's say he faces a related dilemma called the "revenge" of St. Francis, who offers the following speech:

I may never be able to convert Lucifer X, but I shall try very hard to make him repent his evil. Perhaps he is like a vampire in his deathless resolve for ill, but I shall pray for him ceaselessly and perform, through God's grace, acts of mercy and self-giving love. Just when Lucifer X thinks there is no more good that I can do, I shall be given by God new strength to work ever harder against the forces of oppression that afflict my sister and brother creatures. If Lucifer X should destroy me completely, I should still have won, for he will not gain by my freely bowing and serving evil. What if he forces me through drugs and surgery to abandon my faith and serve him? Once again, Lucifer X will not have won me freely, and will have a kind of machine to play with, rather than a living evil soul.

What is Lucifer X to do? As a passibilist the good acts of St. Francis will cause him sorrow and rage. His happiness will be diminished as St. Francis overturns Lucifer X's ill designs. Lucifer X could: (a*) allow St. Francis to do endless good which Lucifer X hates with increasing intensity, or (b*) allow endless good by St. Francis, but decide that he, Lucifer, should only permit himself to hate and be pained by St. Francis to a limited degree, or (c*) send St. Francis to hell, or make moves "d*" and "e*" as above but with his fiendish adjustments. I am not sure which option Lucifer X "ought" to take on the basis of his upside-down value scheme. Still, Lucifer X is not without recourse and can proceed to do that act which will maximize the evil produced, perhaps sticking with his ever-increasing, pained hate for St. Francis until the evil which that represents is outweighed by St. Francis' continued goodness. At that point "e" might be the "best" thing to do, from the standpoint of the netherworld.

I have not sought to offer a way of precisely adding up points that are to be gained from the standpoints of heaven and hell. I simply note that the prospects of the rebel on the one side and St. Francis on the other do not render either passibilism absurd, from their very different standpoints.

5′. The reply at 2′ is appropriate here. Surely one should hope that others do not suffer one's own ill fate. Nonetheless I might well hope that others love me and if love may duly involve sadness, it is far from being selfish or immature to expect others to feel some appropriate degree of sadness over my ills.

6′. The problem of percentages is an interesting one, but not one the emotional passibilist need settle with subtle Divine statistics. Our own emotional life does not admit of clear quantification. Imagine that you love Miriam and feel happiness and sorrow over different features of her life. You may take enormous pleasure in Miriam and feel *tout court*, happiness with respect to her, but you do not thereby fail to be saddened by her bouts of ill health and kleptomania. All this seems quite ordinary and yet you would presumably be hard pressed to analyze your emotions in terms of percentage points. Why expect this to be a matter that the passibilist must settle when it comes to God?

The percentage problem does not reveal the superiority of impassibilism, for one can construct an analogous percentage problem for the impassibilists.

Presumably God has indefinitely many beliefs. How many of these beliefs involve, say, the Atlantic Ocean? God's beliefs about the Atlantic would have to be thought of as infinite, there being infinitely many truths about all the minute components of the ocean, their configurations and constituents, past, present, and future. But these beliefs, even being infinite, are not the whole of God's beliefs, which are thought to range over the whole cosmos, the moral and spiritual world, and so on. What percentage of God's uncountably many beliefs are God's beliefs about the Atlantic? I know of no way we could (even in principle) calculate this. The fact that we cannot satisfactorily calculate the percentages here does not entail that God has no beliefs about the Atlantic. Likewise, the problem of percentages in the case of Divine sorrow and joy does not entail that God has no sorrow and joy.

Creel's percentage objection may be recast not so much as a quandary about formulating precise ratios, but as a problem of viewing the Divine interior life as one of flux. Should we think of God's emotional life as rising and falling with what is, and has been, going on in the world? Two points should be noted briefly in reply. The first is an *ad hominem*. Creel himself acknowledges that God's joy is affected intensively by the world's states. Thus, even if he does not attribute alteration in the extensive scope of Divine happiness, he does not himself avoid positing some fluctuation in the Divine life. Second, the passibilist can conceive of Divine sorrow and joy and their alternation as resting upon a supremely steady, and unchanging, love. The Divine love is changeless, though its manifestations may be uncountable and of endless variety. There is no wild flux in which God is sometimes loving and sometimes not.[30]

Does passibilism still collapse into a form of anthropomorphism? The other Divine attributes of omniscience, goodness, and omnipotence will block attributing to God certain

[30] Even so, there is some theistic motivation for insisting that God's love is informed by the changing world. See Amélie Rorty's illuminating discussion of human love being formed by perceiving alterations in the beloved, "The Historicity of Psychological Attitudes: Love is not Love which Alters not when it Alteration Finds," *Midwest Studies in Philosophy*, ed. French, Vehling, and Wettstein, vol. x (Minneapolis: University of Minnesota Press, 1986.)

emotions like stress, defensiveness, shyness, embarrassment, giddiness, and envy. Insofar as emotions involve making irrational judgments, these will be excluded from a God with maximal cognitive power. It is, in part, because of this that some theists resist attributing anger to God. I agree with them this far: if anger is indeed something which by its very nature is not governed by rational considerations, then thinking of God as angry is problematic. Given a different notion of anger which admits of rationality, then recognizing anger in God becomes more plausible. Of course, my focus has been chiefly on the topic of God's experiencing sorrow and suffering, with some but less attention given to Divine pleasure in the good (as the latter has not been disputed by impassibilists). I know of no reason to see compassionate sorrow as irrational by nature. One may have instances of it, as when someone feels compassion on the basis of certain irrational beliefs, but God would be in no danger of this.[31]

Theistic passibilism also seems to admit of a profoundly nonanthropocentric formulation. A theistic passibilist may, in principle, come to believe that God's loving compassion extends deeply into the sentient world and use this as part of her nonhumanistic environmentalism. Thus, while passibilism needs to be developed in light of our study of humanity in order for us to conceptually grasp the nature of compassion, sorrow, and pleasure, passibilism is by no means intrinsically anthropocentric.

Still, this sixth objection of Creel's has some force, as it does highlight the fact that the impassibilist thesis is difficult to state with precision. In my exposition of passibilism I have freely spoken of God's compassion as constituted in part by sorrow, pain, grief, suffering, and sadness. I believe there is considerable testimony from religious experience that God is experienced as in some fashion grieved, sorrowed, pained by evil, but I don't think we are in any position to map out a kind of intricate

---

[31] I discuss such issues in "The Vanity of God," *Faith and Philosophy* 6:2 (1989), 140–154 and "The Jealousy of God," *New Oxford Review* (Jan.–Feb. 1990), 12–15. See Robert Oakes' defense of Divine anger in "The Wrath of God," *International Journal for Philosophy of Religion* 27 (1990), pp. 129–140.

Divine psychology. It will have to suffice here to characterize theistic passibilism in the broad, general terms, as I have sought to do. I accept theistic passibilism, but I confine the discussion here to defending its coherence and presenting it as a live option notwithstanding the above religious-ethical objections.

I now turn to offer a final portrait of God's integrative presence in light of the passibilism just defended.

GOD'S INTEGRATIVE PRESENCE

Within the classical theistic framework, the cosmos does not function as God's body in some of the ways we have already illustrated. Thus, while your stepping on my toes is to step on me, your stepping on the earth is not to step on God's feet. There is not the causal link between God and cosmos that exists between person and body, whereby bodily mechanisms explain why, say, a person feels dizzy, and the like. Nonetheless, if passibilism is true there is a sense in which the moral welfare of the cosmos, its values and disvalues, does affect God and the cosmos thereby becomes, in a sense, God's moral body. To injure an innocent person is to cause sorrow to God. This is analogous to, though obviously not exactly like, an injury to my body causing an injury to me. The analogy is imperfect not just on the grounds that the effect on me is straightforwardly causal, whereas the effect on God is by way of God's being all good and through caring, affective concern for the cosmos. Another disanalogy is that when you injure my leg, for example, it is not the case that both my leg hurts *and* I hurt as well, while in the passibilist schema, an injury to a creature may cause sorrow both to the creature and to God. Still, the metaphor of creation being God's moral body aptly points to an affective proximity or attachment envisioned by a robust passibilism.

In the course of developing this notion, it will prove useful to consider a passage from Lactantius' *Divine Institutes* (third century) as representative of the theistic reservation over identifying the God–world and person–body relation.

If he [God] made the world, he existed without it. If he rules it, he does not as mind rules the body, but as a master rules a house, a driver a chariot, that is, as not mixed up with the things they rule. If all the things we see are parts of God, because they lack perception he lacks perception also. He is mortal because the parts are mortal.

I can count how often lands shaken by sudden earthquakes have split open or sunk abruptly, how often cities and islands, submerged by waves, have gone to the bottom, how often swamps have swallowed up fruitful plains, rivers and lakes have dried out, and mountains have either cracked or fallen or been leveled with the plains. Hidden unknown fire has consumed many regions and the foundations of many mountains. It is not enough that God does not spare his own members; man is also allowed to act against God's body! Large bodies of water are formed, mountains are cut down and the inner bowels of the earth are dug out to find wealth. Is plowing possible without tearing the divine body? We who violate the members of God are criminals and evildoers. Does God allow his body to be abused and himself weaken it or permit man to do so? Or perhaps that divine understanding that is mingled with the world and all its parts has abandoned the earth's outer surface and buried itself in the depths lest it feel some pain from continuous wounding. If this is vain and absurd, the Stoics are just as lacking in sense as the things of this world. They have not understood that the divine spirit is diffused everywhere and holds all things together, but not in such a way that the incorrupt God himself is mingled with the solid corruptible elements.[32]

In the discussion of God's relation to the world in Chapter 4, I expressed some similar concerns about Jantzen's construal of the God–world relation. Does my employing passibilism to conceive of the world as God's moral body result in an undue mixing of God and world?

It certainly could, though if we assume a reasonable theory of the good and believe God to be perfectly good, I think any resultant mixing is defensible and religiously illuminating. Granted that hitting the earth is not to hit God, where is the absurdity in believing that to hit an innocent person is to cause God sorrow? Lactantius' concern to depict God as master and driver can well obscure appreciating God as fellow sufferer and companion. By describing the world as God's moral body, I am not supposing that the world is God's body in every sense or even most senses. Most important, from the standpoint of

---

[32] *Apocalyptic Spirituality*, an anthology containing work by Lactantius and others, trans. Bernard McGinn (New York: Paulist Press, 1979), pp. 30, 31.

theistic libertarianism, the world is not God's body in the sense that events within it are always the outcome of God's election. (Determinists may see the world as more like God's body than the libertarians). Even so, seeing the world as (in part) God's moral body dramatically captures the passibilist tenet that how you treat the world affects God. This is the key point which characterizes what I term integrative theism as a particular form of classical theism. To see God as merely like a driver or a pilot of a ship (to use Descartes's phrase) does not do justice to God's integral, affective omnipresence in the cosmos.

If we acquire the value-centered, integrative view of God and the cosmos, I think we have gone much of the way to remain within classical theism and reply to critics who accuse us of world-denigrating values. Consider, for example, John Macquarrie's charge that the classic insistence upon a God–world distinction has led to a monarchical outlook, devaluing creation. He comments on one way to formulate the God–world distinction that recalls our modal argument of earlier chapters.

The world minus God = zero
God minus the world = God.

This theological mathematics is designed to underscore that God as a necessary being does not depend on the contingent world, though the world depends on God. Macquarrie comments that this formula expresses an "utter devaluation and profanation of the world ... It seems to me an acosmism."[33] I think we can fully appreciate the force of Macquarrie's charge and insist that as far as values are concerned it is misleading at best to note: "God minus the world = God," for the loss of the world would involve an incalculable loss, perhaps a Divine sorrow which far outstrips our conceptual powers to grasp even faintly. The important point to realize is that the metaphysical

[33] Macquarrie, *Thinking About God* (New York: Harper & Row, 1975), p. 148. Also see his "Classical Theism and its Alternatives," in *In Search of Deity: An Essay in Dialectical Theism* (New York: Crossroad, 1985). I have noted the parallel here with the modal argument for dualism, and add the rider that the thought experiments are not altogether parallel. While the modal argument allows for body switching, Anselmian theists would not want to suppose that it is possible for worlds to switch Gods.

fact that God as a necessary being can exist without contingent beings does not in itself devalue or deny the existence of the contingent beings. By stressing God's affective responsiveness to the goods and ills of this contingent creation, we can recognize the affective identity of God and the world, while avoiding acosmism or some kind of theistic eliminativism. In Chapter 2 we discussed some of the ways in which a dualist philosophy can be illustrated with the mind pictured as floating insubstantially above the body. I suggest that we similarly misrepresent God's presence in the cosmos when we employ a similar picture of remoteness and foggy constitution. The well-being of the cosmos and the life of God are intimately interwoven.

It is worth stressing that the integrative link between God and world may be seen as constituted not only by God's compassionate sorrow, but by God's loving pleasure as well. Taking pleasure in some things can establish a kind of bond or belonging. This is even evident in everyday, trivial cases, as when I might say: "Strawberries are *my* fruit" or "The Twins are my baseball team," or "He's my movie star," in which the possessive term does not signal any mercantile factor, but it does signal a sort of marked identification the speaker has with the object of affection. What makes strawberries and not grapefruit my fruit is that I especially relish the first. I take great enjoyment in one that I do not take in the other. The role that pleasure may have in cases of ownership was highlighted by John Locke, who stipulated that it was vital to love that which is owned. Too often, I think, accounts of Divine ownership of the cosmos are articulated in terms which omit this affective, loving component. Thus, in accord with some theistic philosophers, the cosmos is said to belong to God in virtue of God creating it from nothing and conserving it in existence. A fuller Lockian notion of ownership would insist that God's owning the cosmos consist in such creation and conservation *plus* love, a love that includes appropriate pleasure in the beloved.[34]

---

[34] *Two Treatises of Civil Government.* In the course of developing a contemporary defense of the Lockian notion that God owns the cosmos, B. Brody fails to capitalize on this Lockian theme of love, "Morality and Religion Reconsidered," in *Divine Commands and Morality*, ed. P. Helm (Oxford: Oxford University Press, 1981). I defend the

A theist who recognizes God as taking pleasure in the
creation could reasonably draw on Jean-Paul Sartre's notion
that pleasure and joy have a possessive, internalizing character,
though without suffocation and manipulation.[35] With Divine
joy, this may be understood as internalizing the cosmos into
God. Here the internalization and shared identity that Klein
and others document might serve as a theological reference
point. Klein writes that "Whenever we can admire and love
somebody – or hate and despise somebody – we also take
something of them into ourselves and our deepest attitudes are
shaped by such experiences."[36] Earlier in this chapter I
defended the intelligibility of believing that God is closer to each
person than they are to themselves. The passibilism of integrative theism in this chapter now allows us to envisage this in
profoundly personal terms. I have not offered a sustained
defense of religious experience in this book, but if we allow for
the possibility of our apprehending to some extent God's
affective responsiveness to our interior life, we are further along
the way to understanding claims in Jewish, Christian, and
Islamic spiritual traditions of the good of Divine–human
accord.[37] If I am able to grasp appreciatively God's caring
concern, his approving pleasure and sorrowing compassion, this
can have an empowering, life-enhancing quality. It has the
enriching character that we see in human affairs when persons
are raised under conditions in which they are loved in authentic
ways.

I close with a speculative comment that extends the theme of
God's interior presence. How might the development of our self-
understanding be related to our coming to understand something of God?

notion that God owns the cosmos in "God's Estate," *Journal of Religious Ethics* 2:1
(Spring 1992).

[35] See Sartre's essay "Esquisse d'une théorie des emotions," in *Actualités scientifiques et
industrielles* (Paris, 1935), pp. 38–39.

[36] *Envy and Gratitude and Other Works*, p. 256.

[37] See my *Contemporary Philosophy of Religion* (Oxford: Basil Blackwell, forthcoming) for
more material on religious experience. I try to articulate some of what is involved
with the religious experience of mutual indwelling in connection with some ideas in
Charles Williams' novels in "The Co-inherence," *Christian Scholars Review* 18:4 (June
1989), 333–345.

Recall the theory treated at the outset of this chapter that we develop as persons through a shifting process of attachment and detachment in which others can play an important, formative role. Klein has spoken of the way in which we grow up as a mind within a mind, insofar as we are in growing interpretive interplay as infants with those who care for us, and surround, contain, and (ideally) love us into the identity we have. There is a role for needs not being met, and desires crossed, as part of the process of developing an understanding of ourselves with our own distinct identity. At times the "good enough" care-giver is enough (to use Winnicott's phrase). I think that much of the religious experience recorded in the traditions of Judaism, Christianity, and Islam display a continuing process by which the images we have of God are sometimes blurred, sometimes more focused, in an unfolding, progressive fashion. There are even points where the God described in various sacred Scriptures seems more like a *good enough* God, rather than resplendent with supreme perfection. Our realization of God's perfection is gradual. In Chapter 1 I suggested one way in which one might develop a concept of God in which the theist turns homuncular materialism upside down. Perhaps the gradual realization of God is attainable only by struggling through various stages in the philosophy of God, constantly in need of revision, and doing so in light of religious experience and revelatory narratives as well as independent philosophical reflection. If there is a God along the lines of classical theism with the integrative, affective element I have focused on, then this whole process may be seen in overarching terms where all our explorations do not take place some distance away from God, but in a cosmos surrounded and upheld by God's love.[38]

---

[38] I explore the impact this has on one's philosophical methodology in "Taking Philosophy Personally," in *The Crescent*, forthcoming.

Conclusion

G. E. Moore is reported to have "insisted that he was quite distinct from his body, and one day said that his hand was closer to him than his foot was."[1] This might appear to be a tragicomic plight, and perhaps more like the report of a drug tripper as opposed to a twentieth century, "commonsense" philosopher. I am sympathetic with his stance, however, insofar as I think persons are nonphysical and that it is possible to experience remoteness from parts of one's body and even parts of oneself. In the first three chapters above I defended the thesis that persons are nonphysical, and, in Chapter 6, the claim that a person can be remote from who she is depending upon self-understanding, memory, attentiveness, and so on. Integrative dualism is also well placed to recognize that one can indeed feel remote from one's bodily parts when, say, one's foot is paralyzed and there is no proprioception, feeling, or motor control.[2] Having recognized the ways in which we can be subject to fragmentation, however, I have sought to underscore the integrated, holist relation between persons and bodies. A central aim of the second, fourth, and sixth chapters was to overcome the charge that dualism by its very nature must be conceptually crippling.

Could God be said to be more present to one place in the

---

[1] Moore as reported by Morton White, "Memories of G. E. Moore," *Journal of Philosophy* 57 (1960), 806.

[2] My great-uncle may have felt very much the way Moore did when he lost feeling and control over much of his body and his only way of communicating was with his right hand. A related, but opposite, case would be the plight of Christy Brown, the Irish artist-writer. He suffered from cerebral palsy and was able to write only with his left foot.

cosmos than to another? In other words, is something like Moore's predicament intelligible on a cosmic scale in which some place or thing is closer to God than another? In the theistic framework as outlined in Chapter 5, the answer would be negative in that God's supreme cognitive power takes within its compass all regions of the cosmos and no part of the cosmos can exist without God's creative conservation. Even in places where there is great evil, integrative theism understands God to be affectively present, hating the evil, loving the good. But, as indicated in Chapter 6, there are ethical-religious respects in which our lives may be more or less remote from the God of love envisioned in classical theism. Augustine was prepared to speak of God's having feet and hands metaphorically. "What outward appearance, what form, what stature, hands or feet has love? No one can say; and yet love has feet ... (and) love has hands which give to the poor, love has eyes which give intelligence to him who is in need."[3] From the standpoint of classical Judaism, Islam, and Christianity, when we act cruelly, we cease to act in union with God and there is no sense in which we thereby serve to manifest God's love or could be said to be like God's hands or feet. As far as God's supremely good nature is concerned, we may be more like a paralyzed limb, dead to justice and compassion.

I have written this book about the analogies and disanalogies between the person–body and God–cosmos relationships out of the conviction that the philosophy of mind and the philosophy of religion have resources to challenge and contribute to one another. I am sure that some readers will find my outlook too optimistic in places, especially those who struggle over prior skeptical worries about whether it makes any sense to talk about reality in the first place (rather than referring only to competing conceptual systems) or to speak about moral facts such as the good of compassion. Lycan comments: "Moral facts are right up there with Cartesian egos ... in the ranks of items uncordially despised by most contemporary philosophers."[4] It has not been

---

[3] Augustine, *Homilies on the first Epistle General of St. John*, VII, no. 10.
[4] William Lycan, *Judgement and Justification* (Cambridge: Cambridge University Press, 1988), p. 198.

possible in this book to address fully the plight of moral skepticism, or investigate thoroughly areas outside the philosophy of mind that have a bearing on the philosophy of religion. Despite these deliberate efforts at leaving some issues unsettled, the aim of this project has still been substantial: to address and ultimately overcome some of the philosophical and theological hostility toward dualism and against understanding God as a nonphysical reality. I hope to have overturned some of the skepticism stemming from contemporary philosophy of mind and postdualist theology, and to have articulated, in part, the appeal of an integrative understanding of consciousness and the mind of God.

Select bibliography

Armstrong, D. M., *A Materialist Theory of Mind* (London: Routledge & Kegan Paul, 1968).

Barnes, Jonathan, *The Ontological Argument* (London: Macmillian, 1972).

Boyd, Richard, "Materialism without Reductionism," in *Readings in Philosophy of Psychology*, ed. Ned Block (Cambridge, Mass.: Harvard University Press, 1980).

Bretherton, Inge, "The Origins of Attachment Theory: P. John Bowlby and Mary Ainsworth," *Developmental Psychology* 28:5 (1992).

Chisholm, R. M., *Brentano and Intrinsic Value* (Cambridge: Cambridge University Press, 1986).

On Metaphysics (Minneapolis: University of Minnesota Press, 1989).

Person and Object (La Salle: Open Court, 1976).

Churchland, Paul, *Matter and Consciousness* (Cambridge, Mass.: MIT Press, 1984).

Creel, Richard, *Divine Impassibility* (Cambridge: Cambridge University Press, 1986).

"Radical Epiphenomenalism: B. F. Skinner's Account of Private Events," *Behaviorism* 8:1 (1980).

Dancy, Jonathan, *Contemporary Epistemology* (Oxford: Basil Blackwell, 1985).

Davidson, Donald, *Actions and Events* (Oxford: Clarendon Press, 1980).

Davies, Brian, "Classical Theism and the Doctrine of Divine Simplicity," in *Language, Meaning and God*, ed. Davies (London: Geoffrey Chapman, 1987).

Dennett, Daniel, *Brainstorms* (Cambridge, Mass.: MIT Press, 1978).

Consciousness Explained (London: Allen Lane, 1991).

The Intentional Stance (Cambridge, Mass.: MIT Press, 1987).

Descartes, René, *Philosophical Letters*, trans. Anthony Kenny (Minneapolis: University of Minnesota Press, 1981).

Foster, John, *The Immaterial Self* (London: Routledge, 1991).

Select bibliography 343

Gaskin, J. C. A., *The Quest for Eternity* (Harmondsworth, Middlesex: Penguin, 1984).

Hacker, Peter M., *Appearance and Reality* (Oxford: Basil Blackwell, 1987).

Harrison, Jonathan, "The Embodiment of Mind or What Use is Having a Body?," *Proceedings of the Aristotelian Society* (1973–74).

Hart, W. D., *The Engines of the Soul* (Cambridge: Cambridge University Press, 1988).

Hume, David, *A Treatise of Human Nature*, ed. L. A. Selby-Bigge (Oxford: Oxford University Press, 1965).

Jantzen, Grace, *God's World, God's Body* (Philadelphia: Westminster Press, 1984).

"Reply to Taliaferro," *Modern Theology* 3:2 (January 1987).

Kenny, Anthony, *Religion and Reason* (Oxford: Basil Blackwell, 1987).

Kerr, Fergus, *Theology after Wittgenstein* (Oxford: Basil Blackwell, 1988).

Klein, Melanie, *Envy and Gratitude and Other Works* (New York: Delta, Publishers, 1975).

Love, Guilt and Reparation and Other Works (New York: Delta, Publishers, 1975).

Kripke, Saul, *Naming and Necessity* (Cambridge, Mass.: Harvard University Press, 1980).

Kvanvig, J. "Unknowable Truths and the Doctrine of Omniscience," *Journal of the American Academy of Religion* 58 (1989).

Lepore, E. and R. Van Gulick (eds.), *John Searle and his Critics* (Oxford: Basil Blackwell, 1991).

Levin, Michael, *Metaphysics and the Mind–Body Problem* (Oxford: Clarendon Press, 1979).

Lewis, David, "An Argument for the Identity Theory," *Journal of Philosophy* 63 (1966).

"Counterparts of Persons and their Bodies," *Journal of Philosophy* 68 (1971).

"Mad Pain and Martian Pain," in *Readings in Philosophy of Psychology*, ed. Ned Block (Cambridge, Mass.: Harvard University Press, 1980).

Lewis, H. D., *The Self and Immortality* (New York: MacMillan, 1973).

Locke, John, *An Essay Concerning Human Understanding*, ed. P. H. Nidditch (Oxford: Clarendon Press, 1975).

Lycan, William, "Psychological Laws," in *Mind, Brain, and Function*, ed. J. J. Biro and R. W. Shahan (Norman: University of Oklahoma Press, 1982).

McGinn, Colin, *The Character of Mind* (Oxford: Oxford University Press, 1982).

The Problem of Consciousness (Oxford: Basil Blackwell, 1990).

McPherson, Thomas, *The Argument from Design* (New York: St. Martin's Press, 1972).

Macquarrie, John, *Thinking About God* (New York: Harper & Row, 1975).

Madell, Geoffrey, *Mind and Materialism* (Edinburgh: Edinburgh University Press, 1988).

Miles, Margaret, *Fullness of Life: Historical Foundations for a New Asceticism* (Philadelphia: Westminster Press, 1981).

Miles, T. R., *Religious Experience* (London: Macmillan, 1972).

Morris, Thomas, *The Logic of God Incarnate* (Ithaca: Cornell University Press, 1986).

Nagel, Thomas, "Panpsychism," in *Mortal Questions* (New York: Cambridge University Press, 1980).

The View from Nowhere (New York: Oxford University Press, 1986).

What Does it all Mean? (New York: Oxford University Press, 1987).

Nielsen, Kai, *Scepticism* (London: Macmillan, 1973).

"God, Disembodied Existence and Incoherence," *Sophia* 26:3 (October 1987).

Paulsen, David, "Must God Be Incorporeal?," *Faith and Philosophy* 6 (1989).

Pollock, John, *Knowing and Justification* (Princeton: Princeton University Press, 1974).

Price, H. H. "Survival and the Idea of 'Another World,'" in *Brain and Mind* ed. John Smythies (New York: Humanities Press, 1965).

Thinking and Experience (London: Hutchinson, 1969).

Putnam, Hilary, *Reason, Truth and History* (New York: Cambridge University Press, 1981).

Quine, Willard, *The Pursuit of Truth* (Cambridge, Mass.: Harvard University Press, 1990).

Theories and Things (Cambridge, Mass.: Harvard University Press, 1981).

Robinson, Daniel, *Philosophy of Psychology* (New York: Columbia University Press, 1985).

Robinson, Howard, *Matter and Sense* (Cambridge: Cambridge University Press, 1982).

Rorty, Richard, *Philosophy and the Mirror of Nature* (Princeton: Princeton University Press, 1979).

Ryle, Gilbert, *The Concept of Mind* (London: Hutchinson, 1949).

Searle, John, *The Rediscovery of the Mind* (Cambridge, Mass.: MIT Press, 1992).

Shoemaker, Sydney, "On an Argument for Dualism," in *Knowledge and Mind*, ed. Carl Ginet and Shoemaker (New York: Oxford University Press, 1983).

Shoemaker, Sydney and Richard Swinburne, *Personal Identity* (Oxford: Basil Blackwell, 1984).

Smythies, J. R. "The Inverted Spectrum," *Journal of Philosophy* (July 1982).

Smythies, J. R. and J. Beloff (eds.), *The Case for Dualism* (Charlottesville: University of Virginia Press, 1989).

Stich, Stephen, *From Folk Psychology to Cognitive Science: The Case Against Belief* (Cambridge, Mass.: MIT Press, 1983).

Swinburne, Richard, *The Evolution of the Soul* (Oxford: Clarendon Press, 1986).

The Existence of God (Oxford: Clarendon Press, 1979).

Taliaferro, Charles and Michael Beaty, "God and Concept Empiricism," *Southwest Philosophy Review* 6:2 (July 1990).

Tallis, Raymond, *The Explicit Animal* (London: Macmillan, 1991).

Thatcher, Adrian, "Christian Theism and the Concept of a Person," in *Persons and Personality*, ed. A. Peacocke and G. Gillett (Oxford: Basil Blackwell, 1987).

Van Cleve, James, "Conceivability and the Cartesian Argument for Dualism," *Pacific Philosophical Quarterly* 64 (1983).

Williams, Bernard, *Problems of the Self* (Cambridge: Cambridge University Press, 1973).

Wilson, Margaret, *Descartes* (Boston, Mass.: Routledge & Kegan Paul, 1982).

Winnicott, D. W. "Mind and its Relation to the Psyche-Soma," *Collected Papers* (New York: Basic Books, 1958).

Zimmerman, Dean, "Two Cartesian Arguments for the Simplicity of the Soul," *American Philosophical Quarterly* 28:3 (1991).

Index

DePaul, Michael, 128
Derrida, Jacques, 13
Descartes, René, 5, 15, 20, 45, 98, 99,
  104, 119, 155, 158, 160, 183, 211,
  218–219, 224, 229, 235, 335
Ducasse, C. J., 176, 220
Dummett, Michael, 298

Eccles, John, 93, 164, 222
Eckhart, Johannes (Meister Eckhart),
  1, 297
Edwards, Paul, 4, 225, 226
Ellis, John, 13
Eliot, T. S., 131
Epictetus, 233
Evans, C. Stephen, 220
Ewing, A. C., 23, 103, 220

Feinberg, Joel, 277
Feldman, Fred, 31, 104, 245
Feyerabend, Paul, 25
Firth, Roderick, 123
Flew, Anthony, 4, 5, 113, 176, 225
Fodor, Jerry, 45
Foster, John, 24, 60, 64, 73–74,
  115–116, 132, 135, 140, 166–170,
  196, 224, 246, 274
Freddoso, Alfred, 89
Freud, Sigmund, 13, 34, 35, 191,
  302–304
Fulmer, Gilbert, 279–282

Gale, R., 278
Gaskin, J. C. A., 5, 258–263
Geach, Peter, 246
Gilson, Etinne, 228
Gooch, P. W., 247
Goodman, Nelson, 298
Gore, Al, 57
Gregory of Nyssa, 229, 291

Hacker, P. M. S., 110–111, 120–121,
  126–127, 159
Haeckel, Ernst, 2
Haji, Ishiyaque, 7, 264
Harré, Rom, 223, 281, 299
Harrison, Jonathan, 169, 183, 195, 246
Hart, H. D., 115–116, 176–177, 195
Hebblethwaite, Brian, 88
Hegel, Gottlob, 306–307
Heinamen, Robert, 32
Hick, John, 320

Hildebrand, Dietrich von, 49
Hobbes, Thomas, 7, 26
Hodge, Johanna, 233
Holland, Frederick, 175
Hooker, Michael, 211–212
Hughes, Christopher, 205
Hume, David, 136, 303, 323–324
Husserl, Edmund, 49, 104

Irenaeus, 228
Isaac, 7, 265

Jackson, Frank, 104
Jacob, 7, 265
James, William, 252, 292, 322
Jantzen, Grace, 4, 6, 7, 14, 223–234,
  249–253, 256–264
John of Damascus, Saint, 228
Johnston, Mark, 207
Jones, O. O., 48, 206–207, 218

Kant, Immanuel, 102, 306–307
Kaufman, Gordon, 8
Kenny, Anthony, 9, 10, 12, 98, 120–121,
  225, 229, 258, 283, 295
Kerr, Fergus, 7, 233, 238–239
Kierkegaard, S., 311
Kim, Jaegewan, 128, 165
Klein, Melanie, 159, 302–304, 337–
  338
Kripke, Saul, 62, 145, 201
Kvanvig, J., 150, 288

Lactantius, 272, 333–334
Lash, Nicholas, 7, 267–268
Lear, Jonathan, 302–304
Legennausen, Gary, 8, 253
Leibniz, G. W., 241
Leslie, John, 290
Levin, Michael, 26, 38, 96–98, 100,
  106–111, 122–127, 144–146, 161
Lewis, C. I., 58
Lewis, C. S., 90, 179
Lewis, David, 26, 142–146, 151, 197–
  202, 221–222, 252
Lewis, H. D., 100, 103, 147, 195,
  220, 224, 301
Locke, John, 178, 310, 336
Long, D., 223–224
Loux, Michael, 94
Lovejoy, Arthur, 99, 104
Lucas, John, 119–120